Teaching South Asian Anglophone Diasporic Literature

Teaching South Asian Anglophone Diasporic Literature

Edited by

Nalini Iyer and Pallavi Rastogi

The Modern Language Association of America
New York   2024

85 Broad Street, New York, New York 10004
www.mla.org

To order MLA publications, visit www.mla.org/books. For wholesale and international orders, see www.mla.org/bookstore-orders.

The MLA office is located on the island known as Mannahatta (Manhattan) in Lenapehoking, the homeland of the Lenape people. The MLA pays respect to the original stewards of this land and to the diverse and vibrant Native communities that continue to thrive in New York City.

Options for Teaching 65
ISSN 1079-2562

Library of Congress Cataloging-in-Publication Data

Names: Iyer, Nalini, editor. | Rastogi, Pallavi, editor.
Title: Teaching South Asian anglophone diasporic literature / edited by Nalini Iyer and Pallavi Rastogi.
Description: New York : The Modern Language Association of America, 2024.
Series: Options for teaching, 1079-2562 ; 65 | Includes bibliographical references.
Identifiers: LCCN 2023040491 (print) | LCCN 2023040492 (ebook) | ISBN 9781603296373 (hardcover) | ISBN 9781603296380 (paperback) | ISBN 9781603296397 (EPUB)
Subjects: LCSH: South Asian literature (English)—Study and teaching (Higher) | American literature—South Asian American authors—Study and teaching (Higher) | Caribbean literature (English)—Study and teaching (Higher) | English literature—South Asian authors—Study and teaching (Higher) | South Asian diaspora. | BISAC: LANGUAGE ARTS & DISCIPLINES / Study & Teaching | LITERARY CRITICISM / Asian / General | LCGFT: Literary criticism. | Essays.
Classification: LCC PR9570.S64 T43 2024 (print) | LCC PR9570.S64 (ebook) | DDC 820.9954—dc23/eng/20231226
LC record available at https://lccn.loc.gov/2023040491
LC ebook record available at https://lccn.loc.gov/2023040492

To Ganesh Iyer, for his love and steadfast support.
—Nalini Iyer

To Radha Rastogi and Areendam Chanda,
with much love and gratitude for always being there.
—Pallavi Rastogi

Contents

Acknowledgments xi

Part I: Introduction: Histories and Contexts

Toward a Pedagogy of South Asian Anglophone
 Diasporic Literature 3
 Nalini Iyer and Pallavi Rastogi

South Asian Anglophone Diasporic Writing: Histories
 and Geographies of Dispersion 23
 Nalini Iyer and Pallavi Rastogi

Part II: East Meets South: Africa and the Caribbean

M. G. Vassanji's Fiction in a Transnational, Postcolonial,
 and Social Justice Context 41
 Asma Sayed

Indianness in the Caribbean: Strategies for Teaching
 Indo-Caribbean Anglophone Literature 51
 Anita Baksh

Faulty Stereotypes: Indo-Caribbean Literature and
 a Pedagogy of Social Justice 62
 Mayuri Deka

History, Historiography, Ethnography, and Diaspora
 in Amitav Ghosh's *In an Antique Land* 71
 Dharitri Bhattacharjee

Goa on the Literary Atlas: Questioning Belonging 79
 R. Benedito Ferrão

Part III: East Meets West: Post–World War II Britain

We Are Not All Migrants: Mohsin Hamid's *Exit West*
 and Sunjeev Sahota's *The Year of the Runaways* 93
 Alpana Sharma

Cosmopolitanism and Crisis in South Asian Anglophone
    Diasporic Novels   103
    C. S. Bhagya

Teaching the Cousinship of Experience: The Postcolonial
    Bildungsroman across Time and Cultures   113
    Feroza Jussawalla

Part IV: East Meets North: The United States and Canada

Remembering as Learning: South Asian Histories in
    a Canadian Classroom   123
    Chandrima Chakraborty

"Watch Me Reposition" Bharati Mukherjee's *Jasmine*   133
    Robin E. Field

Race, Citizenship, and Community Formation in Bhira
    Backhaus's *Under the Lemon Trees* and Jhumpa Lahiri's
    Unaccustomed Earth   142
    Rajender Kaur

Teaching Nepali Anglophone Diasporic Literature   152
    Esther Daimari

**Part V: East Meets North: The Sri Lankan
          Refugee Diaspora**

Reimagining the Refugee Crisis through Sharon Bala's
    The Boat People   165
    Umme Al-wazedi

Teaching Sri Lankan American Literature in the
    American South   174
    Dinidu Karunanayake

Navigating the Homeland/Hostland Dynamic: Sri Lankan
    Diasporic Literature   185
    Maryse Jayasuriya

Teaching Sri Lanka in the United States: Human Rights in
    the Literary and Visual Imaginations   194
    Manav Ratti

Part VI: East Meets North: The Pakistani American Diaspora after 9/11

Teaching Pakistani Anglophone Diasporic Literature   207
Mushtaq Bilal

Recontextualizing the Global Diaspora: Mohsin Hamid's
Exit West at a Hispanic-Serving Institution   216
Aniruddha Mukhopadhyay

Resisting Racialization: Mohsin Hamid's *The Reluctant
Fundamentalist* in Ethnic Studies Courses   225
Binod Paudyal

Pakistani Anglophone Diasporic Literature in
Writing-Intensive Seminars   234
Suhaan Kiran Mehta

Part VII: The Forms of Diaspora: Nonfiction, Film, Television, Digital and Creative Writing

Teaching Memoirs: Nonfiction as Public Discourse in
South Asian Diasporas   247
Subhalakshmi Gooptu

Amitav Ghosh's *The Great Derangement*, Close Reading,
and Moments of Recognition   258
Matthew Spencer

Joke's on Us: Indian Americans, Comedy, and Writing America   267
Madhurima Chakraborty

Extimate Pedagogies, Intimate Texts: Teaching Digital South
Asian Diasporas   277
Robyn Carruthers and Asha Varadharajan

"A Temporary Matter": Jhumpa Lahiri and Creative Writing
Pedagogy   287
Amina Gautier

Recovering the Gendered Violence and Trauma of Partition
in the Me Too Era   294
Nidhi Shrivastava

Notes on Contributors   303

Acknowledgments

The idea for this book emerged at the South Asian Literary Association's annual meeting in Seattle in January 2020, where we were part of a panel with Professors Gaurav Desai and John Hawley, who had just published *Approaches to Teaching the Works of Amitav Ghosh*. Inspired by the significance of the book on Ghosh and by the conference's theme, pedagogy and South Asian literature, we approached the MLA with a proposal for this book. Little did we know that in a couple of months the world would be overtaken by a pandemic and that we would see cataclysmic shifts in teaching modality, course design, and pedagogy. Despite the many hardships and challenges of the pandemic, this project moved forward because of the passion and commitment of the teacher-scholars who have contributed essays to this book. Without their hard work, enthusiasm, and expertise in teaching South Asian anglophone diasporic literature, this book would not have been possible.

We extend our gratitude to our many colleagues and friends at the South Asian Literary Association who form our academic community and whom we meet every year at the annual conference for rich conversations about South Asian and South Asian diasporic literature. Our thanks to Lopa Basu, Madhurima Chakraborty, Kavita Daiya, Prathim-Maya Dora-Laskey, Robin Field, Rahul Gairola, Meghan Gorman-DaRif, Sukanya Gupta, John Hawley, Pranav Jani, Maryse Jayasuriya, Priya Jha, Feroza Jussawalla, Cynthia Leenerts, Debali Mookerjea-Leonard, Aniruddha Mukhopadhyay, Moumin Quazi, Asha Sen, S. Shankar, Amritjit Singh, Pennie Ticen, Brian Yothers, and Bonnie Sue Zare. We also thank Gaurav Desai for his support of our early ideas and for generously sharing resources with us as we developed this project.

Thanks also to our colleagues who reviewed drafts of the introduction and other material related to the project, especially Ben Bergholtz, Michael Bibler, Madoka Kishi, Christopher Rovee, and Saumya Lal. We thank Ankita Rathour and Jason Christian for their editorial and research assistance. We cannot adequately convey our immense gratitude to Alexandra Chiasson, whose meticulous editing, research, and formatting skills enabled us to move ahead with the manuscript in a timely way.

James Hatch, our acquisitions editor at the MLA, expertly guided this project. We are very grateful for his enthusiastic support of our work.

Our thanks to the five anonymous peer reviewers of the book at its various stages and to the MLA Publications Committee. Their generous and rigorous readings have sharpened the focus of the book and deepened its theoretical intervention.

Nalini would like to thank Pallavi for her collaborative work on this project. Pallavi's brilliance as a scholar, sharp editorial skills, compassion, wit, and ability to meet deadlines made this project memorable. She is a joy to work with, and Nalini is deeply grateful for her friendship. Nalini would also like to thank her colleagues in the English department at Seattle University, who put their students first and engage enthusiastically in conversations about curriculum, course design, and pedagogy. She has learned much from them. Nalini's students at Seattle University, where she has taught for almost thirty years, inspire her; her work with them is ever-present in this project. Nalini is grateful for the Theiline Pigott-McCone Endowed Chair (2020–22), which helped support her work on this book. A special thanks to Alan Chong Lau, arts editor of *The International Examiner*, who for the last twenty years has been publishing her book reviews and keeping her supplied with literary works from the South Asian diaspora. Last but not least, Nalini would like to thank her family: her parents, Seetha Narayanan and the late J. N. Iyer, who supported her love for reading and her academic aspirations and were her first teachers; her brother and sister-in-law, Ravi Janardan and Chaya Garg, without whom Nalini would not have entered this academic life; her husband, Ganesh, who supports her every day in myriad ways; her daughters, Mallika and Geetanjali, for their love; and Clifford, her beloved cocker spaniel, who ensured that she could write without interruptions from delivery people, squirrels, and neighborhood cats.

Pallavi thanks Nalini, who has been a model of scholarly rigor, intellectual generosity, and editorial acumen. Her knowledge of South Asian literature and culture is awe-inspiring. Pallavi is also grateful to Nalini for her wise advice over the years on parenting two daughters (and a dog) and for constantly assuring her that the kids are all right. Pallavi's life is much richer with Nalini in it. As we say in Louisiana, "Geaux Team Nal-Pal." Pallavi would also like to thank her students, friends, and colleagues at Louisiana State University, all of whom make teaching, and thinking about teaching, a thing of beauty and joy. Finally, this book is for Pallavi's family: her parents, Radha and Aditya Rastogi, for their love, support, and pride in her; her husband, Areendam Chanda; and her daughters, Keya and Anaya. And, finally, to Laska, Pallavi's four-legged third child, who never fails to make her smile.

Introduction: Histories and Contexts

Nalini Iyer and Pallavi Rastogi

Toward a Pedagogy of South Asian Anglophone Diasporic Literature

In April 2021 the delta variant of the coronavirus burned its way through India. The Indian diaspora watched in helpless horror as the virus infected and killed family and friends. Then the medical infrastructure began to collapse. As the stories of death and devastation obtained even more urgency, the diaspora went into action. Indians living abroad raised money for their home country with unparalleled zeal; doctors and nurses in the United States and the United Kingdom stopped sleeping to triage over *WhatsApp*; other medical professionals started telehealth clinics for COVID patients in India; some even risked their lives to return to the subcontinent to work in the trenches there. The mobilization of Indian immigrants in the service of the communities they left behind is not an unusual story for South Asians in the diaspora. Other events—from floods in Bangladesh to tsunamis in Sri Lanka—galvanized Bangladeshi and Sri Lankan diasporic communities to return home and rebuild nations shattered by war, natural disasters, and disease. The South Asian diaspora's immutable connection with the geography of its origin can never be severed, for better or worse.

The dialectic of routes and roots—the back-and-forth movement between the home country and the host country that occurs when individuals settle down in new lands in order to make those lands their own—is a key characteristic of the South Asian diaspora.[1] This tension seeps into the literature of the diaspora and affects how the literature is taught. The pedagogy of South Asian anglophone diasporic literature cannot be separated from the topography of South Asia—a topography that is not only present as place but also manifested in literary registers through South Asian ways of structuring the world: of refracting narrative representation through national origin, language, religion, caste, gender, region, immigration status, and class.

In this essay, the first of our two-part introduction, we tell the story of the pedagogy of South Asian anglophone diasporic literature. It is a young story, even though the body of literature it encompasses is older, but not by that much. This literature found a voice only around the second half of the twentieth century, with the independence of the Indian subcontinent in 1947. In just a few decades, though, it acquired global readerships and literary cachet, partly because of the meteoric rise of writers such as V. S. Naipaul, Salman Rushdie, and Bharati Mukherjee and the awarding of prestigious prizes such as the Nobel, Booker, and Pulitzer to South Asian authors.

Not surprisingly, the boom in literary production led to the slow but steady introduction of South Asian anglophone diasporic texts into higher education curricula across the world—in classes focused on specific writers, genres, and themes; in general education and interdisciplinary courses; and in introductory and advanced undergraduate courses as well as in graduate seminars. Many universities now offer classes focused entirely on South Asian diasporic literature and cultures. Nonetheless, teaching this literature is often challenging for novice and experienced pedagogues because of the multitude of political, religious, cultural, and linguistic factors, or what we call "the intersectionality of diaspora," constituting its subject matter. The subcontinent's internal diversity, its spiritual and ethnonational friction, and the centuries that separate older diasporas from newer diasporas add to the already immense scope of South Asian anglophone diasporic literature. The writers and texts alone constitute an enormous and eternally expanding archive. The historical, theoretical, and political contexts in which this literature emerged—and is taught—are also vast.[2]

What Is the South Asian Diaspora?

The term *South Asia* emerged after World War II and reflects the rise of area studies in the American academy.[3] *South Asia* gestures toward a shared and continuous history in the Indian subcontinent but conceals the hostilities and tensions among the nations and people who are part of that history. South Asians often identify through country of origin, religion, caste, and language, further revealing the cracks in overarching nomenclature such as *South Asia* or *South Asian*. As some critics have argued, South Asia is often associated primarily with India and emphasizes the dominance of Indian, and predominantly Hindu, identities, particularly in North America.[4] We deploy these labels strategically to denote a geographic region with shared histories, cultures, and migratory patterns while also being mindful of the conflicts and power struggles both within and outside of that geographic region.

South Asian migration from the subcontinent commenced on a large scale over 150 years ago under the auspices of the British Empire. A vast number of indentured laborers were transported across the *kala pani*, or the "black waters" of the ocean, to the Caribbean, the Pacific Islands, and Africa. Following the decolonization of the Indian subcontinent (1947 and beyond), migration from South Asia increased as a result of labor scarcity in the United Kingdom, Canada, and the United States. Today, approximately twenty-four million people scattered all over the world trace their heritage to South Asia (Rangaswamy 285). Ancestral roots in the subcontinent entangled with the already complex intersectional experiences of religion, nation, class, caste, gender, sexuality, and geography constitute the subject positions of South Asians in the diaspora. Additionally, political events in the home country, such as the civil war in Sri Lanka, created exilic communities and further transformed diasporic subjectivities.

The histories, demographics, and cultures of the host countries to which South Asians migrated also shaped diasporic selfhood. The rise of Idi Amin and ethnonationalism in Uganda and the subsequent expulsion of Ugandan Asians in 1972 made "double diasporics" out of South Asians, many of whom considered themselves Ugandan or African. New psychic wounds, this time from the trauma of forced expulsion, were etched across generations. On the less dramatic level of daily existence, the life of a working-class Indian in Durban is very different from the life of a South Asian Silicon Valley executive of Indian, Pakistani, or Sri Lankan ancestry. The South Asian diaspora can be imagined in rhizomatic form, as roots become routes and shared geographies of origin transform into a more ambiguous heritage of space.

This complex origin story renders it impossible to craft a full narrative of the literary history of the South Asian diaspora. At the same time, the great diasporic themes of linkages to the homeland, friction and solidarity among different religious and national communities in the diaspora, migration, exile, trauma, nostalgia, memory, identity, gender relations, national belonging and unbelonging, racialization, multiculturalism, and double consciousness resonate across South Asian anglophone diasporic literature. Diaspora is a location, the physical space migrants occupy, and it is also a state of mind—the consciousness of immigrants, émigrés, migrants, and other transplants.

Despite the significant growth and international visibility of South Asian anglophone literature after 1947, critics often do not distinguish between writers residing in South Asia and those living abroad. That many authors sojourn in different parts of the world further complicates the already blurry categorization of resident and migrant. R. K. Narayan lived his entire life in India. Anita Desai lived in India and abroad. Mohsin Hamid lives in Pakistan and the United States. Raja Rao resided in the United States but wrote about colonial and postcolonial India. The work of these authors is often collected under the umbrella category of South Asian literature and taught as a singular entity. The essays in this volume complicate this approach. More specifically, they emphasize that teaching South Asian anglophone diasporic literature requires different pedagogical strategies than those required for teaching South Asian literature, particularly a sharpened engagement with the intersectionality of migration.

Theorizing the South Asian Diaspora Historically

As scholars have long contended, the term *diaspora* is a vexed one. Derived from Greek, *diaspora* literally means "scattering." The term was initially associated with the Jewish Diaspora. In a now classic essay in the inaugural issue of the journal *Diaspora: A Journal of Transnational Studies*, William Safran identifies a desire to return home as one of the defining traits of a diaspora (83–84). While Safran provides a valuable template for diasporic categorization, he uses the Jewish Diaspora as his only model. Moreover, the structuring trope of return manifests itself differently in different diasporas. South Asians born and raised in the United Kingdom probably do not fantasize about returning to the India, Pakistan, or Bangladesh from which their parents or grandparents arrived. Other scholars have conceptualized diaspora more broadly than Safran has (e.g., Brah, *Decolonial Imaginings* and "Multiple Axes"; Vertovec and Cohen). Judith Brown uses the term *diaspora* to "[d]enote groups of people with a common ethnicity; who have left their original homeland for prolonged periods of time and often permanently; who retain a particular sense of cultural identity and often close kinship links with other scattered members of their group" (4). Avtar Brah notes that "diasporas are simultaneously about 'space' and 'place,' about movement as well as settling down" ("Multiple Axes" 164). This dialectical approach informs the crux of this volume's intervention: to reframe diaspora not only as a movement forward to somewhere else but also as a looking back, in myriad ways, at what was left behind.

Beginning with the decolonization of South Asia in 1947, migration from the newly formed nations of India and Pakistan increased dramatically. These nations were formed in the crucible of a bloody partition that forced millions of people to travel across newly articulated borders, and this refugee population created diasporas both within and outside of South Asia.[5] Over the next seventy-five years, diasporic communities emerging from political upheaval in the subcontinent, along with the already existing South Asian communities in East Africa and the Caribbean, were absorbed into existing diasporas in the United Kingdom and North America. The creation of Bangladesh in 1971, the Sri Lankan Civil War from 1983 to 2009, the Sikh movement for an independent homeland, the violence against this community in 1984, and the volatile political status of Kashmir all spurred fresh waves of migration out of South Asia.[6]

Vijay Mishra provides a crucial distinction between the old and new South Asian diasporas: "The old (that is, early modern, classic capitalist or, more specifically, nineteenth-century indenture) and the new (that is, late modern or late capitalist) traverse two quite different kinds of topography" (4–5). But the multiple trajectories of South Asian dispersion and settlements in East Africa and the Caribbean blur the distinction between old and new diasporas. To wit: How would we categorize a writer such as Abraham Verghese? Verghese was born and raised in Ethiopia and migrated to the United States. He wrote two literary memoirs from the vantage point of an infectious disease specialist in the American South and a novel partly about growing up Indian in Ethiopia. Nonetheless, the chronological timeline on which Mishra's definition is predicated allows us to organize the literary narrative of the South Asian diaspora historically and geographically. We suggest theorizing the South Asian diaspora as communities with origins, ancestral or otherwise, in the Indian subcontinent whose subjecthood intersects with the political events, racial upheaval, and social changes in the host and home countries and whose identities are determined by the overlapping vectors of race, religion, language, nation, caste, class, gender, and sexuality, among other matrices.

While it is important to recognize the value of a broad category such as the South Asian diaspora, it is also necessary to acknowledge that diasporic experiences are not homogenous. The chronotropes of departure, the reasons for leaving (e.g., indenture, economic advancement, expulsion, or political unrest), and the public climate in the host country profoundly influence the lives, and thus the consciousness, of diasporic subjects. Thus, Sandhya Shukla asks whether

> the constructed term *South Asian* can adequately bridge the divide between more internationalist conceptions of diaspora and nationalist accounts of racial and ethnic formation, and if so, whether it creates new epistemologies for the consideration of migration in highly globalized political and economic arrangements. In arguing that multiple formations of nationality take place in diasporic culture, this review also intervenes in debates in anthropology about the geographical and conceptual boundaries of community. Finally, in suggesting that gender, sexuality, and generation might profoundly fissure South Asian and other diasporas, the article raises the question of the implicit limits of any category of location or identity. (551)

Extrapolating from Shukla, we also ask if the internationalism of diaspora can generate an understanding of the domestic racialization of the South Asian community in North America, for example. Shukla further warns that "gender, sexuality, and generation" render the experience—indeed the expression—of diasporic life so different as to raise questions about the coherence of the very category of South Asian diaspora. Yet certain emotions, such as those related to national belonging, racial difference, and kinship with other South Asians, appear in diasporic communities across generations, genders, and sexualities. We posit that these cultural signatures constitute some of the unchanging aspects of the South Asian diaspora, even if the signage has adapted across time and geographies. Moreover, the constant overlap between the international and national, the intersectionality of diaspora, shows that migration has always generated new forms of knowledge.

Theorizing the South Asian Diaspora Today

South Asian diasporic experiences have been rendered even more complex over time. The world has become increasingly connected through the easy dissemination of information and culture. Diasporic identity is also created, curated, and expressed through Bollywood films, Internet forums, social media, blogs, websites, emails, smartphones, and other forms of digital communication. New forms of diasporic consciousness that engage these modalities are continually emerging in the twenty-first century.[7]

In *Beyond Bollywood: The Cultural Politics of South Asian Diasporic Film*, Jigna Desai shows how South Asian diasporic lives are bound to some of the most important economic structures of our times, such as "global capital, migration, colonialism, and empire" (3). These world-shaping economic shifts are manifested in blockbuster Bollywood films starring South Asian diasporic characters who consume Western technology and physically traverse continents with utmost ease but still retain their supposedly authentic Indian identity.[8] Through the visual appeal of Bollywood, the South Asian diaspora is often exoticized and fetishized, cinematized into an array of ornamental saris, exotic bindis, and brightly colored spices. Yet Bollywood has also pushed back against promoting only reactionary, nostalgia-infused diasporic sensibilities. Crossover films and television series that borrow aesthetically and thematically from both the hostland and the homeland are on the rise.[9] If nostalgia and prejudice are some of the cultural signatures of South Asian anglophone diasporic literature, then so are political activism and cultural fusion.

Digital media is also enhancing these reactionary and progressive aspects of South Asian diasporic identity.[10] As Radhika Gajjala notes, "[T]he combined logic of digital transnationalism with globalized markets and online technologies allows the emergence of digital diasporas" (12), creating diasporic communities with predetermined sensibilities, even for South Asians only intending to migrate abroad. On the one hand, digital diasporas can be exclusionary, promoting false myths about the nation. They can create closed-off spaces for only some religions, languages, genders, and cultures. On the other hand, digital diasporas can be democratizing. Anyone with access to the Internet can become a participant in South Asian diasporic life and raise diasporic consciousness.

Language and Genre in South Asian Anglophone Diasporic Literature

Several factors influenced our decision to focus on South Asian *anglophone* diasporic literature in this volume. English is the language used in education, government, commerce, and professional and everyday life in almost all the countries to which South Asians migrated, including the Anglo-American world and anglophone Africa. Indeed, the British Empire and its American successor were the primary agents in moving South Asians across the English-speaking areas of the world. Practicality is another issue influencing the choice to write in English. Writers from the South Asian diaspora use the English language to acquire literary capital and to converse with other anglophone cultural producers nationally, internationally, and globally. While linguistic diversity is a hallmark of South Asia and its diaspora, English becomes the default language of many South Asian diasporic writers after fluency in their mother tongues is compromised by years of distance from their home countries. This loss is a shared experience that creates community, forges bonds, and generates literary interaction among South Asian diasporic writers. An anthology like ours cannot reflect the linguistic diversity of the South Asian diaspora, because prioritizing linguistic range would risk tokenism as well as overrepresentation of some languages and underrepresentation of others. It is impossible to solicit essays on teaching literature written in South Asian languages spoken all over the diaspora, which include Tamil, Kannada, Bengali, Hindi, Urdu, Gujarati, and Sinhala, among many others. This volume focuses on those writers likely to be taught across the world, especially those likely to be taught in North American classrooms, where most of our contributors teach and work. The authors with the most pedagogical purchase—those whose books are easily available and inexpensive—often use English.[11] At the same time, English no longer means standard English; it exists in hybrid, impure, "chutneyfied" forms, to modify Rushdie's phrase.[12] Many South Asian anglophone diasporic texts imbue this already hybrid English language with regional or national inflections from the host country—seen, for example, in the use of Zulu words in South African Indian writing.

Genre was another important consideration that shaped this collection. Although we wanted to include essays on a wide range of literary genres—fiction, poetry, theater, and nonfiction—we concluded that the writers taught most often in the American classroom (and whose books were easily available) were primarily fiction writers. The dominance of fiction in the South Asian diasporic canon is not unusual, because it is the most popular genre in almost every field of contemporary literature. Ultimately, this volume focuses on prose narratives, including fiction, memoir, nonfiction, film, and comedy. Our discussions of theory and pedagogy apply to works other than prose fiction alone and provide broad conceptual ideas about how to teach other genres besides fiction. The selection and organization of essays in this book were thus also shaped by the histories and geographies of dispersion and the institutional and curricular locations of the teachers and the courses they offer.

An Intersectional Approach to Teaching South Asian Anglophone Diasporic Literature

The term *intersectionality* is central to the reading and pedagogical practices offered in this collection. Brah notes that "diasporas are inherently intersectional and the study of diaspora and intersectionality is intrinsically connected" (*Decolonial Imaginings* 126). Brah defines *intersectionality* as "historically specific, irreducible, and varied effects which emerge when multiple axes of differentiation intersect with one another" (130), using the term to emphasize diaspora as heritage in a land left behind (roots) and a journey of belonging in the new land that is never complete (routes). Kimberlé Crenshaw's now canonical definition of *intersectionality* underscores the layering of different forms of identity, such as race, gender, class, and sexuality, and emerges from a specifically African American and legal context (1244). *Intersectionality*, as we deploy the term in its relationship to the South Asian diaspora, conveys modes of representation (diasporic literatures themselves are always intersectional) as well as interpretative and pedagogical practices (to teach and read South Asian anglophone diasporic literature is to teach and read intersectionally). Crucially, intersectionality in this body of literature also centers internationalism, migratory status, and diasporic consciousness. The intersectional is thus located at the crossroads of multiple interpretive and disciplinary frameworks. The 9/11 attacks, for example, are the focus of part 6 of this volume. The cataclysmic impact of 9/11, especially the attendant Islamophobia, has forever altered the South Asian diaspora. The ever-present concerns of national belonging and cultural alienation have become even more pressing after 9/11. Self-representation and self-narration in a post-9/11 world are key to understanding South Asian anglophone diasporic literature today.[13]

South Asian anglophone diasporic literature is taught in classrooms scattered across different geographic regions, nations, types of institutions, courses, and programs. Many of the essays in this volume focus on teaching this literature in North American classrooms, where the student population can vary greatly based on regional demographics, class, and politics, such as in a community college in New York City, a large state university on the Texas border, or a prestigious private institution in California. Following Rachel Sagner Buurma and Laura Heffernan in *The Teaching Archive: A New History for Literary Study*, we argue that the theoretical approaches to teaching South Asian anglophone diasporic literature are derived most usefully from the real-life encounters between instructors and students in the classroom. Teaching is a collaborative activity between the teacher and the student, regardless of the size or level of the classes or the pedagogical format (lecture, seminar, or experiential study). Classroom learning, especially when the subject is literature, involves constant reading and rereading, discussion, debate, and analysis. Consciously and unconsciously, teachers and students invoke a range of knowledge, disciplinary backgrounds, and personal histories that create meaningful interpretations and forge connections with literary texts. However, as the essays in *Teaching South Asian Anglophone Diasporic Literature* demonstrate, some theoretical approaches appear more frequently than others do—for instance, postcolonial theory, diaspora studies, cultural studies, critical race studies, and feminist and gender studies. Thus, to teach South Asian anglophone diasporic literature is to teach intersectionally, to always be attentive to internationalism, migration histories, immigration policies, the rise and fall of empires, decolonization, settler colonialism, and engagement with other racial groups in the regions where diasporic communities evolved. Yet, an overarching theory of teaching this literature risks being simplistic and reductive. Our proposal for intersectional teaching simply means paying attention to the historical and material conditions of cultural production, the institutional contexts of pedagogy, and the subject positions of teachers and students.

The last few years have seen a growing demand for decolonizing the curriculum in the Western academy.[14] As Priyamvada Gopal argues, "Precisely because of their location, 'Western' universities can also lead the increasingly vital task of historical self-understanding in the constituent polities and societies of the geo-political 'West,' itself a reaction of the colonial project and its imaginative geography" (878). Decolonization has become increasingly urgent because of the increase in ethnic groups at universities, the need to engage critically with racial politics, and students' search for representation and relevance in their curriculum. South Asian anglophone diasporic literature thus offers a broad range of texts that facilitate diversifying the curriculum. Yet, as Gopal notes, "for some, the project at hand [decolonizing the curriculum] might be driven less by intellectual imperative than market segment satisfaction" (877). Calls to diversify and decolonize can often lead to the tokenistic addition of non-white and non-European authors. Although some teachers may want to decenter the canonical focus of the literature degree, their progress is often hampered by curricular constraints, limited time available in an academic term, and other unforeseeable factors that may disrupt classroom learning. Despite these limitations, an intersectional approach to teaching South Asian anglophone diasporic literature can help diversify and decenter certain types of pedagogical approaches in English classes. Attention to intersectionality underscores the complexity of the origin stories of texts and writers and teaches students to contextualize this literature against political, cultural, and social events in the subcontinent. Moreover, it helps students understand that these writers and the issues they discuss from what seems to be a space that is distant and removed from us are actually near us, with us, and of us.

Intersectionality also involves understanding that different diasporic geographies represent different histories and, crucially, juxtaposing literature with other academic fields. In engaging with the literary representation of the past, present, and future of South Asian diasporic communities, students learn to critique imperialism, hegemonic race and gender relations, and the institutionalization and canonization of certain diasporic texts. Why does anglophone literature dominate the global market? Why do Salman Rushdie, Mohsin Hamid, Monica Ali, and Jhumpa Lahiri appear most frequently in college literature classes? Why do certain genres, such as fiction, predominate? Why are some historical moments (Partition, 9/11) or some nations of origin (India, Pakistan) dominant in the archive of South Asian anglophone diasporic literature? How do we read doubly diasporic texts (Indo-Caribbean Canadian, South Asian African British) differently from single-place migrant texts? And how do literatures from older diasporas and newer diasporas register differently, even as these literatures share some of the same concerns?

For this collection, we have chosen essays that not only represent different geographies of dispersion but also engage intersectionally with literature. South Asian anglophone diasporic literature is often taught in classes that focus on specific geographic regions, such as contemporary Asian American literature or multiethnic British literature. Most important, the very inception of the South Asian diaspora was geographic in origin, with indentured laborers transported to Africa, the Caribbean, and Fiji and later diasporas moving to the United Kingdom and North America. The diasporic story of South Asians in Kenya is very different from the diasporic story of South Asians in Australia. In emphasizing geographies of origin in the organization of this collection, we seek to minimize the risk of flattening the historical, cultural, and political differences within and among distinct diasporas. Moreover, the geographic arrangement of the essays highlights the interplay of South Asian diasporic cultures with local traditions, including language, food, and religious practice.

Our contributors analyze the power involved in canon formation, including the process of organizing collections such as this one, which necessarily foreground some writers, texts, genres, and nations over others. Sonja Thomas argues that, too often, we focus on numerical minorities and overlook the analysis of power (4). Similarly, Patricia Hill Collins and Sirma Bilge propose that in analyzing power, we recognize its interpersonal, cultural, and structural domains (5–13). Rigorous attention to history, politics, and authorly subject positions shows how these different "domains of power" are framed against the civil and international regulations that haunt diasporic subjects (7). However, to truly decolonize the curriculum, the hegemonies within South Asian diasporic studies—such as heteronormativity[15] and caste as well as the often complex relationship between South Asians and Black and Indigenous populations globally—must be addressed.[16]

Caste is a crucial factor in identity and discrimination in the South Asian diaspora and is thus vital to the intersectional framework we propose. Indentured immigrants are an early example of the importance of centering caste in analyzing a South Asian diasporic text.[17] Migrant laborers often faced the prospect of losing caste while crossing the *kala pani* because they were unable to maintain the social practices required to retain caste. After completing their indentureship, some returned to India only to find out that the communities they had left behind no longer accepted them because they had allegedly been polluted. Maintaining caste identities and practices in the diaspora is a significant tension in many South Asian diasporic texts. A novel such as Naipaul's *A House for Mr. Biswas* should be read not just as the story of Naipaul's father but also as a historical narrative that opens a partial, perhaps askew, window into upper-caste Indo-Caribbean migration. Similarly, Amitav Ghosh's Ibis trilogy, particularly *Sea of Poppies*, underscores how caste and class intersect in the life stories of indentured laborers sent to Mauritius. During the post–World War II migration of South Asians to North America and the United Kingdom, upper-caste communities offered their members access to professional networks, which led to advantageous educational and job opportunities, especially for Hindus. Changes in US immigration laws that shifted away from national and racial quotas to skills-based migration favored upper-caste Hindu migrants whose social privileges in the subcontinent translated to increased economic opportunities through emigration abroad. Consequently, upper-caste Hindus often dominate the demographics of the South Asian diaspora in North America, and the caste issues from South Asia are rendered invisible in North America as Hindus morph into South Asian Americans. Thus, when teaching South Asian anglophone diasporic literature, it is important to interrogate caste and pay attention to its history within South Asian immigrant communities.

Additionally, diasporic experiences may produce a race-caste complex wherein racialization is often highlighted at the expense of caste. A bildungsroman such as Lahiri's *The Namesake* explores the intersections of race, nation, and gender in the life of its protagonist, Gogol Ganguli. Even as the novel critiques the racism and xenophobia of the world into which Gogol is born, it does not comment on the family's privileged Brahminic identity, manifested in life rituals such as how the baby is named or the rice ceremony that marks a milestone in his life.[18] In recent times, Dalit diasporic narratives have self-consciously engaged with the triangulation of migration, race, and caste. These include Sujatha Gidla's *Ants among Elephants*, Yashica Dutt's *Coming Out as Dalit*, Suraj Yengde's *Caste Matters*, and the speculative fiction of Mimi Mondal. Teachers will find these books to be a rich repository for discussing caste oppression from the perspective of its victims.

Yet, as the essays in this volume show, caste is but one issue in the tangled web of intersectional identities and histories in which a South Asian anglophone diasporic text is produced, read, taught, and learned about. The best and most effective intersectional teaching accounts for the geographic and institutional contexts and the identities—of writer, teacher, and student—in relation to the South Asian diaspora. Intersectionality is the study of knowledge production and power through overlapping identities and modes of interpretation. Intersectionality is, therefore, not a list of the different vectors of identity that we can summarize here. The intersectional subject positions that South Asian migrants occupy are particularly complex because identities in the geography of origin transform through migration, often appearing not only directly and visibly but also as traces and hauntings. The displacement of caste by race nonetheless reveals the buried or coded but always present presence of caste in many South Asian anglophone diasporic texts and serves as a powerful reminder of the necessity to undertake an intersectional approach to teaching these texts. Instead of attempting to categorize and confine all the various components of intersectionality, this collection shows how some of the many intersectional approaches in teaching South Asian diasporic literature do pedagogical justice to the plurality of the texts and writers we seek to teach.

Essays in This Volume

Teaching South Asian Anglophone Diasporic Literature is divided into seven parts. After this two-part introduction, the next five parts focus on four diasporic locations, Africa and the Caribbean (part 2), the United Kingdom (part 3), and North America (parts 4, 5, and 6), since the place of migration is often a dominant theme in South Asian anglophone diasporic literature. Part 7 focuses on genre, which will allow readers to see the workings of literary forms other than fiction. Taken together, the essays in this collection form a literary silhouette of the South Asian diaspora. Our contributors use a wide range of intersectional approaches in their real-world pedagogies and in thinking about pedagogy in their essays. These critical approaches include postcolonialism, decolonial theory, critical ethnic theory, and social justice strategies, among others. The essays in this volume are not meant to be exhaustive but to serve as a strategically "selective guide to the richness and potential of the field" (Nair 19), specifically to teaching in the field.

Our contributors are teacher-scholars who employ the great diasporic themes of national longing, belonging, and citizenship to challenge stereotypes about South Asia and South Asians in and outside the diaspora but always in the classroom. Many contributors demonstrate how South Asian anglophone diasporic literature can provide students with alternative histories to state-sanctioned narratives of migration. Many also discuss strategies to connect the literatures and histories represented in these texts with the lives of students. All demonstrate intersectional pedagogical and reading practices.

Part 1, "Introduction: Histories and Contexts," consists of two linked essays. These essays provide a general overview of the literary and theoretical approaches to teaching South Asian anglophone diasporic literature and a short but essential summary of the social, historical, and material conditions in which it emerged.

Part 2, "East Meets South: Africa and the Caribbean," focuses on the diasporas of indenture in the Caribbean and Africa and their afterlives in migrations to North America and other parts of the Western world. The opening essay, by Asma Sayed, frames the well-known African Asian writer M. G. Vassanji within the interpretive context of postcolonial, social justice, and critical race studies. Sayed introduces students to concepts such as "double diaspora," which particularly resonate with the South Asian diaspora in Africa. Anita Baksh examines how South Asian diasporic writing from the Caribbean can counter the erasure of this group from mainstream literary criticism. Mayuri Deka's essay focuses on the importance of narrative and imagery, what Deka calls "nonpropositional knowledge," to address student stereotypes of the Indo-Caribbean community. Dharitri Bhattacharjee writes from the perspective of a historian teaching Ghosh's *In an Antique Land*. Her essay shows how a rigorous historical framework can help students deepen their knowledge of the themes resonating in diasporic literary studies: migration, East-South encounters, and the recovery of precolonial cross-cultural interaction. Using a postcolonial perspective, R. Benedito Ferrão invites an understanding of the difference between British and Portuguese colonialism as manifested in literature from South Asian diasporic writers of Goan origin.

Part 3, "East Meets West: Post–World War II Britain," moves to the United Kingdom after World War II. C. S. Bhagya discusses teaching a wide range of South Asian British texts to reveal the connection between political events in the home country and the host country. Alpana Sharma undertakes a paired analysis of Sunjeev Sahota's *The Year of the Runaways* and Mohsin Hamid's *Exit West* to show the difference between the cosmopolitan immigrant and the unmoored migrant. Like Sharma, Feroza Jussawalla pairs American and British texts, but with a different agenda: to understand how Mexican American students may recognize their own experiences in a novel about South Asian British immigrants, such as Monica Ali's *Brick Lane*.

North American geography inevitably forms the center of the volume. Parts 4, 5, and 6 maintain the volume's intersectional approach and its scrupulous attentiveness to the historical specificity of different South Asian groups in North America. Part 4, "East Meets North: The United States and Canada," begins with Chandrima Chakraborty's essay on teaching the 1985 Air India tragedy in Canada as a form of history that challenges official narratives. Robin E. Field examines Bharati Mukherjee's novel *Jasmine* to show how one South Asian diasporic story can be taught from multiple critical perspectives and under different genres. Rajender Kaur discusses teaching Asian American writers through different critical lenses—postcolonial, multicultural, ethnic, and diasporic—to understand how issues addressed in South Asian anglophone diasporic texts overlap with the concerns of other US ethnic communities. Esther Daimari warns teachers against using the easy label of "postcolonial" while discussing Nepali anglophone literature, especially in the North American classroom, as Nepal was not colonized in the way other areas of South Asia were.

Parts 5 and 6 focus on teaching two defining experiences in the South Asian diaspora. In part 5, "East Meets North: The Sri Lankan Refugee Diaspora," Umme Al-wazedi focuses on refugee counternarratives, like many other essays in the volume, in order to challenge students to open their hearts and minds to communities who are forced to flee their homelands. Dinidu Karunanayake juxtaposes mainstream South Asian diasporic writing with Sri Lankan refugee writing to spotlight the specificity of the Sri Lankan refugee experience and to make this work more accessible, primarily to white students. Maryse Jayasuriya undertakes a similar project but brings together Sri Lankan writing with multilingual American literature. Manav Ratti frames teaching Michael Ondaatje's *Anil's Ghost* from the perspective of human rights studies.

The defining experience of the Pakistani American diaspora after 9/11 is the subject of part 6, "East Meets North: The Pakistani American Diaspora after 9/11." Mushtaq Bilal, like many others in this volume, urges teachers to challenge stereotypes about Muslims, using concepts from world literature, feminism, and ecocriticism. Aniruddha Mukhopadhyay discusses how his students, primarily from working-class Hispanic backgrounds, identify with the migratory experience in Hamid's *Exit West*. Binod Paudyal describes how teaching Hamid's *Reluctant Fundamentalist* in an Asian American studies class interrogates depictions of Muslims. Finally, Suhaan Kiran Mehta examines how setting classes against the backdrop of familiar events such as 9/11 can make the life stories of Muslim South Asians in the United States more meaningful to American students.

Part 7, "The Forms of Diaspora," focuses on genres other than fiction. Subhalakshmi Gooptu shows how the formal qualities of South Asian diasporic nonfiction writing open pedagogical spaces to discuss issues of immigration, race, and class that may not best showcase themselves in fiction. Matthew Spencer uses the idea of a global diaspora of discourses in Ghosh's *The Great Derangement* to engage students with climate change. Madhurima Chakraborty analyzes how Indian American stand-up comedy can function as a counterpoint to diasporic fiction to reveal the double consciousness of South Asian immigrants. Robyn Carruthers and Asha Varadharajan bring together pedagogy and digital writing—a juxtaposition predicated on the notion of extimacy, or distance, that digital writing allows rather than the more conventional intimacy created by printed texts. Amina Gautier's essay examines how Jhumpa Lahiri's short story "A Temporary Matter" can be taught in a creative writing course emphasizing craft. Nidhi Shrivastava discusses teaching the 1947 Partition and the ensuing genocidal violence through Bapsi Sidhwa's novel *Cracking India*, originally published as *Ice Candy Man*, and its adaptation into the film *Earth*, directed by Deepa Mehta.

The essays in *Teaching South Asian Anglophone Diasporic Literature* highlight how South Asian diasporic writing is taught nationally and internationally and how theoretical frameworks, curricular and institutional contexts, and teachers' and students' associations with South Asian diasporic communities shape the intersectional pedagogy we propose.

Notes

1. We use the term *South Asia* in this volume to refer to India, Pakistan, Bangladesh, Sri Lanka, Nepal, the Maldives, Afghanistan, and Bhutan.

2. This essay is the first of a two-part introduction presenting an overview of these crucial texts and contexts as well as South Asian diaspora theory, although it is important to underscore the limitations of a précis of this kind. The second essay in part 1 provides a more detailed discussion of the histories and contexts of South Asian anglophone diasporic literature.

3. For a discussion of the term *South Asian*, see Mohammad-Arif.

4. For a nuanced reflection on this naming problem in the context of South Asian diasporic literature, see Singh.

5. This volume studies the literature of these diasporic groups created outside South Asia since Partition and decolonization. We use the term *Partition* to refer to the political division of the Indian subcontinent in 1947 into two nations—India and Pakistan—mainly along religious lines. The Partition was extremely violent, and almost a million people were killed. Many women were abducted on both sides of the border and also experienced sexual assault. Vazira Zamindar notes that some twelve million people on the Punjab border alone and nearly twenty million across the subcontinent were displaced (6). As is the norm in South Asian studies, we capitalize *Partition* throughout the volume when referring to this catastrophic historic event whose repercussions are felt to this day in South Asia.

6. The literary overview we provide of the South Asian diaspora in the second essay in the introduction elaborates on these histories of colonization, shifting immigration laws, political turbulence, culture, and religion.

7. Our pedagogical practices are inevitably adapting to these changes.

8. Examples of such Bollywood films include *Dilwale Dulhania Le Jayenge, Swades,* and *English Vinglish.*

9. Films such as Mira Nair's *Mississippi Masala* and *Monsoon Wedding,* Gurinder Chadha's *Bend It Like Beckham* and *Bride and Prejudice,* and, more recently, the Netflix film *The Wedding Season* and series such as *Indian Matchmaking* and *Never Have I Ever* are examples of these crossover films and television shows.

10. Teachers now have the instant option to assign a digital compendium of material, such as the *South Asian American Digital Archive* (www.saada.org).

11. It is also extremely difficult to procure high-quality translations of diasporic works in the vernacular languages.

12. The term "chutnification" is used by Rushdie in *Midnight's Children* (548). For more on the hybridization of language, see, for example, Gorra.

13. In 2021 the journal *South Asian Diaspora* published a special issue on literary and cinematic representation as a key to defining and understanding the South Asian diaspora (Clini and Valančiūnas).

14. For a useful discussion of decolonial and postcolonial, see Brah, *Decolonial Imaginings* 1–24.

15. Gayatri Gopinath's *Impossible Desires: Queer Diasporas and South Asian Public Cultures* and Kareem Khubchandani's *Queer South Asian Diasporas* are useful resources for unpacking heteronormativity and queer identities in South Asian diasporas.

16. See the four short essays on global South Asian and Black relationships curated by Pallavi Rastogi and Liam O'Loughlin in the journal *South Asian Review* (Bald; Burton; Nasta; Paul).

17. For an extensive discussion of the indentured diaspora and the *kala pani* paradigm, see Bhardwaj and Misrahi-Barak.

18. As S. Shankar and Charu Gupta write in "'My Birth Is My Fatal Accident': Introduction to Caste and Life Narratives," "While not all 'upper-caste' life narratives acknowledge caste as directly as Dalit life narratives, they nevertheless remain marked, even in their silence, by caste. Indeed, it has been argued that such silence is itself a mark of caste privilege—after all, is not the ability to ignore caste in itself a mark of privilege?" (2)

Works Cited

Bald, Vivek. "What Is National Belonging in a Nation That Doesn't Belong?" *South Asian Review,* vol. 43, nos. 1–2, 2022, pp. 155–59.

Bhardwaj, Ashutosh, and Judith Misrahi-Barak, editors. *Kala Pani Crossings: Revisiting Nineteenth Century Migrations from India's Perspective.* Routledge, 2022.

Brah, Avtar. *Decolonial Imaginings: Intersectional Conversations and Contestations.* Goldsmith's Press, 2022.

———. "Multiple Axes of Power: Articulations of Diaspora and Intersectionality." *The Routledge Diaspora Studies Reader,* edited by Klaus Stierstorfer and Janet Wilson, Routledge, 2018, pp. 163–73.

Brown, Judith M. *Global South Asians: Introducing the Modern Diaspora.* Cambridge UP, 2006.

Burton, Antoinette. "See the Noose, Say Their Names: Phyllis Naidoo's *Waiting to Die in Pretoria* (1990)." *South Asian Review*, vol. 43, nos. 1–2, 2022, pp. 144–48.

Buurma, Rachel Sagner, and Laura Heffernan. *The Teaching Archive: A New History for Literary Study.* U of Chicago P, 2021.

Clini, Clelia, and Deimantas Valančiūnas, editors. *South Asian Diasporas and (Imaginary) Homelands: Mediated Exchanges and Representations in the Twenty-First Century.* Special issue of *South Asian Diaspora.* Vol. 13, no. 1, 2021.

Collins, Patricia Hill, and Sirma Bilge. *Intersectionality.* Polity Press, 2016.

Crenshaw, Kimberlé. "Mapping the Margins: Intersectionality, Identity, and Violence against Women of Color." *Stanford Law Review*, vol. 43, no. 6, July 1991, pp. 1241–99.

Desai, Jigna. *Beyond Bollywood: The Cultural Politics of South Asian Diasporic Film.* Routledge, 2004.

Dutt, Yashica. *Coming Out as Dalit: A Memoir of Surviving India's Caste System.* Penguin Books, 2024.

Gajjala, Radhika. *Digital Diasporas: Labor and Affect in Gendered Indian Publics.* Rowman and Littlefield, 2019.

Gidla, Sujatha. *Ants among Elephants.* Farrar, Straus and Giroux, 2017.

Gopal, Priyamvada. "On Decolonisation and the University." *Textual Practice*, vol. 35, no. 6, 2021, pp. 873–99, https://doi.org/10.1080/0950236X.2021.1929561.

Gopinath, Gayatri. *Impossible Desires: Queer Diasporas and South Asian Public Cultures.* Duke UP, 2005.

Gorra, Michael. *After Empire: Scott, Naipaul, Rushdie.* Chicago UP, 1998.

Khubchandani, Kareem. *Queer South Asian Diasporas. Oxford Research Encyclopedias*, 25 June 2019, https://doi.org/10.1093/acrefore/9780190201098.013.807.

Lahiri, Jhumpa. *The Namesake.* Mariner Books, 2004.

Mishra, Vijay. *Literature of the Indian Diaspora: Theorizing the Diasporic Imaginary.* Routledge, 2007.

Mohammad-Arif, Aminah. "Imaginations and Constructions of South Asia: An Enchanting Abstraction." *South Asia Multidisciplinary Academic Journal*, no. 10, 2014, pp. 1–27.

Mondal, Mimi. *His Footsteps, through Darkness and Light.* Macmillan, 2019.

Nair, Supriya M., editor. *Teaching Anglophone Caribbean Literature.* Modern Language Association of America, 2012.

Nasta, Susheila. "'Messy Solidarities': Reflections on the Politics of the Present." *South Asian Review*, vol. 43, nos. 1–2, 2022, pp. 136–43.

Paul, Annie. "Strange Love: South Asians and Blacks in the Caribbean." *South Asian Review*, vol. 43, nos. 1–2, 2022, pp. 149–54.

Rangaswamy Padma. "South Asian Diaspora." *Encyclopedia of Diasporas: Immigrant and Refugee Cultures around the World*, edited by Melvin Ember

et al., Springer, 2005, pp. 285–96, https://doi.org/10.1007/978-0-387
-29904-4_28.

Rushdie, Salman. *Midnight's Children*. Penguin Books, 1980.

Safran, William. "Diasporas in Modern Society: Myths of Homeland and
Return." *Diaspora: A Journal of Transnational Studies*, vol. 1, no. 1, 1991,
pp. 83–99.

Shankar, S., and Charu Gupta. "'My Birth Is My Fatal Accident': Introduction to
Caste and Life Narratives." *Biography*, vol. 40, no. 1, winter 2017, pp. 1–15.

Shukla, Sandhya. "Locations for South Asian Diasporas." *Annual Review of
Anthropology*, vol. 30, Oct. 2001, pp. 551–72, https://doi.org/10.1146/
annurev.anthro.30.1.551.

Singh, Amardeep. "'Names Can Wait': The Misnaming of the South Asian
Diaspora in Theory and Practice." *South Asian Review*, vol. 28, no. 1, 2007,
pp. 21–36.

Thomas, Sonja. *Privileged Minorities: Syrian Christianity, Gender, and Minority
Rights in Postcolonial India*. U of Washington P, 2018.

Vertovec, Steven, and Robin Cohen. *Migration, Diasporas and Transnationalism*.
Edward Elgar, 1999.

Yengde, Suraj. *Caste Matters*. Viking, 2019.

Zamindar, Vazira Fazila-Yacoobali. *The Long Partition and the Making of Modern
South Asia*. Columbia UP, 2007.

Nalini Iyer and Pallavi Rastogi

South Asian Anglophone Diasporic Writing: Histories and Geographies of Dispersion

The first essay in part 1 provided an overview of the collection's scope and rationale and foregrounded intersectionality as a crucial approach to teaching South Asian anglophone diasporic literature. This essay juxtaposes South Asian diasporic literature and literary criticism with the different parts of the world to which South Asians migrated. We focus on geographic areas represented in the essays in this volume in order to establish the historical and literary contexts for the central questions raised across the volume: How do we theorize diasporas emerging from the same region but from different sociopolitical events? What are some common themes in the South Asian diasporic imagination, and what differences do space and time make to literature? How does intersectionality—the transnational assemblage of religion, nation, gender, class, sexuality, caste, and generations—shape this body of writing? We conclude by summarizing select scholarship on teaching South Asian anglophone diasporic literature. The overview of literature and criticism provided here is intended as a necessarily concise starting point for beginning teachers exploring the field. While it would be impossible to summarize all the academic research on the literature of the South Asian diaspora, it is important to note some of the most influential scholarship.

General Scholarship

In *The Literature of the Indian Diaspora: Theorizing the Diasporic Imaginary*, Vijay Mishra offers powerful interpretive terms such as "the girmit ideology" (22) and "the diasporic imaginary" while also focusing on the diasporic mainstream, such as V. S. Naipaul and Salman Rushdie. Other exciting and original scholarship includes Susheila Nasta's *Home Truths: Fictions of the South Asian Diaspora in Britain*. Nasta's book traces the literary arc of South Asian British literature in the late twentieth century and places authors such as Naipaul, Rushdie, G. V. Desani, and Ravinder Randhawa, among others, in a complex matrix of influences such as colonialism, independence, and postcolonialism. Ruvani Ranasinha's *South Asian Writers in Twentieth-Century Britain: Culture in Translation* maps a genealogy of South Asian British writing and explores the emergence of the literary market for British Asian authors. In the American context, Rajini Srikanth's *The World Next Door: South Asian American Literature and the Idea of America* opened the way for the proliferation of scholarship on South Asians in North America. Srikanth situates South Asian writers such as Meena Alexander, Shani Mootoo, and Tahira Naqvi in the context of their homelands to argue that the making of the United States is permanently embedded in the place of origin of the immigrants who helped create the country. Tamara Bhalla's *Reading Together, Reading Apart: Identity, Belonging, and South Asian American Community* examines how diasporic literary works reveal a complex process of identity formation for South Asian Americans. The *South Asian American Digital Archive* recently curated a collection of essays called *Our Stories* that provides historical and cultural contexts for a general audience studying South Asians in America (*Our Stories*). In the wake of the boom in Indian Ocean studies, the last decade has also seen a surge in scholarship on the South Asian diaspora in Africa, including Pallavi Rastogi's *Afrindian Fictions: Diaspora, Race, and National Desire in South Africa* and Gaurav Desai's *Commerce with the Universe: Africa, India, and the Afrasian Imagination*. Rastogi's book focuses primarily on the literature of the Indian diaspora in South Africa and how this body of writing reflects a commitment to South African citizenship rarely seen in other Indian diasporas. Desai expands outward to East Africa and traces the long relationship of mutual exchange between the Indian subcontinent and eastern and southern Africa through an analysis of writers such as Amitav Ghosh and M. G. Vassanji and a wide range of lesser-known authors. The literature of Indians in the

Caribbean is increasingly well represented in the scholarship—and not only in the many studies on Naipaul. *Critical Perspectives on Indo-Caribbean Women's Literature*, edited by Joy Mahabir and Mariam Pirbhai, is but one invaluable example. Other academic research on the Indian diaspora in the Caribbean includes Mitali P. Wong and Zia Hasan's *The Fiction of South Asians in North America and the Caribbean: A Critical Study of English-Language Works since 1950* and Brinda Mehta's *Diasporic (Dis)Locations: Indo-Caribbean Women Writers Negotiate the Kala Pani*. Mehta's book examines anglophone and francophone women writers from the Caribbean. Rahul K. Gairola's *Homelandings: Postcolonial Diasporas and Transatlantic Belonging* challenges heteronormative assumptions about home and belonging and includes sections on South Asian diasporic writing in the United Kingdom. Several journals, including *Wasafiri*, *South Asian Review*, *Postcolonial Text*, *ARIEL*, and *Callaloo*, regularly feature scholarly essays on South Asian anglophone diasporic literature.

South Asian and Indo-Caribbean Literature

South Asians first moved outward in large groups through the transportation of indentured laborers from across the subcontinent to the plantations of the British Empire. Lomarsh Roopnarine identifies three distinct phases of Indo-Caribbean migration: migration under indenture (1838–1917); inter-Caribbean migration (1917–62); and post-1962 migration to the United Kingdom, the United States, and Canada (31). According to Mahabir and Pirbhai, the oceanic voyage and the bonds of fraternity—or *jahaji bhai* and *jahaji behan* ("ship brothers" and "ship sisters")—forged community aboard ships and on plantations (1). The historical wounds of prolonged servitude reveal their marks all over Indo-Caribbean writing and in the literature of other diasporas of indenture. Marina Carter and Khal Torabully's concept of "Coolitude" centers the indentured experience in diaspora studies, pointing to the unique forms of creolization or hybridization that emerge from bonded labor in foreign lands.

Indo-Caribbean writers such as V. S. Naipaul and his younger brother Shiva Naipaul, David Dabydeen, and Sam Selvon migrated to the United Kingdom early in their careers. However, they also wrote about indentured laborers, migration and its sociocultural impact, and negotiating life in England as non-white immigrants. Their work speaks of multiple migrations—from South Asia to the Caribbean and the Caribbean to the

United Kingdom. V. S. Naipaul's fiction, particularly *The Mystic Masseur*, *Miguel Street*, *A House for Mr. Biswas*, and *The Mimic Men*, are considered iconic texts in Indo-Caribbean literature. Dabydeen's novel *The Counting House* is well known for exploring the experiences of indenture and the relationship between Indian migrants and Guyanese of African descent. Similarly, Selvon's *A Brighter Sun*, *Moses Ascending*, and *The Lonely Londoners* are not only foundational Indo-Caribbean novels but also a central part of the Black British literary canon. Shiva Naipaul's *The Chip-Chip Gatherers* won the Whitbread Prize for depicting Hindu-Muslim relationships in rural Trinidad. This first generation of writers was predominantly male. As Mahabir and Pirbhai note, scholarly discussions of Indo-Caribbean writing initially neglected women authors (3–4). Writers such as Ramabai Espinet (*The Swinging Bridge*), Shani Mootoo (*Cereus Blooms at Night* and *Valmiki's Daughter*), Lakshmi Persaud (*Butterfly in the Wind* and *Daughters of Empire*), and Mahadai Das (*I Want to Be a Poetess of My People*) began to gain recognition only toward the end of the twentieth century. In the twenty-first century, Rajiv Mohabir, Gaiutra Bahadur, and Mootoo have written powerfully about multiple migrations, from India to the Caribbean and then to Canada, while raising questions of gender and sexuality in addition to race and class. Mohabir's poetry includes *The Taxidermist's Cut*, *The Cowherd's Son*, *Cutlish*, and *Antiman: A Hybrid Memoir*. *Antiman* narrates Mohabir's childhood as an Indo-Guyanese in Florida, his disaffection as a gay man who is unable to find acceptance in his family, and his struggles to be acknowledged as desi by other South Asians. Mohabir collaborated with Bahadur to translate Bhojpuri diasporic poetry into English in *I Even Regret Night: Holi Songs of Demerara*, marking a significant turn away from the anglophone literary production that is so dominant in the South Asian diaspora.

Bahadur's *Coolie Woman: The Odyssey of Indenture* is a biography of Bahadur's great-grandmother, who was transported from India to Guyana as an indentured laborer. *Coolie Woman* incorporates archival research, oral histories, and storytelling techniques to examine the neglected lives of Indo-Guyanese indentured women. Even with such an illustrious roster of writers, Indo-Caribbean literature has received less attention than its other South Asian counterparts have, as it is usually folded into different literary groupings. Since many Indo-Caribbean writers such as Naipaul, Selvon, and Mootoo migrated to the United Kingdom or Canada, the specificity of the Caribbean experience has often been subsumed under other categories such as "Black British," "queer writing," or "Canadian literature." Paradoxically, individual Indo-Caribbean writers, such as Bahadur and Mootoo, garnered attention because of their nomination for prestigious awards, such as the Giller Prize (Mootoo) and the Restless Books Prize (Mohabir), in North America.

South Asian African Literature

Indenture also transported South Asian laborers to Africa, particularly South Africa, beginning in the 1860s; passenger or trader Indians migrated a few decades later to Kenya, Uganda, and Zambia. The system of apartheid and its legacy in the post-apartheid period shaped South African Asian (or South African Indian, as it is often called) literature. In *Afrindian Fictions*, Rastogi notes that "Indians have been systematically erased in the national consciousness by the apartheid regime that operated primarily on a Black versus white register" (15). Indians thus experienced "a profound unease" about their place in South Africa (16). Racialization, citizenship, and national belonging are vital themes activated in the works of Ahmed Essop (*The Third Prophecy*), Farida Karodia (*Other Secrets*), and Achmat Dangor, who earned international renown for *Bitter Fruit*. Dangor's novel is a searing indictment of post-apartheid South Africa and the rainbow nation's failure to address the anxieties of the communities who fall through its cracks: Muslims, South African "Coloureds," and Indians. Imraan Coovadia is one of the most prolific South African Indian writers today and enjoys a prominent international reputation. Coovadia's *Tales of the Metric System* and *Green-Eyed Thieves* are satirical critiques of post-apartheid South Africa. *The Wedding* narrates the story of Coovadia's grandparents' migration to South Africa. This fictional retelling of an autobiographical past gracefully expands into the history of the passenger Indians who moved to South Africa as traders in the late nineteenth and early twentieth centuries.

South Asian writing in other parts of Africa also reflects the ambivalence of the racial role of this community in a binary black-and-white schema. Writers such as M. G. Vassanji (Kenya), Peter Nazareth (Uganda), Jameela Siddiqi (Uganda), and Shailja Patel (Kenya) explore the discomfort of Asian erasure in the binary of African native versus white settler. Patel's *Migritude*, borrowing its title from Carter and Torabully's *Coolitude*, represents indentured consciousness as a literary genre through a bricolage of memoir, family history, and journalistic essays. Vassanji is perhaps the most distinguished chronicler of this community, having fictionalized the lives of African Asians in several books, including *The Gunny Sack*, *No New Land*, *The Book of Secrets*, and *The In-Between World of Vikram Lall*. Idi Amin's expulsion of Indians from Uganda in 1972—and its ripple effects in neighboring countries—haunts much of contemporary South Asian writing from East Africa. Texts such as Yasmin Alibhai-Brown's *The Settler's Cookbook: Tales of Love, Migration and Food*, Nazareth's *In a Brown Mantle* and *The General Is Up*, and Siddiqi's *The Feast of the Nine Virgins* and *Bombay Gardens* all movingly depict South Asian life in Uganda, referencing the expulsion either directly or obliquely. While writers from other African countries, such as Abraham Verghese, are better known for their American-based memoirs, Verghese's first novel, *Cutting for Stone*, beautifully examines the Ethiopian childhood of its twin protagonists.[1]

South Asian British Literature

South Asian migration to Britain occurred over several centuries spanning the 250 years of British colonization of the subcontinent. Rozina Visram chronicles this long story in *Asians in Britain: Four Hundred Years of History*. In the introduction to *The Cambridge History of Black and Asian British Writing*, Susheila Nasta and Mark Stein discuss the difficulty of separating Black and Asian British writing, which they describe as "an intertwined and polymorphous literary field characterized by both overlap and distinction" (8). South Asian writing in Britain after 1947 reflects many of the concerns of other non-white immigrants, especially racism and xenophobia. Many Indians settled in or traveled to Britain even earlier and wrote about their experiences. Some of the most well-known names include M. K. Gandhi and Cornelia Sorabji. In later years, Kamala Markandaya and Anita Desai rendered the stories of travel and migration to the mother country in vivid fiction and prose. Two literary giants, V. S. Naipaul and Salman Rushdie, sometimes overshadow other South Asian British writers. Although Naipaul's and Rushdie's oeuvres are geographically and thematically diverse, both have written about migration to England in memoirs, such as Naipaul's *The Enigma of Arrival*, and novels, such as Rushdie's *The Satanic Verses*. Rushdie's collection of essays titled *Imaginary Homelands* is also considered a centerpiece in the canon of South Asian diasporic writing in general and Asian British writing in particular.

In *British Asian Fiction: Twenty-First-Century Voices*, Sarah Upstone distinguishes between immigrant writers and writers who were born and raised in Britain, noting that a greater sense of British Asian identity emerged within the second group, who also distanced themselves from a Black British identity. While the category "Black British" crucially acknowledges a shared history of imperialism, decolonization, and migration among people of Asian and African descent, many Asians disclaimed this nomenclature because it obscured the multiplicity of British Asian identities. To be British Asian, for this community, was not just to be born and raised in Britain but also to inherit and embrace the complicated immigrant legacies from India, Pakistan, Bangladesh, East Africa, and the Caribbean.

The fracture between Black Britons and Asian Britons was further exacerbated following the so-called Rushdie Affair in 1987–88. British Muslim identity was discussed and debated at length through British Asian literature after Iran issued a fatwa ordering the assassination of Rushdie for his allegedly blasphemous statements against Islam in *The Satanic Verses*. The impact of the Rushdie Affair on Asian writing in Britain was profound. Some of the most prominent Asian Muslim writers, such as Hanif Kureishi in *The Black Album* and Monica Ali in *Brick Lane*, directly engaged with *The Satanic Verses* controversy. Kureishi is best known for his screenplay for the movie *My Beautiful Laundrette*, a frank discussion of queer sexuality in Thatcherite England, and the novel *The Buddha of Suburbia*, whose opening sentence—"My name is Karim Amir. And I am an Englishman, born and bred, almost" (3)—declares that British-born Muslims can be British and Muslim at the same time. The 9/11 and 7/7 attacks also saw a burst of literature by other Muslim writers, including Kamila Shamsie, whose novel *Home Fire* is now considered one of the most important South Asian diasporic novels of the twenty-first century. *Home Fire* critiques the Islamophobia of the British nation-state through a retelling of Sophocles's *Antigone*. Other works interrogating the position of Muslims in post-9/11 Britain include Nadeem Aslam's *Blind Man's Garden* and Tabish Khair's *Just Another Jihadi Jane*. Recent books such as Sunjeev Sahota's *Year of the Runaways*, a powerful evocation of the lives of poor Indian immigrants in Britain, and *China Room*, about a diasporic Indian's brief sojourn in India to unearth his roots, have also received great acclaim.

British Asian writers are now increasingly diversifying their oeuvre—setting their stories in different geographies and foregrounding themes that their predecessors did not, could not, or would not. *Gifted*, by Nikita Lalwani, set in Cardiff, Wales, examines the challenges a young Indian girl faces. In its depiction of wars and financial collapse and its stories of nations and generations, Zia Haider Rahman's sprawling novel *In the Light of What We Know* stakes a claim to the "encyclopedic narrative" in the mode of Rushdie and Zadie Smith (Bergholtz 84).

South Asian North American Literature

South Asian migration to North America commenced during the American colonial period, as lascars (Indian sailors or militiamen) boarded ships plying imperial trade. However, a migratory surge occurred only in the late nineteenth and early twentieth centuries, particularly on the Pacific coast, with South Asian male workers traveling across Canada to the United States. This history of early South Asian migration on the West Coast is outlined in Joan Jensen's *Passage from India: Asian Indian Immigrants in North America*. Vivek Bald's *Bengali Harlem and the Lost Histories of South Asian America* examines the untold stories of South Asian Bengali migrants who came as traders to the East Coast in the early twentieth century, married Black women, and built lives in cities like New York, Baltimore, and New Orleans. Anupama Arora and Rajender Kaur's *India in the American Imaginary, 1780s–1880s* traces the histories of South Asian arrivals in North America to colonial times. Manan Desai's *The United States of India: Anticolonial Literature and Transnational Refraction* studies the writings of early South Asian immigrants to the United States and their transnational engagement with anticolonialism. Other scholars have focused on the specific regional experiences of South Asian Americans in the post–World War II United States. Amy Bhatt and Nalini Iyer, in *Roots and Reflections: South Asians in the Pacific Northwest*, study South Asians in the Pacific Northwest through oral histories. S. Mitra Kalita, in *Suburban Sahibs: Three Immigrant Families and Their Passage from India to America*, explores suburban New Jersey immigrant life through the stories of a few families, and Himanee Gupta-Carlson, in *Muncie, India(na): Middletown and Asian America*, uses ethnography and personal experiences to show that small-town midwestern experiences were vastly different from those of immigrants to large urban areas on either coast. Literary works such as Chitra Banerjee Divakaruni's *Leaving Yuba City*, Amitava Kumar's *Immigrant, Montana*, Bhira Backhaus's *Under the Lemon Trees*, Anita Rau Badami's *Can You Hear the Nightbird*

Call?, and Rishi Reddi's *Passage West* incorporate historical material from the hybrid Mexican-Hindu communities in California, the Ghadar party, and the Sikh community in Canada, wholly, or in part, to document the experiences of early-twentieth-century immigrants. Khem Aryal's edited collection *South to South: Writing South Asia in the American South* consists of fiction and nonfiction about South Asians in the American South, including Florida, Texas, and Mississippi. The short pieces in this collection interrogate the meaning of South Asian identity in a region often othered in the American imagination; the writers represented here assert, through their bodies and their literary work, the importance of South Asians in the American South.

The earliest corpus of South Asian literature emerged during World War I, after the formation of the Ghadar party in 1913. The Ghadarites, mostly Punjabi farmers and students at West Coast universities, organized politically to fight British imperialism in South Asia and to challenge exclusionary immigration laws in the United States. They also published radical political poetry in Punjabi and Urdu, collected as *Ghadar di Gunj* (1913–14; *Echoes of Mutiny*). Dhan Gopal Mukerji was one of the first commercially successful South Asian anglophone writers. Mukerji arrived as a student at the University of California, Berkeley, after fleeing sedition charges in British India. He wrote a memoir, *Caste and Outcast*, and numerous children's books, including *Gay-Neck: The Story of a Pigeon*, which won a Newberry award in 1928. Similarly, Sadhu Singh Dhami wrote a semi-autobiographical novel, *Maluka*, in which he describes his early years as a young immigrant in the Sikh community in British Columbia before World War II.

The passage of the Immigration and Nationality Act of 1965 (also known as the Hart-Celler Act) reduced most barriers to immigration from the subcontinent and brought thousands of professional immigrants from the newly independent nations of India, Pakistan, and Sri Lanka, with Indians constituting the majority of the diaspora. Anglophone South Asian American writing started to emerge as a distinctive category in the 1970s, with the publication of women writers such as Bharati Mukherjee, Uma Parameswaran, and Divakaruni. Several other authors, such as Zulfikar Ghose, Ved Mehta, Raja Rao, and A. K. Ramanujan, lived in the United States for a significant portion of their lives but wrote mostly about South Asia.

Although the 1965 act opened doors for educated South Asian immigrants, not all South Asian migration to North America was fueled by professional and educated classes looking for economic advancement. Many South Asians, particularly those from Sri Lanka and Punjab, fled political unrest in their home nations. Novels such as V. V. Ganeshananthan's *Love Marriage*, Shyam Selvadurai's *Funny Boy* and *The Hungry Ghosts*, Nayomi Munaweera's *Island of a Thousand Mirrors* and *What Lies between Us*, Sharon Bala's *The Boat People*, Ru Freeman's *On Sal Mal Lane*, Mary Anne Mohanraj's *Bodies in Motion*, and Anuk Arudpragasam's *The Story of a Brief Marriage* and *A Passage North* testify to the devastating consequences of the civil war in Sri Lanka that created an influx of refugees to North America. Similarly, the violence against Sikhs in 1984 following the assassination of Indira Gandhi led to a large wave of Sikh migration very different from the Sikh migration during the Ghadar era. This history of Sikh migration to North America is fictionalized in Badami's novel *Can You Hear the Nightbird Call?* and in Jaspreet Singh's *Helium*. Shauna Singh Baldwin's short story collection *English Lessons and Other Stories* focuses on the diasporic experiences of Sikh women in North America. Since 9/11, many South Asian Muslim writers, such as Mohsin Hamid in *The Reluctant Fundamentalist*, H. M. Naqvi in *Home Boy*, Fatima Farheen Mirza in *A Place for Us*, and Ayad Akhtar in *Disgraced* and *Homeland Elegies*, have highlighted Islamophobia and the war on terror as central concerns in their work. Recent South Asian American novels are now exploring the relationship between South Asians and other ethnic groups. These include Shanti Sekharan's *Lucky Boy* and Devi Laskar's *Atlas of Reds and Blues*. Shilpi Somaya Gowda's *The Shape of Family* and Manjushree Thapa's *Seasons of Flight* also focus on interracial relationships. Queer identities are depicted with great complexity in Rakesh Satyal's *Blue Boy* and *No One Can Pronounce My Name* as well as in SJ Sindu's *Marriage of a Thousand Lies* and in Mootoo's *Moving Forward Sideways Like a Crab*. Megha Majumdar's *A Burning* and Thrity Umrigar's *Honor* powerfully depict the rise of authoritarianism in South Asia, especially Hindu fundamentalism in India, and its consequences on the diaspora.

As this brief overview of South Asian diasporic literary criticism and literature reveals, South Asian migratory experiences vary worldwide. At the same time, the wide assortment of literature that falls under this category also shares many common themes, including "diasporic double consciousness" (Dayal 47), or what Salman Rushdie in his famous essay "Imaginary Homelands" describes as feeling at times "that we straddle two cultures; at other times we fall between two stools" (*Imaginary Homelands* 15). Thus, the connection with the geography of origin, exploration of cultural identity, search for home and belonging, stories of loss and rupture, narratives of struggle and resistance, and experimentation with genre and form all repeat themselves across South Asian diasporic literature.

Scholarship on Teaching South Asian Diasporic Literature

While the scholarly work discussed above offers important analyses of South Asian diasporic literature and culture, no book focused on teaching South Asian anglophone diasporic writing yet exists. The stellar, but small, scholarship on teaching South Asian literature published by the MLA complements this volume well. Deepika Bahri and Filippo Menozzi's *Teaching Anglophone South Asian Women Writers* focuses on women writers from South Asia and includes essays on diasporic women writers. Supriya Nair's *Teaching Anglophone Caribbean Literature* includes essays on Indo-Caribbean writers. Gaurav Desai and John Hawley's *Approaches to Teaching the Works of Amitav Ghosh* examines an important writer in the South Asian diasporic canon. Along with these other MLA volumes, *Teaching South Asian Anglophone Diasporic Literature* provides more pedagogical depth to the vast body of South Asian literature through its selected focus on the anglophone diaspora.

Note

1. Many Indo-Caribbean writers and Asian writers from East Africa migrated to the United Kingdom and North America for political, historical, and economic reasons; we discuss their literary connections in the following sections.

Works Cited

Akhtar, Ayad. *Disgraced*. Back Bay Books, 2013.
———. *Homeland Elegies*. Back Bay Books, 2021.
Ali, Monica. *Brick Lane*. Scribner, 2003.
Alibhai-Brown, Yasmin. *The Settler's Cookbook: Tales of Love, Migration and Food*. Portobello Books, 2010.
Arora, Anupama, and Rajender Kaur. *India in the American Imaginary, 1780s–1880s*. Palgrave Macmillan, 2017.
Arudpragasam, Anuk. *A Passage North*. Hogarth, 2021.
———. *The Story of a Brief Marriage*. Flatiron, 2016.
Aryal, Khem, editor. *South to South: Writing South Asia in the American South*. Texas Review Press, 2023.
Aslam, Nadeem. *The Blind Man's Garden*. Vintage Books, 2013.
Backhaus, Bhira. *Under the Lemon Trees*. Thomas Dunne Books, 2009.
Badami, Anita Rau. *Can You Hear the Nightbird Call?* Knopf, 2006.

Bahadur, Gaiutra. *Coolie Woman: The Odyssey of Indenture*. U of Chicago P, 2013.

Bahri, Deepika, and Filippo Menozzi, editors. *Teaching Anglophone South Asian Women Writers*. Modern Language Association of America, 2021.

Bala, Sharon. *The Boat People*. Anchor Books, 2018.

Bald, Vivek. *Bengali Harlem and the Lost Histories of South Asian America*. Harvard UP, 2013.

Baldwin, Shauna Singh. *English Lessons and Other Stories*. Goose Lane Editions, 1996.

Bergholtz, Benjamin. "The 'Pursuit of Knowledge' and the Paradoxes of Postcolonial Encyclopedism in Zia Haider Rahman's *In the Light of What We Know*." *Genre: Forms of Discourse and Culture*, vol. 53, no. 1, 2020, pp. 79–103.

Bhalla, Tamara. *Reading Together, Reading Apart: Identity, Belonging, and South Asian American Community*. U of Illinois P, 2016.

Bhatt, Amy, and Nalini Iyer. *Roots and Reflections: South Asians in the Pacific Northwest*. U of Washington P, 2013.

Carter, Marina, and Khal Torabully. *Coolitude: An Anthology of the Indian Labour Diaspora*. Anthem Press, 2002.

Coovadia, Imraan. *Green-Eyed Thieves*. Umuzi, 2006.

———. *Tales of the Metric System*. Ohio UP, 2014.

———. *The Wedding*. Picador, 2001.

Dabydeen, David. *The Counting House*. Peepal Tree Press, 1996.

Dangor, Achmat. *Bitter Fruit*. Black Cat, 2001.

Das, Mahadai. *I Want to Be a Poetess of My People*. Guyana National Service Publishing Centre, 1971.

Dayal, Samir. "Diaspora and Double Consciousness." *The Journal of the Midwest Modern Language Association*, vol. 29, no. 1, 1996, pp. 46–62.

Desai, Gaurav. *Commerce with the Universe: Africa, India, and the Afrasian Imagination*. Columbia UP, 2013.

Desai, Gaurav, and John Hawley, editors. *Approaches to Teaching the Works of Amitav Ghosh*. Modern Language Association of America, 2019.

Desai, Manan. *The United States of India: Anticolonial Literature and Transnational Refraction*. Temple UP, 2020.

Dhami, Sadhu Singh. *Maluka*. 1978. Publications Bureau Punjabi University, 1997.

Divakaruni, Chitra Banerjee. *Leaving Yuba City*. Anchor Books, 1997.

Espinet, Ramabai. *The Swinging Bridge*. Phyllis Bruce Books, 2013.

Essop, Ahmed. *The Third Prophecy*. Picador Africa, 2004.

Freeman, Ru. *On Sal Mal Lane*. Graywolf, 2013.

Gairola, Rahul K. *Homelandings: Postcolonial Diasporas and Transatlantic Belonging*. Rowman and Littlefield, 2016.

Ganeshananthan, V. V. *Love Marriage*. Random House, 2008.

Gowda, Shilpi Somaya. *The Shape of Family*. Custom House, 2019.

Gupta-Carlson, Himanee. *Muncie, India(na): Middletown and Asian America*. U of Illinois P, 2018.

Hamid, Mohsin. *The Reluctant Fundamentalist.* HarperCollins Publishers, 2008.

Jensen, Joan. *Passage from India: Asian Indian Immigrants in North America.* Yale UP, 1988.

Kalita, S. Mitra. *Suburban Sahibs: Three Immigrant Families and Their Passage from India to America.* Rutgers UP, 2003.

Karodia, Farida. *Other Secrets.* Penguin Books, 2000.

Khair, Tabish. *Just Another Jihadi Jane.* Interlink Books, 2016.

Kumar, Amitava. *Immigrant, Montana.* Knopf, 2018.

Kureishi, Hanif. *The Black Album.* Scribner, 1995.

———. *The Buddha of Suburbia.* Penguin Books, 1990.

———. *My Beautiful Laundrette.* Bunko, 2000.

Lalwani, Nikita. *Gifted.* Random House, 2007.

Laskar, Devi. *Atlas of Reds and Blues.* Fleet, 2019.

Mahabir, Joy, and Mariam Pirbhai, editors. *Critical Perspectives on Indo-Caribbean Women's Literature.* Routledge, 2013.

Majumdar, Megha. *A Burning.* Vintage Books, 2020.

Mehta, Brinda. *Diasporic (Dis)Locations: Indo-Caribbean Women Writers Negotiate the Kala Pani.* UP of the West Indies, 2004.

Mirza, Fatima Farheen. *A Place for Us.* Hogarth, 2018.

Mishra, Vijay. *The Literature of the Indian Diaspora: Theorizing the Diasporic Imaginary.* Routledge, 2007.

Mohabir, Rajiv. *Antiman: A Hybrid Memoir.* Restless Books, 2021.

———. *The Cowherd's Son.* Tupelo Press, 2017.

———. *Cutlish.* Four Way Books, 2021.

———. *The Taxidermist's Cut.* Four Way Books, 2016.

Mohabir, Rajiv, and Gaiutra Bahadur, translators. *I Even Regret Night: Holi Songs of Demerara.* By Lalbihari Sharma, Kaya Press, 2019.

Mohanraj, Mary Anne. *Bodies in Motion.* Harper Perennial, 2006.

Mootoo, Shani. *Cereus Blooms at Night.* McLelland and Stewart, 1996.

———. *Moving Forward Sideways Like a Crab.* Akashic Books, 2017.

———. *Valmiki's Daughter.* House of Anansi Press, 2008.

Mukerji, Dhan Gopal. *Caste and Outcast.* 1923. Stanford UP, 2002.

———. *Gay-Neck: The Story of a Pigeon.* Dutton, 1927.

Munaweera, Nayomi. *Island of a Thousand Mirrors.* St. Martin's Press, 2014.

———. *What Lies between Us.* St. Martin's Press, 2016.

Naipaul, Shiva. *The Chip-Chip Gatherers.* Penguin Books, 1973.

Naipaul, V. S. *The Enigma of Arrival.* Vintage Books, 1987.

———. *A House for Mr. Biswas.* Vintage Books, 1961.

———. *Miguel Street.* Vintage Books, 1959.

———. *The Mimic Men.* Vintage Books, 1967.

———. *The Mystic Masseur.* Vintage Books, 1957.

Nair, Supriya M., editor. *Teaching Anglophone Caribbean Literature.* Modern Language Association of America, 2012.

Naqvi, H. M. *Home Boy.* HarperCollins Publishers, 2010.

Nasta, Susheila. *Home Truths: Fictions of the South Asian Diaspora in Britain.* Red Globe Press, 2002.

Nasta, Susheila, and Mark U. Stein, editors. *The Cambridge History of Black and Asian British Writing*. Cambridge UP, 2019.

Nazareth, Peter. *The General Is Up*. Goa 1556 Press, 1991.

———. *In a Brown Mantle*. East African Lit Bureau, 1971.

Our Stories: An Introduction to South Asian America. South Asian American Digital Archive, 2021, www.saada.org/ourstories.

Patel, Shailja. *Migritude*. Kaya Press, 2010.

Persaud, Lakshmi. *Butterfly in the Wind*. Peepal Tree Press, 1990.

———. *Daughters of Empire*. Peepal Tree Press, 2012.

Rahman, Zia Haider. *In the Light of What We Know*. Picador, 2014.

Ranasinha, Ruvani. *South Asian Writers in Twentieth-Century Britain: Culture in Translation*. Oxford UP, 2007.

Rastogi, Pallavi. *Afrindian Fictions: Diaspora, Race, and National Desire in South Africa*. Ohio State UP, 2008.

Reddi, Rishi. *Passage West*. Ecco, 2020.

Roopnarine, Lomarsh. "Indo-Caribbean Migration: From Periphery to Core." *Caribbean Quarterly*, vol. 49, no. 3, Sept. 2003, pp. 30–60.

Rushdie, Salman. *Imaginary Homelands: Essays and Criticism, 1981–1991*. Penguin Books, 1992.

———. *The Satanic Verses*. Random House, 1988.

Sahota, Sunjeev. *China Room*. Vintage Books, 2021.

———. *Year of the Runaways*. Picador, 2016.

Satyal, Rakesh. *Blue Boy*. Kensington Books, 2009.

———. *No One Can Pronounce My Name*. Picador, 2017.

Sekharan, Shanti. *Lucky Boy*. G. P. Putnam, 2017.

Selvadurai, Shyam. *Funny Boy*. William Morrow, 1994.

———. *The Hungry Ghosts*. Doubleday Canada, 2013.

Selvon, Sam. *A Brighter Sun*. Hodder Education, 1952.

———. *The Lonely Londoners*. Penguin Books, 1956.

———. *Moses Ascending*. Penguin Books, 1975.

Shamsie, Kamila. *Home Fire*. Riverhead, 2017.

Siddiqi, Jameela. *Bombay Gardens*. Lulu, 2006.

———. *The Feast of the Nine Virgins*. L'Ouverture, 2001.

Sindu, SJ. *Marriage of a Thousand Lies*. Soho Press, 2017.

Singh, Jaspreet. *Helium*. Bloomsbury, 2013.

Srikanth, Rajini. *The World Next Door: South Asian American Literature and the Idea of America*. Temple UP, 2004.

Thapa, Manjushree. *Seasons of Flight*. Aleph Book Company, 2012.

Umrigar, Thrity. *Honor*. Algonquin Books, 2022.

Upstone, Sarah. *British Asian Fiction: Twenty-First-Century Voices*. Manchester UP, 2010.

Vassanji, M. G. *The Book of Secrets*. Picador, 1994.

———. *The Gunny Sack*. Anchor Books, 1989.

———. *The In-Between World of Vikram Lall*. Vintage Books, 2003.

———. *No New Land*. Emblem Editions, 1991.

Verghese, Abraham. *Cutting for Stone*. Vintage Books, 2009.

Visram, Rozina. *Asians in Britain: Four Hundred Years of History.* Pluto Press, 1997.
Wong, Mitali P., and Zia Hasan. *The Fiction of South Asians in North America and the Caribbean: A Critical Study of English-Language Works since 1950.* McFarland, 2010.

Part II

East Meets South:
Africa and the Caribbean

Asma Sayed

M. G. Vassanji's Fiction in a Transnational, Postcolonial, and Social Justice Context

This essay focuses on pedagogical approaches to teaching the works of the anglophone writer M. G. Vassanji. Born in East Africa of South Asian heritage, Vassanji is a Canadian by nationality. He is the author of ten novels, three short story collections, two travelogues, a biography, and numerous articles. He is connected to and has drawn on many places across continents, and these interconnections are evident in the settings of his fiction and nonfiction, for which he has twice won the Giller Prize as well as the Governor General's Award—two of Canada's top literary awards.

Across postsecondary institutions globally, Vassanji's fiction and nonfiction are taught in a variety of classes—for instance, in those that focus on postcolonial and diasporic literatures, South Asian diasporic literatures, travel writing, or Indian Ocean studies. Having taught Vassanji's works often, in this essay I elaborate on how I approach his fiction in my classrooms, especially his novel *The In-Between World of Vikram Lall*, in the context of postcolonial, diasporic, social justice, and critical race perspectives. My students have appreciated and enjoyed reading and analyzing Vassanji's fiction because it enhances their understanding of theoretical concepts (postcolonialism, diaspora, hybridity, hegemony) and allows them to grapple with issues of gender and interracial relations in the context of Afrasian identities (Desai), subjects they are usually unfamiliar with. Some of the questions that my students analyze include the following: How can literature reflect notions of justice? What does justice look like when the ramifications of imperialist practices affect individual choices? These questions offer an opportunity to discuss race relations and the ensuing tensions, matters of gender and class and of complex histories and identities, colonial encounters and anti-colonial revolutions, and Afrasian passages, trade links, and transnational migrations across the Indian Ocean and beyond.

I have included *The In-Between World of Vikram Lall* in undergraduate classes on cross-cultural world literature (the specific topic of which was "Resisting Empires"), diaspora literature, and African literature. I will draw specifically from my experience of teaching the novel in the cross-cultural world literature course to an ethnically diverse group of students in British Columbia. The course is described in the syllabus as follows:

> In this course, students will study works of cross-cultural world literature drawn mainly from the twentieth and twenty-first centuries. They will explore critical concepts and issues that arise in cross-cultural fields of study identified as world literature, postcolonial literature, global anglophone literature, and transcultural literature, such as the influences and effects of colonization and decolonization on world literature. The topic for this term is "Resisting Empires." Through a reading of a wide selection of texts, we will focus on questions of race, migration, language, gender, resistance, and hybridity in literature and other cultural texts.

The course included texts by Chinua Achebe, Binyavanga Wainaina, Warsan Shire, Fatema Mernissi, Frantz Fanon, and Edward Said, among others. Since this is essentially a comparative literature course, and given that I am a comparatist by training, I also include some theoretical underpinning of world literature through readings from David Damrosch's two books: *How to Read World Literature* and *What Is World Literature?* Conversely, when I teach the novel in courses focusing on diasporic literatures, I have centered issues of home, identity, exile, displacement, belonging, and hybridity. In this instance, the theoretical framework was provided through readings from Stuart Hall, Andreas Huyssen, and Benedict Anderson.

Transnational Encounters

When teaching Vassanji's novels, I emphasize the ways in which they lend themselves to issues of transnational migrations across Africa, Asia, Europe, and North America. The novels often deal with those subjects that have not been discussed enough in the literary realm, including but not limited to the migration of South Asian communities from Gujarat to East Africa and their contributions to the development of East African nations as well as the issues of race and ethnicity in the context of Afrasian identities. In particular, I draw attention to the east-to-east migrations, thus decentering the Western narratives of east-to-west movements. While we know much about African and Asian encounters with the West, reading Vassanji's works, especially those that have an East African setting, provides us with an opportunity to study the trade routes between India and East Africa and the long presence of African communities in India known as the Sidis. This history is especially interesting for students who have mostly been exposed to east-west migratory patterns. Gaurav Desai, in his book *Commerce with the Universe: Africa, India, and the Afrasian Imagination*, asks the following in the context of encounters between African nations and India: "What happens to our understanding of Africa—its history, its sense of identity, its engagement with modernity, and the possibilities of its future—if we read its long history as an encounter not only with the West, but also with the East?" (6). Using this quote from Desai's book as a prompt, I encourage students to think about what happens to our understanding of colonialism and of justice, especially in the context of interracial relationships, when we look at east-to-east migration alongside east-to-west interactions. Many of the students in my classes are familiar with migration patterns from South Asia to Western destinations such as the United Kingdom, the United States, and Canada. Nonetheless, most are unaware of the concept of double diaspora and the history of South Asian migrations to the West via African countries or migrations within the Indian Ocean region. Thus, Vassanji's works, both fiction and nonfiction, open new avenues for students to explore the intertwining of roots and routes, a concept examined by Avtar Brah, James Clifford, William Safran, and other diaspora theorists.

Vassanji's Africa Books

Vassanji's novels have different geographic focuses and can be divided into three broad categories: Africa (*The Gunny Sack*, *The Book of Secrets*, *The In-Between World of Vikram Lall*, and *The Magic of Saida*), South Asia (*The Assassin's Song* and *A Delhi Obsession*), and North America (*No New Land* and *Amriika*). When teaching his Africa books, depending on the nature of the course, I outline some concepts connected with postcolonialism, diaspora studies, gender studies, and critical race studies. Vassanji's Africa-focused books offer a nuanced understanding of "the complex histories of and interconnections between Asian and African communities, as well as the European colonists" (Sayed and Murji 7). In our edited collection on Vassanji's works, Karim Murji and I argue that in Vassanji's novels, which have East Africa as the setting and an Asian character at the center, "there never are easy cliches or simple polarities or dualities, which usually are attuned to personal relationships as well as gender and generation differences. Issues of belonging and identity are therefore not settled or ossified in communal cultures; rather, Vassanji locates them in specific historical and political contexts" (Sayed and Murji 8). It is this complexity that my students grapple with and appreciate when they read *The In-Between World of Vikram Lall*.

To begin, students read background material (generally selections from longer works), which allows them to form their theoretical base, followed by an article that analyzes the novel they have read. I use selections from Fanon, Said, Robin Cohen, Ngũgĩ wa Thiong'o, and Gayatri Chakravorty Spivak, among others. To aid our close reading of the novel, I include articles by Nalini Iyer, Françoise Král, Shizen Ozawa, and Aaron Louis Rosenberg.

The Problematics of Interracial Relationships in *The In-Between World of Vikram Lall*

The In-Between World of Vikram Lall focuses on Vikram Lall, a third-generation Kenyan of Indian origin who grows up in a period of decolonization in East Africa and struggles with his identity as an Asian African subject. When the novel begins, Vikram is living in exile in Canada and thinking about the life he has left behind in Kenya. Vikram's grandfather was an indentured laborer from India brought in by the British to work on the railways in East Africa. Growing up, Vikram and his sister, Deepa, befriend a Kikuyu boy, Njoroge. The lives of Vikram and his family members exist at the intersections of Asian and African identities. As the novel progresses, in postcolonial Kenya, Vikram becomes an influential man because his in-betweenness (neither white nor Black) makes it easy for him to help with money laundering and corruption. He comes to be known as "Africa's most corrupt man, a cheat of monstrous and reptilian cunning" (Vassanji, *In-Between World* 1). Personal narrations unfold in the context of political histories, including the ugly legacy of colonization, involuntary labor, and racism. The novel thus deals with the violence of the colonial enterprise as well as justice in multiple ways: through the depiction of the history of indentured laborers brought from India to East Africa, the representation of the brutalities of the Mau Mau uprising set against the violence perpetrated by the colonizers, the role of the Asian African subjects caught in between, and the psychological and emotional violence resulting from the development and destruction of interracial relationships. The novel's depth and complexity allow me to steer students' interests in multiple directions.

One of my approaches is to consider the violence generated by colonization, its role in anti-colonial movements, and its impact on personal relations. The story evolves in the context of the violence brought about by the British occupation of Kenya, the Mau Mau rebellion, and the Kenyan independence movement. It reminds the reader that colonial legacy leaves behind a history of violence and suffering on multiple levels. I guide students to think through the following questions: What is the role of revolutionary anti-colonial violence in independence movements? How does a colonized subject deal with emotional violence evolving from cultural imperialism? Students read Fanon's *The Wretched of the Earth* in order to unpack issues of violence and its role in colonization as well as an anti-colonial resistance. Fanon's book helps students contextualize references to the Mau Mau uprising and the brutality inflicted by British and German colonization of East Africa.

The novel also lends itself to questions of truth, subjectivity, ethics, and justice. Vikram Lall is a product of a society that transitions from a colonial to a postcolonial state, but in the process, he gets caught in the web of corruption and deceit. But, as Vassanji himself has said in multiple interviews, judging Vikram Lall is not easy. How does one decide if Vikram is a victim or perpetrator? Analyzing Vikram's actions and the autobiographical elements of the novel (Vikram narrates the novel) creates some interesting moments for students as they ponder not only the subjectivity of a first-person narration but also the nature of justice in situations where clear dichotomies of right and wrong may not work.

Furthermore, inviting students to focus on the emotional and psychological violence caused as a result of the development and destruction of intimate interracial relationships, which includes those between Indigenous Kenyans and Indian Kenyans, allows for a rich discussion about racial hierarchies and violence. To understand the nuances of these liaisons in the text, we focus on the key characters and close-read a few passages. Students quickly recognize that colonial violence functions on multiple levels. For example, the narrator, Vikram, reminds readers that "[m]any peoples in East Africa resisted the European colonization, but they had early on been subdued by the superiority of rifles against arrows and spears" and that "it was the Kikuyu who paid the harsh price of British countermeasures and settler rage" (Vassanji, *In-Between World* 27). While Vikram's statement focuses on the physical violence generated by arms and the loss of land, identity politics in the text also yields interesting responses. Vikram grows up feeling the in-betweenness and the sense that he is different from Njoroge, whose Blackness allows him to *belong* to Africa, which Vikram, although born in Kenya, cannot claim:

> I do recall that his being different, in features, in status, was not far from my consciousness. I was also aware that he was more from Africa than I was. He was African, I was Asian. His black skin was matte, his woolly hair impossibly alien. I was smaller, with pointed elvish ears, my skin annoyingly "medium," as I described it then, neither one (white) nor the other (black). (25)

Bill is a white settler and a friend of both Vikram and Njoroge. Vikram is caught between Njoroge's Blackness and Bill's whiteness: "In that fateful year of our friendship, when we played together, I couldn't help feeling that both Bill and Njoroge were genuine, in their very different ways; only I, who stood in the middle, Vikram Lall, cherished son of an Indian grocer, sounded hollow like a penny" (54). A close reading of some of the passages in which Vikram muses about his racial identity prompts students to think about racial segregation globally and historically. Students connect this narrative with the civil rights movement in the United States, apartheid in South Africa, and anti-Indigenous racism in Canada. Building on this analysis, the class then moves to discussing the specifics of intimate interracial relationships, especially within a patriarchal context.

The uneasiness that Vikram felt as a Brown child takes another turn in identity formation when he and the other children grow up. The complex racial structures have a long-lasting effect on Deepa, who loves Njoroge but, to appease her mother, eventually marries a third-generation Punjabi man. Alongside Njoroge and Deepa's relationship, the novel offers other examples of African-Asian bonds. Juma Molabux, a Punjabi Muslim and a former indentured laborer, is married to a Maasai woman, Sakina, who has fully embraced Punjabi language, food, and culture. As students read these links closely, they acquire a deeper understanding of the complexities of women's lives in patriarchal cultures. Some students also engage on a personal level by bringing up their biracial identities and their parents' struggles of being in an interracial relationship. The emotional response to the text makes class discussions richer. As students share their personal experiences, they connect with the issues of emotional and psychological violence that originated because of the development and destruction of mixed-race intimacy. At this point, students read some critical scholarship on the novel. For the discussion of race, gender, and patriarchy in the context of a postcolonial nation, we look at Iyer's essay on the novel, which argues that

> Deepa and Njoroge's relationship threatens the very idea of difference that is the foundation of new political power and influence [in Kenya]. . . . [I]f Njoroge wants to rise in the world of politics, he is better served by marrying a Kikuyu; if Deepa's family is to retain the support of its community in times of trouble, it is necessary that she marry an Indian. (209–10)

Students also take this opportunity to discuss the sociocultural role of women. They note that in the novel women make sacrifices to uphold their family's honor. Deepa marries a man in her own community, and Sakina adopts the culture of her husband's family. Both cases push students to think about the patriarchal nature of these relationships and how violence is inflicted on the female body by both the European colonizer and the Asian settler. Here students return to Iyer's argument that "the economic and political power of the Indian community is writ on the bodies and desires of the women whether it is Sakina who fully Indianizes herself or Deepa who loses her love" (210), which prompts them to think further about the intersections of gender and class.

Critical Hope Framework

Finally, I tie all the abovementioned issues together using the analytical frame of social justice and critical hope to understand postcolonial texts as humanitarian texts that serve as counternarratives to historically Eurocentric political discourses. The concept of critical hope is inspired by Paulo Freire's pedagogy of hope, and it calls for teaching and learning approaches that are rooted in social justice and lead to positive sociopolitical change. This approach allows students to think of literary texts as sites for confronting injustice. Over the years, I have found that students respond well to literary texts when they can relate to them in a broader social context. When they read these texts through the lens of critical hope, they see the issues represented in the text as ones that affect them and their society; occasionally, it leads to a desire to change the society by resisting injustice. I am not suggesting that a literary work must have a purpose beyond itself, but if a certain method allows students to absorb a text deeply, it is surely an additional advantage in terms of engaging students and attracting them to literature classes. Students connect all the threads mentioned above and consider the complexity of the idea of postcolonial justice: Who is the colonizer in this context? Is it only the British, or are the Asians equally responsible for denial of justice to the African subject? Where do the second- and third-generation Asians born in Africa belong? While students do not necessarily arrive at specific answers, thinking critically about some of these questions helps them engage with the text more meaningfully.

Pedagogical Challenges

I want to briefly elaborate on some of the challenges associated with teaching Vassanji's work in North American classrooms, especially to students who have not had the opportunity to study South Asian diasporic texts before. I have taught Vassanji's novels only in Canadian classrooms, but I would imagine the challenges would be similar in other North American settings. The difficulties are similar to those encountered by instructors of world literature. My students usually have very little knowledge of the cultural context explored in Vassanji's texts. I spend considerable time explaining the Indian social and religious structures, the history of the British Raj and indentured labor, various anti-colonial movements in East Africa, the Indian Ocean trade routes, and the multilingualism in South Asia (Vassanji uses many words from South Asian and African languages throughout his works). Of course, going through all this background information makes class discussions more engaging. However, doing so means that it takes longer to get to textual analysis. Thus, I would recommend teaching a novel over two weeks (assuming the standard three hours of class time per week) to allow ample time to study the text in an engaging way.

I can envision teaching Vassanji's works in a variety of courses at both the undergraduate and graduate level: in courses on postcolonial literature, global anglophone literature, South Asian diasporic literature, representations of race in literature, African literature, and Canadian literature or in a course on Vassanji. In this essay I have focused on one novel; nonetheless, the approaches I mention above can easily be extended to other works by Vassanji. For instance, *The Book of Secrets*, *The Magic of Saida*, and *The Gunny Sack* all focus on East Africa during and after British and German colonization and can be taught using methodologies similar to the ones I discuss in this essay. Likewise, while some of the specific context discussed above may change, Vassanji's novels set in South Asia, *The Assassin's Song* and *A Delhi Obsession*, can also be explored through the lens of post-colonial and diasporic studies. In the case of these novels, the perspective shifts from interracial relationships to interreligious encounters, especially in the context of Hindu-Muslim tensions in pre- and postcolonial South Asia. Here the focus is on syncretic traditions, the development of nation-alist agendas in the subcontinent, the atrocities of communal violence, and the resulting intergenerational trauma. Vassanji's novels set in South Asia would also prove compelling reads for students who want to explore the South Asian postcolonial context. I have always struggled with selecting one novel to teach; Vassanji's works offer many gateways for students, and it is mostly a matter of personal choice when instructors have to decide on a single novel.

Works Cited

Anderson, Benedict. *Imagined Communities*. Verso, 2006.

Brah, Avtar. *Cartographies of Diaspora: Contesting Identities*. Routledge, 1996.

Clifford, James. *Routes: Travel and Translation in the Late Twentieth Century*. Harvard UP, 1997.

Cohen, Robin. *Global Diasporas: An Introduction*. U of Washington P, 1997.

Damrosch, David. *How to Read World Literature*. Wiley-Blackwell, 2018.

———. *What Is World Literature?* Princeton UP, 2003.

Desai, Gaurav. *Commerce with the Universe: Africa, India, and the Afrasian Imagination*. Columbia UP, 2013.

Fanon, Frantz. *The Wretched of the Earth*. Grove Press, 1963.

Freire, Paulo. *Pedagogy of Hope: Reliving Pedagogy of the Oppressed*. Bloomsbury, 2021.

Hall, Stuart. "Cultural Identity and Diaspora." *Colonial Discourse and Post-colonial Theory: A Reader*, edited by Patrick Williams and Laura Chrisman, Harvester Wheatsheaf, 1994, pp. 392–403.

Huyssen, Andreas. "Diaspora and Nation: Migration into Other Pasts." *New German Critique*, vol. 88, 2003, pp. 147–64.

Iyer, Nalini. "No Place to Call Home: Citizenship and Belonging in M. G. Vas-sanji's *The In-Between World of Vikram Lall.*" *Negotiating Afropolitan-ism: Essays on Borders and Spaces in Contemporary African Literature and*

Folklore, edited by J. K. S. Makokha and Jennifer Wawrzinek, Rodopi, 2011, pp. 205–14.

Král, Françoise. "The Resilient Opacity of Vassanji's *The In-Between World of Vikram Lall*." *Commonwealth Essays and Studies*, vol. 30, no. 1, 2007, pp. 61–72.

Murji, Karim, and Asma Sayed, editors. *The Transnational Imaginaries of M. G. Vassanji: Diaspora, Literature, and Culture*. Peter Lang, 2018.

Ngũgĩ wa Thiong'o. "A Globalectical Imagination." *World Literature Today*, vol. 87, no. 3, 2013, pp. 40–42.

Ozawa, Shizen. "'This Was My Country—How Could It Not Be?': On the Significance of Travel in *The In-Between World of Vikram Lall*." *Tamkang Review*, vol. 47, no. 1, 2016, pp. 121–41.

Rosenberg, Aaron Louis. "Riding the Third Rail: Perpetual Movement and Imagined Return in *The In-Between World of Vikram Lall*." Murji and Sayed, pp. 151–68.

Safran, William. "Diasporas in Modern Societies: Myths of Homeland and Return." *Diaspora: A Journal of Transnational Studies*, vol. 1, no. 1, 1991, pp. 83–99.

Said, Edward. *Orientalism*. Vintage Books, 1979.

Sayed, Asma, and Karim Murji. "Locating M. G. Vassanji in a Transnational Context." Murji and Sayed, pp. 1–16.

Spivak, Gayatri Chakravorty. "Diasporas Old and New: Women in a Transnational World." *Textual Practice*, vol. 2, no. 10, 1996, pp. 245–69.

Vassanji, M. G. *The Assassin's Song*. Doubleday Canada, 2007.

———. *The Book of Secrets*. McClelland and Stewart, 1993.

———. *A Delhi Obsession*. Penguin Random House Canada, 2019.

———. *The Gunny Sack*. Heinemann International, 1989.

———. *The In-Between World of Vikram Lall*. Random House, 2003.

———. *The Magic of Saida*. Doubleday Canada, 2012.

Anita Baksh

Indianness in the Caribbean: Strategies for Teaching Indo-Caribbean Anglophone Literature

Units on Indo-Caribbean literature or stand-alone texts can be incorporated into a variety of college courses, including courses on South Asian literature, Asian American literature, world literature, Caribbean literature, Black British literature, multiethnic literature, and women's literature. Analyzing Indo-Caribbean texts provides an opportunity to foreground dimensions of the Caribbean experience that tend to be elided. Students commonly view the region as the product of encounters between the British, Europeans, and enslaved Africans while overlooking the influences of Asian, Middle Eastern, and Indigenous groups. In addition, Indian indentureship in the Caribbean (1838–1917) establishes a South Asian presence in the Western Hemisphere that dates to the mid–nineteenth century, challenging stereotypes of South Asians as newcomers to the Americas. Examining Indo-Caribbean texts urges students to expand ideas about Caribbean identities and cultures and rethink dominant narratives about South Asians and Asian Americans, including stereotypes of otherness and the model minority myth.

It is particularly important to teach Indo-Caribbean literature in areas where Indo-Caribbean diasporic populations have settled: London, Toronto, and several US states, including New York (New York City and Schenectady), Florida (Fort Lauderdale and Orlando), Georgia, Minnesota, Ohio, and the Washington, DC, metropolitan area. Doing so allows students to engage with the evolving diversity of these spaces and promotes understanding across difference. When I teach Indo-Caribbean texts at a community college in New York City, my students and I discuss relevant information that allows students to connect the literature to real-world circumstances. For example, Guyanese are one of the largest immigrant groups in New York City. The Richmond Hill and South Ozone Park neighborhoods of Queens are called "Little Guyana" because a large population of Indo-Caribbeans from Guyana and Trinidad and their descendants have been settling there since the 1970s. This community is regularly featured in *The New York Times*—for instance, in the newspaper's coverage of the annual Holi, or Phagwah, festival. However, these representations tend to exoticize Indo-Caribbeans as foreign and solely of Indian heritage, overlooking their hybrid cultures and the ways in which Indian cultural practices have transformed, and continue to transform, in Caribbean spaces. Students are sometimes familiar with roti shops (restaurants) and West Indian grocery stores in this area, and some have Indo-Caribbean friends, classmates, or co-workers. Moreover, using literature to connect Indo-Caribbean history and culture to contemporary realities can encourage my students—who are predominantly people of color, immigrants, or both—to reflect on their own migration histories (voluntary or involuntary) and how these have been shaped by race, class, gender, sexual orientation, location, and other factors.

This essay offers approaches to teaching select Indo-Caribbean texts. I touch on historical contexts and theoretical frameworks to assist instructors and students in situating Indo-Caribbean writings. However, it is crucial not to read this literature as sociological documentation of historical or social realities but to consider the aesthetic strategies and generic forms Indo-Caribbean writers employ. My readings of chosen texts model these practices by foregrounding significant themes, language use, narrative modes, and generic experimentations.

Historical Considerations

Between 1838 and 1917, over half a million Indian immigrants were dispersed in large numbers to Guyana (238,909) and Trinidad (143,939) and in smaller numbers to Jamaica, Grenada, St. Vincent, and St. Lucia

(Look Lai 19). This essay focuses on authors with origins in Guyana and Trinidad, countries in which Indo-Caribbeans make up one of the largest ethnic groups of the national population. While most Indian immigrants originated from the United Provinces and Bihar, a significant minority emigrated via the southern port of Madras.

Indentureship was an exploitative system of human capital that confined Indian laborers to the plantation. Moreover, the languages they spoke (Hindi, Bhojpuri, and Urdu), their non-Western clothing, and their Hindu and Muslim religious practices further alienated them from the emerging Afro-Creole culture of colonial West Indian society.[1] The perceptions of Indians as foreigners and interlopers that emerged during indentureship significantly affected the formation of Indo-Caribbean subjectivities and Indo-Caribbean claims to postcolonial citizenship.

To introduce students to this background, I screen the film *Coolies: How Britain Reinvented Slavery,* narrated by Sanjeev Bhaskar. The use of the term *coolie,* an imperial slur used to degrade indentured laborers, suggests a reclaiming of indentured heritage. Featuring the Indo-Guyanese scholar-writer David Dabydeen and the Indo-Fijian historian Brij Lal, the film provides a historical revision based on perspectives from descendants of indentured workers and testimony from a formerly indentured Guyanese woman in her own Creole voice. The film pairs well with Gaiutra Bahadur's nonfiction text *Coolie Woman.* Studying indentureship complicates colonial and labor histories and disrupts the binary between slavery and freedom. It is also important to convey to students the nuanced ways in which indentureship was different from slavery.

Theoretical Frameworks

Several concepts might be useful in framing Indo-Caribbean experiences. Shalini Puri posits "dougla poetics" to theorize "potentially progressive cultural projects" and a political identity, rather than a biological one, that incorporates both the dominant Afro-Creole culture and Indian culture (221). Based on the notion of the *dougla,* the offspring of Indian and African parentage, Puri's theory offers an alternative to *creolization,* which emphasizes African and European traditions. However, it overlooks other groups in the Caribbean, including Chinese, Jewish, and Middle Eastern populations, and has "often glossed over crucial engagements with the specificity of biological *douglas,* who are, ironically, still fighting for national visibility in a very multi-ethnic social milieu" (Mehta 15). Similarly, Rosanne Kanhai offers the concept of a "dougla feminist space" as a means of expanding representation within Caribbean feminist discourse.[2]

Brinda Mehta argues that crossing the *kala pani*, or dark waters from India to the Caribbean, allowed Indo-Caribbean women to renegotiate patriarchal and imperial marginalization in the New World. In Hindu belief systems, transoceanic journeys were viewed as taboo and were associated with the erosion of family, tradition, and caste purity. Mehta's *kala pani* discourse recognizes a shared heritage of oceanic crossings "in the form of Asian indenture, African slavery, and Middle Eastern commercial enterprise" that might unite Caribbean women (15). The scholars Joy Mahabir and Mariam Pirbhai propose *jahaji-bhain* ("ship-sister"), a feminization of the more common Hindi-Urdu term *jahaji-bhai* ("ship-brother"), to describe bonds forged by girls and women traveling across the *kala pani* as indentured labor to the Caribbean and other plantation colonies, relationships that intensified on the plantation. Building on this scholarship, Gabrielle Jamela Hosein and Lisa Outar put forth "postindenture feminism" to understand Indo-Caribbean diasporic experiences in which second- and third-generation Indo-Caribbeans "find themselves in immigrant contexts where their visible Indianness yokes them to subcontinental groupings even as they strive to find the historical and conceptual language to describe their unique specificities as products of indentureship" (9). As the following sections demonstrate, literature has served as a fruitful medium to investigate Indo-Caribbean identities, cultural practices, collective memory, and historical gaps.

Narratives of Colonialism

Courses on Indo-Caribbean literature or South Asian diasporic literature might begin with the foundational diasporic text, *A House for Mr. Biswas*, by the Nobel Prize–winning author V. S. Naipaul. Set in colonial Trinidad between the two world wars, the novel depicts the internal migration of Indians from rural village settlements to more creolized urban spaces and the transformation of Indian culture and religion in the Caribbean context.

Caste is a central concern of the novel. The Indian male protagonist, Mohun Biswas, negotiates masculinity through the Hindu patriarchal values of his upper-caste Brahmin in-laws. In the New World, caste could not dictate the social, political, or economic aspects of life for Indians as it previously did in India (Van der Veer and Vertovec 154). Brahmin men were least desirable as laborers and probably represented only a small percentage of the indentured labor force. Migration also presented opportunities for new beginnings, which led some indentured laborers to claim higher caste affiliations. Brahmin widows, who had often been ill-treated and cast out by in-laws in India, made up a significant number of the women who migrated in the initial phase of indentureship. These women exercised more freedom in choosing partners from other castes, religions, and races (Mehta 5). On plantations, indentured laborers of all castes and religions lived alongside one another, completed the same demeaning tasks, and suffered similar discrimination. However, Brahmins were still revered symbolically as religious leaders, and as Indians became permanent settlers in the Caribbean, they were increasingly sought out as pundits to perform religious functions. *A House for Mr. Biswas* illustrates the irony of this structure as Biswas is selected by relatives during pujas (prayers) to eat before other devotees and to receive gifts but is neglected on other occasions. He is also chosen to marry his wife, Shama, solely based on his Brahmin status, despite his inability to support her on his meager earnings as a sign painter.

Ismith Khan's novel *The Jumbie Bird* also addresses cultural transformation in its foregrounding of the Indo-Trinidadian Muslim festival Hosay (or Hussay), what the scholar Aliyah Khan describes as an "exceptional historical case of Islamic religious creolization in the Caribbean" (20). It features "a public procession of large and small model tombs (*tadjahs*), a red model of the crescent moon and a green model of the moon representing the brothers Hussein and Hasan, respectively, flags, singing, dancing, drumming, and, in earlier days, stick fighting (*gatcar*) and fire dancing (fire pass)" (22). In 1884 colonial authorities attempted to restrict the event.

These novels portray heterosexual Indian males who negotiate culture, family, and home within colonial Trinidad. Although parents and elders might look back to an idealized India as homeland, forgetting their reasons for leaving India or viewing their treatment (and that of their children) within colonial Trinidad as far worse than they previously experienced in India, the protagonists navigate in-between spaces as hybrid colonial subjects born in Trinidad. In her analysis of queer South Asian diasporic texts, Gayatri Gopinath reveals the binary configuration between diaspora and nation often seen in discourses around diaspora:

> Viewing the (home) nation through the analytical frame of diaspora allows for a reconsideration of the traditional hierarchal relation between nation and diaspora, where the former is seen as merely an impoverished imitation of an originary national culture. . . . Indeed while the diaspora within nationalist discourse is often positioned as the abjected and disavowed Other to the nation, the nation also simultaneously recruits the diaspora into its absolutist logic. (7)

The tension between diaspora and homeland arises in *The Jumbie Bird* through Kale Khan, a migrant and former indentured laborer, who initiates a movement among Indians to repatriate, only to be disappointed when a dignitary from the Indian government visits colonial Trinidad and urges Indians to stay there permanently. In this way, the novel complicates the home/diaspora dichotomy and addresses the real-world condition of India's refusal to intervene on behalf of and encourage repatriation of Indian indentured migrants whose crossing of the *kala pani* contaminated their claim to Indian cultural and legal citizenship.

For these early writers, the Indian Trinidadian subject is firmly heterosexual and male; queer characters are omitted, and women are secondary characters. As students examine these texts, they might consider the following questions: How are colonial Caribbean societies organized economically, socially, and politically? In what ways does the Indian male protagonist negotiate connections to self, to family, to community, and to the larger colonial society? How do authors resist stereotypes of Indians? What images of women are presented?

Indo-Caribbean Feminist Consciousness

Indo-Caribbean women's writing emphasizes the perspectives of girls, women, and gender nonconforming individuals. Ramabai Espinet's *The Swinging Bridge* presents an intergenerational tale across time and space as the Trinidadian Canadian protagonist, Mona, traces her female indentured ancestor's journey from India to the New World. In the process, Mona reflects on her own experiences of gender oppression and racism within Trinidad and her family's struggles in Canada as racialized immigrants. Students can examine these themes by answering discussion questions in written responses outside class or in small groups in class, providing passages from the text to support their claims. These low-stakes activities serve as starting points for larger class discussions, promote critical analysis skills, and help students develop materials for future high-stakes assignments. The first theme discussed is how Mona unearths feminist herstories through alternative means of knowledge: letters, rumors, storytelling, memories, and dreams. Students consider how these modes challenge and supplement historical records. A second theme that emerges is racial tension. Mona's family migrates to Canada for economic opportunities and to escape discrimination against Indians in Trinidad. In the novel, her father, Dada, expresses sentiments of marginalization and lack of national unity in a series of letters to a local newspaper. In relation to this theme, students discuss the following questions: In Dada's letters, what tensions seem to exist in Trinidad after independence? How is Trinidadian identity defined in the novel? How do racial tensions affect Dada and his family? A third significant theme that arises is cultural identity; Indianness is defined differently by each character. Questions that address this theme include the following: In the novel, what metaphors depict a sense of Indo-Caribbean identity? What role does religion play in defining identity and culture? A final topic of discussion is land ownership, which drives much of the plot: How is land perceived by each generation? How can Mona's return to Trinidad to buy her family's land be read in relation to the history of Indians as plantation laborers?

In Shani Mootoo's *Cereus Blooms at Night*, elements of magical realism and gothic fiction are used to convey the story of Mala Ramchandani, who is raped by her father, Chandin. Set on a fictional Caribbean island, the novel reveals hidden histories of colonial racism and forbidden sexualities. Christian Canadian missionaries educate Chandin in hopes that he will assist with the conversion of other Indians. But Chandin's experience leads to self-hate and violence. Rejected by Lavinia, the daughter of the white missionary, Chandin marries Sarah, a Christianized Indian woman. However, Sarah escapes to the north with Lavinia, leaving Chandin with two daughters. Silence surrounds Mala's family history: the possibility of her mother's transgressive sexuality, Chandin's abuse of Mala, and suspicions that Mala murdered her father. The most glaring silence is the community's refusal to see her as a survivor of sexual assault instead of as a madwoman and murderer. The novel is narrated by Mala's male nurse, Tyler, who disrupts gender binaries. Tyler cross-dresses, and his love interest, Otoh, is biologically male but is "[n]ot a man and not ever able to be a woman" (Mootoo 77). Mootoo's refusal to label Tyler's and Otoh's identities and their relationship challenges the idea that Western theories of LGBTQI experiences can be mapped onto non-Western sub-jects. Situating these fluid identities in colonial spaces also points to the long existence of queer relations in the Caribbean. Moreover, Mala and Tyler's relationship enables mutual healing, illustrating the power of community and chosen family.

Working-Class and Cross-Cultural Encounters

Indo-Guyanese writers have received less critical attention than their Trinidadian counterparts have. In their works, the Guyanese writers Rooplall Monar, Ryhaan Shah, and Narmala Shewcharan focus on the daily realities of working-class communities. Monar's short story collection, *Backdam People*, depicts Indo-Guyanese communities that emerged from indentureship but continued to live and work on sugar and rice plantations between the 1930s and the 1950s. Indo-Guyanese who had become educated and entered professional careers looked down on the culture and lifestyle of this subgroup. Monar's use of the language of the Indo-Guyanese working class—a mixture of rural Guyanese Creole with Hindi elements—as a mode of narration and dialogue might be challenging for students in Western institutions to fully comprehend. To overcome this challenge, I suggest teachers assign a few stories rather than the complete collection, urge students to use the glossary, and discuss why parts of a cultural text might be inaccessible to readers. Monar's text engages questions about audience: For whom do writers create literature? What purpose does literature serve for communities that are being written about?

Two tales that might be taught are "Masala Maraj" (Monar 38–51) and "Who Is the Real Ole Higue?" (29–37). The first relays the tale of a Brahmin named Maraj who uses his ability to cook delicious Indian Guyanese food—"dal-purri" (a split pea–filled flatbread) and "massala fowl-curry"—to convince the white overseer to give Maraj a less labor-intensive position (39). Originally assigned to work in the *backdam*, the section of the estate in which laborers had to trek for miles in the dark hours of the morning to get to their duties, Maraj hopes that the delightful meal he prepared would persuade the overseer to grant him a carpenter position. As a Brahmin, Maraj believes that "backdam wuk na so prappa for he caste" (backdam work was not proper for his caste; 38). The story engages themes of caste, social relations on the plantation, and techniques employed by workers to resist arduous work conditions. The second story, "Who Is the Real Ole Higue?," depicts a community's attempt to rationalize occurrences of infant mortality. What begins as a quest to find the Ole Higue—an evil spirit in the form of an old woman who preys on the lives of infants—ends with communal violence against a woman. The narrator oscillates between humor, objectivity, and skepticism, concluding that infants were still dying despite the Ole Higue's demise. Invoking the supernatural figure of the Ole Higue, the story shows the Indo-Guyanese working-class community's syncretic beliefs and adoption of Afro-Caribbean folklore.

Shah's *A Silent Life* centers the female activist in the 1930s labor strikes in British Guiana. Focusing on a Muslim family, the narrative provides an alternative to the dominant Hindu-centered perspective emphasized in Indo-Caribbean literature. Shah uses magical realism as a narrative technique to oscillate between time and space and multiple perspectives. Through visions and dreams, the protagonist, Aleyah Hassan, gains insight into the past of her *nani* (the Hindi term for maternal grandmother), who advocates for the rights of cane and rice workers. Students might consider how Nani and her husband uphold or defy prescribed gender roles. Nani is a wife, mother, and fierce activist, and her husband is a dancer who grapples with societal expectations that he be the dominant partner. As a result, he dies by suicide, and Nani becomes a recluse. Another important theme is intergenerational trauma. The following questions encourage students to think more deeply about this issue: How does Aleyah encounter similar gender-related pressures even though she attends college and migrates to England in the 1990s? In what ways does the novel connect intergenerational trauma to indentureship? Lastly, the theme of politics arises through the novel's engagement with Guyana's violent transition from colonialism to nationhood, when racial tensions between Afro-Guyanese and Indo-Guyanese groups were ignited by British and American influences.

Shewcharan's *Tomorrow Is Another Day* presents a cross section of Guyanese society: politicians, smugglers of contraband (clothing and foods), middle-class housewives, and poor and working-class Afro-Guyanese and Indo-Guyanese characters. Set in Guyana's urban capital, Georgetown, the realist novel foregrounds Indo-Caribbean women characters who negotiate life under a tumultuous postindependence fictional governmental regime that resembles that of the former president Forbes Burnham. For example, Chandi, an Indo-Guyanese working-class woman, struggles to care for her four children after her husband is injured while working at a sugar estate. Chandi receives support from several women, including Aunt Adee, an Afro-Guyanese market woman. Speculating on this relationship, students might be asked to ponder these questions: How does Chandi and Aunt Adee's cross-racial solidarity against social and political oppression contrast the country's political structure? A lack of resources and government support leads to Chandi's death by suicide. Students can analyze this act as one of desperation, sacrifice, and resistance; Chandi exerts agency over her body to ensure the survival of her children, who will receive life insurance money after her death. Both Shah's and Shewcharan's novels bring awareness to issues affecting contemporary Guyanese communities: mental health, inadequate support services, and alarming suicide rates that are rooted in Guyana's plantation history.

As this essay demonstrates, Indo-Caribbean texts are integral to the teaching of South Asian anglophone diasporic literature and can be taught in a range of college courses. They allow students to examine the diverse themes of colonialism and its legacy; the social, economic, and political struggles of postcolonial societies; the transformation of Indian culture, religion, and languages in diasporic spaces; feminist resistance; and community, among others.

Notes

1. In this essay I use the term *Creole* to refer to the dominant Anglo-Caribbean culture, which is associated with the hybridization of Afro-Caribbean and European traditions.

2. Kanhai proposed the idea of an inclusive dougla feminist space in a public lecture given at the Centre for Gender and Development Studies at the St. Augustine campus of the University of the West Indies in 1999. For further information, see Mehta 13–14.

Works Cited

Bahadur, Gaiutra. *Coolie Woman: The Odyssey of Indenture.* U of Chicago P, 2014.

Coolies: How Britain Reinvented Slavery. Narrated by Sanjeev Bhaskar, British Broadcasting Corporation, 2003. *YouTube*, uploaded by Germitunitedorg, 11 Nov. 2012, www.youtube.com/watch?v=oxl4q_jfDPI.

Espinet, Ramabai. *The Swinging Bridge.* Harper Perennial Canada, 2003.

Gopinath, Gayatri. *Impossible Desires: Queer Diasporas and South Asian Public Cultures.* Duke UP, 2005.

Hosein, Gabrielle Jamela, and Lisa Outar, editors. *Indo-Caribbean Feminist Thought: Genealogies, Theories, Enactments.* Palgrave Macmillan, 2017.

Khan, Aliyah. *Far from Mecca: Globalizing the Muslim Caribbean.* Rutgers UP, 2020.

Khan, Ismith. *The Jumbie Bird.* 1961. Longman, 1985.

Look Lai, Walton. *Indentured Labor, Caribbean Sugar: Chinese and Indian Migrants to the British West Indies, 1838–1918.* 1993. Johns Hopkins UP, 2004.

Mahabir, Joy, and Mariam Pirbhai, editors. *Critical Perspectives on Indo-Caribbean Women's Literature.* Routledge, 2013.

Mehta, Brinda J. *Diasporic (Dis)Location: Indo-Caribbean Women Writers Negotiate the Kala Pani.* U of the West Indies P, 2004.

Monar, Rooplall. *Backdam People.* Peepal Tree Press, 1987.

Mootoo, Shani. *Cereus Blooms at Night.* Press Gang Publishers, 1996.

Naipaul, V. S. *A House for Mr. Biswas.* 1961. Vintage Books, 2003.

Puri, Shalini. *The Caribbean Postcolonial: Social Equality, Post-nationalism, and Cultural Hybridity.* Palgrave Macmillan, 2004.

Shah, Ryhaan. *A Silent Life.* Peepal Tree Press, 2005.

Shewcharan, Narmala. *Tomorrow Is Another Day.* Peepal Tree Press, 1994.

Van der Veer, Peter, and Steven Vertovec. "Brahmanism Abroad: On Caribbean Hinduism as an Ethnic Religion." *Ethnology,* vol. 30, no. 2, Apr. 1991, pp. 149–66.

Mayuri Deka

Faulty Stereotypes: Indo-Caribbean Literature and a Pedagogy of Social Justice

Coolie—a term often used to identify Indo-Caribbean people—is indicative not only of the history of indentured labor but also of the stereotypes that continue to linger in the present day. While the usage of the term refers to menial laborers and can be traced to the late sixteenth century, Gaiutra Bahadur, in *Coolie Woman: The Odyssey of Indenture*, points out that "after the enslaved were emancipated in the 1830s, the British began to rustle up replacement workers for plantations worldwide, [and] this was the epithet they used for the indentured laborers they enlisted" (xx). *Coolie* represents the deep-seated generalizations about the Brown body within the Caribbean context and is considered pejorative. Used to identify Indo-Caribbean people, especially in the Caribbean, parts of Africa, and within the Caribbean diaspora, *coolie* mislabeled and devalued the immense diversity of the people brought to the Caribbean from India as indentured laborers from 1838 to 1917. This faulty stereotyping continues today: the term is still connected to flawed perceptions of the socioeconomic and cultural realities of Indo-Caribbean people within which it is entrenched, despite attempts to reclaim the word by Marina Carter and Khal Torabully and by Bahadur. Reverberations of the term are heard within the Caribbean classroom as well, where students might use the term without being aware of the sociohistorical and cultural contexts in which it is embedded. Others might recognize the stereotype activated by the utterance of *coolie* but not its effect on their perception and judgment of another individual.

This faulty stereotyping centered on nonpropositional knowledge (apparent in forms such as imagery, figurative concepts, prototypical figures, and ideal or cautionary relational narratives) underlies students' stereotype consciousness and usage. These acts of stereotyping depend on the scripts and schemas (e.g., coolie as "dirty") that students have about Indo-Caribbean people and form the basis of their perceptions and judgments. This is especially evident if the student is socialized within Caribbean cultures or in constant contact with Indo-Caribbean people within the diaspora. Therefore, a consideration of the scripts and schemas that propagate and sustain these faulty stereotypes must focus on not only content but also pedagogical strategies that will lead to prosocial thinking and action. Rhonda Cobham-Sander writes that in the Caribbean "[t]he silence in our school curriculum on the subject of Caribbean writers raised additional doubts about the literary merit of such works as well as the moral standing of their authors, so we tended to talk about them, like the uncle who had fled to Venezuela to escape a little problem with the police, in the past tense, or the subjunctive" (1).

Outside the region, consistent attempts have been made at addressing this question of changing the scope and quantity of texts included in the classroom. However, we now require new strategies for sufficiently understanding, evaluating, and teaching the multiple sociocultural and critical strands influencing the issue so that it leads to prosocial action. A pedagogy that focuses on students expanding their in-groups rather than on difference can result in a subversion of faulty knowledge scripts and schemas that underlie stereotype consciousness and usage. Indeed, instructors in the Indo-Caribbean literature classroom are in a unique position to examine and evaluate the complex history of the Brown body in the Caribbean. A pedagogy that rethinks the politics of social exclusion beyond the terms of the prejudices of the excluders reconfigures this exclusionary framework of self versus other as only a problem of difference and creates ever-widening circles of acceptance.

Self versus Other: Negotiating Stereotypes

One of the persistent and crucial problems faced by the Indo-Caribbean literature instructor lies in the inadequacies of traditional approaches to initiate student interest and a broader base of identification with the Brown other while encouraging a rethinking of students' own stereotype consciousness. Outside the region, this hesitation in identifying with the Indo-Caribbean person is connected to the process of perception and judgment students have of the Brown other and their sense of shared knowledge structures of common ideals (for instance, justice and rights). The Indo-Caribbean figure, while not stereotypically marked as a physical threat, is usually seen as an economic, intellectual, and sociocultural challenger. Bahadur refers to the "Dot Busters" (8), who in the 1980s indiscriminately attacked all people who looked like Indians, and reveals their faulty stereotype scripts and schemas. Groups like these did not discriminate between the Indians from India who recently immigrated to the United States and the Indo-Caribbean community, and narratives reveal the politics (even internal to the American Indians and Caribbean Indians) surrounding the Brown body. Indeed, narratives create and reinforce the sociocultural identities of the group while highlighting the uniqueness and alienness in relation to the white or Black body. Students might feel that these texts are of no use to them, but, more significantly, they might also feel threatened by the unfamiliar cultural codes and knowledges. In the Indo-Caribbean classroom, this is especially true for students of different ethnicities who do not identify with the sociocultural and economic contexts of the texts. Distancing or lack of interest in the content and knowledge presented in the classroom may be indicative of a student's attempts at securing their own sense of self and trying to mitigate the stereotype threat. As Mark Bracher posits, these attempts to secure a sense of self are based on the performance of the core identity-bearing qualities in a person's schemas and scripts of the self and other and on receiving tacit and objective recognition of a coherent and unified identity that is able to effect change. Students, therefore, may implement beliefs and actions that reinforce their sense of self in the form of stereotyping based on nonpropositional knowledge.

Indeed, clinical research by Aaron Beck indicates that people with secure identities are less focused on egocentric monitoring of situations to sustain a coherent sense of self. Beck found that almost all antisocial behaviors reflect the same kind of faulty thought: "the aggressors have a positive bias regarding themselves and a negative bias toward their adversary, often conceived as the enemy" (xiii). Most individuals who display prejudiced attitudes or engage in stereotyping perceive themselves as innocent victims. They must protect themselves by taking certain identity-maintaining steps against the enemy other. This is especially pertinent for a classroom focused on Indo-Caribbean literature. Students with faulty knowledges of the stereotyped other are more focused on identity maintenance than on expanding their circle of similarity. Moving students from this space of vigilance to openness requires pedagogies that not only present novel information but also engage with the underlying nonpropositional emotional structures.

A classroom focused on Indo-Caribbean literature presents an opportunity to create this new form of assessing, evaluating, and judging the other, which leads to prosocial change. This is especially true if students do not belong to the same ethnoracial group as the characters in the texts. In this case, the characters that students read about are neither in their familiar in-group nor present around them. The texts and information presented challenge students' core identities by introducing and asking them to make connections with diverse perspectives. However, as George Lakoff points out, the persuasive power of language comes not from reason but from the "frames, prototypes, metaphors, narratives, images, and emotions" it engages (15). And literature, by its very nature, comprises these narratives and images. Instructors can, therefore, not only appeal to students' logic but also reveal the flaws in their knowledge of the stereotyped other in emotionally compelling ways, thereby helping them become more empathic. By using exercises such as mirroring, journaling, and counterpositioning, instructors can encourage students to see perspectives different from their own. Further, the content of Indo-Caribbean literature provides ample opportunities to read about experiences and identities that reflect collective concerns and beliefs as well as concerns and beliefs that are different from students' own. A pedagogy, therefore, that focuses not only on changing stereotypes by using logic and evidence but also on changing nonpropositional knowledge over time can lead to prosocial thinking and action.

From Theory to Praxis: Reading Bahadur's *Coolie Woman: The Odyssey of Indenture*

Created for a fifty-minute Indo-Caribbean literature class at either the undergraduate or graduate level, the following exercise aims to promote a reassessment of students' reasoning and judgment in relation to the stereotyped other. The diction and complexity of questions in the exercise can be molded to the level of the course, and students are strongly encouraged to participate in both the written reflection and the subsequent class discussion. The exercise assumes that the classroom consists of a diverse student demographic in terms of race, ethnicity, gender, class, and so on. It is possible that some students may belong to the Indo-Caribbean community being discussed in the text, and the exercise encourages them to deepen their understanding of their own relationship to the concepts of self and other. Focusing on the similarities and differences in the affective states and life experiences of the self and other and on the flexibility of the processes of reasoning and judgment, this exercise is one of many possible assignments that can encourage prosocial thinking and action.

The exercise is based on the Guyanese American author Gaiutra Bahadur's *Coolie Woman: The Odyssey of Indenture*. Receiving wide international acclaim since its publication in 2013, the narrative mostly traces the family history of indentureship, recreating the journey of Bahadur's great-grandmother Sujaria, who left Calcutta for British Guiana in 1903. Presented as a historical narrative of an indentured Indian woman in the Caribbean, the text also recounts a personal story. Entwining the ordeals and experiences of her great-grandmother with the larger movement of labor entrenched in the sociocultural landscape of India and the Caribbean, Bahadur recreates a story that focuses on indentured women who struggled to define a coherent sense of self. In its finality, the narrative presents the impossibility of an identity based only on fixed, linear racial or ethnic components. Indeed, I chose Bahadur's text for this exercise because it traces the protagonist's negotiations and struggles in defining a secure sense of self against the other. The text also presents a cultural reality that has a universal resonance as young people struggle to define themselves as unique in this rapidly changing world. The exercise, detailed in what follows, encourages students to vigorously engage with issues of race and ethnicity and the processes of reasoning and judgment:

> *Written Reflection*: Describe a scene in Gaiutra Bahadur's *Coolie Woman: The Odyssey of Indenture* that made you feel sympathy for a character in a difficult situation. Why did you feel sympathy for this character? Was it because of verbal cues, images, or another strategy used by the author? What words made you sympathize with the character? What images allowed you to imagine the character's experience? Now, imagine yourself in the character's situation. How would you feel? Would you feel anger, sadness, or a different emotion? Imagine how you would act in this situation. What would your body posture look like? How would you stand? How would you feel about yourself? What would your mental state be? Would you say something? What would you say? Would you react the same way as the character does,

or would you do or say something different? What changes would you hope to see in the character or situation? Explain in as much detail as possible the reasons for your actions.

Questions for Class Discussion: Can you clearly pinpoint the instigator in this scene? What verbal and nonverbal cues allow you to trace the instigator's action? What words does Bahadur use? What does the instigator's body posture look like? What is their tone like? Now, imagine yourself as the instigator. Why did you act the way you did? What was the reason behind your action? What were your expressions, body posture, and tone of voice like? What do these reveal about your mental state? Why? How do you feel before and after the action? Do you feel happy or sad? If you feel sad, what would you do to reestablish your sense of self? Think about the reasons behind the action. Can you explain in detail the motivation behind the action? Is it justifiable? If yes, why? If no, what would you do differently?

Centered on role-taking, the exercise arouses empathy in students by encouraging them to imagine themselves in the place of not only the character they feel most sympathy for but also the instigator. The cognitive process allows students to see both perspectives and ensures that students do not become self-vigilant and retreat to an inflexible space of self versus other. Imagining the motivation of the instigator and the effect on the victim with affective and physical specificities reduces the likelihood that students will take an aggressive role. This narrative, set in the Caribbean while tethered to India and the Middle Passage, presents a distant culture that challenges students with faulty stereotype consciousness about the Brown body. However, some elements of the story should also be familiar to students, considering that the narrative traces the desires and journey of the characters as they attempt to settle in a new place. It is important to provide sociopolitical and historical context as an introduction to the narrative, which will allow students to see similarities and will undercut the stereotype threat. Because the narrative is based on historical events, instructors could encourage students to do further research on indentureship in the Caribbean and the reasons for the migration away from India. This information would enhance students' ability to see similarities by providing information about the characters' life experiences while reducing the stereotype threat.

The written exercise begins by asking students to pinpoint a scene in the narrative where they feel a character has been treated unjustly and should be sympathized with. The analysis of such a scene will encourage students to think about a similar experience in their own lives and their affective responses to situations. Imagining themselves in the place of the character (for instance, in terms of body posture, mental state, and verbal cues) allows students to experience the same emotions as the character does. Indeed, the connection of students' own distress to the character's situation in the earlier part of the exercise creates an opportune space for an empathic imagining of the other's distress by putting the self in the victim's place. The exercise further engages students by asking them to trace their reactions to the situation. Most students will have a behavioral and action plan of how they will act in a similar situation. If they do not and experience a completely novel situation, this exercise allows students to imagine themselves in the place of the other and to include more diverse scripts and narratives by expanding their sense of self to include a non-stereotypical other. This exercise also prepares students for novel scenes and information, making them more open to new information. Most important, this section of the exercise encourages students to find similarities with another person and to understand their own affective responses to situations that are unfamiliar.

The class discussion attempts to expand students' circle of similarity and to make them aware of the multiplicity of scripts and narratives that affect the decision-making process as they focus on whom they consider the instigator in Bahadur's narrative. This part of the exercise addresses the other, asking students to consider the feelings of the real other in the scene (the instigator) and to imagine themselves in their place. The discussion opens by asking students to think about the motivation for the instigator's behavior by focusing on the various verbal and nonverbal cues that Bahadur provides. This is a primary requirement for deciding to take prosocial action. To act within a framework of social justice, one must feel that the victim needs help. The identification that students already feel with the victim (evident in their written reflections) arouses empathy for that character, allows students to see similarities, and ignites their desire to help that character. This desire would also alleviate the student's own distress that they feel in the process. However, imagining themselves as the instigator and focusing on the minute affective, physiological, and linguistic cues deepens students' empathic response and challenges their stereotype consciousness. An understanding that the instigator is also a product of their socialization and responds according to self-centered needs and desires shaped over a lifetime of experiences is crucial in the process of identification with the other and in reducing students' consciousness of stereotype threat. This understanding is essential in expanding students' in-group to include more diverse others and in ending continued criticism and stereotyping of a distant populace. By imagining oneself in the place of the other and rationalizing objectively the reasons for a character's actions, students may become more accepting of the motivations and actions of a distrusted or distant other. Indeed, the very process of putting oneself in the place of the other makes students more in touch with their own processes and motivations of identity maintenance.

The role-taking encouraged by this exercise inspires students to become aware of the similarity of the identity needs and desires of all people, despite their different behaviors and group memberships, while sustaining their own identities. This assumes that most students in the class do not belong to the groups presented in the text. However, if they do belong to the same groups, this exercise still encourages students to expand their empathic reasoning because it asks them to identify not only with someone they identify with but also with someone they blame. Further, the analysis of the processes of interpreting a situation and forming a judgment and action response that the student will be expected to do in this part of the exercise will encourage them to see the causes of each action. If students understand that all human beings are socialized and act to maintain their sense of self, then it will become much more difficult for them to stereotype anyone for their actions or to alienate them.

Instructors teaching Indo-Caribbean literature recognize the need for including marginalized texts, like Gaiutra Bahadur's *Coolie Woman*, in the classroom and the importance of developing a cohesive framework for converting dominant traditional paradigms into decentered pedagogical strategies. A pedagogy that aims to reconfigure faulty stereotyping must be centered on students' understanding of the Brown other and on changing their nonpropositional knowledge, which underlies their stereotype consciousness and usage. To ensure a coherent identity, this must be done while sustaining the student's sense of self. While a semester of classes with exercises based on this pedagogy would start the process of rethinking the faulty stereotypes underlying concepts of self and other, a more sustained approach to teaching is also required. A pedagogy that is based on expanding students' in-groups rather than on difference alone will encourage prosocial thinking and action.

Works Cited

Bahadur, Gaiutra. *Coolie Woman: The Odyssey of Indenture.* U of Chicago P, 2013.

Beck, Aaron T. *Prisoners of Hate: The Cognitive Basis of Anger, Hostility, and Violence.* HarperCollins Publishers, 1999.

Bracher, Mark. *Radical Pedagogy: Identity, Generativity, and Social Transformation.* Palgrave Macmillan, 2006.

Carter, Marina, and Khal Torabully. *Coolitude: An Anthology of the Indian Labour Diaspora.* Anthem Press, 2002.

Cobham-Sander, Rhonda. "Consuming the Self: V. S. Naipaul, CLR James, and *A Way in the World*." *Anthurium: A Caribbean Studies Journal*, vol. 5, no. 2, 2007, anthurium.miami.edu/articles/10.33596/anth.101/galley/97/download/.

Lakoff, George. *The Political Mind: A Cognitive Scientist's Guide to Your Brain and Its Politics.* Penguin Books, 2009.

Dharitri Bhattacharjee

History, Historiography, Ethnography, and Diaspora in Amitav Ghosh's *In an Antique Land*

Amitav Ghosh's *In an Antique Land: History in the Guise of a Traveler's Tale* serves to remind students what history is, how it's done, how historiography preserves history, the accidental and contingent nature of the discipline, and, finally, how to situate history within the broader framework of the social sciences and even the humanities. How I demonstrate to students the value of these fundamental questions within the scope of an Indian Ocean history course and why I use a key text in South Asian anglophone diasporic literature, Ghosh's *In an Antique Land*, now in print for close to three decades, to look for these critical answers is the main focus of this essay. Ghosh's central focus is an exploration of the world of a twelfth-century Tunisian Jew, Abraham Ben Yiju, who migrated from Fustat (modern-day Cairo) to Mangalore and then to Aden and back to Fustat. Ben Yiju's friends in the Ben Ezra congregation, his family in Tunisia and Italy, his wife and children, and his slave Bomma populate this universe. The pathways that led to this exploration—Ghosh's journey to Cairo and adjoining villages and Mangalore, India, in search of Bomma's history between 1978 and 1990—are a parallel focus. Ben Yiju and Ghosh are both diasporic figures who live and shape interconnected global histories as we know them today. Bringing these two worlds together is the history of how accidental preservation of twelfth-century documents in the Cairo Geniza and inadvertent scholarly writing and citation lured Ghosh deep into Ben Yiju and Bomma's world. *In an Antique Land* is an ode to all kinds of histories: formal disciplinary history, the historical past, the writing of history and historiography that were shaped in large part by the Indian Ocean world. The book reveals all kinds of connections and intersections in this oceanic world enabled by diasporic histories that chafe against narrow, essentialist histories.

The course I teach is upper-level and mainly attracts history majors. I teach Ghosh as a midterm reading assignment. By that time, students have gained familiarity with oceans as methods and conceptual frameworks and the history of the Muslims in the Indian Ocean. The first half of the course ends in the fifteenth century, and the second half starts with the European presence in the Indian Ocean, in particular Vasco da Gama's voyage to Calicut in 1498. Ghosh serves to accentuate the intellectual achievements of the Indian Ocean course from the first half and lay the groundwork to anticipate the history of the Indian Ocean post–European advent in the second half. My course is called Adventures at Sea. In the course description, I underscore the kinds of adventures that historical actors such as merchants, slaves, and pirates embarked on in the Indian Ocean for more than two thousand years and how these movements shaped the space of the Indian Ocean world. Ghosh's narrative complements the course materials and offers itself up for effective conversations with all the other scholars and readings. The course starts with the theme of wanderlust in a significant primary source, George Wynn Brereton Huntingford's edited and translated edition of *Periplus of the Erythraean Sea*. Similar to how the writer of the *Periplus* enables ancient history to come alive, Ghosh captures the history of Ben Yiju's world being preserved by the endeavors of not just the actors but also the historians, enthusiasts, curators, and missionaries, all separated by centuries. Apart from wanderlust, themes such as the rise of Islam and geographic and cultural spheres of influence in the Indian Ocean, the central topics in Patricia Risso's *Merchants and Faith* and Janet Abu-Lughod's *Before European Hegemony*, are also elucidated by Ghosh's variegated cast of twelfth-century Jewish historical actors who are working alongside Muslim trade networks and Islamic spheres of cultural influence. The broader exploration of a strong and affluent network of Jewish traders in the western Indian Ocean coexisting with Muslim networks explains the nature of Islam's presence in the Indian Ocean. The interrogation of the minutiae of Ben Yiju's life as he straddles two very different cultures, that of a patriarchal Jew from Tunisia and of a matrilineal Tulu in western India, is a good example of the fluidities within the spheres of influence. But *In an Antique Land* is as rich an understanding of early modern, modern, and postcolonial histories of the Indian Ocean as it is a portrayal of the twelfth-century world. The book narrates a segment of Ghosh's life from 1978 to 1990 set in Egypt and Mangalore. The nuanced relationship that Ghosh shares with his Egyptian friends, Mangalore with its own past, and Egypt with India are all imbricated with historical themes such as continuity and change, migration, diasporic longing, circulation of knowledge, development of state power, colonialism, and decolonization, all of which students reengage with in further readings by K. N. Chaudhuri, Sunil Amrith, Engseng Ho, and Sanjay Subrahmanyam.

While *In an Antique Land* lends itself exceedingly well to an Indian Ocean course, it does not do so effortlessly. The text may be challenging, particularly for students unfamiliar with global, non-Western, or transnational history, especially of the medieval, early modern world. *In an Antique Land* is a genre-defying text that is in equal measure a history textbook, historiographical literature, and ethnography. It demands deliberate engagement. We read *In an Antique Land* over a week earmarked as "Book *Adda* Week." *Adda* is a Bengali word that can be simply translated as "chat." But as a cultural word it implies a type of unstructured discussion that is deep and sincere and that includes aspects of storytelling. I would like to believe that Ghosh, a Bengali himself, wrote his book as a meandering *adda*, and I try to recreate the informal atmosphere of an *adda* while discussing the book. When we start our discussion, my main goal is to use the text as means to an end, the end being an understanding of the Indian Ocean world, Indian Ocean as framework of historical analysis, and some sense of the discipline of history. By the time we discuss "Going Back" (289–342)—the last section of the book—the means dissolve into the end, and my students are able to appreciate *In an Antique Land* as encompassing within it all the salient points of Indian Ocean history.

In my pedagogical approach, I try to translate my vision of levels of understanding within the text into questions that frame class discussions. At the first level, I encourage an understanding of the macrohistorical contexts that this text relies on, both chronologically and geographically. At the second level, I guide students to piece together the two microhistories that lie at the heart of the book: the twelfth-century story of Ben Yiju, Bomma, and their world and Ghosh's twentieth-century investigation of that story. Straddling these macro- and microhistories, both rooted in the historical experiences of diasporic individuals and communities strewn across centuries, the third level involves theme analysis, focusing on the diaspora and the text as a key diasporic study. At the fourth level, we engage in an intentionally discursive and open-ended discussion of Ghosh's methodology in organizing the text around three distinctive strands: history, historiography, and ethnography. Students write a book review at the end of the week. In the last five years, from reading the reviews, I have found that the approach described above has allowed me to meet students at their level of engagement and comfort. In the book reviews, most students will focus on the levels of macro- and microhistory, unsure how to incorporate the ethnography or the methodology, but a few students will start by exploring the connections between history, historiography, and ethnography. These four levels of discussion, which I elaborate on in what follows, help me teach more equitably.

The sections titled "Prologue" (Ghosh 11–20), "Lataifa" (21–106), and "Nashawy" (107–238) allow students to verify their understanding of historical contexts, covered in the first part of the course, such as human migration, diaspora, transoceanic trade, cross-cultural interaction, and the advent and spread of Islam, and to anticipate structures that led to colonialism and imperialism following European entry into the Indian Ocean region, the subject of the second part of the course. This also helps students form a sense of the chronological rhythm of the book, which swiftly navigates between three different time periods: the twelfth century, the twentieth century, and the nineteenth century. As I lead discussion, I encourage students to take a macrolevel view of historical themes. They are fascinated by the multilocale medieval story set in Ifriqiya (Tunisia), Fustat (Egypt), Sicily (Italy), Aden (Yemen), and Mangalore (India) and connected through trade and migration. While the West is a marginal historical actor in the twelfth-century Indian Ocean world, between the late eighteenth and twentieth centuries, when "Masr (Egypt) had long since ceased to be the master of her own destiny," the West emerged as a "new continent of riches" (80–81). This irony of changed fortune preserved for Ghosh the fragment of history that became the soul of his book. The letters from the twelfth century that ended up purely by chance in the Cairo Geniza because they had the name of God written in them and would not be destroyed were only preserved as historical evidence once they were dispersed far and wide throughout the Western world. These letters made their way from Cairo to Oxford, Saint Petersburg, Paris, Frankfurt, London, Vienna, Budapest, and Philadelphia, a historic dispersal enabled by colonial and imperial financial power. The meteoric rise of the West and its concomitant artistic interest in antiquarian historical pasts, when the West itself was insignificant, changed the dynamic between actors of the Indian Ocean world—as Ghosh would find out during his visits to Egyptian hamlets in the 1980s. It is not lost on students that the letters themselves have been well-received and thrive in their new diasporic destinations.

At the second level, we explore the intricacies of relationships in the chapter titled "Mangalore" (Ghosh 239–88). I encourage students to transition toward a microlevel understanding of the contrasting worlds of Ben Yiju in the twelfth century and Ghosh in the 1980s. Students love the rich descriptions of material life that Ghosh provides. The Cairo Geniza letters mention spices, fabric, paper, sweets, pottery, locks, and cookware. The affluent twelfth-century world of Ben Yiju contrasts with the modest twentieth-century life in Lataifa and Nashawy, hamlets close to Cairo where Ghosh does his ethnographic work, where electricity is still new, a water pump made in India was the occasion of much excitement, and the youth go to the oil-rich Gulf region for jobs. Masr (Egypt) is no longer "umm al-duniya" (80), or "mother of the world," but the change in economic fortunes did not obliterate the familial nature of social relationships within the Indian Ocean world. Students appreciate the opportunity to construct a different narrative of slavery from the letters sent to Ben Yiju by his friends, who also send Bomma "plentiful greetings" (12). Later, of course, Ghosh explains the historical origins of this different kind of slavery, which was more akin to a patron-client relationship. The warm friendships from the twelfth century, most of them long-distance (and long-term), present themselves again in the short span of time in which Ghosh develops similar friendships in Lataifa and Nashawy, especially with Shaikh Musa. When Ghosh visits Lataifa after a gap of eight years and shows up to Musa's house and says "Ana," or "It's me," Musa instantly recognizes Ghosh and is moved to tears (114). The recurrent but varied historical contexts of these diasporic relationships across time and space provide an important backdrop that we explore in greater depth.

Students are expected to have finished the book, the remaining two sections, "Going Back" (Ghosh 289–342) and "Epilogue" (343–54), before our discussion moves toward the third level of engagement with the theme of diaspora. Ghosh, part of the South Asian diaspora himself, narrates a rhythmic parallel between Ben Yiju's and his own Indian Ocean worlds. Ghosh deftly underscores themes that frame diasporic literature, such as belonging, memory, identity, and, specific to the Indian Ocean world, the emergence of the West as a key interlocutor of the global world in the modern era. Ben Yiju, as a patriarchal Tunisian Jew, is hardly a dislocated or displaced diasporic figure in Mangalore and established close relations with Ashu and Bomma, a Nair and a Tulu, both from matrilineal communities. Ben Yiju's longing for his brothers and friends in Africa and Arabia and his desire to be reunited with his family are understandable sentiments, of course. My students are somewhat mystified by Ben Yiju's prioritization of his nephew, Surur, over his old friend, Khalaf Ishaq's son, whom he unexpectedly refers to as "foreigners" when it comes to the marriage of his daughter, Sitt-al-dar (315–17). While identities remain strong in the twelfth century and blood remains thicker than water, the marriage of a Jewish Nair woman to her Jewish Tunisian Sicilian cousin is also possible. Centuries later, enacting a reverse journey from Ben Yiju's, Ghosh lands in Egypt only to show how the Indian Ocean world had transformed. Though Ghosh establishes some genuine friendships, not unlike Ben Yiju's with his trusted slave Bomma, he is often confronted with obstacles. While not a devout Hindu, he is at pains to explain why Hindus burn their dead, remain uncircumcised, and do not shave their pubic hair. He begins to circumvent these barriers when, of all things, an Indian-made water pump, a hallmark of progress and modernity by Western standards, is acquired by one of Lataifa's residents. Ghosh, along with India, finds some credibility. The persistent presence of the West is, however, far more pernicious because the West has created categories of knowledge, such as history and folklore, that disavow entangled historical pasts. This partitioning of knowledge and disciplinary categories is magnificently demonstrated in the scene in which Ghosh visits Sidi Abu Hasira's tomb outside Damanhour, a town close to Lataifa. That a Hindu from India could have any interest in Hasira, a Jewish saint from long ago who converted to Islam, is instantly alarming to the army officer (Ghosh 339). Ghosh was grateful to get his passport back and depart. I ask students to consider how this assimilation of past diasporic histories came to be contested. If friendships between the African Ben Yiju and Arabs in Aden were possible in the twelfth century, why were Nabeel and Ismail, two cousins whom Ghosh had developed friendships with, narrating horror stories of how Egyptians were treated in Iraq in the 1980s? How did the Indian Ocean world, which was shaped by migration, become so intolerant of its many diasporic populations?

While macrohistories, microhistories, and the theme of diaspora are frames of reference through which students can learn about the history of the Indian Ocean as it has been transmitted to us, at the final level, we explore how Ghosh has done history in the "guise of a traveler's tale." It is easy to see almost everyone in this text as diasporic travelers, from Ghosh to the nineteenth-century scholars who visited the Cairo Geniza to Ben Yjiu and his friends and the youth in Egypt. They all have travel tales, and Ghosh creates from them a rich tapestry of historical change and continuity. Ghosh's methods are nonconformist and exemplary. In discussions, I stress above all the tenuous and fragile relationship between historical evidence and historiography and how the latter preserves the former for continuing conversations about the past. Bomma, "the slave of MS H.6," to whom greetings were sent by his master's friends, almost accidentally ended up in a footnote eight hundred years later in a 1942 article by E. Strauss (Ghosh 357). As Ghosh writes, Bomma's appearance was more like "a prompter's whisper than a recognizable face in the cast" (13). It took Ghosh's immaculate research and fifty more years to restore to Bomma a semblance of an identity in the form of this book. While Ghosh's archival evidence is strong, his research also urges an interrogation of the weight of evidence in history. Ghosh constructs Bomma's life but admits to having "only one incident . . . of which we have direct knowledge" (255). Through Bomma's story, Ghosh makes plausible different kinds of histories of slavery in South Asia. In similar fashion, students read Gaiutra Bahadur's unearthing of the journey of about half a million women from colonies to the West Indies to find out about her grandmother, who migrated from Calcutta to British Guiana as an indentured laborer. History teaches in more ways than one. Through ethnography, Ghosh pushes the limits of the historical discipline. Ghosh's is a nonconformist history of the Indian Ocean. For lack of archival evidence, it may have remained unwritten. However, by liberally using words such as "would have" and "possibly," Ghosh leaves it to readers' discretion to reject or be seduced by the past. Our final takeaway in the class is noting the circuitous relationship between past and present and the many ways to honor it.

No other single literary text on the Indian Ocean world offers so many methodological and critical points of engagement for pedagogical purposes as does Amitav Ghosh's *In an Antique Land*. From South Asians in Latin America to Arabs in Indonesia, Indian Ocean history has enabled the creation and consequent study of diasporas in the global landscape. This essay has delved into several pedagogical strategies that I have adopted to teach history through a diasporic literary text such as *In an Antique*

Land. The Indian Ocean world was a magical historical space and still is. It was a world where slaves could be friends and kings could be pirates. It was a world of saints and magic, of understanding and tolerance.

Works Cited

Abu-Lughod, Janet L. *Before European Hegemony: The World System, A.D. 1250–1350*. Oxford UP, 1989.

Amrith, Sunil S. *Crossing the Bay of Bengal: The Furies of Nature and the Fortunes of Migrants*. Harvard UP, 2015.

Chaudhuri, K. N. *Trade and Civilisation in the Indian Ocean: An Economic History from the Rise of Islam to 1750*. Cambridge UP, 2008.

Ghosh, Amitav. *In an Antique Land: History in the Guise of a Traveler's Tale*. Ravi Dayal Publishers, 1992.

Ho, Engseng. "The Two Arms of Cambay: Diasporic Texts of Ecumenical Islam in the Indian Ocean." *Journal of the Economic and Social History of the Orient*, vol. 50, nos. 2–3, 2007, pp. 347–61.

Huntingford, George Wynn Brereton, editor and translator. *The Periplus of the Erythraean Sea*. Hakluyt Soc, 1980.

Risso, Patricia. *Merchants and Faith: Muslim Commerce and Culture in the Indian Ocean*. Routledge, 1995.

Subrahmanyam, Sanjay. "Of 'Imârat' and 'Tijârat': Asian Merchants and State Power in the Western Indian Ocean, 1400 to 1750." *Comparative Studies in Society and History: An International Quarterly*, vol. 37, 1995, pp. 750–80.

R. Benedito Ferrão

Goa on the Literary Atlas: Questioning Belonging

If they have heard of Goa, rare is the American student who knows that this small place was, from the sixteenth century, the capital of *Estado da Índia Portuguesa* (State of Portuguese India), a geography so vast as to be almost mythical. This storied empire, and its resultant literature, sets Goa in what Robert Newman describes as "a gem in a necklace of Portuguese beads stretching from Lisbon, through Africa to . . . Macau and Timor" (91). These historical colonial connections made possible the spread of the Goan diaspora and created the contexts of its multilocale stories. With such displacements as impetus, my course Portuguese India and Its Literary Afterlife uses a postcolonial viewpoint to teach fiction about and from that location and its diasporas in order to challenge how students think about national belonging.

Given its coverage of such themes as imperialism, colonialism and postcolonialism, nationalism, and globalization, my course aptly originated in the town of Colonial Williamsburg, a location historically linked to the founding of the United States. I have consistently made this observation on the first day of classes since 2014, when I began teaching this course at William & Mary. Both the Virginia Colony and the institution I teach at owe their origins to the arrival of Europeans on Turtle Island

(North America); the name of the university derives from a 1693 charter signed by William III and Mary II of England. Royal patronage, I point out to students, similarly allowed Christopher Columbus to happen upon the Americas in his misdirected quest for the Indies.

While this is something they know of the Genovese explorer, my students are less familiar with how Columbus turned to Spain's monarchs for financial support only after being spurned by the Portuguese. Deeming Columbus's notions unscientific, the Portuguese set into motion their own plans to find the sea route that brought them to South Asia in 1498 (Bronner 63). Making connections with the colonial past of the United States, my course uses literary studies to indicate to students that lusophone South Asian coloniality and its diasporas are not without association to their own national history.

Apart from its British royal mandate, William & Mary also prides itself on "its close ties to America's founding fathers," both George Washington and Thomas Jefferson having received instruction at the school in its earlier avatars ("About"). But to tell this glamorous version of William & Mary's connections to British royalty and the American national patriarchy eschews the school's related history of dispossessing Native American tribes of their land and enslaving Africans ("William & Mary"). Paralleling British and Portuguese colonial histories in the Atlantic and Indian Ocean worlds, I additionally underscore the intersections between these spatiotemporalities in my course by noting that enslaved Africans were forcibly removed to both locations by Portuguese-run efforts (Allen 71). Or, to put it differently, there exists not only a Black Atlantic but also a Black Indian Ocean world, histories of enslavement linked by the transcontinental and transoceanic involvement of the Portuguese in Asia, Africa, and the West.

Students, therefore, learn not only about the Black presence in South Asia but also that the literary study of Portuguese India and its diaspora is one that covers multiple geographies and interrelated histories. From the pluricontinental novel *Skin*, by Margaret Mascarenhas, students are informed of the Portuguese imperial connections between Angola, Mozambique, and South Asia, which created a diaspora of enslaved Black people in Goa. One of the most popular novels I teach, its centering of the lives of Black women, and their sexuality as a means of survival, critically jars my students' understanding of early modern African slavery as an exclusively Atlantic phenomenon.

Even as a novel such as *Skin* acts like a literary atlas that contextualizes Goa in its historically global associations, it also subverts glib considerations of identity as being definable only by a single place. If "imagined" (Anderson 6), then the idea of "the nation" intrinsically suggests an affinity with the fictional, the intangibilities of nationally shared heritages making regional and diasporic literatures a rich disciplinary site from which to gauge the construct of such belonging. Placing the conception of national belonging in conversation with literary representations of Portuguese India and its diaspora, my intent is to have students understand how this small South Asian region, with its global entrenchments, can serve as a case study of (un)belonging at multiple locations and times. This, not least, because what became Portuguese India, the presence of its Indigenous communities notwithstanding, had much to do with the arrival and exoduses of diasporic communities, inclusive of and even before and after European contact. These non-Indigenous communities and the region may be understood to be so enmeshed in identity formation as to render the origin stories of either indistinguishable from one another, often with political intent.

To explain, my course situates diaspora in the following ways: internal migrations within South Asia that predate European contact, European colonization as a form of diaspora, migrations of South Asians from Portuguese India to metropolitan and other colonial locations as well as the arrival of colonized and enslaved subjects from elsewhere into Portuguese India, and multiply displaced diasporic subjects and communities, transcolonials, and multilocale diasporic communities. With regard to the first classification, despite the existence of autochthonous communities in Goa, namely the Dhangar, Velip, Gowda, and Kunbi peoples, Saraswat Brahmins stake a mythical claim to the land, as if they were its original occupants. Taking its cue from Frank Conlon's *A Caste in a Changing World: The Chitrapur Saraswat Brahmans, 1700–1935*, my course asks students to consider how this community belatedly constituted itself as a high-caste corporate entity, therein establishing its dominant status in the region. Yet, a more mundane text effectively proves to students how upper-caste narratives are reified in commonplace usage in Goa, even now.

One of the first readings students do is of a page on the Government of Goa's official website, where they encounter the following:

> According to Ancient Indian Mythology . . . Goa was reclaimed from the sea. . . . [The] Sixth Avatar of Vishnu Sage, Parshuram . . . struck an arrow into the western seas. The arrow . . . sent the seas rolling back to create Gomantak or Goa. . . . [Thereupon,] Brahmins were migrated to Goa by Parashurama from Kasmir and the banks of the river Sarawati. ("Culture")

The divinely ordained migration of the riverine Saraswat Brahmins to Goa is an oft told tale that this state media instrument is not the only one to relay. That it is an official source foregrounding this mythology as non-spell-checked truth is concerning.

Illogically, even as this website offers this account of how Goa was created for the arrival of the Saraswats out of the seas, like a promised land, it admits the preexistence of "[o]riginal tribals [who] migrated in [sic] hills due to Aryan arrival" ("Culture"). This becomes students' first lesson on how caste undergirds belonging in South Asia, as illustrated by the aforementioned narrative in official media that fails to account for how tribal communities could have existed on land that allegedly appeared out of the waters only upon the arrival of the Saraswats. It also reveals how a diasporic community instantiates itself as an Indigenous presence though it is, in fact, a group of settlers—their very origin story tells us the Saraswats came to Goa as migrants from elsewhere. To counter upper-caste mythmaking and migration history that eclipses the region's original peoples, my class also includes testimonials by members of Goa's Indigenous communities. Digital media allows me to incorporate contemporary material, as will be the case when a future iteration of this course will feature a statement titled "To Gawda or Not to Gawda," by Favita Dias, a Gawda scholar who bears witness to the travails of identifying, and of teaching in Goa, as an Indigenous person ("Favita Dias").

Although my course can offer only anglophone materials, I make students aware of the diverse linguistic traditions of the region they are studying and of the links between language and identity. Anjali Arondekar's work is useful here because of the historian's research on the multilingual and multilocale (British and Portuguese Indian) community of performers—the Gomantak Maratha Samaj. Arondekar relays how this Bahujan group challenged Brahmin hegemony in Goa in the early twentieth century; that they did so while "embracing rather than disavowing [their] past and present attachments to sexuality" centers the agency of women in this Bahujan community (100). Arondekar surfaces these facts by looking to sources within the community's archives, texts in the multiple languages of the region: Konkani, Marathi, and Portuguese. I highlight this research strategy for students to remind them that, though the language we privilege in the classroom is English, the canon and modes of research need to be diversified to gain an understanding of colonial South Asia's complexities.

To understand the arrival of the Portuguese in South Asia as a form of diaspora, students read works of history and fiction. The Portuguese general Afonso de Albuquerque defeated Adil Shah, the ruler of Goa, in 1510. That Goa was then the domain of a Muslim sovereign again contests the idea that the region's history should only be seen as either Saraswat Hindu or Catholic. Upon taking command, de Albuquerque quickly enacted the *Politica dos Casmentos*, or Marriage Policy. Its goal was to encourage intermarriage, the fair-skinned widows of the vanquished Muslim soldiers being the most desirable, so as to create a progeny of "white" children (da Silva Gracias 32). This new white tribe, created out of racialized and gendered subjugation, would ostensibly form the basis of Portuguese rule in the East. However, the Portuguese inception of whiteness in Goa would require a suspension of disbelief that it was not the product of miscegenation. Just as my course seeks to interrogate caste privilege through a critique of the formation of caste identity, it similarly asks students to contemplate how whiteness was constructed in the early modern encounter between Europe and Asia.

Yet, race-making in the new colony was not predicated on any illusion of erasing difference. Colonial racial identity had as much to do with location as with religion, Iberian Jewish *conversos*[1] often bearing the brunt of the Goa Inquisition (mid sixteenth to early nineteenth centuries), as students find out from reading Jessica Faleiro's short story "The Beginning." In addition to establishing the plight of such converts who were persecuted on suspicion of backsliding into the practice of their previous faith, Faleiro's story helps dispel the myth that the target of the inquisition was specifically unconverted Hindus (Priolkar).

Using fiction, my course underscores for students how European identities are made not only within the Continent but also through colonial contact—identities thus being incapable of belonging only to singular national contexts. Simultaneously, students also grapple with how the colonial encounter affected identity formation in South Asia. As students learn from reading Johny Miranda's *Jeevichirikkunnavarkku Vendiyulla Oppees: Requiem for the Living*, translated into English from the original Malayalam, the Portuguese colonial diasporic presence in South Asia was not specific to Goa; the importance of this lies in dispelling the notion that European colonial cultural influences in South Asia had distinct spatiotemporal boundaries. In the case of Kerala, though the Dutch ousted the Portuguese there in the seventeenth century, a legacy of lusophonic influences persisted. As evidenced by the mixed-race Paranki community of Miranda's novella, set in Kerala, the Malabar Coast was where the Portuguese first landed in the subcontinent in the early modern period. And contrary to de Albuquerque's perception that interraciality would create a diasporic power base for the Portuguese in Asia, the impoverishment of the Parankis leads Josy Pereira, Miranda's protagonist, to lament, "So what if we call ourselves Parankis and have these [Portuguese] surnames, none of us knows English, nor [are clothed]" (12). Availing none of the supposed privileges of being of European descent, as J. Devika notes, the Catholic Paranki community suffers ostracism precisely because "the narrative of local tolerance conceal[s] upper-caste Hindu elitism" despite a much-vaunted Malayalee "cosmopolitanism" (xxiii).

Miranda's novella is instructive not only because of its exploration of regional diversity and its limits but also because it shows how, like Goa's, Kerala's encounters with non-British colonialisms necessitate a look beyond postcolonial studies of South Asian literature that privilege the region's British contexts. In other words, given canonical Indian historiography's predilection for British postcoloniality, minority literatures can offer alternative perspectives about the subcontinent's margins. "To write about Goa is to write about difference," muses Raghuraman Trichur, who goes on to charge Indian history with marginalizing the region, especially due to India's forced annexation of Goa in 1961 after 451 years of Portuguese colonialism (17). When subsumed by Indian history, Goa's Portuguese past and its connections with the lusophone world, past and present, are epistemologically obscured. In turn, Goa's position as a conduit between British and Portuguese empires and colonies is also obfuscated.

One text (and its author) that demonstrates the imbrication of Goan subjects in multiple colonial contexts while conspicuously eschewing any mention of Portugal and Goa is the first Portuguese-language Goan novel, *Os Brahmanes* (*The Brahmans*), by Francisco Luís Gomes, a parliamentarian who represented his native Goa in Portugal. In reading this novel in English translation, students are among a new generation of readers grappling with once exclusively Portuguese texts about Goa. Gomes's novel is allegorical in its critique of colonialism in nearby British India, for it is meant to serve as a cautionary tale to the Portuguese.

Everton Machado argues that Gomes's disavowal of colonialism is of the British variety, the politician's preference being for the Portuguese version and its championing of equality through Catholicism. Yet, Gomes's position, Machado avers, is an overstatement of the enlightened nature of Portuguese colonialism. Nevertheless, Machado holds that Gomes's self-identification as a Portuguese person—paralleled by his South Asian characters' embracing of Christianity—is to be seen only as the "wear[ing] of a 'white mask'" (50). But as students examine the shifting nature of identity throughout the course, they come to view the inherent making of Portuguese identities in a disjointed empire as not having a single geographic origin. Portugueseness outside the metropole, then, like Goanness in diaspora, exists in multiplicity rather than as colonial imitation.

A major difference between British and Portuguese colonialism was that the latter afforded its subjects citizenship rights. Rendered Portuguese, Goans traversed Portuguese and British India as well as between colonial South Asia and Africa. This led to Goans serving as cultural brokers (Irby 98), portrayals of which are seen in novels set in East Africa such as *The Book of Secrets*, by M. G. Vassanji, and *The General Is Up*, by Peter Nazareth. Students read these works to understand how Goan subjects used their nationally and culturally ambiguous identities to navigate multiple colonial and postcolonial polities as minority subjects who were sometimes agents of empires and other times their victims.

Nazareth's oeuvre is in the genre of the roman à clef and takes from his lived experience, echoing how literature chronicles marginalized histories. Employed by the Idi Amin administration, Nazareth fled Uganda after the 1972 publication of *In a Brown Mantle*; it foretold the expulsion of Asians in the same year as the novel's release. Like his roving characters, Nazareth lived in exile in England and now resides in the United States. He is one of the few scholars to teach the anglophone literature of the Goan diaspora in the United States (Nazareth, "Interview") and was responsible for anthologizing such work, in his edited collection *Pivoting on the Point of Return*. Indeed, in my exchanges with academics in other countries, there is little evidence to suggest that there are many instances of such literature being taught in Goa itself (Pinto; Rocha) or in Europe (Melo e Castro, Email interview).

That many of the efforts to collect and thereby preserve Goan-authored anglophone (Nazareth, *Pivoting*) and lusophone (Melo e Castro, *Lengthening Shadows*) literature of earlier periods are undertaken by academics outside Goa contributes to and is, perhaps, the result of the nonengagement with such material in the region itself. This also transpires because Goa's educational institutions are beholden to the curricular dictates of a nationalist, post-British Indian system. Despite identifying "a vibrant community of researchers with diverse interests . . . not evident in the rest of India," Trichur points out how a lack of institutional support in Goa toward inculcating theoretical scholarship about Goa has led to "a silo or tunnel effect," leaving such extrainstitutional efforts by Goan researchers in academic limbo (11).

Because of Nazareth's anthological efforts, the work of the seldom published, and now deceased, Mozambican-born Goan writer Violet Dias Lannoy was saved from obscurity. This raises questions of canonicity, especially as my course regards how and why the writing of a woman who lived in multiple polities and continents likely kept her from being classifiable as a writer of a given national origin, again reiterating my pedagogical theme of (un)belonging. Not set in her African birthland, Dias Lannoy's posthumously published novel, *Pears from the Willow Tree*, has echoes of her time as an acolyte of Gandhi's in India.

I guide students to read *Pears* as the novelist's critique of post-British India, which, despite its own anti-colonial struggles, annexed Goa and curtailed its path to self-emancipation (Lannoy xix). Dias Lannoy was also vocal about the Israeli occupation of Palestine, no doubt seeing in it the predicament of her own Goan compatriots. As Richard Lannoy, her spouse, describes it, the novelist considered Palestinians "her Eastern brethren" (xvii). The connection to be made here is between two communities, Goans and Palestinians, who have not gained sovereignty over their colonized homelands. The deep irony for Goa, as Dias Lannoy observes, is that her homeland was wrested from one colonizer, only to be recolonized by a nation that itself had decolonized, making Goa "a colony of a postcolony" (Ferrão).

Recently published texts used in my class illustrate for students that the diasporic concerns and displacements of Goans are not just subjects of a foreclosed past. My involvement in various cultural forums in Goa, such as its literary events, has put me in touch with Goan and diasporic writers, many of whom have graciously shared textual materials not readily available in the United States. For example, Savia Viegas provided my class with her novel *Let Me Tell You about Quinta*, a multigenerational and part diasporic family saga about land rights in present-day Goa, while Roanna Gonsalves's Australia-set stories, which she shared ahead of their publication in *The Permanent Resident*, caused students to think about settler colonial immigrant identity formation. Other authors have videoconferenced into my classroom. This includes Suneeta Peres da Costa, whose *Homework* is a magically real tale about a Goan girl born in Australia with antennae on her head; that her father is an anti-Portuguese Goan nationalist complicates matters. Tony D'Souza gamely took questions from my

class about his US-based *The Konkans*, which wrestles with colonial legacies in the region of the novel's naming. Newer works broaden students'
awareness of post-Portuguese India and contemporary diasporic lives in
diverse locations.

Through its chronological trajectory, the course establishes how the
study of the literature of South Asia and its diasporas functions as a cultural
record of Portuguese India that is not only of the past but also continues
to unfold. Diaspora and transnationalism being mainstays of the literary
works studied, the displacements of characters in these texts registers
an ever-evolving index of interconnected histories and multiple sites of
(un)belonging. Thus, the course asks students to scrutinize not only how
identities are made, remade, and unmade within the multiplicity of places
and histories engaged but also how these complexities of identity formation, in turn, ask for a reconsideration of history and place.

Notes

Research for this essay was supported by a fellowship from the American Institute
of Indian Studies.

1. Even when translated as "convert," this approximation in English does not
fully capture the meaning of *converso*.

Works Cited

"About W&M." *William & Mary*, 2023, www.wm.edu/about/history/index.php.
Allen, Richard B. "The Constant Demand of the French: The Mascarene Slave
Trade and the Worlds of the Indian Ocean and Atlantic during the Eighteenth
and Nineteenth Centuries." *Journal of African History*, vol. 49, no. 1, 2008,
pp. 43–72.
Anderson, Benedict. *Imagined Communities: Reflections on the Origin and
Spread of Nationalism*. Verso, 2006.
Arondekar, Anjali. "In the Absence of Reliable Ghosts: Sexuality, Historiogra-
phy, South Asia." *Differences: A Journal of Feminist Cultural Studies*, vol. 25,
no. 5, 2015, pp. 98–122.
Bronner, Fred. "Portugal and Columbus: Old Drives in New Discoveries." *Medi-
terranean Studies*, vol. 6, 1996, pp. 51–66.
Conlon, Frank. *A Caste in a Changing World: The Chitrapur Saraswat Brah-
mans, 1700–1935*. U of California P, 1977.
"Culture and Heritage." *South Goa*, 2021, southgoa.nic.in/culture-heritage/.
da Silva Gracias, Fatima. *Kaleidoscope of Women in Goa, 1510–1961*. Concept
Publishing, 1996.
Devika, J. "The Delicate Task of Recovering Cochin-Creole: Johny Miranda's
Requiem for the Living." *Jeevichirikkunnavarkku Vendiyulla Oppees: Requiem
for the Living*, by Johny Miranda, translated by Sajai Jose, Oxford UP, 2013,
pp. xxi–xxxvii.

Dias, Favita. "To Gawda or Not to Gawda." *Savari*, 28 Nov. 2015, www
.dalitweb.org/?p=2963.

Dias Lannoy, Violet. *Pears from the Willow Tree*. Edited by C. L. Innes, Three
Continents Press, 1989.

D'Souza, Tony. *The Konkans*. Houghton Mifflin Harcourt, 2008.

Faleiro, Jessica. "The Beginning." *Afterlife: Ghost Stories from Goa*, by Faleiro,
Rupa Publications, 2012, pp. 107–22.

"Favita Dias, Assistant Professor Speaks about Being an Adivasi Teacher in the
Caste Society of Goa." *YouTube*, uploaded by Dalit Camera, 11 June 2021,
www.youtube.com/watch?v=eJCHyGjdJbI.

Ferrão, R. Benedito. "Hong Kong and the Promise of Protest." *The Good Men
Project*, 3 Oct. 2019, goodmenproject.com/featured-content/hong-kong
-promise-protest-kvnw/.

Gomes, Francisco Luís. *The Brahmans*. 1866. Translated by the Dr. Francis Luis
Gomes Centenary Committee, Sindhu Publications, 1971.

Gonsalves, Roanna. *The Permanent Resident*. University of Western Australia
Publishing, 2016.

Irby, Charles. "Challenge of Goan Literature." *Souvenir Publication of the International Goan Convention, Toronto*, 1988, pp. 98–100.

Lannoy, Richard. "Biographical Introduction." *Pears from the Willow Tree*, by
Violet Dias Lannoy, edited by C. L. Innes, Three Continents Press, 1989,
pp. xi–xxxiv.

Machado, Everton. "Against British Rule and Indian Castes: The First Portuguese-
Language Goan Novel, *Os Brahmanes* (1866) by Francisco Luís Gomes."
Colonial and Post-colonial Goan Literature in Portuguese, edited by Paul Melo e
Castro, U of Wales P, 2019, pp. 41–60.

Mascarenhas, Margaret. *Skin*. Penguin Books, 2000.

Melo e Castro, Paul. Email interview. Conducted by R. Benedito Ferrão, 4 July
2021.

———, editor. *Lengthening Shadows: An Anthology of Goan Short Stories Translated from Portuguese*. Goa 1556 / Golden Heart Emporium, 2016. 2 vols.

Miranda, Johny. *Jeevichirikkunnavarkku Vendiyulla Oppees: Requiem for the Living*. Translated by Sajai Jose, Oxford UP, 2013.

Nazareth, Peter. *The General Is Up*. TSAR Publications, 1991.

———. *In a Brown Mantle*. Kenya Literature Bureau, 1972.

———. "Interview: Author Peter Nazareth on Working with Idi Amin, the Goan
Diaspora in East Africa and More." Conducted by R. Benedito Ferrão. *Scroll.in*,
22 Aug. 2021, scroll.in/article/1003177/interview-author-peter-nazareth
-on-working-with-idi-amin-the-goan-diaspora-in-east-africa-and-more.

———, editor. *Pivoting on the Point of Return: Modern Goan Literature*. Goa
1556 / Broadway Publishing House, 2010.

Newman, Robert. *Of Umbrellas, Goddesses and Dreams: Essays on Goan Culture
and Society*. Other India Press, 2001.

Peres da Costa, Suneeta. *Homework*. Bloomsbury, 1999.

Pinto, Augusto. Email interview. Conducted by R. Benedito Ferrão, 4 July 2021.

Priolkar, Anant Kakba. *The Goa Inquisition: Being a Quartercentenary Commemoration Study of the Inquisition in India*. Bombay UP, 1961.
Rocha, Prema. Email interview. Conducted by R. Benedito Ferrão, 8 July 2021.
Trichur, Raghuraman. *Refiguring Goa: From Trading Post to Tourism Destination*. Goa 1556, 2013.
Vassanji, M. G. *The Book of Secrets*. McClelland and Stewart, 1994.
Viegas, Savia. *Let Me Tell You about Quinta*. Penguin India, 2011.
"William & Mary Land and Slavery Acknowledgments." *Decolonizing Humanities Project*, 2021, www.wm.edu/sites/dhp/.

Part III

East Meets West: Post–World War II Britain

Alpana Sharma

We Are Not All Migrants:
Mohsin Hamid's *Exit West* and
Sunjeev Sahota's *The Year of the Runaways*

In this essay I undertake a paired reading of two South Asian diasporic texts, Mohsin Hamid's *Exit West* and Sunjeev Sahota's *The Year of the Runaways*. I present this paired reading as a pedagogical exercise intended to produce critical distinctions between the mobility of the immigrant subject and the immobility of the migrant subject. Both subjects aspire to move—away from an oppressive situation toward something promising freedom from oppression—but while the immigrant often succeeds in this aspirational endeavor, migrants seem doomed to fail because of the precarity of their undocumented status. Thus, the twin poles of mobility and immobility encapsulate the irreducible difference between migration (an event) and migrancy (a condition). Characters in both novels may be termed *refugees*—travelers from foreign countries seeking refuge—but while Hamid's refugee characters aspire to and obtain state protection as a prelude to legal residence, Sahota's refugee characters live in precarity outside the law; lacking state support, they are migrants in imminent danger of deportation by the host country. They are "refugees . . . without refuge," Donna Haraway's characterization of those displaced by the ravages of the Anthropocene (160).

My pedagogy is informed by the emerging body of Latin American decolonial theory formulated by the likes of Walter Mignolo, Catherine Walsh, Arturo Escobar, Aníbal Quijano, Boaventura de Sousa Santos, Nelson Maldonado-Torres, Chela Sandoval, and Sylvia Wynter. These decolonial thinkers critique what they term *coloniality*, typified by Mignolo as a racist and patriarchal form of power that outlives the historical experience of the actual colonization process. As such, coloniality is inscribed in Eurocentric forms of government and economic structures, which continue to order life in the ex-colonies long after nations there declared their formal independence from European colonial powers. Mignolo sees this coloniality as constitutive of modernity itself; it is not merely an incidental by-product of European modernization. Modernity and coloniality, or what Mignolo calls the "colonial matrix of power" (9), are deeply entangled and mutually complicit historical formations whose disentanglement involves a call to action to resist the forces of Western capitalist homogenization and development and to preserve and revitalize nonmodern, subaltern, and other ways of being human (see, e.g., Mignolo 17–21). Thus, decolonial theory entails the delinking of coloniality and modernity.

As such, decolonial thinking departs from its related field, postcolonial studies, which has been shaped by the experience of non-settler colonialism in South Asia, an experience that is largely, though not exclusively, seen as belonging to the past. To do the work of decentering Europe, postcolonial critique mobilizes the resources of European critical theory (e.g., Antonio Gramsci, Michel Foucault, Jacques Derrida) against mainstream European-style academic knowledge production, highlighting how such knowledge production renders invisible the subjectivities and self-understandings of the colonized other. In so doing, postcolonial critique is primarily an internal critique of modern academic knowledge production in the humanities and social sciences. Decolonial critique, however, has been shaped by the experience of settler colonialism in the Americas, an experience that continues to the present day. It exposes the continuing existential ramifications of a European coloniality of knowing and being, whereby globalizing forces of capitalist growth and development perpetuate the racialized subordination of Indigenous and other subaltern peoples, a subordination that is held to be constitutive of modernity as a whole. To resist this modern coloniality of knowing and being, decolonial critique mobilizes the non-European epistemological resources of Indigenous peoples against the very metaphysical foundations of European modernity. In so doing, decolonial critique is primarily an activist critique of modernity as a whole, one that insists on the possibility of a pluriverse of experience, where more sustainable modes of life can be in other worlds. Whereas postcolonial theory is typically associated with hybrid forms of modernity among those who adapted to Western ways, decolonial theory responds to the ongoing experience of colonialism—hence, coloniality—among those whose nonmodern world still survives alongside the world of capitalist modernity.

Thus, while on the face of it Mignolo's delinking of the complicities of modernity and coloniality appears to have little to do with the teaching of South Asian diasporic texts in the North American classroom, it usefully addresses, first, that institutions of higher learning have increasingly become sites of neoliberal power, corporations governed by the modern Western corporate logic of profit and gain (Zembylas 255–56). How will our pedagogy be attentive to issues of racial, economic, and social inequities when we are embedded in such institutions and the modern Western epistemologies they support? The ethics of a decolonial pedagogy that situates itself in the United States begins by acknowledging its situatedness in modern Western systems of knowledge production. The task from there is to attempt to read through a different, what I would call an "adjacent," lens: one that can accede to many diverse and contradictory worlds and that rejects the singularity of dominant Western paradigms. As they read South Asian diasporic literature, I encourage my midwestern American undergraduate students to learn to read through a lens adjacent to that of contemporary American culture. While they cannot entirely jettison their Western mindset and the foundational modern Western ways of knowing and being that naturalize and normalize that mindset, they can interrogate their reading practice and learn to read from the perspective of the text and its complexities of gender, sexuality, class, nationality, indigeneity, race, and region.

With its focus on subordinated and racialized subjects caught within a coloniality they must nevertheless overcome, decolonial theory also captures more accurately the precarity of the migrant-refugee position. True, it is not the same as the position of Indigenous people that is the focus of decolonial theory. But coloniality persists in the trope of the migrant-refugee that these texts develop. Hamid even goes so far as to universalize the trope, stating that "[i]f we are all migrants, then possibly there is a kinship between the suffering of the woman who has never lived in another town and yet has come to feel foreign on her own street and the suffering of the man who has left his town and will never see it again" ("We"). In the classroom, Hamid's hypothetical formulation ("If we are all migrants, then . . .") must be turned into a question ("Are we all migrants?") so that Western assumptions about the refugee as "subhuman" (as in non-white, non-Western, stateless, homeless, and destitute) may be questioned and overturned. For, in fact, in decolonial terms it is the refugee who demands to be treated as a human. Following this dictate, albeit divergently, both *Exit West* and *The Year of the Runaways* humanize refugees while attesting clearly to the fact that the twenty-first century is the century of refugees. Characters in these novels come from regions of the earth that have been rendered unlivable because of the traumatic effects of civil war, poverty, environmental degradation, and gender- and caste-based violence. Inevitably, then, these regions are haunted by the elusive promise of someplace better. And, as a result, every "someplace better" is drawn into new and unwelcome proximities, a condition Judith Butler calls "upagainstness": the product of "populations living in conditions of unwilled adjacency, the result of forced migration or the redrawing of the boundaries of a nation-state" (134).

Within the informing framework of decoloniality, this essay aims to reveal the slippages between the terms *refugee, immigrant*, and *migrant* as evidenced in the paired reading of *Exit West* and *The Year of the Runaways*. Both novels feature characters escaping from circumstances in their native countries that they deem to be life-threatening. In *Exit West*, the protagonists Saeed and Nadia meet and fall in love against the backdrop of an unnamed country hurtling toward religious militancy, insurrection, and civil war. They have heard of mysterious doors that turn into portals, instantly transporting people into other, perhaps safer, countries. The secular and liberal-minded pair take their chances and pay an agent to escape through one of these portals. The journey carries them first to a refugee camp on the island of Mykonos, Greece, then to London, and, finally, to Marin, California, where the couple part ways. Saeed begins a romantic relationship with an African American woman, the daughter of a preacher, while Nadia redefines her sexual orientation and finds stability with another woman.

The Year of the Runaways narrates the journey of three men from India to England. Randeep Sanghera and Avtar Nijjar arrive somewhat legally from Punjab, Randeep through a so-called fixed marriage to a British citizen and Avtar through a student visa partly purchased by the sale of his kidney. The third man, Tarlochan "Tochi" Kumar, is a Dalit. Having lost his entire family to a gang of Hindu fundamentalists taking power in the state of Bihar, he saves enough money to be smuggled to England in a perilous and harrowing journey. The novel's fourth perspective is that of Narinder Kaur, a devout Sikh woman and a British citizen who married Randeep to fulfill her *seva*, her Sikh duty. The end of the novel finds Randeep and Avtar uneasily settled into bourgeois life in a new housing complex in Sheffield, Narinder liberated from the hidebound shackles of her patriarchal family, and Tochi in Kanyakumari, on the southernmost tip of India, "the end of the country" (Sahota 76).

Beyond their shared focus on refugees seeking refuge, however, little ties these texts together. Hamid's speculative novel about a couple escaping an unnamed civil war by going through magical portals to instantly enter new countries could not be more different from Sahota's realist fiction about four Indian characters variously escaping caste-based violence, gender discrimination, religious extremism, and poverty by escaping to England. Hamid's instantaneous dispersal of characters across the globe departs radically from Sahota's lengthy descriptions of the migrant's perilous and painful passage, by boat, by plane, by truck, to the shores of the so-called promised land. And while *Exit West* is fundamentally an optimistic narrative about people banding together to achieve social harmony, *The Year of the Runaways* steadfastly rejects a utopian future in favor of a bleak reckoning with the present. As I suggest, *Exit West* remains problematically tethered to the modern Western liberal narrative of post-racial progress and success, while *The Year of the Runaways* lends itself to a decolonial dismantling of those same universalist narratives. In what follows, I treat each of the above differences as a deliberately polemical discussion topic for students; these topics or prompts may form the basis either for spirited class discussion or for short, informal response papers. While my pedagogy fosters students' critical thinking by promoting multiple textual interpretations and opposing viewpoints, my aim here is to push against students' typical reading practice: they expect that what they read is or should be about them and their own perceived homogeneous system of shared thoughts, perceptions, and values. They read to escape rather than to be returned to reality, they prefer a quick read to a slow read, and they prefer happy endings to sad endings. If they can better comprehend the respective colonialist and decolonial trajectories of the two novels, they may begin to read differently. In other words, they may learn to read the text on its own terms rather than the terms shaped exclusively by and for a twenty-first-century American perspective.

I should clarify that my pedagogy has developed over the past twenty years at a midsize, midwestern university that caters primarily to first-generation college students. While the student body is racially diverse, our English majors are primarily white. The kind of course on South Asian diasporic literature I have in mind here is one that is made up of senior English majors and beginning MA students. The course presents difficulties because of the different levels of learning that students bring to the class and their lack of prior exposure to South Asian diasporic writers. But an advantage of such a course is that I can assign complex secondary readings (in literary criticism and critical theory, for example) and place responsibility on graduate students for leading the presentation and explication of this secondary material to the class. So, for instance, we will read literary criticism by Mai Al-Nakib and Yogita Goyal alongside Hamid's *Exit West* and Sahota's *The Year of the Runaways*. Al-Nakib and Goyal read Hamid very differently, creating an opening for Sahota to fill in what Hamid leaves out or occludes. We also read excerpts from genre theory and critical theory that help to delineate what is at stake in our readings (Moynagh; Mignolo).

Defining Genres: Speculative Fiction versus Realist Fiction

To help students understand how their reading is grounded and informed by genre, I familiarize them with generic distinctions between speculative fiction and realist fiction. *Speculative fiction* is an umbrella term embracing fantasy, science fiction, horror, the supernatural, and the like. Many students are already familiar with its popular incarnation in such works as *The Lord of the Rings*, *Star Trek*, the Marvel comic and film series, and *The Handmaid's Tale*. Genre theorists maintain that its what-if quality makes it a powerful medium through which alternative worlds may be imagined. These alternative worlds, according to R. B. Gill, reflect either "one's mode of engagement with the ordinary world or one's replacement of it" (81). Increasingly, however, speculative fiction has been associated with issues of social, political, and economic justice, undertaking, according to Maureen Moynagh, "a critical exploration of the gap between the ideals of liberal democracies and their oppressive acts" (212). With its depiction of magical portals, instant transportation, and indeterminate spatial and temporal modalities, *Exit West* qualifies as a work of speculative fiction. It goes beyond mere escapism to offer what Al-Nakib claims is a trenchant critique of contemporary society and politics, against which individuals must come together to forge new, nonbinary global alliances transcending race, class, gender, religion, and sexual orientation (see, e.g., Al-Nakib 243). Hamid seems to signal that if everyone is a foreigner, then no one can lay claim to an autochthonous nativeness: "we are all migrants through time" (Hamid, *Exit West* 209).

Realist fiction, by comparison, is often viewed as a provincial genre. But, reading Goyal, students will recognize that its evocation of everyday life lived in a specific place at a specific time adds a necessary verisimilitude. As Goyal points out, "[I]f realist novels traditionally evoke a sense of place by providing detailed descriptions of locations and characters that allow the reader to immerse herself in a recognizable culture, *Exit West* jettisons such a project of recognition, emplacement, or geopolitical specificity" (247). The realist text dwells, often chronologically, on the mundane and everyday aspects of the life it seeks to mirror, more or less faithfully. Its this-is-how-it-is quality may suggest a passive engagement with the world, as if the author were a mere commentator or bystander instead of the one actively shaping, rearranging, and transforming reality on the page. Students who read Sahota's text will see things differently. While it is clear that there is no alternative world to the one in which his characters are forced to endure, with no new alliances or convivial political communities to be forged and no what-if scenarios, it is through the banal casual racism suffered daily by Brown people at the hands of the white "natives" that Sahota steadily mounts his case against racist, patriarchal Western society (and, relatedly, against the dominant upper-caste, patriarchal Hindu society). In place of Hamid's planetary solidarity that transcends oppositions, students must reckon with Sahota's age-old binaries—poor/rich, Brown/white, female/male, outcaste/upper caste, migrant/citizen—which are so deeply entrenched that the best Sahota's characters can do is barely survive with some shred of humanity. While Randeep and Avtar become British citizens, their journey to citizenship has irretrievably scarred them. To give students a critical angle on what to them may appear to be an unquestioned good, I ask them whether citizenship is worth all the pain, sacrifice, and humiliation that goes into attaining it: What is the self that survives? For Tochi, a sense of release comes only when he returns to the southernmost tip of India, not to any homeland. Of the four, Narinder's is the most optimistic trajectory: she finally lives her life as a financially independent and single woman. But she, of course, never was a migrant.

Treatment of Time: The Slow Read and the Quick Read

Hamid's and Sahota's treatment of time is also very different. As noted, Hamid's magical portals are instantaneous. In a flash, characters leave one country and are placed in another. Yet, strangely, even with this collapsing of space and time we find that the novel proceeds chronologically. Saeed and Nadia's narrative is sporadically interrupted with the accounts of other travelers: soldiers arrive through the portals to join the militants in Saeed and Nadia's unnamed country; a suicidal British accountant finds himself at a seaside in Namibia; two elderly men—one Dutch, the other Brazilian—meet in Amsterdam and decide to travel together to Rio de Janeiro, where they become a couple. But all these travelers are placed in the same time frame, in the same historical moment; they are all escaping together, as if they are fleeing a common threat.

Students attracted to the quick read should be asked why time is made so inconsequential in *Exit West* as to suggest that events occur automatically. By contrast, *The Year of the Runaways* takes time seriously, and, for their part, students must take the time to appreciate this feature of the novel. They read of characters who must earn wages to assemble the funds needed to migrate. Some characters must make a reluctant deal with the devil to procure those funds. Planning and travel take time, even months, especially when one is being transported illegally across multiple borders using different modes of transport (plane, truck, boat). And what the migrant has to look forward to after such a long journey and all that frenetic movement is the realization that they are stuck in limbo: they cannot travel, because they have no car; they must rely on others to get to a job; if they do not get to their job on time, they are fired; they have outstayed their visa (if they even had one), so they must work illegally; and they cannot see a National Health Service doctor if they are sick or wounded, because they lack identification papers. Thus, ironically, while Hamid intends to portray characters who are (vaguely) disenfranchised, he gives them the privilege of mobility. But while Sahota portrays characters who are escaping specific forms of persecution, in realistic terms he must withhold from them such freedoms as those of movement, choice, and self-determination. Instructors might ask students why Sahota chose to title the novel's sections by season ("Winter," "Spring," "Summer," and "Autumn," which together make up the year alluded to in the book title). How does this structuring principle underscore the temporality that governs the lives of his characters?

Book Endings: Happy and Sad

Ultimately, *Exit West* is an optimistic novel. It ends with the platonic re-union of Saeed and Nadia in the city of their birth, where they reminisce about the past and express a joint desire to travel together to the deserts of Chile. The refugees have averted a face-off with the military forces and have settled and attained legal residency. The novel's utopian and idyllic ending reflects Hamid's own worldview. In an interview with *The Observer* in 2018, Hamid stated, "I've come to the belief that pessimism is a deeply conservative and reactionary position. It tends to lead towards deference, towards the strong and powerful, towards powerlessness and a kind of surrender. . . . Putting forth an optimistic vision . . . makes that vision, in some small way, more likely to come true" ("Interview"). This optimism is open to debate in the classroom. The debate would certainly not be complete without considering Sahota's ostensibly pessimistic ending to *The Year of the Runaways.* His characters' legitimate fight for the restora-tion of their humanity was not sanctioned by the forces of the state or the arm of justice. Contrary to Hamid's insistence that "we are all migrants," Sahota demonstrates that some of us are made migrants by virtue of the oppressive and intolerable conditions under which we labor.

This essay has attempted to trouble conventional views of the dia-sporic, typically understood as the immigrant subject, by turning to an-other other: the migrant. In contrast to the commodified immigrant, who is arguably folded into the national narrative of the host country, the mi-grant cannot aspire to a seamless absorption into bourgeois nation-bound society. It is imperative that we demonstrate to our students that both subjects—the immigrant and the migrant—occupy the South Asian dias-pora and that both have transformed it. But if the immigrant version of the South Asian diasporic experience has found a refuge of sorts in the canon of the West, then we, and our students, must find the outermost edge of the diaspora in the figure of the migrant, the one who did not find that refuge.

Works Cited

Al-Nakib, Mai. "Finding Common Cause." *Interventions,* vol. 22, no. 2, 2020, pp. 228–45.

Butler, Judith. "Precarious Life, Vulnerability, and the Ethics of Cohabitation." *Journal of Speculative Philosophy,* vol. 26, no. 2, 2012, pp. 134–51.

Gill, R. B. "The Uses of Genre and the Classification of Speculative Fiction." *Mosaic,* vol. 46, no. 2, June 2013, pp. 71–85.

Goyal, Yogita. "'We Are All Migrants': The Refugee Novel and the Claims of Humanism." *Modern Fiction Studies*, vol. 66, no. 2, summer 2020, pp. 239–59.

Hamid, Mohsin. *Exit West*. Riverhead Books, 2017.

———. "Interview: It's Important Not to Live One's Life Gazing toward the Future." Conducted by Alex Preston. *The Observer*, 11 Aug. 2018, www .theguardian.com/books/2018/aug/11/mohsin-hamid-exit-west-interview.

———. "We Are All Migrants in the Twenty-First Century." *National Geographic*, Aug. 2019, www.nationalgeographic.com/magazine/2019/08/we -all-are-migrants-in-the-21st-century.

Haraway, Donna. "Anthropocene, Capitalocene, Plantationocene, Chthulucene: Making Kin." *Environmental Humanities*, vol. 6, 2015, pp. 159–65.

Mignolo, Walter D. *The Darker Side of Western Modernity: Global Futures, Decolonial Options*. Duke UP, 2011.

Moynagh, Maureen. "Speculative Pasts and Afro-Futures: Nalo Hopkinson's Trans-American Imaginary." *African American Review*, vol. 51, no. 3, fall 2018, pp. 211–22.

Sahota, Sunjeev. *The Year of the Runaways*. Vintage Books, 2017.

Zembylas, Michalinos. "The Entanglement of Decolonial and Posthuman Perspectives: Tensions and Implications for Curriculum and Pedagogy in Higher Education." *Parallax*, vol. 24, no. 3, 2018, pp. 254–67.

C. S. Bhagya

Cosmopolitanism and Crisis in South Asian Anglophone Diasporic Novels

Salman Rushdie's *Midnight's Children* and Monica Ali's *Brick Lane* are two important texts that feature regularly in different courses in the United Kingdom, including but not limited to courses on modernist and postmodernist writing, postcolonial and world literature, and twentieth- and twenty-first-century British writing. In this essay I discuss how migration and diasporic identities can become a productive part of classroom conversations on South Asian anglophone diasporic writing by introducing migration, exile, and itinerancy as conceptual rubrics that expand the discourse around the textual forms of works that test the limits of generic conventions. The teaching methods used to unpack these two texts benefit from a contextualization of the generic structure of the texts as a product of the novel's own migratory history as a genre. Moreover, I underscore that the formative itinerant underpinnings of these texts, not least the featured characters' journeys or the evolution of hybrid diasporic identities, are shaped by seminal political events in the Indian subcontinent and global crises such as 9/11, which have affected life in the diaspora in significant ways. Further, cosmopolitanism and its literary expression need to be read and taught as shaped by the global anglophone literary market, which commodifies exoticized cultural narratives from and about the Indian subcontinent. Such framing techniques not only illustrate characters' life trajectories as part of a world system affected by the circulation of capital and the effects of uneven development but also highlight the need to view these texts as literary objects that accrue power through these material disparities.

When teaching a novel as highly canonized and well-known in postcolonial literary studies as *Midnight's Children*, particularly in an undergraduate course, I find it useful to start in the obvious places. A mammoth narrative that spans twentieth-century India, including late colonial and postcolonial India, *Midnight's Children* has frequently been read as a straightforward national allegory. I typically introduce the text using Fredric Jameson's famous piece "Third-World Literature in the Era of Multinational Capitalism" and Aijaz Ahmad's equally well-known rebuttal, "Jameson's Rhetoric of Otherness and the 'National Allegory.'" This sets the stage for thinking through the structure of the text, its chronology, and pivotal narrative markers that draw on the history of the Indian subcontinent. In courses on modernist and postmodernist literature, the vast time frame of the text, its multiple plots and subplots, and its nonlinear narrative segues provide the critical contexts for debating postmodernist claims and contestations related to truth, authenticity, and history. In South Asian literature courses, framing the text through debates around national allegory helps swiftly address the conceptual beast of the nation and its persistence as a sociohistorical marker in fiction from South Asia and its diaspora. However, focusing on Rushdie's status as a diasporic British writer is essential for reframing these debates in light of Rushdie's own reflections on the process of writing the novel. As Graham Huggan has noted, writers like Rushdie and V. S. Naipaul are rarely thought of as British writers: "Even the most culturally sensitive of critics have been known to persist in the view that Naipaul and Rushdie originally come from 'other' places—to suggest that in some deep-rooted, almost atavistic sense, they are immigrant writers who 'really belong' somewhere else" (160). Acknowledging the perils of dismissing Rushdie's stake in British identity and contextualizing Rushdie as a writer distant from India, his "imaginary homeland," are both important to understanding the generic structure, style, and linguistic coding of *Midnight's Children*. Rushdie has admitted that while writing his novel in North London, he was looking at "a city scene totally unlike the ones I was imagining on paper" (*Imaginary Homelands* 10). He was therefore obliged to confront in the text the idea that what he was producing was "a novel of memory and about memory"

(10). This is why, he notes, he made his narrator, Saleem, "suspect in his narration": "his mistakes are the mistakes of a fallible memory compounded by quirks of character and circumstance, and his vision is fragmentary. It may be that when an Indian writer who writes from outside India tries to reflect that world, he is obliged to deal in broken mirrors, some of whose fragments have been irretrievably lost" (10–11). Underscoring Rushdie's migrant status in classroom discussions resituates the narrative contour and stylistic specificity of the novel as haunted by diasporic concerns about disrupted authenticity, memory, and dislocation, which also otherwise mark postmodernist literary texts.

In February 2021 I taught *Midnight's Children* to two different students for a set of similar major tutorials on South Asian literature.[1] A student in a third-year tutorial read the novel through Jameson and Ahmad as potentially deconstructing the national allegory, which led us to organize the discussions around ideas of nation and how they are borne out in the novel. In a tutorial on literatures from 1900 to the present, we discussed alternative historiography in the novel and, following a student comment, considered how Rushdie's position as a migrant metropolitan writer cast a shadow over *Midnight's Children* and how the postcolonial public sphere envisioned in the text embodies an ideal produced by the distant location of the diasporic writer. This let us segue into discussions on the idealistic and aspirational project of the Nehruvian pluralist, heteroglot, and secular nation that forms the basis for the protagonist Saleem's vision of India. As seen in the latter parts of the novel, this crystallizes in the Midnight Children's Conference—here also a metaphor for the presumed polyvocality of postcolonial Indian parliamentary democracy.[2]

Moreover, Rushdie's investment in venerating Nehruvian idealism in these instances paves the way for an affective politics of pessimism about the evolution of postcolonial Indian democracy, as seen in the final chapters of the novel, which depict the Indian Emergency. Declared during Prime Minister Indira Gandhi's stewardship, the National Emergency (1975–77) was a period when democratic governance was suspended and civil liberties curbed. Written in its immediate aftermath in 1981, *Midnight's Children* was in some ways a direct response to the political crisis and tackles concerns around freedom of speech foregrounded by the Emergency state's censorship policies. The long time frame of the novel, moreover, is strategically constructed so as to allow comparisons between the violence of the colonial regime during the British Raj in India and the neocolonial apparatus of the Congress (R) government thirty years after independence.[3] This time frame allows Rushdie to contrast the moment of Indian independence and the promises of democracy enshrined during this optimistic time with the dark days of the Indian Emergency, which emblematized the failure of democracy.[4]

In classroom discussions, reading *Midnight's Children* through the prism of the Emergency facilitated the appraisal of discourse around the seeming predictability of the decline of postcolonial democracies. It provided an inroad for students to discuss the relevance of rhetoric about so-called failed states and democracies in decline for contexts outside India. This line of thought had been reiterated around the time I was teaching these sessions, albeit with some self-reflexivity, in media coverage of the United States Capitol attack in January 2021. As Patrick Gathara pointed out in a *Guardian* article on the attack, the idea that "the globe is divided between those who have achieved democratic nirvana and those of us seeking enlightenment at the feet of Western gurus" is, unfortunately, widely accepted. This was very much part of the international discourse around what many see as India's democratic failure during the Emergency, captured by Rushdie's novel and other literature on the period.[5] In related classroom discussions, teaching *Midnight's Children* by foregrounding political crises—such as the Partition of India, the Bangladesh War of Independence, and the Emergency—illustrated the effectiveness of adopting postcolonial and comparative pedagogical methods to study diasporic South Asian novels. These methods were crucial for understanding how such literature contests accounts of postcolonial South Asia as messily delayed in its arrival at modernity as well as in its adoption of the emancipatory aspects of liberal democracy. Moreover, it allowed my diverse—South Asian, British, and American—student cohort unique and meaningful access to contemporary global politics, demonstrating how reading diasporic South Asian literature helps in the critical comprehension of present-day contexts in which texts are read and consumed.

Political crises are not conjured up with the same degree of immediacy in Ali's *Brick Lane* as they are in *Midnight's Children*; however, two important events watermark the backdrop of the narrative. The turbulent lead-up to the 1971 Bangladesh war and an effort to escape its violence were, in fact, the direct causes of Ali's own very early excursive journey to the United Kingdom with her family. The novel's time span covers 1967 through the early 2000s, concluding just after the 9/11 attacks in the United States. It is set in London, though it provides snapshots of life in Dhaka through the letters of the protagonist Nazneen's sister, Hasina.

The novel straddles personal and political crises through the lives of these two women. Discussing the representation of women in *Brick Lane* has typically proven to be an effective technique for unpacking the text and its thematic concerns. In a tutorial I conducted in 2020 at Oxford, it proved useful to read parts of Jameson's *Postmodernism; or, The Cultural Logic of Late Capitalism* alongside excerpts from Jean-François Lyotard's *The Postmodern Condition* in order to examine the narrative claims of postmodernism and how these may get subtly rearticulated in a novel that does not formally enunciate such tendencies through circuitous narration or the interplay of Indigenous cultural texts (such as the *Mahabharata*), as Rushdie's novel does.

One student's essay on the novel's framing of women and choice in diasporic and Bangladeshi contexts initiated discussion on how the intersectional structures of racial and patriarchal oppression in London constrain Nazneen's ability to express herself fully. Based on a cross section of London's Brick Lane, within a self-contained, almost insular locality, Ali's narrative shows that the tantalizing possibilities of cosmopolitan life in the city do not reach fruition for Nazneen until the very end of the novel, signaling the limits of multiculturalism. Reading *Brick Lane* alongside Leila Aboulela's *Minaret*, which features another woman, Najwa, fleeing from the Sudanese civil war to start a new life in London, would provide narrative and discursive parallels. Both novels are similar in that they portray Nazneen's and Najwa's relationships to their faith and their fraught connections with the illusory liberties offered by capitalist-consumerist cosmopolitan London life in the wake of rising Islamophobia after 9/11.

While the majority of the discussion in this tutorial dwelt on gender-based discrimination in both the United Kingdom and Dhaka, analysis of Ali's usage of nonstandard forms of English was also intellectually provocative. At that time, the student and I were both uncertain why Ali used a different, syntactically ruptured form of broken English in Hasina's letters to Nazneen when it was evident from the sisters' impoverished background that they had not had access to proper education, let alone education in English. In an interview I conducted with Ali in January 2021, she shed light on some of her writing choices. For her, using broken English was not about the logic of translating Bangla (the language in which the sisters' correspondence takes place) into English. It was, rather, an expression of her desire to "convey some of the naivety, the chaos, the brokenness of [Hasina's] life" (Ali, "In Monica Ali's Worlds"). The appearance of crisis as a structuring presence in Ali's novel therefore also seeps into the forms of English used to show how standard English is inadequate to mediate the multicultural and multilingual lives of characters who populate South Asian anglophone diasporic narratives.

This interview was conducted for *Writers Make Worlds,* an open educational resource project helmed by Elleke Boehmer and Erica Lombard at Oxford. Its online archive has a large repository of profiles on Black and Asian British writers. The website is primarily aimed at A-level readers in the United Kingdom but can easily be used to introduce more advanced readers to South Asian anglophone diasporic writers. Moreover, the website provides a rich multimedia archive that is particularly useful for online teaching. I have frequently used this archive in teaching diasporic literature by writers such as Moniza Alvi, Kazuo Ishiguro, and Linton Kwesi Johnson. Using online resources, especially images or audio and video recordings of poetry, has been pivotal in making these writers' work accessible to students as it relies heavily on code-switching, incorporation of musical forms, and ekphrastic responses to art.

In teaching *Midnight's Children,* too, attention to language and code-switching is indispensable for appreciating the text's formal power and its diasporic genealogy. I usually ask students to read aloud Rushdie's bulky, exploding sentences as part of an active classroom exercise in order to underscore how the author disrupts conventional syntactic order, thereby unsettling rational, Eurocentric expectations of reality and authenticity. The expansiveness of sentences (which some of my students have often described as "incoherent") and their peculiar diction highlight Rushdie's attempts at linguistically embodying "chutnification" (642), or cultural hybridity, by referencing hybrid forms of English—such as Hinglish—commonly spoken in the Indian subcontinent and its diaspora. Both Ali's and Rushdie's novels could, therefore, be understood as products of itinerant migratory aesthetics, including the circumambulatory history of the postcolonial novel form, circulating global Englishes, and traveling authors and characters.[6] Paying attention to this itinerancy is important for contextualizing overlapping concerns in diasporic and postcolonial literary studies: as Ato Quayson has pointed out, "[T]he salience of the diaspora" cannot be overstated in "understanding the primary conditions of production and reception of much that falls under the rubric of postcolonialism" (140). I emphasize this disciplinary proximity when teaching these texts, which I have included in courses on both subjects. Here, a self-conscious discussion of the recurrence of authors and theorists facilitates debates on framing.

What is even more important to foreground during discussions of *Midnight's Children* and *Brick Lane* is the cosmopolitan privilege of authors like Rushdie and Ali. Both authors are Oxbridge-educated and have been lauded in international prize circuits, and their frequent canonization should not be elided when thinking about representation and claims of representativeness in their works. For a writer like Rushdie, who was bombastically feted by critics for producing a narrative in which the continent had supposedly found its voice (Blaise), the processes of canonization of his novel are complicit in the erasure of other writers from the Indian subcontinent and the diaspora who may not have access to the same privileged structures of education, publicity, and reception. Moreover, both *Midnight's Children* and *Brick Lane* are embedded within the global anglophone literary industry, which enables the easier circulation of texts in English compared with counterparts in other languages from the subcontinent.

In the case of *Brick Lane*, questions of representation ought to take center stage in order to acknowledge the controversy surrounding the novel and its connection with the Bangladeshi community in Brick Lane.[7] To open up questions of representation, a strategy I have found useful is to read portions of Gayatri Chakravorty Spivak's "Can the Subaltern Speak?" with students. A notoriously difficult essay, it allows a metatextual discussion of the politics of representation and giving voice as seen in literary representation. Further, it carves out space to contemplate the privilege inherent in reading and teaching these novels in institutions like Oxford and Cambridge, exercises that may reinforce the same forms of privilege that contribute to the canonization of texts while obscuring imbalances of representation both in the texts being read and the people reading. It compels responses to difficult questions that ought to shape students' critical analysis: How do the social, cultural, and economic positions and identities of students and tutors affect reading practices within such institutions? What are the limitations of scholarship produced by upper-class, upper-caste academics in British and American universities? And how do other axes of privilege (e.g., being white or male) culturally and socially foreclose interactions with South Asian anglophone diasporic fiction?

The tutorial format, its constraints and flexibility, has informed how I have been able to frame some of these debates. Usually structured as an intense one-hour discussion on a single text, the tutorial is organized around an essay on the text submitted by the student before each meeting. Framing discussions through the critical works of thinkers such as Jameson,

Ahmad, Lyotard, and Spivak has certainly been key in setting the pedagogical mise-en-scène. Typically, visiting students from US institutions, who are unfamiliar with the format, take time to acclimatize to it and the rather large workload, which is compounded by mandated enrollment in multiple courses each term. In these instances, I adjust the course design to focus primarily on the literary texts: I introduce theoretical debates on representation by illustrating core ideas through a close reading of the selected narratives. I invite students to speak on their sense of the text and its themes, which they often, productively, read as an invitation also to reflect on the text from their own sociocultural positions. These exercises in reading and discussion offer reflective spaces where students are able to read themselves, also, as historically and politically formed readers of South Asian anglophone diasporic texts.

Notes

1. Tutorials at Oxford consist of one-hour sessions with a single student or a small group (two to three students). Major tutorials involve eight sessions over eight weeks—the typical length of a term at Oxford. Minor tutorials have four sessions, one every other week during the term. For more on the Oxford tutorial format from the perspective of critical pedagogy, see Ashwin; Horn.

2. See Srivastava; Morton; and Kortenaar for more on secularism in the Indian novel, on metaphors of secularism in Rushdie's novel, and on Saleem's relationship with the nation and the state in postcolonial India, respectively.

3. The Indian National Congress split into two factions in 1969. A major section of the original party challenged Indira Gandhi, who retaliated by forming the "New Congress" to demonstrate her popularity among the masses. This new organization was called the Indian National Congress (Requisitionists). Eventually, the other faction, Congress (Organisation), led by K. Kamaraj, merged with the Janata Party. Congress (R) is now the Indian National Congress.

4. I have written earlier about the representation of the Emergency in the Indian author Shashi Tharoor's *The Great Indian Novel*. Tharoor takes his cue from Rushdie to reproduce the same time frame for similar effect. For a longer engagement with the implications of this framing, see Bhagya.

5. See Sahgal's characterization of Mr. Neuman, the foreign businessman in *Rich Like Us*, who disparagingly surveys Delhi under Emergency rule in the opening pages of the novel. See also Watson on how common modes of representing state tyranny in postcolonial literature may be complicit in naturalizing conceptions of postcolonial authoritarianism.

6. See Mukherjee on how the novel was introduced in the Indian subcontinent during the colonial period and was later adapted by Indian writers, therefore meriting Mukherjee's evocative phrase "twice born fiction."

7. See Ali's response to the controversy ("Outrage Economy") and Islam's article on reading *Brick Lane*.

Works Cited

Ahmad, Aijaz. "Jameson's Rhetoric of Otherness and the 'National Allegory.'" *The Post-colonial Studies Reader*, edited by Bill Ashcroft et al., Routledge, 2003, pp. 91–109.

Ali, Monica. *Brick Lane*. Doubleday, 2003.

———. "In Monica Ali's Worlds." Interview conducted by C. S. Bhagya. *Writers Make Worlds*, 2021, writersmakeworlds.com/interview-monica-ali-worlds/.

———. "The Outrage Economy." *The Guardian*, 13 Oct. 2007, www .theguardian.com/books/2007/oct/13/fiction.film.

Ashwin, Paul. "Variation in Students' Experiences of the 'Oxford Tutorial.'" *Higher Education*, vol. 50, no. 4, Nov. 2005, pp. 631–44.

Bhagya, C. S. "'The Reign of Error': Tropes of Exception in Shashi Tharoor's *The Great Indian Novel*." *Journal of Postcolonial Writing*, vol. 56, no. 6, 2020, pp. 761–74, https://doi.org/10.1080/17449855.2020.1766854.

Blaise, Clark. "A Novel of India's Coming of Age." *The New York Times*, 19 Apr. 1981, www.nytimes.com/books/98/12/06/specials/rushdie -children.html.

Gathara, Patrick. "Papa Don's Failed State: The US as Seen from Kenya." *The Guardian*, 9 Jan. 2021, www.theguardian.com/us-news/2021/jan/09/ capitol-storming-us-failed-state-kenya-patrick-gathara.

Horn, Julia. "Signature Pedagogy / Powerful Pedagogy: The Oxford Tutorial System in the Humanities." *Arts and Humanities in Higher Education*, vol. 12, no. 4, Oct. 2013, pp. 350–66.

Huggan, Graham. *The Postcolonial Exotic: Marketing the Margins*. Routledge, 2001.

Islam, Sanchita. "Monica Ali: 'Brick Lane' - 2003." *London Fictions*, Nov. 2016, www.londonfictions.com/monica-ali-brick-lane.html.

Jameson, Fredric. *Postmodernism; or, The Cultural Logic of Late Capitalism*. Duke UP, 1991.

———. "Third-World Literature in the Era of Multinational Capitalism." *Social Text*, no. 15, 1986, pp. 65–88. *JSTOR*, www.jstor.org/stable/466493.

Kortenaar, Neil ten. *Self, Nation, Text in Salman Rushdie's* Midnight's Children. McGill-Queen's UP, 2004.

Lyotard, Jean-François. *The Postmodern Condition: A Report on Knowledge*. 1979. U of Minnesota P, 1984.

Morton, Stephen. "Metaphors of the Secular in the Fiction of Salman Rushdie." *Metaphor and Diaspora in Contemporary Writing*, edited by Jonathan Sell, Palgrave Macmillan, 2012, pp. 151–69.

Mukherjee, Meenakshi. *The Twice Born Fiction: Themes and Techniques of the Indian Novel in English*. Heinemann, 1971.

Quayson, Ato. "Postcolonialism and the Diasporic Imaginary." *A Companion to Diaspora and Transnationalism*, edited by Quayson and Girish Daswani, Wiley-Blackwell, 2013, pp. 139–59.

Rushdie, Salman. *Imaginary Homelands: Essays and Criticism, 1981–1991*. Granta Books / Penguin Books, 1991.

———. *Midnight's Children*. 1981. Vintage Books, 2010.

Sahgal, Nayantara. *Rich Like Us*. 1985. HarperCollins Publishers, 2016.

Spivak, Gayatri Chakravorty. "Can the Subaltern Speak?" 1985. *Marxism and the Interpretation of Culture*, edited by C. Nelson and L. Grossberg, Macmillan, 1988, pp. 271–313.
Srivastava, Neelam. *Secularism in the Postcolonial Indian Novel*. Routledge, 2007.
Watson, Jini Kim. "Stories of the State: Literary Form and Authoritarianism in Ninotchka Rosca's *State of War*." *Contemporary Literature*, vol. 58, no. 2, 2017, pp. 262–89. *Project Muse*, muse.jhu.edu/article/689868.

Feroza Jussawalla

Teaching the Cousinship of Experience: The Postcolonial Bildungsroman across Time and Cultures

One of the challenges of teaching South Asian diasporic literature is making it relevant to students across cultural backgrounds. Underscoring the commonalities among the student-readers, the characters, and the authors while also teaching the development of the genre is essential to advancing the pedagogical relevance of South Asian diasporic literatures in the US classroom. At my university, we welcome students from New Mexico's ethnically diverse populations, including Hispano and Native American students. In all my classes, particularly Introduction to Literature and a course I developed entitled Introduction to Postcolonial Literatures, I use South Asian and South Asian diasporic literatures in conjunction with Chicanx literatures. I do this to show the commonalities among my students' experiences—what I call the "cousinship of experience"—as students navigate their differences in cross-cultural situations.

Even when they are far from literal borders, people living in the diaspora still exist in a borderland condition. In her book *Borderlands / La Frontera*, Gloria Anzaldúa beautifully articulates this condition of unbelonging and living in liminal spaces: "Borderlands are physically present wherever two or more cultures edge each other, where people of different races occupy the same territory, where under, lower, middle and upper

113

classes touch, and where the space between two individuals shrinks with intimacy" (3). Students from the US Southwest might easily recognize themselves in the works of South Asian diasporic writers, even if they initially assume they have no connection to writers like Monica Ali, Bapsi Sidhwa, and others.

Many Hispanic students see themselves and their experiences in the Indian novelist R. K. Narayan's *Swami and Friends*. This is a text foundational to my teaching of both the genre of the bildungsroman and the comparative experience. *Swami and Friends*, one of the early postcolonial novels in English, established the pattern for many books that followed in its footsteps in India and beyond. When read closely together with the US southwestern writer Rudolfo Anaya's *Bless Me, Ultima*, *Swami and Friends* shows the parallel experiences of the two young protagonists, who grow up in a culturally foreign, hegemonically dominant educational system. The colonizing systems were similar in India and the US Southwest. Students were taught in English and prohibited from speaking their native languages. While Narayan's novel is an example from colonial times, the practice can also be seen in postcolonial diasporic texts. All of these texts—colonial, postcolonial, and diasporic—make students aware of the continuing difficulties of interacting in colonialist or cross-cultural situations. The protagonists of these novels and their coming-of-age experiences are similar to my students' experiences, which shows that such experiences are not only universal but also mutually illuminating. This is what I call the "cousinship of experience."[1] The experiences of inclusions, exclusions, and consequent confusions continue to plague students in my classrooms. Therefore, looking at their lived experiences in the context of these literary works helps us understand the dilemmas of our students, which further helps us teach more effectively. The profound cultural connections between the Latinx or Chicanx and South Asian cultures depicted in Anaya's *A Chicano in China*[2] show the historical background of the connections between Asia and the southwestern United States. When students read texts that resonate with their own experiences alongside texts of the South Asian diaspora, they can recognize a deep connection and cousinship between the two cultures. Understanding that which is seemingly foreign helps students learn to make sense of their own experience as something universal. This is important to me as an immigrant faculty member from South Asia who also lives the cross-cultural encounter.

The plot of the postcolonial bildungsroman can be summarized as a young protagonist's coming-of-age experience in a cross-cultural environment, either under colonialism or in the new postcolonial home country, that centers around learning language, inhabiting borderland spaces, searching for identity, and coming into an awareness of where they belong. There is always a journey of introspection, either metaphorical or actual, that culminates in the "aha" experience of belonging. As students read, the cousinship of experience is established. This cousinship includes the following: learning English as a second language; navigating cultural differences, both in school and beyond; undertaking a journey, either physical or introspective, that culminates in knowing where one belongs, and therefore coming to an awareness of rootedness in one's own culture.[3]

This comparative strategy opens students up to questions about their own culture and sense of belonging, how they relate to differences in their own cultures and environments, and the consequent movements of peoples: How is one's culture different from the culture depicted in the text? Or, most important, how do students read a text? What do they see as its theme or message? How does this relate to students' lives? What do they find foreign or different? All these become prompts for response papers. Students often take away from a text whatever fits within the framework of their own experiences and within contemporary contexts.

My strategy here relies on Stanley Fish's theorizing of reading and making meaning of a text in *Is There a Text in This Class? The Authority of Interpretive Communities*. Fish argues that students make sense of a text based on their interpretive community and personal experiences. "The personal is political," as bell hooks would say, since personal engagement, including students' gut reactions, is essential in their scholarly reading. Fish argues that the reader's activities give meaning to what is embedded in the text (2). For Fish, the student's experience is essential to reading the text. Fish argues that "the act of interpretation is often . . . removed from the act of reading" (52). Fish reasons that because a reader who is also a critic feels compelled to translate their experience into critical principles, the reader's personal experience of the text is important to the making of meaning (5–6). While it could be argued that such a strategy creates an affective fallacy, using it in class validates students' reading experiences and gives students power over the text. This is crucial in teaching ethnically diverse students, whose responses to texts are often invalidated based on their supposed lack of knowledge of literary history and literary critical practices. It is essential in a classroom made up of ethnically diverse students to validate students' readings. The personal is important in allowing students to make sense of the text and its history. Students can then use the text to better understand their own circumstances. Though E. D. Hirsch, in *Validity in Interpretation*, would contest this, Fish provides the idea of establishing an interpretive community. Students who are allowed to read a text through the lens of personal experience can establish such a community from their own "context of situation"[4] and their in-class learning communities and group activities.

Students react to the texts in different ways. Therefore, I always ask students to write a response paper, of the reader-response variety, in which they describe their gut reaction to the text. This shows how a text speaks to students, either culturally or in terms of students' own experiences. Consequently, there is always an immediate connection with the characters' coming-of-age experiences. My experiences have shown me that most, if not all, students identify with the experiences of being othered or bullied and feeling different.

Students strongly identified with the struggle to learn and communicate in the English language, with moments of embarrassment at lunchtime, and with differences in meals. All students wrote about how the characters, despite their vastly different circumstances, searched for freedom and how each created strategies aimed at increasing self-awareness.

The experiences of students from Hispanic and Native American communities are often similar to the experiences of people from South Asian cultures. They often come from conservative, joint-family homes; speak their mother tongue at home; and struggle to negotiate school, friendships, and familial expectations. The journeys of the protagonists and those of the students themselves are similar in their negotiation of cross-cultural territories. Hence the students identify with this literature.

Students in New Mexico often speak Spanish as their mother tongue, and sometimes Diné. While English is the predominant first language in the South Asian diaspora, some literature still reflects code-switching and code-mixing, words from the mother tongue, sometimes Hindi, Bengali, or Gujarati, sprinkled throughout English texts. This is also true of Chicanx and Native American texts. The eminent South Asian writer Raja Rao wrote that writing in a second language is never easy. I always share this passage with my students: "One has to convey in a language that is not one's own the spirit that is one's own" (Rao vii).

In the South Asian diasporic context, Monica Ali's *Brick Lane* is a bildungsroman that tells the story of two young sisters with Bangladeshi parents growing up in London. Together with their mother, the sisters journey through the in-between cultural space that they find themselves inhabiting. Bapsi Sidhwa's *American Brat* is a story about a journey toward Americanization in predominantly white rural Wyoming. Feroza, the character caught between cultures, tries desperately to hold on to her religious practices while attempting to mix with the Americans, just like the Parsis in India always said that when they arrived from Iran, they mixed with the people of Gujarat like milk mixes with sugar, to dissolve and assimilate.

To assimilate or not, to preserve one's culture or not, and most of all, to maintain one's strength as a woman in a challenging cross-cultural environment is the theme of Ali's *Brick Lane*. Shahana and Bibi struggle with their sense of belonging in a cross-cultural environment. Their father, Chanu, is an immigrant in the United Kingdom who aspires to a better life than that of a taxi driver. A product of British colonial education, he feels entitled to a better job. He had sent for a wife from his home in Bangladesh. Nazneen, unwanted in her own family, becomes his unwitting wife and eventually becomes the liberated heroine of the novel. The young daughters feel the embarrassment related to their parents' unbelonging and their father's lack of success and are caught amid the debates in their school and community in Brick Lane, the predominantly Bangladeshi district in London. In a way, the novel is a double bildungsroman. It is also the journey of the mother's awakening, the immigrant Nazneen, who realizes she does not want to return to Bangladesh and prefers the freedom of living in the United Kingdom, despite the discrimination she experienced. I teach this text alongside Sandra Cisneros's *The House on Mango Street*. Like the characters in *Brick Lane*, Esperanza Cordero struggles to learn English, to experience a sense of belonging in her school in Chicago, to make sense of her environment, and to understand how her parents belong in both a cross-cultural and cross-class setting.

Whether Hispanic, Latinx, or South Asian, the characters in these novels and the readers of these novels all have the same angst: Where do they belong, and how do they belong? This is often the condition of minority students in the United States as they negotiate their way in a dominant culture. This can become the focus of our teaching, allowing students to explore their experiences alongside those of the characters they read about. We, as teachers, can also explore how we, too, belong. All this is captured in the experiences of Shahana and Bibi. Their experience is very similar to that of Esperanza Cordero, the protagonist of *The House on Mango Street*. She is the daughter of an immigrant house cleaner, while Shahana and Bibi's mother takes on sewing projects at home. They all negotiate similar situations at school, interact with the society around them, and attempt to find themselves.

In these contexts, education becomes a polarizing factor. This is particularly true of the schools the characters attend. Shahana and Bibi attend a school that wants to retain its Britishness and supposedly not commit "multi-cultural murder" (Ali 181). The "Multicultural Murder" pamphlet asks the residents of the neighborhood, "How long before the extremists are putting veils on our women and insulting our daughters for wearing short skirts? Do not tolerate it! Write to the council!" (186). Annoyed by the attack on multiculturalism in his daughters' school, Chanu says to his wife, "You see, they feel so threatened. . . . Because our own culture is so strong. And what is their culture? Television, pub, throwing darts, kicking a ball. That is the white working-class culture" (184). The issue of multiculturalism in the schools becomes a central concern of *Brick Lane*. Chanu, who had yearned to belong in the United Kingdom, dreams of going back to Dhaka to teach, of all things, Shakespeare (186). The immigrant culture is pitted against the host culture in Ali's novel.

This incident of Chanu and multiculturalism further reflects the cousinship of experience and includes the issue of culture wars common to all South Asian and US minority communities. In his book *Culture Wars in British Literature: Multiculturalism and National Identity*, Tracy J. Prince writes that Ali's novel provides insight into the contemporary culture wars between white working-class communities and non-white ethnic communities, especially immigrants: "*Brick Lane*'s characters grapple with multiple layers of class and race conflicts faced by today's immigrants to Brick Lane, as they try to fit into Britain's image of itself" (124). In the novel, Nazneen—as an immigrant, a woman, a Muslim woman belonging to a lower class than some of her neighbors—is the subject of discrimination, even from her more assimilated Muslim neighbors. Immigrants and minorities in the United States, even those who have long been settled, such as Hispanics and Native Americans, face rejection from dominant majority cultures. Making students aware of this extra layer of othering is essential to our new societies.

Students can connect their own educational experiences with those of the characters, which shows that education, as practiced in the schools, can be a polarizing factor, pitting the immigrant culture against the host culture schools, in general, become contested territory. In *"There Ain't No Black in the Union Jack,"* Paul Gilroy writes, "The attachment to non-British cultures, which endures in black communities and from which much of their apparent strength and cohesion derives, is cited as the final proof that the entry of aliens into the national community is not only hazardous but practically impossible" (61). To me, this encapsulates the conditions of both diasporic communities and existent minority communities. The bildungsroman genre has become my preferred genre for teaching because it is also the preferred genre of many postcolonial novels, particularly diaspora novels. It is central to the experience of finding home in a cross-cultural setting, whether as a consequence of colonialism, of migration, or simply of connections across borders. The question of belonging raised in this genre can become the focus of our teaching, allowing students to explore their experiences alongside the characters they read about. This can enable us, as teachers, to explore how we can communicate culture, despite presenting the similarities and the senses of foreignness.

My students reacted to the violence against women depicted in *Brick Lane*, and they admired Nazneen's journey and growth. One student wrote with sympathy about how Nazneen is thrown into a "foreign culture" as a result of an arranged marriage. She noted that Nazneen had to adapt to both her husband and the world around him, find strength in herself, and make the best possible life for her family. Another student praised Nazneen's ability to adapt. The stable family environment of another student, who was from a majority culture, contrasted with what was depicted in the novel and shifted the student's understanding of family. Most of the women students read *Brick Lane* as Nazneen's journey to freedom, which in turn liberated her daughters to be themselves in the cross-cultural environment they were raised in. For my students, the last scene, in which Nazneen and her daughters make snow angels, was a symbol of freedom and coming into one's own.

The cultural contrast in the reception of the novels is striking. Some students gravitated toward the strength of the women and identified it with the strength of their own mothers. Others were fascinated by the coping strategies that the women characters used.

Overall, comparing and contextualizing the bildungsroman experiences made students more sensitive to cross-cultural encounters in their daily lives. They saw the ultimate growth of the characters as growth into themselves, and they learned to understand that everyone finds happiness and identity in their own way and that individuals find their own ways of coming together. I hope that this strategy helps students achieve greater self-acceptance and learn to accept one another and create bridges of relationships. I believe that my choice of texts and strategies developed empathy in students for others from different backgrounds, thus establishing the cousinship of experience.

Notes

1. A similar experience can be seen in the Native American context in the works of Sherman Alexie, particularly *Ten Little Indians*.

2. Similar to Anaya's exploration of the connection between the Chicanx and Chinese peoples is the Native American writer Gerald Vizenor's *Griever: An American Monkey King in China*. While we tend to exoticize the Native American experience, *Harold of Orange*, directed by Richard Weise, is a filmic text that not only shows the ordinariness of the Native American experience but also the similarities of the experience of growing up in the shadow of a hegemonic culture.

3. I first wrote about this strategy in "Teaching R. K. Narayan's *Swami and Friends*" and in "Colonialismo y la respuesta al colonialismo: La experiencia comparartida de Anaya, Ngugi y R. K. Narayan" (Jussawalla).

4. I developed this idea in Jussawalla, *Family Quarrels* 29–30 and 183–84.

Works Cited

Alexie, Sherman. *Ten Little Indians*. Grove Press, 2004.

Ali, Monica. *Brick Lane*. Scribner, 2003.

Anaya, Rudolfo. *Bless Me, Ultima*. Tonatiuh-Quinto Sol, 1984.

———. *A Chicano in China*. U of New Mexico P, 1986.

Anzaldúa, Gloria. *Borderlands / La Frontera: The New Mestiza*. 1987. Aunt Lute, 1999.

Cisneros, Sandra. *The House on Mango Street*. 1984. Vintage Books, 2016.

Fish, Stanley. *Is There a Text in This Class? The Authority of Interpretive Communities*. Harvard UP, 1982.

Gilroy, Paul. *"There Ain't No Black in the Union Jack": The Cultural Politics of Race and Nation*. U of Chicago P, 1991.

Harold of Orange. Directed by Richard Weise, screenplay by Gerald Vizenor, Vision Maker Media, 1984.

Hirsch, E. D. *Validity in Interpretation*. Yale UP, 1973.

Jussawalla, Feroza. "Colonialismo y la respuesta al colonialismo: La experiencia comparartida de Anaya, Ngugi y R. K. Narayan." *Culturas hispanas de los Estados Unidos de América*, edited by María Jesús Bux Rey and Tomas Calvo Buezas, Ediciones de Cultura Hispánica, 1990, pp. 557–67.

———. *Family Quarrels: Towards a Criticism of Indian Writing in English*. Peter Lang, 1984.

———. "Teaching R. K. Narayan's *Swami and Friends*." *Teaching Postcolonial and Commonwealth Literatures*, special issue of *College Literature*, edited by Kostas Myrsiades, vols. 19–20, nos. 3–1, Oct. 1992–Feb. 1993, pp. 219–24.

Narayan, R. K. *Swami and Friends*. 1935. U of Chicago P, 1980.

Prince, Tracy J. *Culture Wars in British Literature: Multiculturalism and National Identity*. McFarland, 2012.

Rao, Raja. *Kanthapura*. New Directions Publishing, 1963.

Sidhwa, Bapsi. *The American Brat*. 1993. Milkweed, 2012.

Vizenor, Gerald. *Griever: An American Monkey King in China*. U of Minnesota P, 1990.

Part IV

East Meets North: The United States and Canada

Chandrima Chakraborty

Remembering as Learning: South Asian Histories in a Canadian Classroom

Inadequate attention to the ongoing legacies of colonialism in the curriculum of Canadian postsecondary institutions inhibits both public education and cross-cultural learning in Canada. My pedagogical practice involves making marginalized histories visible, with the intent of facilitating the formation of a shared, collective history. Drawing on anglophone South Asian diasporic texts, I strive to cultivate in students an openness to encountering new—that is, unfamiliar and othered—stories and to guide them to responsibly engage with lesser-known voices, histories, and texts.

I am committed to a public pedagogy of remembrance in the form of teaching and learning from little-known and little-remembered South Asian histories. Central to my teaching practice is curating counterhistories by drawing on anglophone South Asian diasporic texts that bear witness to the experiences of people of South Asian descent residing in Canada. For me, as bell hooks writes, "The classroom, with all its limitations, remains a location of possibility . . . that allows us to face reality even as we collectively imagine ways to move beyond boundaries, to transgress" (207). Over the last decade I have focused the critical attention of my students as well as the scholarly community and the wider public on a "Canadian tragedy" that resonates with few (Commission): the 1985 bombing of

Air India Flight 182, en route from Toronto to New Delhi, which killed 329 people, mostly Canadians of Indian heritage, and its aftermath.[1] The bombing resulted in the longest and most expensive criminal investigations in Canadian history and has been belatedly acknowledged as "the largest mass murder in Canadian history" (Commission 21).

Following the critical pedagogy and memory scholar Roger Simon, whose scholarship was dedicated to exploring the role of pedagogy in addressing historical trauma, I use a pedagogy of remembrance to create openings for conversations on legacies of the Air India bombings that are being marginalized, if not erased, by official forms of remembering in Canada. I employ anglophone South Asian diasporic texts that engage with remembrances of the Air India tragedy in order to interrogate dominant versions of national histories and to invite students to build connections between this tragedy and other historical events that are hazily remembered in Canada. Anglophone South Asian diasporic texts offer my students creative modes of engagement with South Asian diasporic lives as well as a diasporic history of loss, grief, pain, resistance, and survival in relation to other groups—Indigenous, Black, and Asian—alongside whom South Asians live, think, and form communities. Informed by scholarship on memory, postcolonialism, critical race, gender, and critical pedagogy, my pedagogical approach prepares students to be open to the affective encounter with "difficult knowledge," a concept developed by the educational theorist Deborah Britzman that alerts us to the internal struggles that occur when we are faced with knowledge that fractures our sense of self and creates emotional discomfort.[2] Acknowledging and leaning into this discomfort in the classroom can offer valuable opportunities for collective learning and unlearning. It can work "to provoke their [students'] inquiry and challenge their existing views of the way things are and should be" (Simon, *Teaching* 47).

Remembering Air India Flight 182

On 23 June 1985, luggage bombs detonated on Air India Flight 182 in Irish airspace, killing all passengers and crew members. The Canadian government promptly dismissed this mass murder as a foreign tragedy. Even though the act of terror was conceived and executed in Canada and most of the victims were Canadians, the government's response promptly pushed the bombing into the margins of Canadian public consciousness and did not facilitate national mourning (Chakraborty et al., "Art" xiii;

Rae 2; Razack 104–08). Following the 9/11 attacks and the war on terror led by the United States, however, there were significant efforts to reframe the bombing as "the single worst act of terrorism in Canadian history" (Prime Minister 153): in 2005, 23 June was declared the National Day of Remembrance for Victims of Terrorism, and the 2010 report of the Commission of Inquiry into the Investigation of the Bombing of Air India Flight 182 was titled *Air India Flight 182: A Canadian Tragedy* (Chakraborty et al., "Art" xiv).

The public inquiry finding that a "cascading series of errors" by the Canadian government and official agencies had contributed to the Air India tragedy (Commission 21) was followed by a federal government "apology for the institutional failings" and "the treatment of the victims' families thereafter" (Prime Minister 155). Yet in official forms of remembering, the Air India tragedy has emerged as a story of Canada's vulnerability to terrorism; what are not recognized are the racial injuries repeatedly noted by the families in trial testimonies, interviews, and press reports as well as the ongoing experiences of loss for successive generations living with the legacies of this tragedy (Chakraborty et al., "Art" xiv–xviii). As a result, while the terrorist act has been incorporated into public memory, the grief of those who lost loved ones and the violence of indifference and systemic racism remain unacknowledged.

Therefore, my pedagogical imperative is to create opportunities for classroom conversations on how the past continues to shape our present, so that the loss and grief of those who lost loved ones on Air India Flight 182 can become part of Canadian public memory.[3] Anglophone South Asian diasporic texts that engage with this little-known Canadian tragedy point to both the Canadian state's and the general public's indifference to the pain of fellow Canadians. They demonstrate that what remains invisible is the grief not only of losing one's child, wife, husband, friend, or neighbor but also of knowing that those South Asian Canadians who died in the bombing were not recognized as Canadians and that their loss was not considered worthy of public mourning.

Remembrance as Pedagogy

To prepare students to be open to learning about the Air India tragedy (23 June 1985 and its aftermath) and to engage with official and artistic memorializations of the Air India events, I tell them how I came to research the tragedy. Interestingly, my experiences teaching anglophone

South Asian diasporic texts in undergraduate and graduate courses led me to research how the Air India tragedy is remembered in Canada. In teaching fiction and film that engages with the tragedy, I discovered that most students were unfamiliar with these events. At the same time, students were open to the possibility of encountering unfamiliar stories and histories. Inspired by students' questions and driven by both the dearth of scholarship on and the hazy public memory of the tragedy, I began conducting interviews with Air India families and other critical witnesses and collecting archival materials for an Air India public memory archive at McMaster University Library (airindiaflight182.humanities.mcmaster .ca). The goal of the archive is to document and educate Canadians about a history that risks disappearing when elderly Air India family members are no longer able to share what they know. The work of critical race and memory studies scholars prompts me to consider that I have ethical as well as pedagogical responsibilities in terms of what I might do with my newfound historical knowledge—and with the interviews and archival materials that I have been gathering over more than a decade. To care for and honor the memories of those who died, I strive to transmit difficult and erased historical knowledge (e.g., interviews, photographs, memorial books, artwork, etc.) and carefully prepare students to be open to the affective encounter with such difficult knowledge.

Studying creative remembrances of the Air India tragedy involves not only increasing students' knowledge of the past but also fostering critical learning by requiring students to learn from the discomfort occasioned by comprehending unknown pasts and grappling with new perspectives (Britzman; hooks; Simon, *Pedagogy, Teaching*, and *Touch*). As Simon and colleagues write in "Between Hope and Despair," "As a difficult return, remembrance attempts to meet the challenge of what it might mean to live, not *in* the past but *in relation with* the past, acknowledging the claim the past has on the present" (12). Remembrance can offer an opening into establishing relations with a past that is unfamiliar or not yet known to us and therefore into unlearning stories that we have accepted as truth. In the struggle to work through their own affiliations with and differences from the inherited narratives or memories, students recognize the historical character of partial and mediated remembrance. Invoking remembrance as a pedagogy calls for a "'reckoning' not only with stories of the past but also with 'ourselves' as we 'are' (historically, existentially, ethically) in the present" (15).

Following Simon and colleagues, I use remembrance as a pedagogical praxis for engaging with historical knowledge, so that creating new, shared histories and altered subjectivities also becomes possible. I am encouraged by hooks's insistence that "[t]he classroom remains the most radical space of possibility in the academy" (12). To foster a commitment to responsibility, I employ anti-colonial, feminist, and critical race studies approaches to motivate students to revisit and reassess the stories and histories "they have accepted as truths all their lives by becoming mindful of the dialectical relationship" between the self and the other (Aegerter 143).

My pedagogical approach works to create fissures in students' historical consciousness. I include scholarly essays on loss, trauma, nationalism, race, and multiculturalism to develop students' understanding of how Canada's past is continually reframed through the present. To encourage students to be cautious about the truth claims of official history, I often include in the course readings Sherene Razack's expert witness testimony, which holds systemic racism responsible for the Air India bombings. Razack's testimony was commissioned by a lawyer representing the Air India families for the public inquiry. Interestingly, it was excluded from the Commission of Inquiry's official report. This "clear indication of how the state endeavours to deflect attention away from allegations of racism" (Chakraborty et al., "Art" xviii–xix) invariably results in animated classroom discussions about how our understanding of the Air India event (and other historical events) is limited by dominant frames of remembering of those events. Razack's testimony encourages students to evaluate the recognition granted to official historical records and attend carefully to the strategic exclusion of documents from official archives. For, as Judith Butler reminds us, "the frame does not simply exhibit reality, but actively participates in a strategy of containment, selectively producing and enforcing what will count as reality" (xiii).

The frame-setting power of official documents and public figures provokes robust classroom conversations when I pair the text of the Air India apology (Prime Minister) or pictures of the current Canadian prime minister donning Indian attire ("'It'") with Bharati Mukherjee's short story "The Management of Grief," the first published fictional representation of the grief of losing family in the bombing. The juxtaposition of performative official multiculturalism with a short story that delineates the failures of multiculturalism—from the perspective of communities that make Canada's self-characterization as a multicultural nation possible—leads to rich conversations. It provokes a look back at the adoption of multiculturalism as state policy in Canada through an exploration of the increasing frequency of government apologies and the work apologies do. In addition, it asks students to reflect on the official account of the Air India tragedy as "an exceptional or aberrant event" in Canadian multiculturalism (Chakraborty 113). When a fictional text such as Mukherjee's short story is placed alongside official records such as the Air India apology, the radically different versions of the Air India tragedy suggest to students that creative works also function as knowledge—as witness to Canada's past and present.

Canadian official discourse routinely traces the Air India bombings to the Sikh separatist movement seeking an independent Khalistan, or a Sikh homeland, in India.[4] In contrast, many anglophone South Asian diasporic writings trace the Air India bombings to an earlier history of British imperialism and to attempts at maintaining a white Canada. Such attempts include anti-Asian riots in Vancouver, British Columbia—the site of the first Asian settlement in Canada—and the turning back of South Asian immigrants on the *Komagata Maru* from Vancouver Harbour. Anita Rau Badami's novel *Can You Hear the Nightbird Call?*, Uma Parameswaran's poem "On the Shores of the Irish Sea," and Padma Viswanathan's novel *The Ever After of Ashwin Rao* reference the *Komagata Maru*, yet another largely forgotten part of South Asian immigration history, in relation to the Air India tragedy (Dean 19–20). The ship, the *Komagata Maru*, with 376 passengers aboard—mostly Sikh men who were subjects of British India— was denied entry to Canada because of a racist immigration policy and sent back to India (Dean 4). Badami's novel, for example, which begins with the *Komagata Maru* and ends with the bombing of Air India Flight 182, connects a grandfather's aborted journey on the ship to his immigrant grandson's disaffection with Canada, which incites his grandson to participate in the Air India bombing (Chakraborty 123–25). Badami's novel, like Parameswaran's poem and Viswanathan's novel, invites students to consider how Canada's racializing practices are as much a part of the history of the Air India bombings and its aftermath as is the oft cited 1947 British Partition of India or the 1984 anti-Sikh violence in India (Dean).

Anglophone South Asian diasporic literature offers students a more complex understanding of the racial and imperialist histories that produced the clashes around class, race, masculinity, and religion that underpinned the Air India bombings. By tracing the history of the bombings to other events and histories in India and Canada, anglophone South Asian diasporic texts reveal how remembrance—both personal and collective— plays an indispensable role in a historical accounting of the past. Informed by critical readings on memory and memorialization, students explore various aspects of the process of remembering, including how both Indian and Canadian state-sanctioned memory projects inhibit other possibilities of memorialization and how facts and truth are contested and negotiated through artistic creations.

Many family members who lost loved ones on Air India Flight 182 have employed art to express social realities and demand justice. To privilege their personal proximity to the losses, I regularly include in my course materials creative remembrances by family members, such as Eisha Marjara's docudrama *Desperately Seeking Helen* and Renée Saklikar's collection of elegies *Children of Air India*.[5] I also teach anglophone fiction by diasporic South Asians who did not suffer direct losses from the bombing (e.g., Mukherjee or Viswanathan) to demonstrate the impact of the Air India events on the wider South Asian community and successive generations.[6] Such recognition of the effects of the bombing and its aftermath on others beyond the immediate family members of those killed on Air India Flight 182 is missing in the Commission of Inquiry findings and the Canadian government's apology. Anglophone South Asian diasporic texts play a significant role in this regard by helping broaden a sense of inheritance of the tragedy. When students recognize the ongoingness of grief, loss, grievance, and racism, it opens up possibilities to attend to the profound impact of the tragedy and to care for past and present others.

Difficult Encounters

My courses enroll a racially diverse student population, including many diasporic South Asians who can be further differentiated based on their status as international students, second- or third-generation Canadians, or recent immigrants to Canada. These diasporic South Asians enter the classroom with different lived experiences and familial, community, and national memories of critical historical events. However, they hold a shared awareness that they are perceived as other in postsecondary Canadian institutions and in Canada. Therefore, although my pedagogy derives from the obligation to represent inconvenient histories, my goal is not to gather persuasive historical narratives to compel students to remember (or to remember differently). Rather, recognizing students' differential vulnerabilities to fraught South Asian histories and lived experiences in the diaspora, I aim to curate counterhistories that support the possibility of generative dialogue within, between, and beyond South Asian diasporic communities. Our multifaceted exploration of the suffering, activism, and survival of differently positioned diasporic South Asians in relation to similar experiences of other racialized groups in Canada (Black, Indigenous, and Asian) helps historicize the presence of South Asian diasporic youth in the Canadian classroom. It makes students' participation in the study of Canadian literature and global anglophone literature meaningful, because it fosters an openness to both learn from unfamiliar stories and unlearn the familiar.

Increasing awareness of the events of 23 June 1985—that is, what preceded and followed the Air India bombing—calls for a responsive attendance to this historical event. It solicits students' active participation in public discourse, so that "remembrance becomes a form of difficult learning . . . demanding both responsibility and a response" (Simon, *Pedagogy* 204). Simon believes that remembrance practices can lead to transformative learning in which "words and images not only bear witness to specific histories of violence and violation, but are given over as a difficult inheritance to those called to receive it" (*Touch* 4). In bearing witness to silenced South Asian and South Asian diasporic histories through my teaching of anglophone South Asian diasporic texts that memorialize the Air India tragedy in varied ways, similar to Simon (*Pedagogy* vii–viii, 203–04), I hold on to the hope that pedagogy can play a role in supporting students to learn from and carry forward difficult histories.

My pedagogical practices invite students to encounter the loss, grief, and calls for recognition of South Asian Canadians as forms of difficult knowledge, with the hope of contributing to the production of alternative social memories and historical sensibilities. The scholarly and creative works that form the basis of my course materials encourage students to be open to listening to and discovering other histories and other memories. I believe that in the affective encounter with difficult, hazy, or forgotten histories lies the potential of pedagogy to contribute to public education by supporting responsive and responsible engagement with othered voices, histories, and texts.

Notes

1. Another bomb, intended for Air India Flight 302, detonated while in baggage transfer at Tokyo's Narita International Airport, killing two baggage handlers.

2. For a discussion of the concept of "difficult knowledge," see Pitt and Britzman.

3. According to a June 2023 study by the Angus Reid Institute, nine in ten Canadians have "little (61%) or no (28%) knowledge of the worst single instance of the mass killing of their fellow citizens, with three-in-five (58%) of those younger than 35 saying they have never even heard of it" ("Air India Anniversary").

4. The two suspects put on trial for the bombing were alleged to be involved in the Khalistan movement. This strengthened the view that the bombings were an act of retaliation against the Indian government for atrocities against Sikh separatists in the 1970s and 1980s, the Indian Army's storming of Sri Darbar Sahib (The Golden Temple) in what was known as Operation Blue Star (6 June 1984), and the Congress government's complicity in the violence perpetrated against Sikhs in India following the assassination of Prime Minister Indira Gandhi by two of her Sikh bodyguards (31 October 1984).

5. Marjara's mother and sister and Saklikar's aunt and uncle died on Air India Flight 182.

6. Other anglophone South Asian filmmakers and novelists who have referenced the Air India bombing in their works include Srinivas Krishna, Salman Rushdie, and Farzana Doctor. For a complete list of cultural productions, see airindiaflight182.humanities.mcmaster.ca.

Works Cited

Aegerter, Lindsay Pentolfe. "A Pedagogy of Postcolonial Literature." *College Literature*, vol. 24, no. 2, 1997, pp. 142–50.

"Air India Anniversary: 60% of 18- to 34-Year-Olds Have 'Never Heard of' Nation's Deadliest Terror Attack." *Angus Reid Institute*, 22 June 2023, angusreid.org/air-india-bombings-anniversary-canada-memorial/.

Badami, Anita Rau. *Can You Hear the Nightbird Call?* Alfred A. Knopf, 2006.

Britzman, Deborah. *Lost Subjects, Contested Objects: Toward a Psychoanalytic Inquiry of Learning.* State U of New York P, 1998.

Butler, Judith. *Frames of War: When Is Life Grievable?* Verso, 2009.

Chakraborty, Chandrima. "Official Apology, Creative Remembrances, and Management of the Air India Tragedy." *Studies in Canadian Literature*, vol. 40, no. 1, 2015, pp. 111–30.

Chakraborty, Chandrima, et al. "The Art of Public Mourning: An Introduction." Chakraborty et al., *Remembering*, pp. xiii–xxxii.

———, editors. *Remembering Air India: The Art of Public Mourning.* U of Alberta P, 2017.

Commission of Inquiry into the Investigation of the Bombing of Air India Flight 182. *Air India Flight 182: A Canadian Tragedy, Final Report.* Vol. 1, Minister of Public Works and Government Services, 2010.

Dean, Amber. "Remembering in Relation: The Air India and the Komagata Maru Disasters." Chakraborty et al., *Remembering*, pp. 3–28.

Desperately Seeking Helen. Directed by Eisha Marjara, National Film Board of Canada, 1999.

hooks, bell. *Teaching to Transgress: Education as the Practice of Freedom.* Routledge, 1994.

"'It Feels Like a Weeklong Indian Wedding': Trudeau Gets a Dressing-Down over India Outfits." *CBC Radio*, 22 Feb. 2018, www.cbc.ca/radio/asithappens/as-it-happens-thursday-edition-1.4547153/it-feels-like-a-weeklong-indian-wedding-trudeau-gets-a-dressing-down-over-india-outfits-1.4547159.

Mukherjee, Bharati. "The Management of Grief." Chakraborty et al., *Remembering*, pp. 221–38.

Parameswaran, Uma. "On the Shores of the Irish Sea." Chakraborty et al., *Remembering*, pp. 29–32.

Pitt, Alice, and Deborah Britzman. "Speculations on Qualities of Difficult Knowledge in Teaching and Learning: An Experiment in Psychoanalytic Research." *Qualitative Studies in Education*, vol. 16, no. 6, 2003, pp. 755–76.

Prime Minister of Canada. "Statement by the Prime Minister of Canada at the Commemoration Ceremony for the Twenty-Fifth Anniversary of the Air India Flight 182 Atrocity." Chakraborty et al., *Remembering*, pp. 153–57.

Rae, Bob. *Lessons to Be Learned: The Report of the Honourable Bob Rae, Independent Advisor to the Minister of Public Safety and Emergency Preparedness on Outstanding Questions with Respect to the Bombing of Air India Flight 182.* Air India Review Secretariat, 2005.

Razack, Sherene H. "The Impact of Systemic Racism on Canada's Pre-Bombing Threat Assessment and Post-Bombing Response to the Air India Bombings." Chakraborty et al., *Remembering*, pp. 85–117.

Saklikar, Renée Sarojini. *Children of Air India: Un/Authorized Exhibits and Interjections.* Nightwood Editions, 2013.

Simon, Roger I. *A Pedagogy of Witnessing: Curatorial Practice and the Pursuit of Social Justice.* State U of New York P, 2014.

———. *Teaching Against the Grain: Texts for a Pedagogy of Possibility.* Bergin and Garvey, 1992.

———. *A Touch of the Past: Remembrance, Learning, and Ethics.* Palgrave Macmillan, 2005.

Simon, Roger I., et al. "Between Hope and Despair: The Pedagogical Encounter of Historical Remembrance." *Pedagogy and the Remembrance of Historical Trauma*, edited by Simon et al., Rowman and Littlefield, 2000, pp. 9–15.

Viswanathan, Padma. *The Ever After of Ashwin Rao.* Random House Canada, 2014.

Robin E. Field

"Watch Me Reposition"
Bharati Mukherjee's *Jasmine*

Jasmine is Bharati Mukherjee's most well-known and most often taught novel (Maxey 54). While the novel—and Mukherjee herself—are controversial, *Jasmine* offers students a quick and engaging read that may be understood through multiple lenses and contexts: as a South Asian diasporic text, US immigrant fiction, quintessentially American literature (in the figure of the rebel and renegade), trauma writing, and cosmopolitan literature that eschews parochialism and transcends national borders and cultural integrity. Whether taught in introductory classes or in seminars for English majors, *Jasmine*, with its provocative protagonist, exposes students to "the wonder!" of great literature while challenging them to understand cultural, historical, and literary issues (Mukherjee, *Jasmine* 21).

Mukherjee's novel, with its simple and direct narration, is an accessible text for beginning students in introductory literature classes. In my core literature class for first- and second-year students titled Immigrant Fictions, I use *Jasmine* as an example of South Asian diasporic literature. Because my students usually know little about South Asian culture and history, I offer a short lecture with slides to introduce the history of British colonialism and the division of the subcontinent in 1947; the myriad languages, religions, ethnic groups, and castes in India; and the five important tenets of Sikhism. Alternatively, students may read a short article on South Asian history and culture, such as Aminah Mohammad-Arif's "Imaginations and Constructions of South Asia: An Enchanting Abstraction?," and then write a brief reflection paper addressing what they have learned and why they believe they have not previously encountered this history and culture in their education. When discussing their experiences in class, they reflect further on how literature may expand their worldviews. During these discussions, I make sure to question the stereotypes about Sikhs that appear in the novel. Mukherjee depicts Sukhwinder Singh as a one-dimensional terrorist whose desire for a separate Sikh nation-state leads him to attack Hindus indiscriminately. His reappearance as a hot dog vendor in Central Park years later solidifies the violent stereotype; J (I use this abbreviation for the protagonist so as not to prioritize any one identity, for the character uses multiple names throughout the novel: Jyoti, Jasmine, Jazzy, Jase, and Jane) asserts that "he'd kill [Taylor], or Duff, to get at me" and immediately flees New York (Mukherjee, *Jasmine* 189). When discussing this Sikh character with students, I underscore the importance of being a critical reader and resisting stereotypes presented by authors, even when the subject matter (here, Sikhism) may be new to them.

The protagonist's migration from India to the United States allows students to explore the concepts of immigration and American individualism in *Jasmine*. In introductory classes such as Immigrant Fictions and Rebels and Renegades in American Literature and Film, we read Mukherjee's novel, in its presentation of the immigrant who sheds her past to strive for a better life, as quintessentially American. In Immigrant Fictions, students write a short paper comparing the protagonist of *Jasmine* to another female immigrant character, such as América in T. C. Boyle's *The Tortilla Curtain* or the Dominican woman in Junot Díaz's "Edison, New Jersey." Both women are undocumented, like J, but they have very different experiences in the United States: América yearns to return to Mexico after months of homelessness, and the Dominican woman endures domestic and sexual slavery in a white American man's home. Such comparisons underscore to students the variability of Brown immigrant women's experiences. J's success in obtaining financial security, respect from her community, romantic and familial love, and personal agency comes in part because of her "genuine foreignness" (Mukherjee, *Jasmine* 26); unlike América and the Dominican woman, her Brownness does not limit her life possibilities. Time permitting, students may productively complicate positive readings of J's assimilation by digging into erin Khuê Ninh's provocative argument that J embodies pervasive global stereotypes about Asian women as gold diggers, sex workers, and mail-order brides (148). A discussion of Ninh's work helps students realize the importance of resisting stereotypes about Sikhs and Asian women more generally.

Just as *Jasmine* maps the traditional immigrant narrative of achieving the American dream of prosperity and freedom, the protagonist, J, also fits the American archetype of the rebel and renegade. In my American studies core class titled Rebels and Renegades in American Literature and Film, *Jasmine* serves as a counterpoint to the story of the white cisgender heterosexual male protagonist who strikes out on his own. Mukherjee's protagonist expands the category of who can be an American renegade: she is an undocumented Brown woman who, like the archetypal American renegade Huck Finn, leaves attachments behind to head west to "the frontier" (Mukherjee, *Jasmine* 240). Additionally, Mukherjee's protagonist shifts identities as she moves from place to place, like the trickster figure so prevalent in multiethnic American literature. Thus, in one novel, students in introductory courses may study postcolonial literature and American literature—which demonstrates that Mukherjee may be categorized as a cosmopolitan writer as well, since her novels do not fit neatly into any one national tradition.

Jasmine also appeals to more advanced students in courses for English majors. In sophomore-level courses such as Twice-Told Tales and The History of Literature in English, English majors explore how twentieth-century and contemporary authors respond to canonical authors such as Joseph Conrad, Charlotte Brontë, and Charlotte Perkins Gilman. In *Understanding Bharati Mukherjee*, Ruth Maxey outlines these connections to Conrad and Brontë, delineating Mukherjee's "simultaneous disregard for, yet reliance upon, the British canon and its complex position within her multilayered use of intertextuality" (69). Students may read Asha Nadkarni's essay linking *Jasmine* to Gilman's "The Yellow Wallpaper," which argues that "even a 'multicultural' feminist progress narrative can contain a eugenic impulse" (219). Students may spend a class period unearthing the many connections between *Jasmine* and Brontë's *Jane Eyre* or "The Yellow Wallpaper," or they may write a paper that discusses how Mukherjee's novel builds on and challenges Brontë's novel or that parses the variations of feminism in Mukherjee's and Gilman's texts. In addition to discussing *Jasmine*, students examine Mukherjee's 1988 *New York Times* article, "Immigrant Writing: Give Us Your Maximalists!," in order to debate the author's positionality as an American writer, a diasporic Indian author, a cosmopolitan writer, or some combination of the three—discussions that allow students to ponder the importance, and lack thereof, of any author's biography and intentions for how their work is received. Finally, students may read Shazia Rahman's essay, which analyzes the covers of Mukherjee's novels with regard to their "orientalist cosmopolitanism" (407), in order to learn about peritexts and epitexts, the former being those images and texts closely related to the book (such as dustcovers, blurbs, and forewords), the latter statements about the book (such as interviews, reviews, and essays). The various editions of *Jasmine* that students obtain lead to a fascinating discussion about how the publishing industry presents Mukherjee's work as "all highly exoticized and focus[ing] on exactly the ethnicity that Mukherjee insists is insignificant" (413).

Jasmine is also an excellent text for advanced English majors to study as trauma writing. In my Senior Seminar in Literature, students explore the scene of rape, often read metaphorically by critics such as Ralph J. Crane, who argues that J's rape is "an almost clichéd symbol in colonial and post-colonial fiction of the brutal relationship between colonizer and colonized" (126). Many students resist a primarily metaphorical understanding of this scene, focusing instead on the physical and psychological trauma experienced by the young woman. I teach this text as a rape novel, a new genre that emerged in the 1970s that depicts the victim-survivor's experience of sexual violence and its physical and psychological repercussions instead of the perpetrator's pornographic and salacious perspective (Field 10). Mukherjee's explicit depiction of rape and post-traumatic stress disorder (PTSD) aligns with other rape novels of the 1980s, such as Alice Walker's *The Color Purple* and Sandra Cisneros's *The House on Mango Street*, in that it educates readers about the trauma of rape. *Jasmine* pairs well with excerpts from Judith Herman's psychological treatise *Trauma and Recovery* because J experiences the symptoms of PTSD (such as constriction, intrusion, and hyperarousal) that Herman so lucidly describes. Reading *Jasmine* as a rape novel provides another compelling explanation for J's reinventions, renamings, and journey westward. Until J attends to her psychological recovery from the sexual violence she endured from Half-Face and the multiple rapes "in boats and cars and motel rooms," she cannot recover in any meaningful way from sexual trauma and will continue to leave her "lives" behind (Mukherjee, *Jasmine* 127). This interpretation of a lack of healing negates J's multiple identities as positive expressions of individualism and free will, instead locating her new identities and westward trajectory as attempts to escape the trauma of her past. For students who resist this less hopeful interpretation, Suzanne LaLonde's essay "Healing and Post-Traumatic Growth" helpfully explores the possibilities of healing not narrated in Mukherjee's novel. Given Mukherjee's optimistic description of J's next venture westward at the end of the novel, students eagerly debate whether *Jasmine* offers a hopeful new life for J or whether the protagonist will remain enmeshed in her traumatic past.

Students may also examine the influence of another traumatic event on J and her family: the 1947 Partition of the Indian subcontinent. Advanced English majors are intrigued by the application of memory studies to this novel and by the "gothic perspective" of "unspoken/unspeakable grief [and] trauma" that Andrew Hock Soon Ng argues applies to the teaching of Asian American literature (237–38). I introduce students to the theoretical work of Marianne Hirsch, Stef Craps, and Irene Visser, particularly their theorization of the "postgeneration," the generation after those persons who lived through trauma, who instead experience a kind of remembering through the "stories, images, and behaviors among which they grew up" (Hirsch 4–5). Students then analyze how J's childhood is saturated by her family's remembrances of Lahore and Partition and how J herself is so affected by her parents' experience of Partition that she inadvertently replicates the physical and psychological aftereffects of trauma in her own life.

Productive discussion occurs when students analyze how the novel depicts the trauma experienced by J; her mother, Mataji; and her father, Pitaji. In small groups, students analyze one or all three characters and find details demonstrating Herman's categories of PTSD. They note how J's narration of her mother's remembrances demonstrates the trauma Mataji endured:

> Mataji, my mother, couldn't forget the Partition Riots. Muslims sacked our house. Neighbors' servants tugged off earrings and bangles, defiled grottoes, sabered my grandfather's horse. Life shouldn't have turned out that way! I've never been to Lahore, but the loss survives in the instant replay of family story: forever Lahore smokes, forever my parents flee. (Mukherjee, *Jasmine* 41)

The timelessness of the final line underscores the trauma this family lived through. Students recognize that J's parents are still fleeing from their past, which makes Partition an omnipresent reality for their children as well. Students also point to the line "my father . . . had given up long before I was born," noting that Pitaji is unsatisfied with everything about his new life after Partition (42). Students link Pitaji to his daughter through this dissatisfaction; although J is critical of her father's longing for his past life, she also replicates his inability to be satisfied in the present, both in her childhood in Punjab and in her adulthood in the United States. Students note how J regularly refuses to accept her life circumstances: As a poor village girl she dreams of becoming a doctor, and as a young wife of co-owning a business with her husband, Prakash. In Flushing, New York, J is dissatisfied with the limitations of life with Professorji's family, who demands she enact the duties of a widow; and in Iowa she wants more to life than being Jane, the common-law wife of a middle-aged banker, Bud, even though she is pregnant with his child. J's refusal to accept her current life circumstances thus mirrors her father's refusal to accept his new life circumstances in the Indian village of Hasnapur. Students often find Joya Chatterji's idea of the "partial citizenship" of members of the Indian diaspora helpful in explaining the characters' dissatisfaction. Chatterji notes that for South Asians in the diaspora, "their sudden rebranding as citizens of two different and hostile countries" caused them "to grapple in new ways with questions of belonging" (311).

The aftereffects of the violence of Partition on identity are also relevant to J's own life decades later, as she negotiates her diasporic subjectivity in the United States. As Nalini Iyer argues, South Asian diasporas contain multiple narratives of displacement and arrival (54); hence, *Jasmine* demonstrates how the displacement of Partition maps onto the immigration narrative of South Asians to North America. J's journey to the United States is instigated by the legacy of Partition; the bombing that kills her husband, Prakash, results from Sikh militants demanding their own nation-state, just as Muslims demanded an independent Pakistan at the time of Partition. The primary figure of violence, Sukkhi, plants a bomb in the sari shop where J and Prakash are shopping. Students point to J's narration of the bombing as an example of a symptom of trauma known as "intrusion," given its narration in the present tense: "Instant replay in slow motion. I can't turn the VCR off. The sidewalk surges, men scream. I am screaming. My hands touch a red wet cheek, my eyes are closed, Prakash and I stumble together, Sukkhi guns the motor, shouting, 'Prostitutes! Whores!'" (Mukherjee, *Jasmine* 93). Some students even notice that the phrase "instant replay" is also used in J's description of the family's memory of Partition: "the loss survives in the instant replay of family story" (41). Both the trauma of Partition and the bombing that kills Prakash occur in the present tense, indicating the lack of historicity for these two events. As in discussions of *Jasmine* as a rape novel, students discuss the implications of a violence that is not relegated to or integrated into the past. Herman explains that survivors of trauma may compulsively place themselves in harm's way to try to rescript the violent events they have survived (39). J appears to want to rescript her past when she decides to travel alone to Florida, a dangerous journey that results in multiple rapes. Students point to Half-Face's words about her suitcase to explain the link between J's past and the violence in her present: "You carried all this shit halfway around the world? You crazy or what? Travel light, sweetheart, always travel light. If you had not been carrying this bag, you wouldn't be in the deep shit now" (Mukherjee, *Jasmine* 114). J carries the past with her—not only her suitcase but also the traumas that spur her movements across the globe—therefore placing herself in dangerous circumstances. I underscore that we should not blame J for being raped, as Half-Face clearly makes the choice to assault her. However, this discussion demonstrates that J is vulnerable and alone because of the chain of events that leads back to Partition. As Iyer notes, "The characteristic rootlessness of diasporic subjects . . . may sometimes be traced back to Partition experiences" (66).

J's diasporic subjectivity is foregrounded during the scene in Central Park, where J sees Sukkhi. This scene—which highlights a quintessential moment of PTSD related to the bombing that killed Prakash—may be examined in class or used as the basis for a short paper or an exam question. Students note that J has not been in a romantic relationship since her marriage and that her last experience with sex was the rape by Half-Face. Once Taylor confesses his romantic feelings for her, J is faced with the prospect of both sex and love. She then has a panic attack, ostensibly because she sees Sukkhi, the Sikh militant whose bomb killed her husband, across the park. Students and I note how unrealistic it would be for this Brown hot dog vendor to be Sukkhi, although Mukherjee told me in a 2008 interview that she did intend for Sukkhi to be the hot dog vendor (Interview). Regardless, J's belief that the hot dog vendor is Sukkhi links her flight to Iowa to the violence and trauma of the Partition. In their close readings of this scene, students connect J's past traumas to her panic about sex and her fear that Taylor will be killed by Sukkhi, just as Prakash was. They tie the end of *Jasmine*, where a pregnant J leaves Iowa with Taylor to go to California, to J's ongoing struggle with PTSD; she needs to leave Jane behind by any means necessary, and Taylor is her mechanism to escape Iowa. Trauma and PTSD prove persuasive explanations for the origins of

J's actions and motivations throughout the novel. Despite Mukherjee's insistence that *Jasmine* is an American story (Maxey 85), students come to recognize the novel's diasporic and transnational underpinnings.

A provocative novel by an equally provocative author, *Jasmine* offers myriad pedagogical possibilities. Just as J whispers "Watch me reposition the stars" at the end of the novel (Mukherjee, *Jasmine* 240), referring to her multiple identities and improbable life trajectory, instructors teaching *Jasmine* may utilize the multiple positions this novel occupies in order to challenge accepted narratives and enrich conversations about literature and contemporary life.

Works Cited

Boyle, T. C. *The Tortilla Curtain*. Penguin Books, 1995.

Brontë, Charlotte. *Jane Eyre*. 1847. *Project Gutenberg*, 1 Nov. 1999, www .gutenberg.org/ebooks/1260.

Chatterji, Joya. "Partition Studies: Prospects and Pitfalls." *The Journal of Asian Studies*, vol. 72, no. 2, 2014, pp. 309–12.

Crane, Ralph J. "Of Shattered Pots and Sinkholes: (Female) Identity in Bharati Mukherjee's *Jasmine*." *SPAN: Journal of the South Pacific Association for Commonwealth Literature and Language Studies*, vol. 36, Oct. 1993, pp. 122–30.

Craps, Stef. *Postcolonial Witnessing: Trauma Out of Bounds*. Palgrave Macmillan, 2013.

Díaz, Junot. "Edison, New Jersey." *Drown*, by Díaz, Riverhead Books, 1996, pp. 119–38.

Field, Robin E. *Writing the Survivor: The Rape Novel in Late Twentieth-Century American Fiction*. Clemson UP, 2020.

Gilman, Charlotte Perkins. "The Yellow Wallpaper." 1892. *Project Gutenberg*, 1 Nov. 1999, www.gutenberg.org/ebooks/1952.

Herman, Judith. *Trauma and Recovery: The Aftermath of Violence—from Domestic Abuse to Political Terror*. Basic Books, 1992.

Hirsch, Marianne. *The Generation of Postmemory: Writing and Visual Culture after the Holocaust*. Columbia UP, 2012.

Iyer, Nalini. "Multiple Migrations: Partition and South Asian Canadian Writing." *South Asian Review*, vol. 37, no. 1, 2016, pp. 51–69.

LaLonde, Suzanne. "Healing and Post-Traumatic Growth." *Trauma and Literature*, edited by J. Roger Kurtz, Cambridge UP, 2018, pp. 196–210.

Maxey, Ruth. *Understanding Bharati Mukherjee*. U of South Carolina P, 2019.

Mohammad-Arif, Aminah. "Imaginations and Constructions of South Asia: An Enchanting Abstraction?" *Ideas of South Asia: Symbolic Representations and Political Uses*, special issue of *South Asian Multidisciplinary Academic Journal*, edited by Mohammad-Arif and Blandine Ripert, vol. 10, 2014, https://doi .org/10.4000/samaj.3800.

Mukherjee, Bharati. "Immigrant Writing: Give Us Your Maximalists!" *The New York Times Book Review*, 28 Aug. 1988, p. 1+.

———. Interview. Conducted by Robin E. Field, 28 Dec. 2008.

———. *Jasmine*. Grove Press, 1989.

Nadkarni, Asha. "Reproducing Feminism in *Jasmine* and 'The Yellow Wallpaper.'" *Feminist Studies*, vol. 38, no. 1, spring 2012, pp. 218–44.

Ng, Andrew Hock Soon. "Teaching the Intangible: Reading Asian American Literature in the Classroom through the Gothic." *Pedagogy: Critical Approaches to Teaching Literature, Language, Composition, and Culture*, vol. 12, no. 2, 2012, pp. 235–52.

Ninh, erin Khuê. "Gold-Digger: Reading the Marital and National Romance in Bharati Mukherjee's *Jasmine*." *MELUS*, vol. 18, no. 3, fall 2013, pp. 146–59.

Rahman, Shazia. "Cosmopolitanism, Internationalization and Orientalism: Bharati Mukherjee's Peritexts." *Journal of Postcolonial Writing*, vol. 49, no. 4, 2013, pp. 405–18.

Visser, Irene. "Decolonizing Trauma Theory: Retrospect and Prospects." *Humanities*, vol. 4, no. 2, 2015, pp. 250–65.

Rajender Kaur

Race, Citizenship, and
Community Formation in
Bhira Backhaus's *Under the Lemon Trees*
and Jhumpa Lahiri's *Unaccustomed Earth*

I often begin my class on Asian American literature by asking the question "What then is the American, this new man?," famously posed by J. Hector St. John de Crèvecoeur in *Letters from an American Farmer*. Crèvecoeur posits that the American is "a mixture of English, Scottish, Irish, French, Dutch, Germans, and Swedes. From this promiscuous breed, that race now called Americans have arisen" (43). The celebration of transnational hybridity in this statement should not blind us to the fact that whiteness is the unequivocal assumption of American racial identity in Crèvecoeur, as traced in the introduction to this volume of letters. The Naturalization Act of 1790 restricted citizenship to "free white people" (United States), effectively excluding people of all other races. Although immigration and naturalization policies would become more expansive over time, it was only in 1952 that racial restrictions regarding naturalization were lifted; it is not surprising, then, that citizenship, race, and community formation are fraught issues in the Asian American context.

These issues are further complicated by recent scholarship, not just on pioneer immigrants from Punjab who settled on the West Coast in the early twentieth century but also on "East Indian"[1] servants, slaves, and lascars in the early national period, which reveals plebeian histories of arrival

142

that belie the model minority myth embraced so avidly by the generation of professional elites who came in the wake of the 1965 Immigration and Naturalization Act.[2] Advertisements for runaway slaves and petitions against their wrongful enslaved status by some of these runaway servants and slaves of South Asian origin are testament to a prehistory of South Asian Americans in the United States dating back to the seventeenth century.[3] A petition by Sick Keesar, a Bengali lascar, on behalf of himself and his company of thirty-five men to Benjamin Franklin in 1786, for instance, makes an eloquent plea for redress against exploitative labor practices and is evidence of earlier transatlantic maritime economies and circuits of labor in which people from the Indian subcontinent came to the United States (Kaur). Accordingly, I structure my Asian American literatures course to highlight some of these early histories. I organize the South Asian American literature module around Bhira Backhaus's *Under the Lemon Trees* and Jhumpa Lahiri's *Unaccustomed Earth*, texts that present two diametrically opposed portraits of the South Asian American community. *Lemon Trees* is rooted in the very local and particular history of Sikh pioneers who settled in the fertile valleys of California—San Joaquin, Sacramento, and Imperial—at the turn of the twentieth century, while *Unaccustomed Earth* focuses on the urban, well-educated community of doctors, engineers, and academics who came to the United States in the late 1960s and 1970s. Pairing these two texts allows me to draw a sharp contrast between two radically different narratives of arrival, community formation, and identity that are prevalent in the South Asian American community.

I situate South Asian American community formations such as the Mexidus, the unique community born out of the union of Punjabi immigrants and Mexican women, represented in *Lemon Trees* within the triangulated relations between Britain, the United States, and India borne of colonial circuits, and I connect these colonial networks to the presence of "East Indian" lascars, servants, and slaves in colonial and postrevolutionary America.[4] Such a context gestures to the understudied currency of India in the American imaginary dating back to the early national period.[5] *Unaccustomed Earth*, in contrast, with its cast of upwardly mobile, successful characters, serves to complicate students' understanding of race as a social construct by highlighting the discriminatory underpinnings of such apparently meritocratic terms as *model minority*.[6]

I supplement a study of *Lemon Trees* and *Unaccustomed Earth* with online resources such as those hosted by the *South Asian American Digital Archive*, an invaluable resource on South Asian American history, especially the archival materials (e.g., early immigration documents) collected as part of the site's early immigration series (www.saada.org). *Free African Americans of Virginia, North Carolina, South Carolina, Maryland and Delaware*, a digital database created by Paul Heinegg that includes a special section titled "East Indians in Colonial Maryland, Virginia and North Carolina," is another valuable resource: here one can peruse advertisements for runaway slaves and servants of South Asian origin (www.freeafricanamericans.com). There were several petitions for freedom by people with anglicized names like James Dunn and others who are identified as being of Indian origin in the Pennsylvania Abolition Society's archives ("Petition"). I complement the advertisements with petitions of protest filed by many of these slaves and lascars, such as the aforementioned Sick Keesar, to trace the long but little-known presence of South Asians in early America. The petitions protesting wrongful confinement or unfair labor practices gesture to a long history of dissent against uncivil laws.

My pedagogical aim in this class is threefold. My first aim is to use these archival materials to construct an alternative genealogy of South Asian Americans, one that dates back to the early European settlement in the seventeenth century, and to highlight the humble, working-class roots of this genealogy. I encourage students to ask why this history has been erased in histories of colonial America. What bearing does it have on notions of American identity? on South Asian American identity? And what are the implications of supplementing early American history with the forgotten histories of the raced bodies of servants, slaves, and lascars from the Indian subcontinent? This permits me to demonstrate the ideological force of whiteness that bleaches out the presence and contributions of the raced bodies of Asians in conventional narratives of early American history.

In guiding students to explore advertisements for "East Indian" runaway slaves, the second aim is to trace the slipperiness of race as a social construct.[7] I supplement the study of these advertisements by referencing the changing designation of South Asians in US census forms, where they were first classified as white based on the assumption that they were Caucasian. People from the Indian subcontinent were called "Hindus" on the census form from 1920 to 1940, regardless of their religion. Beginning in 2000, people could select from among six different Asian groups in addition to "Other Asian," with the option to write in a specific group. We study successive US census forms across the past century to trace the shifting racial designation of South Asians.

The third aim is to chart the changing community formation of South Asians from the stray members who mixed with Africans Americans, traces of which can only be found in the Heinegg archive, to the hybrid community of Mexidus of the 1930s and 1940s to a community that has come into its own politically with Vice President Kamala Harris, whose own mixed-race heritage harkens back to this early history.[8]

I also make it a point to focus on the aesthetics of the two texts, so that I don't fall into the common practice of reading literature as a mining expedition for social and historical context only. I urge students to examine how Backhaus structures her novel, juxtaposing the bildungsroman of Jeeto's quest for independence with Uncle Avtar's immigrant narrative in order to provide a layered portrait of community formation. We study the tropes of planting and "unaccustomed earth" in the titular story of Lahiri's collection in order to examine issues of acculturation and assimilation. In many ways, then, Lahiri's tropes, which evoke the dislocations of the immigrant experience, tie in nicely with the concerns of the community of Sikh farmers presented in Backhaus's novel.

Mapping Diasporic Roots and Inscribing Self in Backhaus's *Under the Lemon Trees*

As a prelude to reading *Lemon Trees*, I have students research the Punjabi community in California today, which, at over 250,000 people, constitutes one of the largest Punjabi diasporas in the world. The roots of this large diasporic community stretch back to the 1890s, when the first significant numbers of Punjabi immigrants (seven to eight thousand), a majority of them Sikh farmers, first arrived, before anti-immigrant anxiety about "the Hordes of Hindus" and the "Tide of Turbans" led to the passing of a series of exclusionary acts, which effectively stopped their arrival.

Backhaus's *Lemon Trees* presents in poetic detail the poignant history of this phase of South Asian migration through two complex, intersecting narratives. The stories are of Jeeto, a young second-generation Punjabi American girl living in the small town of Oak Grove, California, in the 1970s, and of her uncle, Avtar, who arrived in 1946 as a peasant youth from Punjab because of straitened family circumstances in British India. I divide the class in two working groups to tease out the narrative arc of Uncle Avtar's and Jeeto's stories. After this, we discuss how the novel avoids the familiar pitfall of Asian American immigrant narratives that lapse into cheerless docudramas by interweaving Avtar's saga of grit and survival with Jeeto's coming-of-age story in ways that move beyond the common themes of troubled acculturation and intergenerational ruptures between parents and their Americanized children. Jeeto and Avtar constitute the two narrative foci of the text, and their stories telescope two distinct historical periods of Sikh migration, one facilitated by the 1946 Luce Cellar Act, the other by the 1965 Immigration and Naturalization Act. While the latter mitigated the outright ban of Asians enacted by the 1924 Immigration Act by allowing a quota of one hundred people to emigrate from India, the latter abolished immigration based on national origins and established a new immigration policy based on uniting families and encouraging skilled labor to the United States. While Avtar's story gestures to the hybrid community of Mexidus of the 1940s, Jeeto's narrative, which centers on her conflicted relationship with her mother, who is determined to marry her off to a suitable boy from Punjab, is located in the 1970s. The two plots function contrapuntally to present a polyphonic and expansive family history that is also at once a history of the United States and of the South Asian American community that has been an integral part of it. I ask students to write on how the dialogic subjectivities of Jeeto and Avtar reflect a multivoiced cultural situation that allows the narrator to represent the personal and communal experience in order to comment on issues of identity politics and rewrite history.

A critical pedagogical task in teaching Asian American literature is to raise student awareness of the strategies writers use to stake a claim to new homelands, to build bridges between homes left behind and new homelands in order to consolidate a sense of self that transcends a hyphenated identity. I establish the theoretical context of these issues through a guided reading of Uma Parmeshwaran's essay "Dispelling the Spells of Memory: Another Approach to Reading Our Yesterdays," which advocates for "making space in the cathedral" of the adopted homeland by forging interconnections between history and memory of the two cultures (lxi). Students note the insistent mapping of local spaces within the milestones of a larger arc of American history that sprinkle the narrative in *Lemon Trees*. By noting the names of the numerous towns and geographic landmarks of Northern California, historical events such as the gold rush, and the important immigration acts that the text makes mention of, students are encouraged to engage in a close reading of *Lemon Trees*. I ask students to analyze the purpose of such mapping and to reflect on how Backhaus frames Jeeto's and Avtar's stories as American stories. I follow this up with a mini lecture on how *Lemon Trees*—by insistently inscribing the quintessentially American small town of Oak Grove within the landscape and history of California—uses cartography to move beyond the familiar frames of Asian American fictions in which memory and history are invoked primarily in terms of victimization and loss.

I make sure to focus students' attention on literary aspects of the texts while encouraging them to note how the text negotiates the personal in terms of the political. To that end, students are reminded to anchor their analyses of the texts using a cardinal discussion question I pose in all my literature classes: How is what said? Students parse the way *Lemon Trees* juxtaposes an array of novelistic modes—bildungsroman, autoethnography, family romance—in order to forcefully encode itself both spatially and temporally as an American story, mapping the history of the Punjabi community of Oak Grove in the deep time of American history. Once they have a clear understanding of how the text deploys different genres and tropes, we move to a reflective writing prompt: "How does *Lemon Trees* juxtapose different literary tropes and genres in fresh combinations to chronicle not just the legislative history of immigration acts but also the psychosocial development of Jeeto and Avtar mediated by different gendered expectations and hence identity formation?" Students reflect on the changing face of the Punjabi community and its growing heterogeneity, shown through the death of its pioneering fathers, men like Mohta Singh who married Mexican women but who are now perceived ambivalently. Mohta Singh is a pillar of the community, respected for his courage and patronage but feared as well. More pertinently, mixed-race children, like Hari, are not seen as suitable marriage material by the newer arrivals, like Jeeto's family. Other fissures can be seen in the text's critique of the more rigidly orthodox Sikh priests, for whom the gurdwara is not a place of communal gatherings but a place of worship. *Lemon Trees* registers the changing function of the gurdwara by referring to the first Sikh temple built in Stockton in 1912, which was a safe haven for new immigrants and was instrumental in consolidating a sense of community. It was also a hotbed of political activism, mobilizing the community against discriminatory immigration laws and helping initiate the Ghadar movement, a translational anti-colonial movement that organized resistance against British rule in India.

A Quest for Literary Forebearers and Hardy Offspring
in Lahiri's *Unaccustomed Earth*

I conclude the module on South Asian American literature by teaching Lahiri's short story "Unaccustomed Earth" (3–59). Lahiri uses the American writer Nathaniel Hawthorne not just to suggest the title and epigraph for the collection but also, more importantly, to articulate "her desire to be seen as writing fully within the American literary tradition and her confidence in positioning herself within the American literary pantheon," as Rajini Srikanth notes (55). The epigraph signals issues of belonging and roots so central to immigrant lives in adopted homelands. Lahiri herself has famously commented that "I would like to see myself as an American writer. When I was raised, I was told I was not to see myself as an American. It was important for my mother to raise her children as Indian. . . . Even now it is hard for me to say I am American" (qtd. in Rothstein).

I ask students to analyze the epigraph. What does it mean to gesture to Hawthorne, a quintessential canonical American writer? What is the function of the metaphor of "unaccustomed earth"? Does it have the same valency and determined patriarchal optimism that informs Hawthorne's statement in "The Custom House," or does the metaphor of transplanting gesture to a more gendered experience of dislocation and struggle, especially as contextualized within what Susan Koshy calls the "filial gothic" engendered by neoliberalism (362)? I urge students to pay attention to textual details that capture the texture of immigrant lives. How does "Unaccustomed Earth" represent the angst of estrangement between Ruma and her father as they struggle to communicate with each other? While the story lays out with nuance and subtlety the silences and gaps, thwarted parental ambitions, and stunted emotions that mark the relationship between father and daughter, we are a world away from Backhaus's feisty Jeeto. What function does class and education play in the choices the female protagonists make in "Unaccustomed Earth" and *Lemon Trees*? I persuade students to analyze the seeming contradiction of Ruma's decision to be a stay-at-home mother and, ironically, follow the model of her domesticated mother despite her professional qualifications as well as Jeeto's struggle to break free from the gendered expectations of her mother. A spirited discussion usually follows when I lead students to connect the shift in immigrant perspectives as a coming-of-age of the South Asian American community itself. I nudge students to think about how literary form itself mirrors material and historical shifts—for example, in the ways the bildungsroman and immigrant narrative of Backhaus are replaced by the far subtler psychological crises of communication, of love unfulfilled, and the enervating search for rootedness and belonging in Lahiri's focus on the lives of the South Asian diaspora in the contemporary era. While Backhaus maps the mountains, valleys, and quotidian markers of small-town California, Lahiri, with equal skill, maps Boston, Seattle, and New York, the metropolitan urban habitats of aspirational desis. Ruma is privileged by virtue of her upper-class status and the accepted gender norms associated with motherhood in making the choice to be a stay-at-home mother, a far cry from the constraints Jeeto faces as she struggles to get an education and be independent. Lahiri complicates the intergenerational conflicts stemming from the contradictions of the model minority ethos as internalized by South Asian Americans.

I urge students to reflect on the metaphor of the fragrant lemon tree growing in Jeeto's backyard juxtaposed with the image of the hardy hydrangeas planted by Ruma's father. The act of transplanting nursery-bought hydrangea plants and the variable color of the hydrangea flowers, which depends on the alkalinity of the soil, function as symbols of the adaptability of immigrants, just as the metaphor of "unaccustomed earth" speaks of a larger geological scale and human mutability. I conclude my discussion of these two texts by returning to Crèvecoeur's question, "Who is an American?," and shift the answer from race to other claims to citizenship that Crèvecoeur emphasizes—grit, enterprise, determination, and an identification with forgotten antecedents—so that identity is inscribed by present-day South Asian immigrants through continuing in the footsteps of the Mexidus, lascars, servants, and farmers who settled here and called it home.

Notes

1. Individuals from the Indian subcontinent were labeled "East Indians" to distinguish them from Native Americans in eighteenth-century print culture.

2. A cursory demographic analysis of early immigrants from South Asia, a group that largely consisted of lascars, indentured servants, domestic help, slaves, and farm, railroad, and lumber mill workers, provides a strikingly different portrait of the South Asian community than the affluent, upwardly mobile self-image embraced by post-1960s immigrants from the Indian subcontinent. While scholarly work has done much to illuminate the little-known history of early South Asians in North America (see, e.g., Jensen; Takaki; Leonard, *Making*, *Roots*; Prashad; Shah; Bald; Kaur), cultural amnesia about the working-class history of the earliest pioneers continues to persist.

3. In "Indian Slaves in Colonial America," Francis C. Assisi cites 2006 archaeological reports from the Colonial Williamsburg Foundation that identify Tony, an "East Indian" servant bought to America as headright by George Menefie, a wealthy English merchant, in 1622. Menefie was granted 485 hectares of land near Jamestown because he had paid the passage of twenty-four immigrants, including Tony. *Headright* refers to the legal grant of land, usually fifty acres, that was given to settlers during the earliest phase of European settlement in North America.

4. For more information on the Mexidus, see Karen Leonard's field-defining research in *Making Ethnic Choices: California's Punjabi-Mexican-Americans*. According to Leonard, "In California in the early twentieth century, some 400 immigrant men from India's Punjab province married Mexican and Mexican-American women. These couples and their children formed a biethnic community in rural California. Called by others 'Mexican-Hindus,' 'Mexidus,' 'Punjabi Mexicans,' or 'half-and-halves,' they generally called themselves 'Hindus'" ("Intermarriage" 147).

5. For more on India and Indians in the early American imaginary, see Kaur and Arora.

6. The term *model minority* was coined in 1966 by the sociologist William Petersen in an article he wrote for *The New York Times* titled "Success Story, Japanese-American Style." Petersen stressed that family structure and a cultural emphasis on hard work allowed Japanese Americans to overcome discrimination and achieve success. The term has been widely critiqued for a problematic deployment of cultural traits to displace racial characteristics; see, for example, Wu.

7. Beyond what Ian Haney López has argued, racial attitudes tended to be much laxer in the fluid and chaotic social world of postrevolutionary America. Consider, for instance, the case of Thomas Law, an employee of the British East India Company who chose to settle in America in order to give his mixed-race children born of an Indian woman a better chance of integrating and being accepted into polite society.

8. For one such mixed-race family whose ancestors were from India, consider the Weaver family, of "East Indian" origin. A fascinating discussion thread of a search for roots by descendants of the Weavers can be found at www.afrigeneas .com/forum-fpoc/index.cgi?md=read;id=2450.

Works Cited

Assisi, Francis C. "Indian Slaves in Colonial America." *India Currents*, 16 May 2007, indiacurrents.com/indian-slaves-in-colonial-america/.

Backhaus, Bhira. *Under the Lemon Trees*. Thomas Dunne Books, 2009.

Bald, Vivek. *Bengali Harlem and the Lost Histories of South Asian America*. Harvard UP, 2015.

Crèvecoeur, J. Hector St. John de. *Letters from an American Farmer*. Fox, Duffield, 1904. *Library of Congress*, www.loc.gov/item/04012106/.

Haney López, Ian. *White by Law: The Legal Construction of Race*. New York UP, 1996.

Jensen, Joan M. *Passage from India: Asian Indian Immigrants in North America*. Yale UP, 1988.

Kaur, Rajender. "The Curious Case of Sick Keesar: Tracing the Roots of South Asian Presence in the Early Republic." *Journal of Transnational American Studies*, vol. 8, no. 1, 2017, pp. 1–26.

Kaur, Rajender, and Anupama Arora. "India in the American Imaginary, 1780s–1880s." Introduction. *India in the American Imaginary, 1780s–1880s*, edited by Arora and Kaur, Palgrave Macmillan, 2017, pp. 3–37.

Keesar, Sick, et al. "Memorial and Representation of the Underwritten Mr. Sick Keesar First Lieutenant, in Behalf of Himself and Thirty Four Others." 14 Dec. 1785. *Papers of the Continental Congress*, no. 69, vol. 2, p. 537.

Koshy, Susan. "Neoliberal Family Matters." *American Literary History*, vol. 25, no. 2, summer 2013, pp. 344–80.

Lahiri, Jhumpa. *Unaccustomed Earth*. Alfred A. Knopf, 2008.

Leonard, Karen. "Intermarriage and Ethnicity: Punjabi Mexican Americans, Mexican Japanese, and Filipino Americans." *Ethnic Studies*, vol. 16, no. 2, July 1993, pp. 147–63.

———. *Making Ethnic Choices: California's Punjabi-Mexican-Americans.* Temple UP, 1994.

Parmeshwaran, Uma. "Dispelling the Spells of Memory: Another Approach to Reading Our Yesterdays." *Diaspora and Multiculturalism: Common Traditions and New Developments*, edited by Monika Fludernik, Rodopi, 2003, pp. xxxix–xliv.

Petersen, William. "Success Story, Japanese-American Style." *The New York Times*, 9 Jan. 1966, timesmachine.nytimes.com/timesmachine/1966/01/09/356013502.html.

"Petition of James Dunn, an East Indian Boy 1790s." Pennsylvania Abolition Society papers, The Historical Society of Pennsylvania, collection 0490, series IV, box 2, folder 13.

Prashad, Vijay. *The Karma of Brown Folk*. U of Minnesota P, 2001.

Roots in the Sand. Directed by Jayasri Majumdar Hart, 1994.

Rothstein, Mervyn. "India's Post-Rushdie Generation; Young Writers Leave Magic Realism and Look at Reality." *The New York Times*, 3 July 2000, www.nytimes.com/2000/07/03/books/india-s-post-rushdie-generation-young-writers-leave-magic-realism-look-reality.html.

Shah, Nayan. *Stranger Intimacy: Contesting Race, Sexuality and the Law in the North American West*. U of California P, 2011.

Srikanth, Rajini. "What Lies Beneath: Lahiri's Brand of Desirable Difference." *Naming Jhumpa Lahiri: Canons and Controversies*, edited by Lavina Dhingra and Floyd Cheung, Lexington Books, 2012, pp. 51–74.

Takaki, Ronald T. *Strangers from a Different Shore: A History of Asian Americans*. Little, Brown, 1998.

United States, Congress. A Bill to Establish an Uniform Rule of Naturalization, and to Enable Aliens to Hold Lands under Certain Restrictions. 4 Mar. 1790. *Library of Congress*, www.loc.gov/item/rbpe.21301100/.

Wu, Ellen D. *The Color of Success: Asian Americans and the Origins of the Model Minority*. Princeton UP, 2014.

Esther Daimari

Teaching Nepali Anglophone Diasporic Literature

At Tezpur University, where I teach literature, a revision of the syllabus saw the introduction of Manjushree Thapa as part of an undergraduate elective course in South Asian literature. The teaching of her novel *Seasons of Flight* invites questions about the representation of migration, home, diaspora, and postcolonialism in Nepali anglophone diasporic literature. As is evident from classroom discussions on the text, students seem to ignore the layered historical context of Nepal as a country that was "never formally colonized by the British" but "has some kind of colonial legacy" (Kerr 2). In this regard, a teacher could highlight Nepal's nuanced relationship with colonialism so that students develop a more intricate understanding of the context and the politics of Nepali anglophone diasporic writings. As Bishupal Limbu highlights, "[T]he 'enabling violation' of colonization that gave rise to literary production in English in countries such as India was never part of Nepal's inheritance" (86). Limbu argues that Nepali anglophone literature cannot be considered part of the "postcolonial banal" (87) and that these works do not ask the same questions as anglophone Indian literature, even if they might seem to. In light of this argument, can *Seasons of Flight* be read as a postcolonial text? If yes, how? Instructors can teach postcolonialism in *Seasons of Flight* through themes of diaspora, migration, globalization, and neocolonialism in Nepal. I suggest that students read about Nepal's history (I recommend John Whelpton's *A History of Nepal*, which presents a concise history of Nepal from the eighteenth century to the twenty-first century) before diving into the literary texts. Lectures and assignments on the history of Nepal, from the Anglo-Nepalese War of 1814–16 to the present, help students explore the historical and political contexts of the texts.

Instructors can use the Anglo-Nepalese War and the subsequent Treaty of Sagauli, signed in 1816, as an entry point to explain Nepal's relationship with the British and with the English language. The British recruitment of Gurkha soldiers after the treaty allowed the spread of English education in Nepal as well as Nepali migration to various parts of British imperial outposts. It is important to remember that modernity reached Nepal not directly through colonialism but mainly through contact with other nations as a result of globalization as the country gradually opened up to the outside world in the 1950s. The country's close connection and unrestricted movement to previously colonized countries like India also initiated its population, especially the middle class, to imbibe Indian and Western patterns of consumption of modernity. Instructors might highlight how Thapa, in *Seasons of Flight*, refers to America as an "agent of corporate capitalist expansionism" (66) and shows the gradual infiltration of Western development models in Nepal. Thapa's protagonist, Prema, works for an NGO in Nepal whose mission is to teach villagers the philosophy and practice of conservation—"to offset the carbon footprint of a British corporation" (16). Prema soon begins to question the validity of such developmental projects based on Western models because, first, the talk about conservation sounds futile in a world destroyed by war, and second, because "they were coaxing the poor, who already consumed so little, to consume even less" (16). Therefore, while the concern of Nepali writing in English does not seem to react to or critique the colonizer and the empire explicitly, the text hints at a critique of neocolonialism, the wide divide between developed and underdeveloped countries, and Western ideas of development that rarely lead to genuine development in developing countries. Contemporary Nepali diasporic authors who write in English, such as Thapa, write with a sense of urgency to translate to the world the experience that emerges from the disturbed sociopolitical conditions of a nation straddling age-old traditions and the newfound and supposedly superior modernity of the West.

Nepali migration to the West—to the United States and the United Kingdom, for example—is a recent phenomenon compared with other South Asian countries that have experienced emigration since the 1950s. Poverty, lack of economic and educational opportunities, and political unrest in Nepal—its struggle with nationalism, insurgency, and democracy—are the main reasons for migration. Thapa highlights the limited choices available to individuals; they can either flee the country or be embroiled in poverty and various politics in society and state. Thapa's *Seasons of Flight* is an excellent text to explore the poetics and politics of Nepali migration and diasporic literature because it pays equal attention to cultural and historical specificities. The novel deals with the experiences of a first-generation Nepali immigrant in America named Prema and highlights her struggles with a different culture and with her sense of self. The text raises provocative questions about both Nepali and Western society and the anxiety of a Nepali immigrant in these contexts. Instructors can lead the discussion on the text by asking questions such as "Why does Prema migrate to America?" or "Why does Prema leave Nepal?"

These questions help students focus on the nature of diaspora. The nature of diaspora, Nepalis' relationship with the hostland and the homeland, is largely determined by the conditions of the dispersal: Were Nepalis forced out of their homeland (as, for example, in the case of Africans or Jews), or did they flee from Nepal? Or were they taken as prisoners? The novel suggests that in the case of Nepalis, more specifically Prema, diaspora results from voluntary exile because of problematic situations at home or emigration in search of job opportunities. Instructors can ask students to read the first nine chapters of the novel and to discuss how these chapters show poverty, war, human rights abuses, and a desire for freedom as the main reasons for Prema's decision to migrate to America. Prema recounts how from the very beginning she had conceived of Nepal as a land of sorrows and limited opportunities, especially for poorer families like hers. Thus, when her friends leave Nepal before she does, she finds herself rationalizing their decision: "There was so little in Nepal, everyone just wanted to leave" (Thapa 17). Instructors might also cite the episode from the chapter "The Boy Who Disappeared" (60–65) in which the cybercafe owner, Kancha, is abducted by the army, never to be found again, as an instance that connects the act of migration with human rights abuses and Maoist insurgency in Nepal.

However, Prema's final decision to leave Nepal for America is facilitated by her winning the Diversity Visa lottery available to people from countries with low levels of immigration to the United States. Once in America, she juggles jobs and works for a long time as the caretaker of a white woman named Esther. Thapa highlights that Nepali migrants' positions in Western countries demonstrate a pattern that responds to the British and American demand for labor. Unlike other South Asian migrants, such as Indian migrants, who arrive in America primarily as students or professionals, Nepali migrants tend to be mainly working-class. The novel highlights how America's multiculturalism and more open and inclusive policies regarding immigrants make it a much sought-after destination for Nepalis in terms of ease of arrival and as a permanent place to settle. The instructor could initiate a discussion on the arrival of Nepalis as immigrants in America and their journey toward becoming a diaspora. Prema seems to prefer to assimilate rather than hold on to her ethnic identity and culture. Thapa juxtaposes Prema's die-hard effort to become an American (and not a hyphenated Nepali American) by adjusting, assimilating, and adopting American culture with the preferences of Little Nepal's residents. Prema's foremost hosts in America—Sushil and Neeru, who live in Little Nepal—value keeping close contact with other Nepalis and Nepali culture. The chapter "Little Nepal" (107–14) illustrates the formation of small Nepali communities in America that ironically provide nothing close to the American dreams of the immigrants. The chapter presents Little Nepal as a closed Nepali community of about twenty families, and while in Little Nepal, "Prema did not feel that she had actually reached America" (112). The Nepalis there are "half-modern, half-traditional" people (108), struggling to make a living in America. Sushil works as a pizza deliveryman, and Neeru works in a shopping complex. The novel suggests that the residents of Little Nepal stick to jobs as drivers or waitresses and hardly mingle with outsiders. They seem to participate in what Bandita Sijapati calls "reverse assimilation," or "reinforcing ethnic or national identity, especially in benign terms, rather than assimilating into mainstream America" (249). Perhaps the practice of conservatism and assertion of their original identity in an alien landscape gives them a sense of belonging and connection with their homeland. Instructors might invite students to ponder how Thapa's representation highlights hardships in America and how low wages and job instability force Nepali immigrants with lower educational qualifications to stick to ethnic neighborhoods in order to increase their chances of employment. Sticking together, however, reduces their chances of assimilation with the mainstream culture.

Subsequent discussions of the text might consider Prema's aspirations to leave Little Nepal and reach the America of her dreams. As Prema moves into a more multicultural space in America, the instructor could raise questions about what Prema's experiences in America are like, what challenges Prema faces, and how she constructs her identity in America.

The first thing that Prema does to pose herself as an American is to challenge herself to get out of Little Nepal and find a job and accommodations. Prema's struggles in this endeavor suggest that assimilation in America is more complex than she had imagined it might be. For Prema, the process of learning a new language and imbibing American ways and manners is a humiliating experience, and she is not readily accepted as an American. Identity is a major issue for Prema. She desires to escape her Nepali identity, and at the same time, she is equally disturbed by Americans' ignorance and misinterpretation of Nepal.

Thapa suggests that one of the main problems a Nepali immigrant faces in America is that people seem oblivious to the existence of a country called "Nepal." Prema tries to help the Americans by providing cues such as "'It is near India' or 'Where Mount Everest is,' 'You have heard of the Sherpas?'" (Thapa 11). Sometimes, Americans even mistake Nepal for *nipple* or for the Italian city of Naples. Most writings from Nepal seem to evolve from this sense of uneasiness at being ignored or oversimplified and mostly misunderstood by the rest of the world.

Here, the instructor could introduce Edward Said's theory of Orientalism to elucidate Prema's experiences in America. In *Orientalism*, Said highlights how colonialism molded a relationship between the dominant West and the Middle and Far East, seen as inferior, by positioning the two as opposites—the superior Occident and the inferior Orient. This relationship is based on the European colonizers' dominance over and oppression of the colonized territories. It has led to racial binaries that posit "us" against "them" and "self" against "other." Said's theory is relevant to a discussion of the tendency to other those seen as inferior in dominant Western culture, including in the American context, and how this leads to prejudice and racism that affects the lives of migrants even in the twenty-first century. Even in this age of globalization, such hegemonic worldviews persist. Said explains as follows:

> It is hegemony, or rather the result of cultural hegemony at work, that gives Orientalism the durability and the strength I have been speaking about. . . . [It is] a collective notion identifying "us" Europeans against all "those" non-Europeans, and indeed it can be argued that the major

component in European culture is precisely what made that culture hegemonic both inside and outside Europe: the idea of European identity as a superior one in comparison with all the non-European peoples and cultures. (7)

Prema begins an affair with Luis Reyes, who explains his attraction to her by saying, "There's something so *elemental* about you" (Thapa 102); his notion of "elemental" represents Western ways of seeing people from South Asia. Luis uses the term "elemental" to highlight the contrast between his own cultural background and Prema's Nepalese heritage. It refers to something basic or fundamental in Prema that conveys to Luis a sense of authenticity untouched by modern influences. Their discussion of Nepal foregrounds the country as a seemingly backward place devoid of modern amenities like electricity, mobile phones, television, and so on. Prema's relationship with Luis ultimately fails because Luis never fails to remind Prema of her Nepali origins through his exotic associations with both Nepal and Prema. Even as Prema moves to a more multicultural space, she is always conscious of her difference. Prema sometimes blends in with her fair skin but never entirely escapes othering or exoticization. She is sometimes assumed to be a Mexican or an Indian, and she does not challenge such assumptions; instead, she often assumes an Indian identity, rejecting her Nepali identity. Prema herself seems to place the immigrant Nepali identity at the bottom of the hierarchy of American immigrant identities and struggles with an urgent desire to escape that identity, even though Nepal is "deep-set in her psyche" (Lahiri 80) and is, therefore, inescapable.

It is interesting to note that Prema herself participates in exoticization of the other, constantly exoticizing America and her boyfriend—"You are exotic" (Thapa 102). Prema wishes to give up Nepal for America, to move from the traditional to the modern and from a regressive world to a progressive one. She aims to reinvent herself in America, severing ties with anything that is Nepali. Instructors could ask students to make a list of the things that Prema does to reinvent herself. (Students could also write an essay on this topic.) The list might include Prema's decision to sever ties with Rajan, to leave Little Nepal, to date an American man, and to adopt a more wanton sex life. Prema believes that she has reached America after she starts dating and living with the American Luis Reyes. However, after the two break up, Prema is overcome by a sense of rootlessness, and she even considers going back to Nepal. However, a chance meeting with Fiona, an environmentalist actively engaged in search of an endangered species of butterflies called El Segundo Blues, introduces her to a new group of friends and associates from various professions who recognize her experience and skills as a conservationist. She is later hired by a nonprofit organization, which allows her to become part of the group of skilled Nepali migrants and facilitates a higher-level and seemingly successful assimilation into mainstream American culture. However, until the end, Prema continues to straddle a Nepali identity and an American identity, which results in what Homi Bhabha calls "cultural hybridity." Using Said's ideas of the self and the other, Bhabha propagates the idea of "hybridity" and the "Third space" that allows the interaction between cultures that brings about a "cultural hybridity" (36–37). Bhabha asserts that perfect assimilation is not possible; rather, there is always a hybridity of some sort in the postcolonial condition of migration, diaspora, displacement, and relocation. Prema is finally reasonably assimilated into the American world, though her Nepali roots continue to show themselves in the form of her values, habits, and language.

Nevertheless, she resolves to remain in America. Does Prema suffer from guilt? A part of her does seem to suffer from guilt for leaving Nepal and for not being hopeful about Nepal like Rajan or her Maoist sister, Bijaya, which is also reflected in her interest in and sense of affinity to the people and histories of Guatemala. And although Prema considers going back to Nepal, she ultimately chooses to remain in America. For her and others she represents, America, despite all the challenges, evolves into the place where they want to live.

The novel suggests that since Nepalis migrate from a place of social and political unrest, they look for shores that offer permanent settlement. Prema is representative of those migrants who choose to leave the ancestral homeland in order to make a home elsewhere. In this regard, students should be encouraged to understand the author's treatment of the concept of "home" and how *Seasons of Flight* perpetuates or challenges traditional ideas of home. How important are home and nation to Nepali immigrants in the novel? What is their approach to returning to the homeland? Sara Ahmed's article "Home and Away: Narratives of Migration and Estrangement" can be used to approach the concept of "home" and to address how the idea of home is interlaced with images of migration, identity, estrangement, and community. Ahmed highlights the possibility of "many homes," nevertheless differentiating between the "real home," a lost home that is tied to the past, and a new home in the future (330). A link between the subject and the real home is the memory of home, which seems to fail over time. Thapa suggests in *Seasons of Flight* that although Nepal may be part of the living memory of Nepalis, they do not wish to return to it.

In this regard, students could be encouraged to consider that migration is a heterogeneous phenomenon and that it is the individual or the community to which that individual belongs that gives meaning to migration. *Seasons of Flight* highlights the complexity of Nepali migration to the West, showing how immigrants negotiate between viewing migration as a way of breaking away from local cultures, as a state of permanent exile (where nowhere is truly home), and as a strong desire to escape to some other home. Given the circumstances in Nepal, Prema strives to recreate her identity in America and make America her new home; however, her original homeland remains a constant frame of reference as she compares her experiences in America with those in Nepal. *Seasons of Flight* dramatizes the complex relationship that most immigrants from Nepal have to their homeland. The novel does not feature the kind of nostalgia for the homeland seen in the works of writers from other South Asian countries— a kind of "reductive desire for home through painful recollection" (Tolia-Kelly 59). Instead, there is a strong sense of escape and relief at being able to give up the original homeland, no matter how difficult it was initially to arrive at the decision.[1]

The following question could be posed toward the end of a discussion of *Seasons of Flight*: Do Nepali anglophone diasporic writers like Thapa add another dimension to the meaning of home and diaspora? William Safran's examination of different types of diaspora is useful in answering this question. The idea of diaspora originated with the Jews' search for their original homeland, suggesting that the desire for connection (real or imaginary), return, and memory of the original land remains intact in diasporic individuals and communities. Safran suggests that while the concept of diaspora once had a "very specific meaning: the exile of the Jews from their historic homeland and their dispersion throughout many lands, signifying as well the oppression and moral degradation implied by that dispersion" (83), today the term *diaspora* can be applied to various communities or groups that have experienced forced or voluntary dispersion from their original homeland and have established new communities in different parts of the world.

According to Safran, some diasporic communities "regard their ancestral homeland as their true, ideal home and as the place to which they or their descendants would (or should) eventually return—when conditions are appropriate" (83–84). Safran cites the example of those in the Chinese diasporas in Southeast Asia who wish to make enough money to return to their homeland (89). Still, Safran writes, "some diasporas persist—and their members do not go 'home'—because there is no homeland to which to return; because, although a homeland may exist, it is not a welcoming place with which they can identify politically, ideologically, or socially; or because it would be too inconvenient and disruptive, if not traumatic, to leave the diaspora" (91). For the characters in *Seasons of Flight*, Nepal is an undesirable place of return. Despite all the challenges it presents for the Nepali immigrant, the hostland is where characters choose to settle. *Seasons of Flight* suggests that the Nepali diasporic experience is unique because of the desire of Nepalis to be accepted as global citizens. They do not want to be constantly reminded of their roots in Nepal. The Nepali migrant characters in the novel go through a drastic process of readjustment, and they reconstruct themselves through the dynamic processes of cultural mixing, changing, and becoming. Therefore, the quest for Prema in the novel is also for Nepal to be conceptualized as part of the global collective and not as other, to generate more tolerance and acceptance among diverse nations and traditions, and to merge and assimilate. In this way, Thapa's text brings in overlooked aspects of Nepali life and experience and adds a great deal to a course on South Asian literature.

Note

1. See Lahiri 82, which also reads *Seasons of Flight* as a narrative of escape from Nepal to America.

Works Cited

Ahmed, Sara. "Home and Away: Narratives of Migration and Estrangement." *International Journal of Cultural Studies*, vol. 2, no. 3, Dec. 1999, pp. 329–47.

Bhabha, Homi K. *The Location of Culture*. Routledge, 1994.

Kerr, Rosemary. *Planning and Practice: Factors Impacting on the Development of Initial Education in Nepal, with Special Reference to English Language Teaching, 1950–1995*. 1999. Victoria University of Technology, PhD dissertation.

Lahiri, Himadri. "Diaspora from the Himalayan Region: Nation and Modernity in Select Literary Works." *Asiatic*, vol. 11, no. 1, June 2017, pp. 69–85.

Limbu, Bishupal. "Democracy, Perhaps: Collectivity, Kinship, and the Politics of Friendship." *Comparative Literature*, vol. 63, no. 1, winter 2011, pp. 86–110.

Safran, William. "Diasporas in Modern Societies: Myths of Homeland and Return." *Diaspora: A Journal of Transnational Studies*, vol. 1, no. 1, spring 1991, pp. 83–99.

Said, Edward W. *Orientalism*. Penguin Books, 1978.

Sijapati, Bandita. "Being and Belonging: Mapping the Experiences of Nepali Immigrants in the United States." *Globalization in the Himalayas: Belonging and the Politics of the Self: Governance, Conflicts, and Civic Action*, edited by Gerard Toffin and Joanna Pfaff-Czarnecka, vol. 5, Sage, 2014, pp. 233–63.

Thapa, Manjushree. *Seasons of Flight*. Aleph, 2012.

Tolia-Kelly, Divya Praful. *Landscape, Race and Memory: Material Ecologies of Citizenship*. Routledge, 2010.

Whelpton, John. *A History of Nepal*. Cambridge UP, 2005.

Part V

East Meets North: The Sri Lankan Refugee Diaspora

Umme Al-wazedi

Reimagining the Refugee Crisis through Sharon Bala's *The Boat People*

Migration crises brought on by mass refugee movements are transforming societies worldwide, including the South Asian diaspora in the United States and Canada. Refugee settlements in the South Asian diaspora bring together a history of violence, marginalization, and the classifications of refugees. Nicholas Van Hear argues that such mass displacements have led to what is known as "refugee diasporas" (180). This essay focuses on the complex nature of the South Asian refugee diaspora and of refugee diasporas in general, which are made up of legal immigrants from the same country as the refugees, asylum seekers, and their children. My goal is to help students reimagine and recontextualize who a refugee is. Most often, the residents of the host country, including those who have migrated legally from the same country as the refugees, may look at such diasporas suspiciously because "the role of diasporas is now more often seen as ambiguous" (181). Sharon Bala's *The Boat People* reflects the ambiguity identified by Van Hear. The novel shows how often the Sri Lankan diaspora is questioned regarding its support of the Tamil Tigers. At the same time, the novel shows the diaspora supporting the refugees and thus protesting the images of "the queue-jumper, the terrorist and the breeder" (Krishnamurti 140) that are created for the national imaginary. I teach Bala's novel as part of my honors course, Migration Fiction, in order to point out some of these ambiguities and stereotypical images. In addition, many people in North America, including college students, have shown skepticism over the increasing inflows of refugees. Not all refugees arrive by boats, however. Arriving through airports can also be a site of discrimination for refugees. Yet, there is a lack of understanding as to why people leave their homelands. At the same time, many do not understand that "one's capacity to migrate is shaped by class or socioeconomic standing, access to resources, and associated network" (Van Hear 181; see also Martin 136–37). The anti-immigrant and anti-refugee rhetoric of persecution, incrimination and confrontation is widespread in today's media and in the rhetoric of some policymakers. Having noticed such sentiments, I focus on what Robert Hattam and Danielle Every advocate: "practices that are inflected by notions of restorative justice" (422). The center of restorative justice, as I see it, is ethical development and reflecting on what is "good" or on who a "good citizen" is.

A series of fundamental questions guide my pedagogical approach to Bala's novel. These questions have been asked by countless others, particularly by Alice Bloch. First, what was the refugee's life like before migration, and what stories of that life and the journey are shared? How are these stories perceived by the recipients? (For my class and this essay, the recipients are the Canadian people, refugee lawyers and social workers, and the Sri Lankan diasporic population.) Second, "how does the second generation from the refugee [or legal immigrant] backgrounds make sense of silences and narrative gaps" (Bloch 648)? In this essay I discuss how I use Bloch's two questions to frame the teaching of Bala's novel and the impact of the novel on students' understanding of the effect of wars and displacement—and the subsequent creation of the refugees—and their observations on ethical, political, geographic, and imaginative articulations of home in an era of mass mobilities and geopolitical crises. *The Boat People* is a challenging counternarrative about refugees that helps students interpret contemporary media and current events that focus on the Global South that students are anxious to understand and respond to. I use two assignments to assess the impact of Bala's novel. The first assignment asks students to lead a discussion. As discussion leaders, students assume the role of a debater, and they bring discussion questions to class. The second assignment is a written reflection of one to two pages (single-spaced) that asks students to respond to the following prompt:

> Imagine that you own a small publishing company and that you decide to write a review, the purpose of which is to convince people to read a book that you have published, in this case Bala's *The Boat People*. Convince your readers by making arguments about why they should read *The Boat People*. Do not summarize the plot or list themes or ideas from the novel. In writing this review, discuss at least one of the following: the poem "Refugees," by Brian Bilstone; the song "Borders," by M.I.A.; or Timothy K. August's "The Refugee Image" (*Refugee Aesthetic* 25–54).

I begin class by asking students to read texts that focus on the debate on the contemporary refugee crisis. We read former president Donald Trump's 2016 speech. In this speech, Trump spoke of an elusive caravan coming from the southern border to take over the United States, urging his listeners to be prepared to defend themselves against this unknown and invisible mass. Then we look at Michèle Lamont, Bo Yun Park, and Elena Ayala-Hurtado's study, which focuses on the rhetoric of Trump's campaign messages. We discuss how Trump "equated immigrants to criminal aliens" when he said that they were "guilty of murder, assault, rape, and all manner of violent crime" (Lamont et al. 169). Even though the immediate impact of such rhetoric is felt in the United States, similar sentiments can be seen in Canada. For instance, Bala's novel presents the voice of a government official who states, "The vessel and its illegal passengers are part of a larger criminal organization. Make no mistake, there are terrorists on board. We must not let the smugglers win" (145). To challenge these stereotypes, I have students read "Refugees," a palindrome poem by the *Twitter* poet Brian Bilstone that needs to be read from top to bottom and then from bottom to top, with the last line becoming the first. Reading this poem allows students to see the stereotypical image of refugees that has been cultivated in Trump's *Twitter* posts and the right-wing media's representation of refugees. For my students, the most emphatic lines of the poems were the following: "These haggard faces could belong to you, or me / Should life have dealt a different hand / We need to see them for who they really are." Students were surprised by the form of the poem, but on further reflection, they came to understand the poet's attempt to subvert the stereotypical portrayal of the displaced people. They noticed that the poem doesn't have a single punctuation mark, as if the poet is trying to finish speaking in one breath and thus advocating an urgent response. When they read from the bottom up, students were able to see the other side of the story. With the stereotypical images shattered and Bilstone's counterimages in mind, students began reading Bala's novel, which brought the refugee characters alive.

Along with Bilstone's poem, I give a lecture on how the West sees refugees and on the history of the phrase *boat people*. It is important for students to know that migration by boat or ship is linked to indentured labor. The phrase *boat people* was also used to refer to the Vietnamese who came to the United States as refugees following the end of the Vietnam War in 1975. Refugees are often seen as "object[s] of concern," "speechless emissaries," "mute victims," or as individuals without "unique identities" (Karunanayake 184). Such epithets deny refugees the authority to provide credible narrative testimony about their condition. To explain the significance of such epithets, I introduce the phrase "crimmigrant nations," coined by Robert Koulish and Maartje van der Woude. According to Koulish and Van der Woude, "these sentiments are being translated into actual policies and practices that contribute to a merger of crime control and migration control, with devastating effects for those falling under its reach. This merger has been referred to as the phenomenon of 'crimmigration'" (1). Koulish and Van der Woude's argument helps students see how refugees have been framed within a nation. Making students aware of a process whereby a refugee comes to be considered a criminal is one way that I focus on advocating for restorative justice. Restorative justice is a different way of thinking that goes beyond judging and blaming refugees; it is about caring for refugees and reflecting on the national imaginary. So, when students read Grace and Blair's narrative about the Tamil Tigers being "terrorists" (Bala 41), their awareness of how refugees are framed as criminals, as underscored in Karunanayake's and Koulish and Van der Woude's arguments, helps them think about restorative justice.

Before the discussion of *The Boat People*, it is essential to highlight the history of the Sri Lankan Civil War and the role of the Tamil Tigers. Otherwise there is a danger of seeing the Tamil Tigers as terrorists, as noted above, a controversy discussed in detail by Maryse Jayasuriya in her book *Terror and Reconciliation: Sri Lankan Anglophone Literature, 1983–2009*. Therefore, a lecture on the civil war and the Tamil Tigers requires careful researching of multiple sources such as websites and critical articles to avoid biases and help students understand what life was like before this group of people became refugees. Bala notes some of the prominent sources that she used to write *The Boat People* in a section at the back of the book titled "Author's Note" (326–35). Bala also discusses the Liberation Tigers of Tamil Eelam and the Sri Lankan Civil War from an outsider's perspective. Fred Blair, a conservative politician, defines the Liberation Tigers of Tamil Eelam as "the separationist group better known as the Tamil Tigers, who had been waging war against the Sri Lankan government for more than twenty years," and accuses them of regrouping in Canada (Bala 40). Blair's description certainly sets up the Tamils as the enemy of the state, one that had influenced Priya's father, a legal immigrant in Canada who didn't allow Priya to have anything to do with the Tamils (47). The scene where Priya recalls her father forbidding her to have anything to do with Sri Lankans enables students to connect the incident to Van Hear's argument about the ambiguous nature of diasporas.

When teaching *The Boat People*, I highlight what occurred before migration or displacement, which is a fantastic way to help students connect with a particular character's life. For example, Bala describes the reasons why the main character, Mahindan, leaves Sri Lanka with his son. While Mahindan tells his story about the conflict in Sri Lanka, readers simultaneously see how he is perceived by people in Canada—individuals in immigration offices such as the immigration lawyer, Gigovaz. For example, Mahindan is asked to shave cleanly before appearing in court as we hear Gigovaz claim, "A brown man with a beard begging for asylum? Not on my watch" (Bala 51). Here Bala demonstrates the multiple levels of identity that a refugee like Mahindan must juggle—between being a noncitizen with perceived criminal intentions, a "conditional citizen" (Lalami 22), and a future model citizen. Through a close reading of the novel, students come to understand that Mahindan is set against Prasad, another refugee, because Prasad was a "journalist in Columbo, he had a degree and spoke fluent English. . . . He's our bet. Our model migrant" (Bala 51). This is a critical place to stop and help students critique the role of multiculturalism in Canada, "a contested space where legal and policy frameworks intersect with immigration policies, settlement services, and hegemonic discourses of nation-building" (George 462). Students realize that only the English-speaking educated person can be a citizen of a civilized country—this is the narrative that Mahindan picks up, which ultimately affects his personality. It is also important to closely read the chapter "Judge, Jury, and Executioner" (Bala 259–61). Grace—whom students and I struggle to understand because she seems to lack empathy for both her mother, who was taken to the Japanese internment camp, and the asylum seekers whom she deals with—thinks that if the refugees follow the rules, then they should have no problem proving themselves innocent of any crime (261). But Mitchell draws attention to the complexity of the situation, noting that refugees may be coerced into doing illegal things, and points to child soldiers who can't decide for themselves whether they want to join the war or not (261). In the course of our discussions, students come to see how ambiguous the situation is for Mahindan, who thought that if he could escape war-torn Sri Lanka, he would be able to find peace and a safe home in Canada. Students realize that Mahindan faces a terrible reality: his "relationship to the state is at least partly determined by the color of [his] skin, the nature of [his] creed, [his] gender identity, or [his] national origin" (Lalami 22).

To help students understand refugee children's complex and ambiguous situations, I ask the class to closely read the passages showing Mahindan's struggles as a father. Helping students connect to the children's experiences is another way for me to encourage students to advocate for restorative justice. Mahindan's son, Sellian, is taken away from his father, since a young boy cannot live in a prison cell. Mahindan initially protests but eventually agrees because he sees the possibility of a new life for his son. Yet Sellian's new life presents challenges: Sellian doesn't do well in his foster home; he "started taking things—colored chalk, a classmate's ruler, the chocolates from schoolchildren's lunches. Nothing of value, just small-small things. They had found the box under his bed where he hoarded his treasures" (Bala 213). There was nothing Mahindan could do, students thought, and they were bothered by it. On one visit to the prison, a happier Sellian tells Mahindan about all his accomplishments. Mahindan feels a pang in his heart at the thought of his son moving on: "this boy who was his son but looked and spoke like someone else's" (329). Students link Mahindan's frustration with Sellian to his rejection of Prasad's bright future. Students sense the anger Mahindan feels toward Prasad, who seems well positioned to transition to a free life in Canada, yet students are surprised by the hostility Mahindan harbors toward him: "What Mahindan wouldn't give to trade places with him. Was there anything he wouldn't do? . . . [B]y summer Prasad would have picked up the accents too. He would pass to the other side, while Mahindan remained stuck here" (247–48). Students feel empathy for Mahindan and see that his loss of his son and his thwarted dream of a successful future in Canada make him think negatively about the prosperity of others. Students notice that coming to Canada may have given Mahindan one kind of imagined freedom, yet his past restricts his real freedom.

While thinking about Charlie, Priya, and Grace and their relationship with the Tamil refugees, one student, the leader of the discussion that day, posed the following questions: Do victims of intergenerational racial trauma have a responsibility to be activists? If they decide not to be activists, are they part of the problem? How do children of immigrants balance those two sentiments? These questions lead me to encourage students to analyze how each of the characters, second-generation children of immigrants each with their own historical incarceration stories, react, develop, and deliver messages about the refugee condition as well as the policies they see being enacted in front of them. This leads to Bloch's second question. We spend some time examining two characters, Priya and Charlie. Through Priya's first reaction to refugees and her subsequent change and Charlie's care and ethical responsibility for refugees, students get another look at what restorative justice may look like. While Priya is the daughter of a Sri Lankan immigrant, Charlika, or Charlie, is the Tamil Alliance interpreter, "someone both fluently Canadian and authentically Sri Lankan, one of those third-culture people who slipped in and out of identities like shoes" (Bala 46). Priya, however, can't even speak Tamil. Her parents never encouraged her "fraternizing with other Sri Lankans" (47). Her father explicitly asks her not to "get mixed up in all of that" when she tells him she wants to join the Tamil Alliance group on her college campus (47). In the beginning, Priya doesn't understand why her parents feel the way that they do and thinks that perhaps this is their way of assimilating into Canadian society. Later, however, she learns that her uncle came to Canada as a refugee on a boat. Priya doesn't necessarily try to figure out a story from the silences of her uncle's journey. Yet, her conversation with her father and her description of the present-day refugee situation help her father see the need to aid the refugees. As a result, he decides to donate to the Tamil Alliance. Unlike Priya, as students point out, Charlie is very vocal about the conditions of the Tamil refugees. Charlie is against putting them in prison because she thinks they will suffer from post-traumatic stress disorder and depression, which students agreed with (50). As an example, students point to Ranga, a young man who arrives with Mahindan and who later dies by suicide in prison. Charlie is the only one who makes it a point to say, in a whisper, that the Tamil refugees were being "led in chains like slaves!" (51). Therefore, students were very much inclined to point out that Charlie is the model who carries restorative justice in her heart.

I reinforce the notion of multiple complexities by showing the music video for the song "Borders," by M.I.A. (Maya Arulpragasam), a famous rapper, singer, designer, producer, and refugee from Sri Lanka. Yet the video does not escape students' critique with respect to its sensationalism. The first question students ask after seeing the video is "Where are the women?" We take some time to discuss the video's presentation of faceless masses of dark-skinned people and how the video obscures female refugees. We talk about migration statistics (male versus female) and we go back to the perceived images of the refugees ("speechless emissaries," "mute victims") to deconstruct what may have been the reasons for M.I.A. to make this video. Then students read August's analysis of the song. August's argument helps students understand the role that novels like *The Boat People* play in destabilizing the traditional image of a refugee by "shift[ing] the refugee image away from serving as a signifier of otherness" and reconceptualizing the actual refugee as a person who suffered the effects of war and displacement (54). The refugees, no longer imagined as huddled masses or enemies of the state, acquire specific names and characteristics in students' minds after they read the novel and watch the music video. Students travel with Charlie, Priya, and Gegovaz, who tackle the tremendous job of translating correctly to ensure the officials record the refugees' authentic papers. As Bala writes, "The legal back-and-forth progressed with infinite slowness, each person speaking only a couple of sentences at a time to allow for translation" (55). It is essential to focus on a sentence or passage like this one in order to help students think about restorative justice—the idea that one should have empathy for refugees and understand the difficulty of the process of entering a country and the implementation of policies that automatically consider the refugees as "criminals." In the process, students learn to challenge assumptions about refugees and to ask thoughtful questions about why people become refugees.

Students realize that a novel like *The Boat People* requires them to recognize "the refugee claimant beyond the discursive images" (Krishnamurti 153). One student wrote that the novel helps readers see not only the refugees' perspectives but also that people of the host country react differently to these perspectives. Another student, while contemplating the ethical, political, geographic, and imaginative articulations of home in an era of mass mobilities and geopolitical crises, saw the relevance of reading Bala's novel. The student felt that when people think that they belong to a certain group, it is easy to see others who do not belong to that group as different, yet those people may have more in common with them than they initially believe. Thus, by the end of the novel and our class discussion, students understand refugees' struggles for fundamental human rights and protection and that their travels and subsequent settlement histories are complex.

Works Cited

August, Timothy K. *The Refugee Aesthetic: Reimagining Southeast Asian America*. Temple UP, 2021.

Bala, Sharon. *The Boat People*. Anchor Books, 2017.

Bilstone, Brian. "Refugees." *National Poetry Day*, nationalpoetryday.co.uk/poem/refugees. Accessed 9 Aug. 2023.

Bloch, Alice. "Talking about the Past, Locating It in the Present: The Second Generation from Refugee Backgrounds Making Sense of Their Parents' Narratives, Narrative Gaps, and Silences." *Journal of Refugee Studies*, vol. 31, no. 4, 2018, pp. 647–63.

"Borders." *YouTube*, uploaded by Vevo, 17 Feb. 2017, www.youtube.com/watch?v=r-Nw7HbaeWY.

George, Glynis. "The Canadian Tamil Diaspora and the Politics of Multiculturalism." *Identities*, vol. 18, no. 5, 2011, pp. 459–80.

Hattam, Robert, and Danielle Every. "Teaching in Fractured Classrooms: Refugee Education, Public Culture, Community, and Ethics." *Race Ethnicity and Education*, vol. 13, no. 4, 2010, pp. 409–24.

Jayasuriya, Maryse. *Terror and Reconciliation: Sri Lankan Anglophone Literature, 1983–2009*. Lexington Books, 2012.

Karunanayake, Dinidu. "Reclaiming Home and 'Righting' Citizenships in Postwar Sri Lanka: Internal Displacement, Memory, and Human Rights." *The Subject(s) of Human Rights: Crises, Violations, and Asian/American Critique*, edited by Cathy J. Schlund-Vials et al., Temple UP, 2020, pp. 180–200.

Koulish, Robert, and Maartje van der Woude, editors. *Crimmigrant Nations: Resurgent Nationalism and the Closing of Borders*. Fordham UP, 2020.

Krishnamurti, Sailaja. "Queue-Jumpers, Terrorists, Breeders: Representations of Tamil Migrants in Canadian Popular Media." *South Asian Diaspora*, vol. 5, no. 1, 2013, pp. 139–57.

Lalami, Laila. *Conditional Citizens: On Belonging in America*. Pantheon Books, 2020.

Lamont, Michèle, et al. "Trump's Electoral Speeches and His Appeal to the American White Working Class." *British Journal of Sociology*, vol. 68, 2017, pp. 153–80.

Martin, Susan. "Migration and Refugee Studies: A US Perspective." *Migration Studies*, vol. 5, no. 1, 2017, pp. 136–39.

Van Hear, Nicholas. "The Rise of Refugee Diaspora." *Current History*, vol. 108, no. 717, 2009, pp. 180–85.

Dinidu Karunanayake

Teaching Sri Lankan American Literature in the American South

Even as the South Asian American community becomes increasingly visible, Sri Lankan America holds a peripheral position in Asian American studies and the public imagination of the United States. South Asians are no longer a "crypto group," as Rajiv Shankar put it over two decades ago (x). Nor are they insulated from the trauma experienced by East and Southeast Asian communities in relation to the US empire, a lack of which once put South Asians outside the house of Asian America (ix). Moreover, hate crimes directed at South Asian communities, ranging from micro-aggressions to mass killings, surged in the post-9/11 context, necessitating alliances among disparate Asian communities and with Indigenous, Black, and Latino movements invested in social justice and civil rights. However, the heterogeneity, hybridity, and multiplicity of South Asian America—which Lisa Lowe recognized as attributes of Asian America—are yet to be adequately acknowledged, impelling a historically underrepresented culture like that of Sri Lanka to be at worst overlooked and at best misrepresented or conflated with the dominant Indian American culture.[1]

As the field of Asian American studies rapidly expands in tandem with the growth of the Asian American community across the United States, student demographics in the Asian American studies classroom are also

174

changing. Whereas early classrooms mainly attracted Asian Americans born in the United States (Chan 28), many classrooms today enroll students from a broad range of ethnic and racial backgrounds. At a time when diversity, equity, and inclusion are becoming cornerstones of college campus curricula across the United States against the backdrop of new forms of racism, white supremacy, and rising hate crimes, it has become even more important to bring critical awareness to the nuances of Asian American experiences. To foster such awareness, instructors must endeavor to put overlooked sites on the map of Asian American pedagogy. Reflecting on two courses I designed and taught at Centre College in Kentucky and Elon University in North Carolina in 2020, this essay maps how I navigate the pedagogy of Sri Lankan American literature in the US undergraduate classroom. In response to the major investments of this volume, I discuss my goals in teaching Sri Lankan American literature while also concentrating on student dynamics and effective pedagogical practices.

The traditional borders of the Asian American studies classroom are changing. The two courses I consider in this essay were advertised as English courses, not Asian American studies courses. Such cross-disciplinary traffic is important to accentuate the relevance of Asian American literature in academia today. At a time of shrinking ethnic American studies programs across the United States—a phenomenon that has only been exacerbated by the COVID-19 pandemic—interdisciplinary disciplines like English make a welcoming environment for Sri Lankan American literature. From a disciplinary perspective, it is useful to unmoor Asian American texts from an exclusively Asian American studies classroom. As Cathy Schlund-Vials reminds us, Asian American studies and ethnic studies cannot "nostalgically rely on history and memory, nor can [they] continue to exist in a monolithic racial vacuum" ("Re-seeing Race" 104). As such, a literature classroom is a pragmatic space to understand the global and historical interconnectedness of race relations.

Sri Lankan America in the College Syllabus

As a faculty member in English who has been trained in the fields of postcolonial literature and Asian American studies, I contextualize Asian American inquiry as mutually constitutive of postcolonial and global neoliberal experiences. To this end, I invoke the work of both Rajini Srikanth and Inderpal Grewal. As Srikanth puts it, on the one hand, South Asian American literature is charged with "supply[ing] the narrative and images that are compelling enough to make readers in the US aware of the gaps in their consciousness, and intriguing enough to move them to fill these gaps by reading with care and living with vision" (33). South Asian literature thus punctures the bubble of disinterest, disengagement, and depersonalization that relatively entitled readers in North America may develop vis-à-vis the far corners of the world that work night and day to ensure a life of convenience for them. Grewal, on the other hand, investigates this exchange from the Asian side in her study of "transnational America": "America functioned as a discourse of neoliberalism making possible struggles for rights through consumerist practices and imaginaries that came to be used both inside and outside the territorial boundaries of the United States" (2). She delineates the production of "American" subjects in postcolonial spaces like South Asia through economic, political, and ideological means (2–3). Therefore, she argues that America cannot be studied singularly within the US territories, and the field of postcolonial studies provides valuable methods to examine the tryst between US imperialism and global culture (2).

I translate Srikanth's and Grewal's ideas into Sri Lankan American literature pedagogy. Sri Lanka and its literature occupy a marginal space in US secondary and postsecondary education. Before starting a discussion of Sri Lanka, I ask students to locate Sri Lanka on a world map and inquire how familiar they are with the country's history, culture, and literature. For many students, Sri Lanka turns out to be an uncharted territory. Srikanth's words, therefore, animate my teaching philosophy, which uses literary and cultural works to fill the gaps in students' consciousness. If the post–World War II global ethos has been permeated by "American" ideas in line with Grewal's argument, it is important to expose students to a nuanced reading of America at home and abroad by engaging them in comparative critical inquiry. This aligns well with the broader institutional vision of current US higher education that seeks to offer students a global experiential education.

But why Sri Lanka in particular when there are other dominant South Asian sites, such as India and Pakistan, which have witnessed recalibrations of postcolonial nation-building endeavors that pay tribute to American ideals? Here, David L. Eng's deliberations on canon formations are illuminative: "Each time Homer's poem appears on a syllabus, each time it is cited in a student essay, and each time it is critiqued by a figure of authority (even a teacher like me), it accrues a bit more prestige, a bit more history, a bit more citational power" (14). This idea is applicable to a minority literature syllabus: when certain texts and experiences predominate, other texts and the experiences represented in those texts are marginalized. Canons are always in the making and can leave gaps in our consciousness. My objective as a teacher, then, is to urge students to think beyond the familiar borders of the Western canon as well as newly emerging regional canons in ethnic American literature.

Students enroll in literature classes for various reasons, ranging from a desire to explore diverse literary traditions to the necessity of fulfilling degree requirements. It is essential to introduce them to both canonical and noncanonical traditions. To this end, Eng's advocation of a "both/and" approach in lieu of an "either/or" approach is effective in teaching Sri Lankan American literature (13). This approach provides a more comprehensive inquiry into literary and cultural traditions and convinces students of the validity of minority literature. It also allows English departments to offer courses on minority literary traditions alongside traditional curricula.

These objectives underscored the two courses I use as touchstones in this essay. I taught the first course, Unmaking Asian America: Literature and Cinema of Genocide, in the winter term of 2020 at Centre College. The course probed Asian American relations and connectivities in the genocidal contexts of Kashmir, Cambodia, and Sri Lanka. Students read Shyam Selvadurai's novel *Funny Boy* together with literary work by Agha Shahid Ali and scholarly work by Schlund-Vials (*War*) and by Gananath Obeyesekere. They also watched several films, including Gurinder Chadha's *India's Partition: The Forgotten Story* and Rithy Panh's *The Missing Picture*. I designed and taught the second course at Elon University in fall 2020. Entitled World Literature: Other Narratives of Post/Colonial Encounters, it examined literary and cultural representations of the colonial imprint in the postcolonial spaces of Africa, the Caribbean, South Asia, and their diasporas. Students read a range of texts, including Chinua Achebe's *Anthills of the Savannah* and Selvadurai's *Funny Boy* and critical prose by Edward Said, Frantz Fanon, and Ngũgĩ wa Thiong'o, and watched such films as Gillo Pontecorvo's *The Battle of Algiers* and Pippa Scott and Oreet Rees's *King Leopold's Ghost*.

In both courses, *Funny Boy* was students' favorite text, as was evident in their enthusiastic engagement in class discussions and in their responses to a survey I shared with them as part of research for this essay. Students' interest in the novel was due in part to the novel's ability to transcend the borders between the local and global. After the discussion of the first chapter, titled "Pigs Can't Fly" (1–39), which traces the enforcement of heteropatriarchal gender norms on the young queer protagonist, a white male student born and raised in Kentucky related to the fictional experience. In the survey, another white student from Texas raised in Europe drew parallels to William Faulkner's *The Sound and the Fury* and Harper Lee's *To Kill a Mockingbird*. Other students made connections to Barry Jenkins's film *Moonlight* and to the work of the Afghan American novelist Khaled Hosseini. These examples reveal the effectiveness of the bildungsroman narrative, which resonates with young adults. For this reason, I have continued to assign *Funny Boy* and have received similar responses. A student in a class I taught at Elon University in winter 2021, for instance, appreciated the book for unmooring queer politics from hegemonic white centricity.

Teaching students how to read with care and empathy is one of the responsibilities of instructors of literature. Most students in the two courses had first heard of Sri Lanka in middle school, but their knowledge of the country and its culture was rather limited, and none had read Sri Lankan American literature prior to taking the class. As such, when introducing them to Sri Lankan literature, I engaged them in a "process of cross-cultural translation" (Couser 23). The stakes are high in this endeavor, especially when the material under discussion is premised on genocidal postcolonial politics in non-Western spaces. If after reading a non-Western text like *Funny Boy* that documents human rights violations and warped democratic politics a student makes a sweeping generalization of Sri Lanka as an antithesis of Western democratic values—thus invoking the hackneyed Orientalist binaries of the Western canon—it is an undoing of the course objectives. Cross-cultural reading, therefore, is a type of literacy that a student must be trained in (Saravia-Shore and Arvizu).

Reading *Funny Boy* across Cultures

Training students to read *Funny Boy*, a text set in an unfamiliar historical, geopolitical, and cultural milieu, requires support from comparative texts and contexts. To this end, carefully sequencing the material in the syllabus is helpful. For example, the winter-term class used Schlund-Vials's thesis on Cambodian American cultural work that "reimagine[s] *alternative* nonhegemonic sites for justice by way of heterotopic negotiations in film, literature, hip-hop, and visual culture" as a heuristic to study post-genocide literature (*War* 20). Students read Schlund-Vials's work on memory and justice in *War, Genocide, and Justice*; watched several films premised on the Cambodian genocide, including David Munro's *Year Zero: The Silent Death of Cambodia*, Roland Joffé's *The Killing Fields*, and Panh's *The Missing Picture*; and visited the National Museum of the US Air Force in Dayton, Ohio, where they interrogated the officialization of memories of the Vietnam War and the Cambodian genocide. Introducing Selvadurai's text was effective on the heels of this discussion. Students applied Schlund-Vials's ideas to study how Selvadurai—in tune with Cambodian and Cambodian American artists like praCh Ly and Panh—uses writing to articulate justice outside official venues that are complicit in genocidal violence.

Schlund-Vials's argument also became a rubric for the fall postcolonial literature course. The course started with a discussion of the discursive power of writing and cultural productions using sections from Said's *Orientalism* (1–28, 92–110). Rudyard Kipling's poem "The White Man's Burden" and Hollywood creations including Indiana Jones and John Rambo translated well into textual references. Next, I introduced students to the politics of decolonization through Fanon's framework in *The Wretched of the Earth*. Students applied these two theoretical frameworks to the first primary literary text, Achebe's *Anthills of the Savannah*. Achebe's examination of the postcolonial West African nation that inherits its administrative system from the former British colonizer and the novel's search for a voice for African subjects urged students to think beyond their familiar images of Africa. This conversation set the stage for Selvadurai's novel. Using Achebe's critique comparatively, students placed Sri Lanka within residual legacies of British colonialism and US neoliberalism. They observed the role of the United States in transforming postcolonial locales in West Africa and Sri Lanka that are mired in "transnational connectivities" (Grewal 3). The protagonist's hotelier father, for instance, despite his second-class citizenship, succeeds under economic liberalization practices introduced to the country in 1977. But his success makes him a target of rival nationalists' envy. When his family is victimized in the 1983 pogrom, America becomes both an idea and tangible means of refuge. America plays a different role in Achebe's novel, in which the postcolonial military dictator seeks to build an affinity with American emissaries to legitimize his rule. A comparative reading of the two contexts gave students an in-depth understanding of America's position in the postcolonial consciousness. Furthermore, following Schlund-Vials's idea, students analyzed Achebe's and Selvadurai's reimaginations of an alternative space on behalf of subjects who are disavowed by heteropatriarchal postcolonial values. Achebe's protagonist, Ikem, shouts, "Writers don't give prescriptions . . . They give headaches!" (161). Achebe's treatise invigorated classroom conversations about why writers from marginalized positions write. Students applied Ikem's words to Selvadurai's political mission as a queer Tamil Sri Lankan American writer.

Interdisciplinary inquiry and intersectional methods are at the core of cross-cultural reading practices. My literature classroom attracts more non-English majors than English majors. The winter-term course, which enrolled eleven students, had only two English majors, and the fall course, which enrolled thirty students, had four. An interdisciplinary focus offers nonmajors a sense of belonging in the literature classroom. The use of audiovisual texts, legal documents, and public speeches is effective in making literary texts more accessible for nonmajors. To this end, I paired *Funny Boy* with former Sri Lankan president J. R. Jayewardene's 1984 speech at the White House hosted by then US president Ronald Reagan ("President Reagan's Remarks"), Obeyesekere's anthropological writing on the Black July violence, and Sritharan Someetharan's documentary *Burning Memories* ("Burning Memories"). Multiple perspectives promote intersectional thinking that "accounts for connections between power, authority, and identity, destabilizes categories of difference and productively opens up the discussion of systemic racism, sexism, and homophobia" (Schlund-Vials, "Re-seeing Race" 106). This methodology also urges students to be mindful of their own subjectivities as they interpret texts. Students are compelled to challenge a binary, Orientalist view of the world and to see Sri Lanka as a site that is historically and ideologically tied to former colonial Europe and neoliberal America.

What's more, students find the interdisciplinary nature of Sri Lankan American literature pedagogy compelling and relevant. One student, an economics and finance major, appreciated how *Funny Boy* challenged his previous study of Sri Lanka in the US classroom. The novel, he claimed, enabled him to understand that people have "individual experiences, emotions, and reactions" that are often missing from larger historical narratives of war. He mentioned that the literature classroom was instrumental in giving him a nuanced understanding of Sri Lanka, forcing him to think beyond his familiar perceptions. This is a testimony to Srikanth's assertion that South Asian American literature makes North American readers aware of "the gaps in their consciousness."

Recalibrating the Sri Lankan American Literature Classroom

The success of Sri Lankan American literature pedagogy owes much to the diversity of the student body, reflected in students' cultural, ethnic, racial, and gender identities as well as their individual experiences. The winter-term course included students of Bhutanese, Cambodian American, Haitian American, Indian, Mexican American, Nepalese, and European descent. Similarly, the postcolonial literature course brought together Black, white, and Asian American students as well as two international students from Cypress and Germany. Such cultural diversity and previous global exposure contributed to an environment of reading with care, responsibility, and sensitivity.

Robust class discussions benefit from an experiential learning environment. For instance, the visit to the National Museum of the US Air Force during the discussion of the Cambodian genocide set a precedent for studying the politics of memory in Selvadurai's *Funny Boy*. When I taught an iteration of this course at Elon University in the winter semester of 2021, I scheduled a field visit to a local site of contested memory—a Confederate monument in the neighboring city of Graham. This visit had a significant impact on the ongoing class conversations. When students started reading *Funny Boy*, they saw the literary text as not only a window into but also an extension of a larger political discourse that invited inter-contextual comparisons between Sri Lanka and the United States.

The Region as a Variable

Asian American studies has been traditionally central to the West Coast, where many Asian communities established their first roots in North America. As the communities have spread nationwide, so have teacher-scholars of the field. Against this backdrop, it is worth asking if such historical and political boundaries as the North and the South matter in Sri Lankan American literature pedagogy. To the Asian American scholar-teacher Jennifer Ho, teaching Asian American epistemology in the American South demands special attention because such spaces have historically approached race in black-and-white terms (15). Speaking of her teaching experience in North Carolina, she says, "Asian Americans, by and large, remain an invisible minority group within the university environment as well as the larger conversations about race happening around the state" (22–23). There is reason to believe that Ho's observations have changed since they were made in 2009. Asian Americans' increasing visibility in the corporate world, in information technology, and in national politics—epitomized by the election of Kamala Harris as vice president—has evidently challenged the conventional binary vision of ethnic relations in the United States. However, their status as "perpetual foreigners" (Lee and Kumashiro 9) continues to prevail nationally, as attested by the mass shooting in Atlanta in 2021 and the rising anti-Asian hate crimes in New York and California, among other states.

When academic institutions see an interstate and international inflow of students, the location of the institution—whether in the North or in the South—can be less significant. Labels that harken back to the Civil War and its aftermath can be inadequate to understanding the rapidly shifting upwardly political mobilizations in the "ex-Confederate" states or new forms of racism in the northern states. Academic institutions with a dedicated liberal arts mission have a profound positive impact not only on the general environment on campus but also on their neighborhoods. In such contexts, Sri Lankan American literature pedagogy, which coexists with a constellation of other disciplinary endeavors that are invested in transformative education, works to challenge students to think beyond their personal and disciplinary comfort zones, thereby enabling them to fill the gaps in their consciousness and to become citizens with global accountability.

Note

1. A recent example of this can be seen in the casting choices made by the Canadian Indian filmmaker Deepa Mehta in her cinematic adaptation of Shyam Selvadurai's novel *Funny Boy*, in which all major Sri Lankan characters (except for one) are played by Indian actors.

Works Cited

Achebe, Chinua. *Anthills of the Savannah.* 1987. Heinemann, 1988.
Ali, Agha Shahid. *The Country without a Post Office: Poems, 1991–1995.* W. W. Norton, 1997.
The Battle of Algiers. Directed by Gillo Pontecorvo, Rialto Pictures, 1966.
"Burning Memories—Burning of Jaffna Library 1981 English Version (2007) by Someetharan." *YouTube*, uploaded by Somee Tharan, 1 Feb. 2020, www.youtube.com/watch?v=e21mnFWgL2A.

Chan, Sucheng. *In Defense of Asian American Studies: The Politics of Teaching and Program Building.* U of Illinois P, 2005.

Couser, Thomas G. "Indian Preservation: Teaching *Black Elk Speaks.*" *Teaching American Ethnic Literatures*, edited by John R. Maitino and David R. Peck, U of New Mexico P, 1996, pp. 21–36.

Eng, David L. "Queer/Asian American/Canons." *Teaching Asian America*, edited by Lane Ryo Hirabayashi, Rowman and Littlefield, 1998, pp. 13–23.

Fanon, Frantz. *The Wretched of the Earth.* Translated by Constance Farrington, Grove Press, 1963.

Funny Boy. Directed by Deepa Mehta, Array, 2020.

Grewal, Inderpal. *Transnational America: Feminisms, Diasporas, Neoliberalisms.* Duke UP, 2005.

Ho, Jennifer. "Letter from an American Professor: An Asian American Education in the South." *The United States South and the Pacific Rim*, special issue of *The Global South*, vol. 3, no. 2, 2009, pp. 14–31.

India's Partition: The Forgotten Story. Directed by Gurinder Chadha, BBC Two, 2017.

The Killing Fields. Directed by Roland Joffé, Warner Bros. Pictures, 1984.

King Leopold's Ghost. Directed by Pippa Scott and Oreet Rees, Linden Productions, 2006.

Kipling, Rudyard. "The White Man's Burden." 1899. *Rudyard Kipling's Verse: Inclusive Edition, 1885–1918*, Doubleday, Page, 1919, pp. 371–72.

Lee, Stacey J., and Kevin K. Kumashiro. *A Report on the Status of Asian Americans and Pacific Islanders in Education: Beyond the "Model Minority" Stereotype.* National Education Association, 2005.

Lowe, Lisa. "Heterogeneity, Hybridity, Multiplicity: Marking Asian American Differences." *Diaspora: A Journal of Transnational Studies*, vol. 1, no. 1, 1991, pp. 24–44.

The Missing Picture. Directed by Rithy Panh, Strand Releasing, 2014.

Ngũgĩ wa Thiong'o. *Globalectics: Theory and Politic of Knowing.* Columbia UP, 2012.

Obeyesekere, Gananath. "The Origins and Institutionalisation of Political Violence." *Sri Lanka in Change and Crisis*, edited by James Manor, Croom Helm, 1984, pp. 153–74.

"President Reagan's Remarks at the Arrival Ceremony for President Jayewardene on June 18, 1984." *YouTube*, uploaded by Reagan Library, 5 Aug. 2019, www.youtube.com/watch?v=v6seLaSTfmc.

Said, Edward. *Orientalism.* Vintage Books, 1979.

Saravia-Shore, Marietta, and Steven F. Arvizu, editors. *Cross-Cultural Literacy: Ethnographies of Communication in Multiethnic Classrooms.* Routledge, 2019.

Schlund-Vials, Cathy J. "Re-seeing Race in a Post-Obama Age: Asian American Studies, Comparative Ethnic Studies, and Intersectional Pedagogies." *New Directions for Teaching and Learning*, no. 125, 2011, pp. 101–09.

———. *War, Genocide, and Justice: Cambodian American Memory Work.* U of Minnesota P, 2012.

Selvadurai, Shyam. *Funny Boy.* 1994. Harcourt Brace, 1997.

Shankar, Rajiv. "South Asian Identity in Asian America." Foreword. *A Part, Yet Apart: South Asians in Asian America*, edited by Lavina Dhingra Shankar and Rajini Srikanth, Temple UP, 1998, pp. ix–xv.

Srikanth, Rajini. *The World Next Door: South Asian American Literature and the Idea of America.* Temple UP, 2004.

Year Zero: The Silent Death of Cambodia. Directed by David Munro, ATV Network, 1979.

Maryse Jayasuriya

Navigating the Homeland/Hostland Dynamic: Sri Lankan Diasporic Literature

The study and teaching of diaspora and diasporic literature are inherently shaped by diffusion and distance, but in the classroom, they can also be a source of connection among the experiences of widely disparate groups of people. My teaching experience has shown that South Asian diasporic literature can speak to students with no familial connections to South Asia and, indeed, little prior awareness of South Asia's history, politics, cultures, or literatures, precisely because the concept of diaspora resonates across a range of identity categories.

This essay examines how I teach South Asian—specifically Sri Lankan—diasporic writing in the English department of the University of Texas, El Paso, a state university in the United States–Mexico border region where there are no specific South Asian courses on the curriculum. The majority of students at my institution are Mexican American first-generation college students. Located as we are in the border region, students face issues relating to migration and border crossings, immigration status, and the competing imperatives of assimilation and preservation of language and cultural identity on a regular basis. This ongoing negotiation makes diasporic literature of particular interest to them. As a result, my students are not fully representative of the general category of North American university students, but they are representative of an especially important and growing subset of students in North American universities: urban student bodies where students of color form a majority and where there are often strong recent connections to histories of immigration and diaspora.

In class discussions and journal responses to reading assignments, students have shared stories about how their parents and grandparents were forced to abstain from using Spanish in school, to the point of being subjected to corporal punishment if they spoke Spanish, a practice that resembles the teaching of English in South Asia during the British colonial period. Students have also shared their own uneasy experiences of diaspora: many of them report feeling like outsiders in the hostland of the United States, but when they return to their parents' or grandparents' homeland of Mexico, even when it is to a city that is just a few miles away from where they live and one that can be seen from campus, they feel that they are defined more by their associations with the United States than by their associations with Mexico in the eyes of friends and relatives. Finally, whether they are US citizens or permanent residents, residents with DACA status, or undocumented immigrants, they all are keenly aware of the ways in which immigration status shapes what it means to be a diasporic subject. They find each of these issues—language, homeland/hostland dynamics, and immigration status—reflected in the Sri Lankan and South Asian literary texts that I teach.

In incorporating into my courses both Sri Lankan writers specifically and South Asian writers more broadly, I ensure that students encounter a broader range of experiences through which they can engage with their own stories. My classes all include a mix of Sri Lankan writing and South Asian writing from India, Pakistan, and Bangladesh because the size and structure of my department do not allow for devising classes solely on Sri Lankan writing and because it seems important to me to consider South Asian writing in a transnational context.

Diasporic Writers in Undergraduate Surveys

To incorporate texts by South Asian diasporic writers, I create suitable modules in many of the courses that I teach. In undergraduate courses such as Postcolonial Literature, I incorporate modules that deal with the effects of colonization and imperialism, education, language issues, and cultural hegemony (I assign extracts from Ngũgĩ wa Thiong'o's *Decolonizing the Mind* [4–33] and Gauri Viswanathan's *Masks of Conquest*

[1–22]), independence and attempts at decolonization, issues of identity and hybridity, first nations, and diaspora. In the unit on postindependence conflicts, I include A. Sivanandan's novel *When Memory Dies* since it outlines how the status quo does not necessarily change when the former colonizers depart—as Frantz Fanon has argued in *The Wretched of the Earth*, the native bourgeoisie tends to take control and maintain the structures imposed during the colonial period, which does not lead to the necessary decolonization or to genuine liberation for most people in the new nation. Sivanandan's novel also delineates the way in which the divide-and-rule policy of the British colonizers exacerbated ethnic and religious divisions, ultimately resulting in conflict in the postindependence era. This novel, written by a diasporic writer who remained invested in the homeland and focused on matters of race and class, spans three generations of a Sri Lankan family comprising Tamil and Sinhalese characters, from the preindependence period through postindependence disenfranchisement of minority groups by the majority that led some to go into exile in other countries and that also led to the eruption of the ethnic conflict in 1983. The fact that Sivanandan was an important theorist of race and class in a Black British context makes it relatively easy to make broader connections using his fiction and theoretical work in tandem. The novel pairs well with Partition narratives such as Bapsi Sidhwa's *Cracking India* and Khushwant Singh's *Train to Pakistan* and with Chimamanda Ngozi Adichie's *Half of a Yellow Sun* and Tahmima Anam's *A Golden Age*. I include shorter works by writers residing in Sri Lanka (such as Jean Arasanayagam's poetry, available through the Library of Congress, and Vivimarie Vanderpoorten's poetry, available through the poet's blog site [vivimariev.blogspot.com]). The work of some Sri Lankan writers can be difficult to obtain in North America, meaning that digital publications and reproductions are an essential part of making available the range of texts that my students need.

I also take the opportunity to include modules on South Asian diasporic literature in other undergraduate courses such as World Literature, Literary Theory, Literature and Film, and Women and Literature, which can be cross-listed with women's and gender studies and Asian studies. In a unit on feminist and gender theory in my Literary Theory course, I use Shyam Selvadurai's novel *Funny Boy*, a coming-of-age narrative about a young gay Sri Lankan Tamil boy. (The film adaptation, directed by Deepa Mehta, was released in 2020, and I anticipate that it could become a part of future discussions of the novel.) Issues of gender performativity as theorized by Judith Butler can be examined particularly through the first chapter of the novel (1–39). Chapter 1 pairs well with Ismat Chugtai's short story "The Quilt," since both interrogate the concept of gender through the eyes of a child.

In Literature and Film, I focus on immigrant fiction and film. In certain cases, I pair a novel with its film adaptation, and in other cases, I pair novels and films that deal with similar themes. Shobasakthi's novel *Gorilla*, for example, can be paired with the film *Dheepan*. The novel follows a young Sri Lankan Tamil man who was a child soldier with the Liberation Tigers of Tamil Eelam (LTTE) and eventually migrates to Paris as an undocumented immigrant seeking refugee status. The film (starring the writer himself in this semi-autobiographical role) concentrates on the protagonist's time in Paris as an undocumented immigrant doing menial work while experiencing racism in French society. Other pairings include Sidhwa's *Cracking India* and Mehta's adaptation *Earth*. Meera Syal's *Life Isn't All Ha Ha Hee Hee* can be paired with *Bhaji on the Beach* and *My Beautiful Laundrette*, which deal with issues relating to gender and sexuality in South Asian communities in Britain.

Diasporic Writers in Graduate Seminars

I also created various iterations of period- or theme-based graduate classes in order to include South Asian diasporic literature. Works that deal with the complicated expectations surrounding ethnic identity and intersectionalities resonate with my students at the University of Texas, El Paso, most of whom identify as either Mexican American or Chicanx and many of whom grapple with questions of identity in relation to race, class, gender, sexuality, and immigration status. In my Diasporic Literature course, I focus on first- and second-generation immigrant narratives in North America, Britain, and Australia. These narratives explore how first-generation immigrants deal with homesickness and nostalgia for what they have left behind; the disorientation, culture shock, racism, prejudice, and precarity they experience in the hostland; and the pressures they face to assimilate and survive in their new environment while attempting to preserve the language and traditions of the homeland or even to ameliorate conditions in the homeland. My students and I also discuss intergenerational conflict that can come into play between first- and second-generation immigrants because of the pressure imposed by the former on their offspring to conform to parental and cultural expectations and because of the efforts of the latter to straddle two or more cultures in their private and public lives. I include novels such as Yasmine Gooneratne's *A Change of Skies*, which focuses on a middle-class Sri Lankan couple who move to Australia as economic migrants and reinvent themselves in the new milieu, and Nayomi Munaweera's *Island of a Thousand Mirrors*, which deals with a young girl who moves with her family to the United States and attempts to assimilate while trying to understand the ethnic conflict going on in her homeland. Selvadurai's *Hungry Ghosts* and SJ Sindu's *Marriage of a Thousand Lies* both focus on first- and second-generation immigrants dealing with non-heteronormative sexual identities in a conservative diasporic community that polices its borders and continues to adhere to the misogynistic double standards and homophobia operating in the homeland. In response to these texts, students have shared their own challenges in negotiating questions of sexuality and gender identity with family members who hold more conservative views.

I juxtapose fiction with poetry: in poems such as "Persistence" (Piepzna-Samarasinha 3–4) and "I Didn't Want the End Times to Be Like This: 9/11 in Seven Slams" (50–53), Leah Lakshmi Piepzna-Samarasinha explores the ways in which hybrid identities can affect second-generation immigrants. In the first poem, the speaker attempts to figure out her multiracial identity as she confronts assumptions about her appearance and ethnic origins casually made by people she encounters in New York City; in the second poem, the speaker deals with ethnic profiling along with the racist epithets and threats hurled at her and her family after the 2001 terrorist attacks. My students have shared their own anger and frustration in the face of negative stereotypes and casual racism regarding immigrants from Mexico and reflected on the implications of members of the South Asian diaspora being referred to as "the model minority."

The intersection of violence and diasporic issues has proved particularly compelling for my students given our proximity to Ciudad Juárez, a major site in the drug war in Mexico and a place that many people in El Paso have family and personal connections to; some of my students were compelled to move from Juárez to El Paso because of the drug war. In a course titled The Literature of War, Violence, and Terrorism, I teach contemporary depictions of violence and conflict that also frequently lead to internal and external displacement. My students and I reflect on the process of retrieving or recovering hidden or forgotten histories of war, the relationship between trauma and memory, and the significance of grieving and mourning.

The protagonist of Michael Ondaatje's *Anil's Ghost* is a diasporic Sri Lankan who represents an international organization and investigates possible human rights violations by the government during a phase of Sri Lanka's long-running conflict. The protagonist, Anil, who prides herself on her cosmopolitan identity, is challenged by Sri Lankan characters with whom she comes into contact to consider diasporic responsibility to the homeland.

Anuk Arudpragasam's *The Story of a Brief Marriage* depicts the life of Dinesh, an internally displaced young man caught between the Sri Lankan military and the LTTE in the closing days of the war, and challenges simplistic notions about the effects of empathy. The novel enables me to discuss with students the impact of consistent violence and loss on individuals and to examine prevalent Eurocentric notions of single-event trauma through the work of theorists of postcolonial trauma such as Stef Craps, who focuses on trauma caused on a daily basis over a period of time by factors such as colonialism, racism, and slavery. Unlike those who experience a single traumatic event and are therefore unable to return to normal life, Dinesh and others like him endure a series of endless traumatic events as part of their everyday lives, which are full of "chronic suffering and structural violence" that contrast with "the Western standard of normality" (Craps 53). Both *Anil's Ghost* and *The Story of a Brief Marriage* interrogate the ethics of representation as well as the ethics of empathy on the part of both writer and reader.

Written from the vantage point of the Tamil diaspora in the United States and Canada, V. V. Ganeshananthan's *Love Marriage* provides the perspective of Yalini, a young woman born to Sri Lankan Tamil parents who left their home country to escape the growing disenfranchisement of the minority Tamils by the majority Sinhalese following independence. Khachig Tölölyan has argued that what differentiates the "diasporic" from the "ethnic" is an involvement or investment in the homeland (13); when her uncle, a member of the LTTE, arrives in North America, Yalini unwittingly gets drawn into the conflicts of her parents' homeland. She attempts to gather the stories of her family members in order to investigate the sociopolitical situation in Sri Lanka that forced some relatives into exile and compelled others into an armed struggle. Sharon Bala's *The Boat People* interrogates the predicament of Sri Lankan asylum seekers coming to Canada who are viewed as possible terrorists by immigration officials, a story that resonates with recent controversies about asylum seekers at the United States–Mexico border. I juxtapose these novels with other considerations of war, violence, and terrorism, such as the 9/11 novel *Falling Man*, by Don DeLillo; *Sozaboy*, an experimental novel about the Biafran War by Ken Saro-wiwa; *Home Fire*, by Kamila Shamsie, which focuses on immigration, homeland security, racial profiling, and surveillance in the United Kingdom; and *The Reluctant Fundamentalist*, by Mohsin Hamid. These combinations allow students to trace thematic connections across national literatures and beyond the conventional context of the US war on terror while also examining the particularities of violence in specific contexts.

Assignments include daily journal responses to reading assignments as well as term papers. In addition, I have asked students to do mini presentations on journals related to the field so that they can become familiar with relevant publications and share with classmates what they need to remember in writing a paper that might be submitted to such a journal. For example, in my postcolonial literature course, students are assigned an academic journal that relates directly or indirectly to postcolonial studies and are asked to familiarize themselves with the journal and make a short presentation to the class. Students are assigned journals such as *South Asian Review*, *MELUS*, *ARIEL*, *Callaloo*, *Interventions*, *Journal of Postcolonial Writing*, *Wasafiri*, *Journal of Commonwealth Literature*, and *Contemporary Women's Writing*, journals that typically publish essays on diasporic literature. Another mini presentation asks students to examine a literary or theoretical text they have read outside class in light of an article discussed in class or to examine a current news story in light of an article from class in order to put theory into practice and put texts in conversation with each other.

Another assignment broadens students' familiarity with the range of South Asian diasporic writers and works beyond what is in the course syllabus. Students are asked to research a South Asian or South Asian diasporic novelist and, ideally, to read a work by that novelist in preparation for a class presentation. Collectively, these assignments enable students to connect with their own experiences of diaspora and to deepen their knowledge of South Asian history and culture and postcolonial theory, which informs their readings of individual texts.

Teaching South Asian diasporic literature at a university without a South Asian studies program is challenging, but it also has certain advantages: I am able to infuse works by South Asian and, specifically, Sri Lankan diasporic writers into the English department curriculum at large, and my students are often able to bring these works into conversation not only with the global anglophone literature that I teach but also with the multilingual literatures of the Americas and with their own diasporic experiences. I am also able to consider the various ways in which diasporic fictions can function. These works are understood as immigrant literature in the hostland, and they offer an opportunity to delve into the various homeland/hostland dynamics that appear in the novels by Ganeshananthan and Bala. These works also illustrate that diasporic fiction is not *only* immigrant fiction: many are deeply concerned with—and, in Qadri Ismail's phrase, "abid[e] by"—the homeland and thus address emigration, exile, and circulation as well as the sociopolitical circumstances that lead to such movement rather than immigration as such, as in Ondaatje's and Arudpragasam's novels and Romesh Gunesekera's novels *Reef* and *Noon Tide Toll*. Finally, the works I teach connect questions of diaspora, immigration, and exile and matters of gender and sexuality, which appear in works by Selvadurai, Mary Anne Mohanraj, and Sindu. In this way, the circulations of the South Asian diaspora enable students to consider the circulation of questions of race, ethnicity, culture, and sexuality within the curriculum of my department.

The question of how to "abid[e] by" a homeland gains an added piquancy for many of my students, who can quite literally step outside the classroom building and see people walking and biking across the river in Ciudad Juárez. A recurring topic of conversation involves the parallels and differences between the South Asian diaspora, whose members are scattered across the globe, and the Mexican American or Chicanx diaspora, whose members may live within just a few miles of where their parents grew up on the Juárez side of the border or indeed may commute from Juárez despite having US citizenship. My students learn through their encounters with Sri Lankan diasporic writing and its relation to their own experiences in a borderland community that diaspora is a central rather than a peripheral concern in the literary production of the twenty-first century.

Works Cited

Adichie, Chimamanda Ngozi. *Half of a Yellow Sun*. Anchor Books, 2007.
Anam, Tahmima. *A Golden Age*. 2007. Harper Perennial, 2009.
Arudpragasam, Anuk. *The Story of a Brief Marriage*. Flatiron Books, 2016.
Bala, Sharon. *The Boat People*. Anchor Books, 2018.
Bhaji on the Beach. Directed by Gurinder Chadha, Film4 Library, 2011.
Butler, Judith. *Gender Trouble: Feminism and the Subversion of Identity*. Routledge, 2006.

Chugtai, Ismat. "The Quilt." *Women Writing in India, 600 B.C. to the Present*, edited by Susie Tharu and K. Lalita, vol. 2, Feminist Press, 1993, pp. 126–37.

Craps, Stef. "Beyond Eurocentrism: Trauma Theory in the Global Age." *The Future of Trauma Theory: Contemporary Literary and Cultural Criticism*, edited by Gert Buelens et al., Routledge, 2014, pp. 45–61.

DeLillo, Don. *Falling Man*. Scribner, 2008.

Dheepan. Directed by Jacques Audiard, Canal+ / Cine+ / France 2 Cinema, 2015.

Earth. Directed by Deepa Mehta, New Yorker Video, 2003.

Fanon, Frantz. *The Wretched of the Earth*. 1961. Translated by Richard Philcox, Grove Press, 2004.

Funny Boy. Directed by Deepa Mehta, Netflix, 2020.

Ganeshananthan, V. V. *Love Marriage*. Random House, 2008.

Gooneratne, Yasmine. *A Change of Skies*. Picador, 1991.

Gunesekera, Romesh. *Noon Tide Toll*. Penguin Books, 2014.

———. *Reef*. Penguin Books, 1994.

Hamid, Mohsin. *The Reluctant Fundamentalist*. 2007. Harvest, 2008.

Ismail, Qadri. *Abiding by Sri Lanka: On Peace, Place, and Postcoloniality*. U of Minnesota P, 2005.

Mohanraj, Mary Anne. *Bodies in Motion*. Harper Perennial, 2006.

Munaweera, Nayomi. *Island of a Thousand Mirrors*. Perera-Hussein, 2012.

My Beautiful Laundrette. Directed by Stephen Frears, Criterion Collection, 2015.

Ngũgĩ wa Thiong'o. *Decolonizing the Mind*. James Currey, 1986.

Ondaatje, Michael. *Anil's Ghost*. Alfred A. Knopf, 2000.

Piepzna-Samarasinha, Leah Lakshmi. *Consensual Genocide*. TSAR, 2006.

Saro-Wiwa, Ken. *Sozaboy: A Novel in Rotten English*. 1985. Pearson College Div., 1995.

Selvadurai, Shyam. *Funny Boy*. Harcourt Brace, 1994.

———. *Hungry Ghosts*. Penguin Books, 2013.

Shamsie, Kamila. *Home Fire*. Riverhead Books, 2017.

Shobasakthi. *Gorilla*. 2001. Translated by Anushiya Sivanarayan, Random House, 2008.

Sidhwa, Bapsi. *Cracking India*. 1991. Milkweed, 2006.

Sindu, SJ. *Marriage of a Thousand Lies*. Soho Press, 2017.

Singh, Khushwant. *The Train to Pakistan*. 1956. Grove Press, 1994.

Sivanandan, A. *When Memory Dies*. Penguin Books, 1997.

Syal, Meera. *Life Isn't All Ha Ha Hee Hee*. 1999. Picador, 2001.

Tölölyan, Khachig. "Rethinking *Diaspora*(s): Stateless Power in the Transnational Moment." *Diaspora*, vol. 5, no. 1, 1996, pp. 3–36.

Viswanathan, Gauri. *Masks of Conquest: Literary Study and British Rule in India*. Columbia UP, 1989.

Manav Ratti

Teaching Sri Lanka in the United States: Human Rights in the Literary and Visual Imaginations

This essay discusses my approach to teaching Michael Ondaatje's *Anil's Ghost* in a seminar at Salisbury University designed for master's and advanced undergraduate students. I examine how teaching South Asian diasporic literature can help students unlearn and relearn beliefs and ideas about distant nations and cultures; recognize the ethical and political sensitivities and insensitivities that shape diasporic authors, instructors, and students; and understand the tension between the diasporic novel as aesthetic object and the material needs, including the human rights, of peoples in South Asia.

In addition to novels by Ondaatje (*The English Patient* and *Anil's Ghost*), I taught works by Salman Rushdie (*Haroun and the Sea of Stories* and *East, West*) and Amitav Ghosh (*The Shadow Lines* and *The Hungry Tide*). These writings coalesced around several themes, including nation, diaspora, religion, and violence. The course consisted of twenty-one undergraduates; nearly a third of the students had previously taken a course with me, meaning that they were already familiar with some of the values and sensibilities of postcolonial and South Asian studies. This familiarity allowed me to invoke vocabularies and discourses that might not be as easy to teach in a lower-division or introductory course.

194

As I told students at the outset of the course, the "diasporic" in South Asian diasporic literature was, in this course, inseparable from the post-colonial. Diasporic literature is, of course, not always postcolonial. I emphasized for students the personal and international dimensions of diasporic writing. In other words, diasporic authors have a personal connection to a particular nation (through birth, upbringing, ancestry, or some combination of the three) but are writing about that nation while living in another nation. This writing about another, distant nation helped students understand the internationalism of diasporic writing. Postcolonial and South Asian literature were also an entry point for understanding diasporic literature: How do writers represent other cultures, and how do we understand other literatures and cultures that might seem foreign? To help students relate to diasporic writing (since relatability to literature is an important criterion for student readers), I asked them to reflect on distant moments in their lives and thus to be sensitive to how memory works. What experiences and relationships, both positive and negative, did they remember? How did they now relate to those experiences and memories? Did they feel a sense of nostalgia, or did they feel some other emotion? How had those experiences shaped who they were now? How faithfully and sensitively could they describe those experiences and the conditions that produced them? Would describing those experiences help them understand the experiences? Was their ability to remember and narrate those experiences shaped by their present circumstances? Asking these rhetorical questions helped students understand and relate to South Asian diasporic literature. Throughout the course, we discussed diasporic literature as both an aesthetic product and a form of representation that tackles difficult political issues. This well-known tension between aesthetics and politics is especially relevant in a novel such as Ondaatje's *Anil's Ghost*, which reflects on the highly political topic of human rights.

The tension between aesthetics and politics also plays out in the role of the instructor, since South Asian diasporic literature educators based in the West (like diasporic authors and even some diasporic students) are often cast in the role of native informant with regard to South Asian cultures. The constraints, however, of the informant's position (especially as cultural nativism, essentialism, and exoticism) can be somewhat mitigated by naming its hegemonic power, making it visible, and showing the limitations and biases of its knowledge production. For instance, Qadri Ismail has argued that "no single Sri Lanka can, by definition, succeed in capturing or encompassing the infinitude of its significance; thus, no two Sri Lankas are likely to coincide, though some will certainly overlap" ("Speaking" 304). For instructors, this can mean adopting a certain humility by not presuming to speak *for* national cultures and by incorporating scholarship in their courses that explains some of these burdens and fissures of representation. I have found that such a self-consciously modest position adds to the instructor's authenticity and helps them connect with students, for the students can then also recognize, and perhaps practice, humility. Such humility could even foster ethical formation, for it counteracts Orientalist representations of Sri Lanka and South Asia. At the same time, being unable to fully know or understand the material should not become an alibi for disinterest or intellectual irresponsibility. I strove to cultivate in students interest and intellectual responsibility as values for understanding and representing difference.

Since *Anil's Ghost* explores differences among nations, including how they shape diasporas and human rights, I began the course with a lecture and discussion on nations as sociopolitical constructs. Benedict Anderson's *Imagined Communities* was central to this discussion. This grounded the course in an analysis of nations and nationalisms as not only socially constructed and contestable (the latter especially from perspectives that are minoritized, whether on the basis of race, ethnicity, religion, language, or otherwise) but also politically powerful, including perniciously so. These topics led some students to question their deeply held beliefs about the naturalness, benevolence, and even desirability of nation and nationalism. This critical questioning provided a conceptual, discursive, and ethical framework for the rest of the course and closely informed our discussions of *Anil's Ghost*.

Diaspora as a Teaching Tool: Seeing Characters, Seeing Ourselves

The protagonist of *Anil's Ghost* is Anil Tissera, a forensic pathologist born in Sri Lanka, educated in the United Kingdom, and based in the United States. Anil visits Sri Lanka during its civil war as part of a United Nations human rights investigation into allegations that the government has murdered civilians. Anils's diasporic identity as an insider and outsider in Sri Lanka was useful in teaching students about diaspora, particularly its liabilities to insensitivity and ignorance about the home nation. Anil's identity as a diasporic subject allows the novel to meditate on the international politics of human rights investigations. While Anil is a kind of emissary of

Western human rights, her lived connection with Sri Lanka adds a personal dimension to her visit there. The novel shows Anil's processes of unlearning and relearning. This includes reflecting on what counts as truth and evidence and gaining a more nuanced understanding of how they operate in Sri Lanka. For example, when the Sri Lankan archaeologist Sarath says that "political secrets are not powerless," Anil asserts that "truth comes finally into the light. It's in the bones and sediment" (Ondaatje, *Anil's Ghost* 259). Sarath replies that truth lies "in character and nuance and mood" and that "for the living it is the truth" (259).[1] Sarath (and Ondaatje) may well be speaking to readers who, like Anil, are (North American) outsiders with regard to Sri Lanka. Observing Anil's potential for learning and unlearning proved pedagogically effective for students. They used it as a model for becoming conscious of, and perhaps revising, their own assumptions about Sri Lanka and South Asia. I encouraged students to consider this similarity between Anil's and their own processes of learning about Sri Lanka. Through Anil, students could begin to see parts of themselves. Internationalism was part of this similarity, for both students and Anil were outsiders with respect to Sri Lanka and based in the United States. I expanded the similarity by asking students to reflect on whether the process of unlearning and relearning could be a model for the West (particularly the United States) to better understand Sri Lanka and South Asia.

The concept of diaspora was thus useful for helping students think about national and global locations, the distance between nations, personal connections to nations (whether homeland, hostland, or both), and the attachments (or lack of attachments) those connections can foster. The thread running through each of these aspects of diaspora is how seemingly abstract and unrelatable political features of nations (and the relations between nations) can be grounded in the personal. These personal processes consist of unlearning and revising beliefs, knowledge, and assumptions. Diaspora also served as a teaching device: I reminded students that the novel was a result of Ondaatje's diasporic upbringing (across the United Kingdom and Canada) and location (Canada). Thus, for all the virtues of his characters' unlearning and relearning, such processes are not unproblematic, including for the author. Ondaatje himself is liable to diasporic insensitivities toward and misperceptions of Sri Lanka. For example, several critics have noted the novel's political insensitivities (Ismail, "Flippant Gesture"; Jazeel; Ratti, *Postsecular Imagination* 109). Ismail observes that the novel has no Muslim or Burgher characters and only four Tamil characters, all in minor roles, and only one of the Tamil characters is named ("Flippant Gesture" 24). This was a pedagogically useful point for students. It showed them that while South Asian diasporic literature can be discursively self-aware of its limitations (for instance, through its characters' words), there are almost unavoidable blind spots in the construction of the novel itself. Such blind spots bring us back to the continuous need for unlearning and relearning from observing others, which includes authors and their literature.

"Speaking to Sri Lanka"

I began the unit on *Anil's Ghost* with a *PowerPoint* lecture on some historical and political contexts of Sri Lanka, particularly as such contexts are relevant to the novel and issues of human rights. My lecture was informed in content and spirit by Sri Lankan scholars' call to avoid orientalizing Sri Lanka and to instead respect the country's agency and complexity (Abeysekara; Ismail, "Speaking"; Jeganathan). Teaching and learning about diaspora from outside Sri Lanka allowed us to practice Ismail's concept of "speaking to Sri Lanka" ("Speaking"). Ismail argues that we should view Sri Lanka as having a subjectivity rather than as something passive and static with no dynamism or meaning beyond its objectifications by political science and anthropology (298). I thus strived to show multiple and diverse aspects of Sri Lanka while teaching key facts surrounding ethnopolitical conflicts such as the 1956 Sinhala Only Act and the July 1983 pogrom against Tamils in Jaffna and Colombo. This multiplicity mirrored Ondaatje's novel, which depicts not only violence but also Sri Lanka's landscapes and religious monuments. I showed photos from my visits to religious sites such as the Temple of the Sacred Tooth Relic (Sri Dalada Maligawa) in Kandy, the sacred city of Anuradhapura, and the caves at Dambulla with their Buddhist paintings. I also showed photos of everyday settings, such as tea plantations (including in the hill city of Nuwara Eliya), street vendors, bookstores, university buildings, and Galle Face Green, a sea-facing park in Colombo that features in *Anil's Ghost*.

After this introductory lecture, we analyzed the novel chronologically across its first, second, and last thirds. These discussions invited students' interpretations and reflections. Each of our class meetings began with my asking students for their reactions to the part of the novel assigned for that day. I also played for students several interview clips in which Ondaatje discusses the novel ("Michael Ondaatje Interview (2000)") and his wider work ("Michael Ondaatje Interview: We"). Among the backbones of our analyses of the novel were the literary techniques used by Ondaatje. Students learned to use terms such as *imagery, voice, perspective, metaphor,* and *atmosphere* in order to describe these techniques. This attentiveness to the novel's formal dimensions allowed me to remind students that the novel, in addition to its political and historical content, is an aesthetic object—and not primarily a political or historical tract. Our analysis of literary form enabled me to present the aesthetics versus politics debate in diasporic and postcolonial studies. We discussed the aesthetic and political meanings of the word *representation,* and I asked students the following questions: Who speaks and writes? Who listens and reads? Who makes issues visible, and how? I shared the following excerpt from Ismail's article:

> What is this thing, this object Sri Lanka? Do we know it? How do we know it? Do we know it other than an object of anthropology (a place of cultural difference and violence)? Or cartography (a miniature on a map)? Is it doomed to be forever object? Could it be conceived as subject? And, as an even more cardinal priority: Is it a task of postcoloniality to make objects subject? ("Speaking" 298)

In this context I invoked the issue of human rights and the idea of "speaking to Sri Lanka." In my scholarship on the novel, I examine the West's understanding of Sri Lanka through human rights, as if Sri Lanka was constituted only by human rights violence and violations (Ratti, "Michael Ondaatje's *Anil's Ghost*" 126–28, *Postsecular Imagination* 87–117, "Representing China" 98–101). Having shared this scholarship with students, I asked them what such understanding meant for us as readers of the novel, for we ourselves are understanding Anil (through Ondaatje), who is in a process of understanding human rights in Sri Lanka. I also argued that the novel's representation of human rights is not the delivery of human rights. By this I meant that the novel is a representation (an aesthetic, imaginative creation) and not an immediate solution that meets urgent material needs and protections in Sri Lanka, the nation at a diasporic distance. I connected this argument to my previous assertion that the novel's representation of a character's unlearning and relearning does not mean that the author or we ourselves as readers actually or automatically go through such a revision of views and beliefs. I then asked the class what would constitute the fulfillment of human rights in Sri Lanka. What do people in Sri Lanka need, materially and otherwise? This was a turning point in our discussions. The room became silent. It was evident to me that students realized the gravity of the material need in Sri Lanka. Perhaps they became more conscious of their relative privilege as people who, unlike Anil, are not caught in a civil war. This paved the way for our documentary screenings and concluding reflections on the novel.

Documentaries of the Sri Lankan Civil War: Visualizing Human Rights

After our discussions of the novel, we watched two documentaries: *Sri Lanka's Killing Fields*, directed by Callum Macrae, and *No More Tears Sister*, directed by Helene Klodawsky ("No More Tears"). *Sri Lanka's Killing Fields* was broadcast in the United Kingdom by Channel 4 and documents the final months of the civil war, showing graphic footage taken by soldiers. I gave trigger warnings to students. While lauded by some Western organizations (such as the Tom Lantos Human Rights Commission, based in the United States), the documentary was criticized by the Sri Lankan government for what it claimed was fabricated footage. Watching this documentary was a watershed moment in some students' understanding of Sri Lanka, the civil war, and human rights. Many commented that the documentary brought alive for them the extent of the devastation and suffering in Sri Lanka. *No More Tears Sister*, produced by the National Film Board of Canada, chronicles the life of the human rights activist Dr. Rajani Thiranagama, a professor of anatomy at the University of Jaffna who was critical of the use of violence by the Liberation Tigers of Tamil Eelam. Dr. Thiranagama was assassinated by the Tamil Tigers in 1989. The film contains interviews with Dr. Thiranagama's family members, and her character is played by her anthropologist daughter Sharika Thiranagama (Thiranagama 1–40). These documentaries became teaching moments for the novel, revealing two distinct visual approaches to representing Sri Lanka and its crises. I showed these documentaries after we studied the novel, so that students could first "speak to" Sri Lanka and human rights on their own terms. After watching the documentaries, we returned to a discussion of the novel. I asked students the following questions: Like Anil, have you unlearned and relearned anything? If so, what? How do you now interpret Sarath's assertion to Anil that truth lies in character, nuance, and mood? In what ways do the documentaries construct Sri Lanka through both their content and their tone? After reading Ismail's article "Speaking to Sri Lanka," what are some of your questions and concerns about the civil war and human rights in Sri Lanka? What blind spots could Anil and

Ondaatje, situated in the diaspora, have about Sri Lanka? Educators can take inspiration from and teach Nimanthi Perera-Rajasingham's critique of witnessing Sri Lanka's civil war. Perera-Rajasingham argues that such witnessing reproduces inequalities in the neoliberal capitalist international division of labor (126). I thus asked my students, What, if anything, do authors, readers, and people in the South Asian diaspora owe South Asia? Whose and what interests, political and otherwise, could such diasporic literature privilege and serve? What ethical and political responsibility, if any, should authors, readers, and people in the South Asian diaspora have toward South Asian nation-states and peoples? How does a documentary about South Asia produced in the diaspora assist or thwart unlearning and relearning about South Asia?

Learning about the need for human rights through multiple modes—a novel, documentaries, interviews, raw footage, an illustrated lecture, and class discussions—mirrors the heterogeneity and diversity through which we can "speak to" difference, rather than "speak for" it, in a process of genuinely learning about difference. As I have argued elsewhere about the teaching of human rights, such pedagogy risks being constructed by "the rights machine" as merely, among other reifications, the concerns of only racialized peoples and expressions of South Asian essentialism (Ratti, "Representing China" 99–101). Of course, human rights and their violations are not only Sri Lankan or South Asian problems—they are universal. Writing about Sri Lanka and human rights, Debjani Ganguly argues that the "information technology revolution has radically transformed our threshold of responsibility to our distant others" (250). Let us recall that the documentaries on the Sri Lankan Civil War include cell phone footage by soldiers and that these documentaries are available online, including as clips on *YouTube*. Responsibility is one of the common threads in the scholarship on Sri Lanka and diaspora that I have cited in this essay. Novels and documentaries mediate Sri Lanka, its civil war, and human rights—but they also carry an immediacy. For the instructor of South Asian diasporic literature, that immediacy is a call to keep learning and teaching how to speak to Sri Lanka and human rights from the diaspora. The Western-based South Asian diaspora—which includes authors, readers, instructors, and students—can bring visibility to South Asian issues through its privileged, powerful platforms (such as its global publishing forums and prizes, its educational and political institutions). Such representation can also become a misrepresentation, even an obfuscation, especially of political nuance and reality. If instructors of South Asian diasporic literature can communicate this duality of privilege and liability to students, then teaching diasporic literature can perhaps teach critical thinking and even ethical formation. What is Sri Lanka? How do we speak to Sri Lanka? What are human rights? How do we address human rights in Sri Lanka?

Note

1. For further analysis of this exchange, see Ratti, *Postsecular Imagination* 114.

Works Cited

Abeysekara, Ananda. "Sri Lanka, Postcolonial 'Locations of Buddhism,' Secular Peace: Sovereignty of Decision and Distinction." *Interventions*, vol. 14, no. 2, 2012, pp. 211–37.

Anderson, Benedict. *Imagined Communities: Reflections on the Origin and Spread of Nationalism*. Revised ed., Verso, 2006.

Ganguly, Debjani. *This Thing Called the World: The Contemporary Novel as Global Form*. Duke UP, 2018.

Ghosh, Amitav. *The Hungry Tide*. HarperCollins Publishers, 2004.

———. *The Shadow Lines*. Ravi Dayal Publishers, 1988.

Ismail, Qadri. "A Flippant Gesture towards Sri Lanka: A Review of Michael Ondaatje's *Anil's Ghost*." *Pravada*, vol. 6, no. 9, 2000, pp. 24–29.

———. "Speaking to Sri Lanka." *Interventions*, vol. 3, no. 2, 2001, pp. 296–308.

Jazeel, Tariq. "Geography, Spatial Politics, and Productions of the National in Michael Ondaatje's *Anil's Ghost*." *Spatialising Politics: Culture and Geography in Postcolonial Sri Lanka*, edited by Catherine Brun and Jazeel, Sage, 2009, pp. 122–45.

Jeganathan, Pradeep. "The Postnational, Inhabitation and the Work of Melancholia." *Economic and Political Weekly*, vol. 44, no. 10, 2009, pp. 54–57.

"Michael Ondaatje Interview (2000)." *YouTube*, uploaded by Manufacturing Intellect, 16 Aug. 2016, www.youtube.com/watch?v=r3yxgL4TB0E.

"Michael Ondaatje Interview: We Can't Rely on One Voice." *YouTube*, uploaded by Louisiana Channel, 16 June 2015, www.youtube.com/watch?v=3gBVILOsetU.

"No More Tears Sister - Defining Human Rights 1/3 – POV | PBS." *YouTube*, uploaded by POV, 5 Nov. 2015, www.youtube.com/watch?v=R6I0Wst-uxA.

Ondaatje, Michael. *Anil's Ghost*. Picador, 2000.

———. *The English Patient*. Picador, 1992.

Perera-Rajasingham, Nimanthi. *Assembling Ethnicities in Neoliberal Times: Ethnographic Fictions and Sri Lanka's War*. Northwestern UP, 2019.

Ratti, Manav. "Michael Ondaatje's *Anil's Ghost* and the Aestheticization of Human Rights." *Ariel: A Review of International English Literature*, vol. 35, nos. 1–2, 2004, pp. 121–39.

———. *The Postsecular Imagination: Postcolonialism, Religion, and Literature*. Routledge, 2013.

———. "Representing China and Asia: Translating Outside in 'the Rights Machine.'" *Teaching Human Rights in Literary and Cultural Studies*, edited by Alexandra Schultheis Moore and Elizabeth Swanson Goldberg, Modern Language Association of America, 2015, pp. 96–107.

Rushdie, Salman. *East, West*. Jonathan Cape, 1994.

———. *Haroun and the Sea of Stories*. Penguin Books, 1990.

Sri Lanka's Killing Fields. Vimeo, uploaded by Forensic Architecture, 16 Feb. 2012, vimeo.com/36888107.

Thiranagama, Sharika. *In My Mother's House: Civil War in Sri Lanka*. U of Pennsylvania P, 2011.

Part VI

East Meets North: The Pakistani American Diaspora after 9/11

Mushtaq Bilal

Teaching Pakistani Anglophone Diasporic Literature

This essay is based on my experience teaching an undergraduate course titled Introduction to Pakistani Literature at Binghamton University in the fall of 2020. Undergraduate courses dedicated to South Asian literature—anglophone or vernacular—are rarely offered at Binghamton, and this course was the result of my initiative. It was offered through the Department of Asian and Asian American Studies. Since it was a new course, I was apprehensive that the student body might not find it appealing enough. But the multiple general education designations (humanities, global interdependencies, and composition) made the course attractive for prospective students. I advertised the course online and answered students' queries, and the Pakistani Student Association promoted the course through social media and word of mouth. The class size was limited to 25, and 24 students enrolled.

Of those 24 students, 13 could broadly be considered heritage students, which means that they were part of the South Asian diaspora in the United States, and 11 were nonheritage. Of the 13 heritage students, 7 were of Pakistani origin, 5 Indian, and 1 Bangladeshi. One student of Pakistani origin identified as a lesbian and as an Ahmadi, and another student identified as an Ecuadorian Pakistani. The cohort of nonheritage learners was also diverse and included various ethnicities (African American, Asian American, Chinese, Hispanic, white) and religious groups (Jewish, Jehovah's Witnesses). The class comprised 12 freshmen, 3 sophomores, 7 juniors, and 2 seniors. Thirteen students were majoring (or planning to major) in STEM, 6 in social sciences, 2 in business and accounting, 1 each in nursing and English literature, and 1 student was undecided. In terms of gender, 15 students identified as women and 9 as men.

In our first class, I asked students about their motivations for enrolling in the course. Most nonheritage students said they were interested in learning about different cultures. Michelle Keown, professor of postcolonial literature at the University of Edinburgh, writes about the desire among students (in her case, white, middle-class, British students) to "learn more about other cultures" through the study of literature (103). Keown observes that while "well-meaning, liberal sentiments" undergird students' intention to enroll in a course on postcolonial literature, the assumption "that one can gain knowledge of a culture by reading fictional or poetic meditations of 'reality'" is "highly problematic" (103). Most nonheritage students in my class, much like Keown's students, assumed that the course was meant to offer an "ethnographic 'window'" onto Pakistani culture (103). Most heritage students assumed the same, the only difference being that instead of learning about different cultures, they were interested in learning about their own culture. If nonheritage learners treated the course as a form of what Keown calls "intellectual or cultural tourism" (103), for heritage learners it was the academic equivalent of what certain social scientists call "roots tourism," in which second-generation migrants return to their parents' homelands with a desire to stay connected to their "roots" (Bolognani 107).

I structured the course in reverse chronological order; I started with literary works that explored relatively recent events and worked backward to 1947, the year Pakistan was created. The reverse chronological order enabled me to start with a text that required relatively little historical and cultural context; as a result, I was able to ease students (especially the nonheritage students) into the course. I also wanted to ensure that class time was devoted to developing different readings of the texts and not spent on explaining historical facts (e.g., the Partition of India in 1947 and of Pakistan in 1971) or providing answers to googleable questions (e.g., what the difference is between Muslims and Arabs or if Pakistan was in South Asia or the Middle East). For this purpose, I encouraged peer learning among heritage and nonheritage students. The emphasis on peer learning prompted an enterprising student to create a virtual group for the class on the messaging app *GroupMe*. All twenty-four students were part of this virtual group.

Our class met twice a week for an hour and a half. I dedicated two weeks (four class meetings) to every text. Students were required to read the assigned chapters and post a comment and a question related to the reading on the *Blackboard* discussion board before the start of a class. These comments and questions ranged from a few lines to several lengthy paragraphs in which students expressed their candid opinions about their individual reading processes and the difficulties they faced. I commented on some of the questions and encouraged students to respond to their peers, which many of them did. Moreover, I prepared my lectures in light of the questions and comments on the discussion board.

We started with Mohsin Hamid's novel *The Reluctant Fundamentalist*. There were three reasons for starting the course with this text. First, since the protagonist in Hamid's novel is a young Pakistani man who goes to college in New Jersey and moves to New York City after graduation, I assumed the novel would help me ease students into the course material. Second, the novel's length—fewer than two hundred pages. Third, unlike many novels by South Asian anglophone writers, *The Reluctant Fundamentalist* contains very few non-English words and cultural expressions, a feature that made the novel a useful point of entry in a course like this. I increased the level of cultural specificity with every subsequent reading. The fact that thirteen students chose the novel for their response papers and seven chose it for their final paper validated my decision to begin the course with this text. In an informal survey conducted at the end of the course, fifteen students said *The Reluctant Fundamentalist* was one of the two literary works they found "most interesting." Some students found the novel so intriguing that they read more than the assigned chapters. In addition, I assigned two critical essays about the novel: Anna Hartnell's "Moving through America: Race, Place and Resistance in Mohsin Hamid's *The Reluctant Fundamentalist*" and Priyamvada Gopal's "Of Capitalism and Critique: 'Af-Pak' Fiction in the Wake of 9/11." I also recommended my own interview with Hamid, included in my book *Writing Pakistan: Conversations on Identity, Nationhood and Fiction* (Bilal 153–73). Although it was not mandatory, some students read the interview and cited it in their response papers.

Hamid's novel lends itself well to Wolfgang Iser's phenomenological approach to reading, which understands reading as a collaborative process between a text and a reader. Iser prescribes that a literary writer must conceive a text in a manner that encourages such a collaboration by including certain unwritten parts, which will get written by the reader. Commenting on his writing process, Hamid says that the power of the novel as a genre is "rooted in the enormous degree of co-creation it requires on the part of its audience": "If the novel was special because it allowed writers and readers to create jointly . . . I should try to write novels that maximised this possibility of opening themselves up to being read in different ways, to involving the reader as a kind of character, indeed as a kind of co-writer" ("Mohsin Hamid").

Without making them overly self-conscious, I encouraged students to read the novel creatively by bringing their own personal experiences and worldviews to the process of reading as a type of cowriting. They found the phenomenological approach useful and empowering. One student found it liberating that she could use the first-person pronoun *I* while talking and writing about the novel. For another student, the absence of the "stress of getting it right" proved particularly productive. To write the unwritten parts of the novel, I told students they had to pay close attention to the way Hamid arranges his text and to the kinds of literary devices and narrative techniques he uses. Thus, we approached the process of writing the unwritten parts through close reading.

Before the start of our first class, I posted two comments on the discussion board in which I asked students to pay close attention to Changez (the protagonist's name), its meaning, and its spellings. One student commented that *Changez* meant "prosperous"; another said that it meant "firm, solid" and related it to how Erica (the American woman with whom Changez falls in love) tells Changez that he gives off a "strong sense of home," which makes him feel "solid" (Hamid, *Reluctant Fundamentalist* 19). A student of Pakistani origin said Changez was "not really a Pakistani name" and wondered if Changez changed his name after coming to America. For my part, I said I had always been intrigued by the way the name resembles the word *changes*.

This exercise served two purposes: first, students became cognizant of "the polysemantic nature" of the protagonist's name and, by extension, the text (Iser 290); and second, by paying close attention to Changez's name, they realized that the names of characters in a literary work serve denotative as well as connotative functions. One student commented on how similar Erica's name sounded to *America* and how Chris, Erica's deceased boyfriend, who had an "*Old World* appeal," made the student think of Christopher Columbus (Hamid, *Reluctant Fundamentalist* 27). The deceased Chris, I added, could also be read as a symbolic representation of the Christianity that America (Erica) was still in love with. Another student wondered about the significance of Juan-Bautista's name, and other students responded by mentioning biblical references to the name (John the Baptist is called "Juan-Bautista" in Spanish) and how the name aligns with his role as someone who helps Changez get rid of his "blinders" (145).

Having realized the various semantic possibilities of characters' names, students began to think critically about words such as "hungry," "shark," and "soldier," words that Jim, Changez's boss, uses to describe Changez (Hamid, *Reluctant Fundamentalist* 12, 70, 153). Close reading, therefore, led students toward defamiliarization. By the time I brought up the word *fundamentalism*, most students already seemed skeptical of the way it was generally understood. But instead of explaining it, I asked if anyone knew about market fundamentalism. I wanted to draw on students' knowledge of basic economic principles, but since no one had a background in economics, I googled "market fundamentalism" and projected the definition on the screen. We all read it together. One student commented on the limits of market fundamentalism and free market economy and cited the Coronavirus Aid, Relief, and Economic Security (CARES) Act as an example. This helped students make sense of the kind of fundamentalism Changez was "reluctant" to embrace.

From paying close attention to individual words and then sentences, students gradually moved toward an examination of form in *The Reluctant Fundamentalist*. The novel is a long dramatic monologue delivered by Changez to an unknown, unnamed American man who, at times, seems like he might be a CIA agent. The American never gets to speak, and whatever the reader learns about him is filtered through Changez's narrative voice. Halfway through the novel, one student wondered if he would ever hear directly from the American, and another asked why Hamid chose to write the novel this way. Many students seemed puzzled as to why Changez insists on narrating his life story to an American who appears uninterested.

Instead of answering directly, I asked students what they knew about the 9/11 attacks before reading the novel. Some students said that in school they were taught only about how 9/11 affected America, not about the impact America's reaction had on the world. Hamid's novel, they then realized, provided them with the perspective of someone who had been affected by America's reaction. Next, I asked students if any of them knew how to play counterpoint on the piano. A student who was a trained pianist explained how two melodic lines interweave to create polyphony in counterpoint. Once students had understood the idea of counterpoint, I invited them to consider what they were taught about 9/11 in their schools as one melodic line and Changez's monologue as another; this way, I said, they could make their own worldviews polyphonic. This particular way of reading a text, I told them, was called "contrapuntal reading" (Said 51).

Hamid's novel was a relatively easy read, but Sara Suleri's memoir, *Meatless Days*, which is "a feminized re-narration of the [Pakistani] national allegory" (Koshy 45), proved to be one of the most abstruse and challenging texts for students. Since we had only read novels (*Our Lady of Alice Bhatti*, by Mohammed Hanif; *Noor*, by Sorayya Khan; and *The Reluctant Fundamentalist*) before reading *Meatless Days*, many students presumed that it, too, was a novel. A couple students alerted their peers that the book was, in fact, a memoir. Although it was a necessary and useful correction, the mention of the word "memoir" made some students assume that it was the kind of book American celebrities and politicians write in which they offer lessons learned throughout their lives. Further, many students approached *Meatless Days* with an implicit formalist distinction between story (the events in a narrative) and discourse (the organization and rendition of the events in a narrative). As a result, they found Suleri's nonlinear narrative rendered in a densely metaphorical language "disorganized," "extremely confusing," "hard to read," and "full of tangents," which made it difficult for them to understand the "gist" of the story.

Since we read *Meatless Days* in the second half of the semester, students already knew that the kind of literary texts we had been reading required a rigorous engagement with the text that could only be achieved through multiple readings. Several students mentioned in their comments how rereading helped them make better sense of these texts. But with *Meatless Days*, even rereading did not help them much. Nor did they find particularly helpful (at least initially) the two critical essays I assigned— Shazia Rahman's "Orientalism, Deconstruction, and Relationality: Sara Suleri's *Meatless Days*" and Susan Koshy's "Mother-Country and Fatherland: Re-Membering the Nation in Sara Suleri's *Meatless Days*."

The pedagogical challenge, then, was to enable students to develop a mode of reading that helped them engage productively with Suleri's stylized prose, which interweaves memory with metaphor and womanhood with nationhood. I asked them to think of Suleri not as an author of the book they were reading but as an old, distant aunt who had traveled the world, met with different kinds of people, and had all sorts of stories to tell. This distant aunt came to their house and while sitting at the dinner table started recounting her experiences, which they had to listen to out of politeness. This pseudofamilial bond with the author and the imaginary compulsion of politeness significantly transformed students' relationship with the text. Instead of treating *Meatless Days* as a book they were reading in a literature course, they started imagining themselves as part of Suleri's family. I asked them to pay close attention to the kind of language Suleri uses instead of trying to get to the "gist" of the story. A sense of enjoyment then replaced students' initial confusion, although, as one student put it, it was a different kind of enjoyment. On the discussion board students also talked about their favorite chapters. Their favorite chapters were "Papa and Pakistan" (109–39), in which Suleri explores her father's role in the creation of Pakistan; "The Immoderation of Ifat" (131–50), which is about the death of her sister, Ifat; and "What Mama Knew" (151–69), a chapter dedicated to her Welsh mother who moved to Pakistan and taught English literature.

Another aspect of *Meatless Days* that students found challenging was Suleri's polyphonic metaphors, which, although rendered in English, contain residual traces of Urdu. While a close reading of certain metaphors, such as Ifat's having been "emptied" (174) and "living in language" (177), led to productive discussions, Suleri's extended metaphor of woman as absence, which she not only mentions explicitly but also enacts through the form of her self-effacing memoir, proved particularly difficult for students. "[T]he concept of woman was not really part of an available vocabulary" in Pakistan, Suleri asserts (1), and students asked what this meant. To answer this question, I told them we needed to look at the etymology of the word *aurat* in Urdu—Pakistan's national language. Of Arabic origin, this word is generally used as an equivalent to "woman" in Urdu, but literally it means a place of shame that needs to be kept hidden. Many heritage students who were familiar with the word were shocked at this revelation, but now they were able to appreciate how Suleri's remark was a comment on the way the Urdu language not only bestowed a sense of shame on the existence of a woman but also endeavored to keep women hidden.

Although close attention to metaphorical language in *Meatless Days* as well as the pseudofamilial bond with the author had altered for the better the way students engaged with the text, the nonlinearity of Suleri's narrative still frustrated them. One student even remarked that the book seemed to have suffered from poor editing. In an in-person class I asked students if anyone would like to share a memory. One student volunteered and narrated an incident from his childhood. We then discussed the complex portrayal of time in his narration, and I showed students the nonlinear presentation of time in the narration. During the discussion, the student added that while he did remember the incident from his childhood, there were certain details that had become part of his memory because they were narrated to him by his mother. There were also certain other details that he thought he misremembered. I repeated this exercise a few more times with different students. Then I asked students to narrate a memory to a friend and to see if their narration followed a neat chronology.

After students realized that the narration of memories is not always ordered chronologically, we went back to *Meatless Days*, and students immediately recognized that Suleri's text imitates the form memories take in human minds. One student commented that in her narration she filled the "gaps" in memories with her interpretations, which was similar to what Suleri had done in her book. Another student remarked that reading Suleri's book made her see the value in narrating and recording her own memories. Yet another student wondered if memory could exist independently of narration. Over the course of the two weeks during which we read and discussed *Meatless Days*, many students gradually moved away from the formalist distinction between story and discourse with which they had initially approached the text. One aspect of the book that resonated particularly strongly with many heritage students was Suleri's comments on her life in the diaspora and how she could express in Urdu what she could not in English.

Over the course of the semester, several students commented that our readings of texts like *The Reluctant Fundamentalist* and *Meatless Days*, which focused not on gleaning historical or cultural information about Pakistan and the Pakistani diaspora but on grappling with the moral, ethical, and political questions raised in these texts, was a form of critical reading they had never practiced before. This mode of engagement with literary texts, which positioned students as active cowriters rather than passive readers, enabled them to acquire a new set of reading skills that they could use not only in other academic courses but also in life in general. A sustained focus on reading as a creative process combined with critical pedagogical practices that were continuously recalibrated to suit different literary texts enabled me to impart what one student called an "introspective education."

Works Cited

Bilal, Mushtaq. *Writing Pakistan: Conversations on Identity, Nationhood and Fiction.* HarperCollins Publishers, 2016.

Bolognani, Marta. "Visit to the Country of Origin: How Second-Generation British Pakistanis Shape Transnational Identity and Maintain Power Asymmetries." *Global Networks*, vol. 14, no. 1, 2014, pp. 103–20.

Gopal, Priyamvada. "Of Capitalism and Critique: 'Af-Pak' Fiction in the Wake of 9/11." *South-Asian Fiction in English: Contemporary Transformations*, edited by Alex Tickell, Palgrave Macmillan, 2016, pp. 21–36.

Hamid, Mohsin. "Mohsin Hamid on Writing *The Reluctant Fundamentalist*." *The Guardian*, 13 May 2011, www.theguardian.com/books/2011/may/14/mohsin-hamid-reluctant-fundamentalist-bookclub.

———. *The Reluctant Fundamentalist.* Harcourt, 2007.

Hanif, Mohammed. *Our Lady of Alice Bhatti.* Jonathan Cape, 2011.

Hartnell, Anna. "Moving through America: Race, Place and Resistance in Mohsin Hamid's *The Reluctant Fundamentalist*." *Journal of Postcolonial Writing*, vol. 46, nos. 3–4, 2010, pp. 336–48.

Iser, Wolfgang. "The Reading Process: A Phenomenological Approach." *New Literary History*, vol. 3, no. 2, 1972, pp. 279–99.

Keown, Michelle. "Teaching Postcolonial Literature in an Elite University: An Edinburgh Lecturer's Perspective." *Journal of Feminist Scholarship*, vol. 7, no. 7, fall 2014-spring 2015, pp. 102–09.

Khan, Sorayya. *Noor.* Publishing Laboratory, 2006.

Koshy, Susan. "Mother-Country and Fatherland: Re-Membering the Nation in Sara Suleri's *Meatless Days*." *Interventions: Feminist Dialogues on Third World Women's Literature and Film*, edited by Bishnupriya Ghosh and Brinda Bose, Garland Publishing, 1997, pp. 45–57.

Rahman, Shazia. "Orientalism, Deconstruction, and Relationality: Sara Suleri's *Meatless Days*." *Literary Interpretation Theory*, vol. 15, no. 4, 2004, pp. 347–62.

Said, Edward W. *Culture and Imperialism.* Vintage Books, 1993.

Suleri, Sara. *Meatless Days.* U of Chicago P, 1989.

**Aniruddha Mukhopadhyay

Recontextualizing the Global Diaspora:
Mohsin Hamid's *Exit West*
at a Hispanic-Serving Institution

When teaching South Asian diasporic texts in American universities, we need to be cognizant of the location and nature of the institution and the backgrounds of the students and the instructor. This essay is based on my experience teaching Mohsin Hamid's novel *Exit West* at Texas A&M University, Kingsville. I argue for a pedagogical approach to help students recontextualize the global diaspora represented in the novel by drawing upon their own life experiences—in this case, growing up in South Texas, often in border towns, in a Hispanic-majority region with a complex political, linguistic, and cultural history.

Texas A&M University, Kingsville, is a designated Hispanic-serving institution (HSI), with around 70% of the student population identifying as Hispanic as of the fall semester of 2020 ("Interactive Campus Data"). It is important to understand the role that HSIs play in higher education in the United States. HSIs were first formally recognized in 1992 as part of the reauthorization of the Higher Education Act (Malcom-Piqueux and Lee 2). While Hispanics are the largest minority in the United States and the fastest-growing ethnic group according to the 2015 United States Census (Vela and Gutierrez 1–2), at 16%, the bachelor's degree completion rate of Hispanic American students lags behind both white American

216

(40%) and African American students (20%; Arbello Marrero and Milacci 219). However, studies show that Hispanic American students enrolled in HSIs perform better and have lower dropout rates than their counterparts at non-HSIs, and the completion rate for exclusively full-time students at HSIs is higher than the national graduation rate.

I joined the university in 2016 to teach twentieth- and twenty-first-century global anglophone literatures in the English program as an international faculty member of South Asian (Indian) origin specializing in postcolonial literatures and theories. While I had limited exposure to the southwestern region of the United States before joining the university, I soon developed a sense of the student body, the overall institutional environment focused on teaching and mentoring, and the cultural values of South Texas. This knowledge was facilitated through conversations with other faculty members, a transculturation workshop, and an intensive two-year orientation. Many of our students are first-generation and from working-class backgrounds, rural areas, or both. Students are often employed full- or part-time, many transfer from local community colleges, and many struggle with academic writing (Vela and Gutierrez 4–5). They bring to the classroom recognizably postcolonial anxieties such as lack of self-confidence, cultural and linguistic dissonance, and limited exposure to noncanonical literature. My main pedagogical goal is to spark students' interest in literary-cultural studies, to get them to start conversations, to read more, and to connect new ideas to their own contexts. This pedagogical focus informed my approach to teaching Hamid's *Exit West* in my upper-division undergraduate Postcolonial Literature and Theory course in the spring semester of 2020.

I also argue for a rethinking of postcolonial pedagogy and a recontextualizing of the global diaspora in the US classroom by reimagining the classroom itself and the students. By and large, prominent voices in postcolonial studies are located in major, research-focused institutions with primarily homogeneous, monocultural, and white student bodies from middle-class backgrounds. Let us imagine teaching postcolonial literature in South Texas, where over two-thirds of the students come from bicultural and bilingual backgrounds and have some sense of Gloria Anzaldúa's "nepantla," of living in between, living in the borderlands. The location then changes your pedagogical approach when you learn, even before you teach, of the history of the annexation of Texas and of the continuing political, linguistic, and cultural challenges of the Chicanx population. And so, here, the literature of the margin in a different context can be taught more effectively to address the concerns of the margins at home. Following Jacques Derrida, I encourage students to bridge the "aporia" of the subaltern (the other that is erased, is prefigured in its absence) in the literary text to the liminal figures they recognize in their own contexts, to recognize the "haunting" of borders/limits shared across time and space.[1]

Exit West has generally been hailed as a timely literary intervention in the growing global refugee crisis, and Ben De Bruyn describes it as "a migration novel that humanizes future migrants by accentuating the everyday character of displacement" (4). Hamid's novel narrativizes the migrations of a young couple, Saeed and Nadia, from an unknown city in an unnamed nation facing civil war. As their city and their middle-class lives descend into chaos and violence, the two protagonists use a "special door" to instantaneously transport themselves to the Greek island of Mykonos. Simple everyday doors are randomly transformed into magic doors that allow large numbers of people to cross borders into mostly "First World" nations. Saeed and Nadia join an eclectic group of migrants in a refugee camp in Mykonos. Soon, they use the doors again to join a global community of migrants in a palatial house in London. The novel also focuses on the reactions of the "First World" host nations and their citizens to this influx of refugees. The novel concludes with Saeed and Nadia finally teleporting to California, where their trajectories separate, and they seek different but hopeful futures.

I conducted the discussion of the novel over four class sessions while transitioning to distance learning because of the exigencies of the COVID-19 pandemic that forced all courses at my institution to go online. I structured the discussion of the novel around the following: introducing diaspora and diaspora theory, contextualizing the refugee crisis, analyzing the trope of doors in the novel, and analyzing the differences in migrant experiences based on location, class, and gender. I also used different interactive class activities to help students stay engaged, particularly since they were negotiating technological difficulties with distance learning amid growing concerns about a potentially deadly epidemic. I now discuss my experiences teaching each of the four abovementioned themes.

Introducing Diaspora and Diaspora Theory

I used Hamid's background and the depictions of migrancy in the novel as an opportunity to introduce students to diaspora theory. I showed them how to search for "diaspora" on the university's library website, and, together, we went over a couple of encyclopedia entries on the term. I explained how the term was originally used to refer to the Jewish, Armenian, and Greek diasporas (also known as "classical diasporas") as well as Africans displaced by slavery. We discussed the reinvention of diaspora theory in postcolonial studies and the difference between old and new diasporas. Students brought up the concept of hybridity, which we had previously discussed, and we talked about the diasporic subject's "insider-outsider perspective."

I also summarized for students R. Radhakrishnan's caution against the "de-racination" of the metropolitan diaspora that allows the celebration of radically ahistorical hybridity (175). We discussed the fact that Hamid never names Saeed and Nadia's hometown or nation, and while their names provide clues to their ethnic identity, the magic doors transport many other unnamed migrants from all over the world. I explained to students Radhakrishnan's argument for reterritorializing the diaspora through the situated hyphenation of the "ethnic self" (175). This understanding continued to inform students' recontextualization of immigrant identities throughout the rest of our discussion of the novel.

For this session's class activity, I had students read Hamid's interview in *The Day* ("Mohsin Hamid") and the poem "Refugees," by Brian Bilston, and then watch a *YouTube* video of Denice Frohman reading her poem "Borders" ("Denice Frohman"). Students then wrote a short paragraph or two connecting these texts to *Exit West*. In this activity, I particularly used Frohman's powerful oratory and "presence" to encourage students to think about borders, emphasizing Frohman's identity as a Latina and queer educator, writer, and activist. One of the students, in her response paper, connected our discussion of diaspora theory and borders to Anzaldúa's theory of "borderlands." So, students were already exploring the "haunting" of contexts in order to respond to and analyze the migration narrative of *Exit West*. They were recontextualizing the global migrations of Hamid's novel through their own knowledge and understanding of border crossings and border living in South Texas.

Contextualizing the Refugee Crisis

I created a slideshow of images of refugees from Syria, Iraq, and African nations; before-and-after images of neighborhoods devastated by war; a drawing by Michel Kichka of Alan Kurdi, the young Syrian boy who tragically drowned during his family's attempt to reach Kos by boat from

Turkey, surrounded by news crews with video cameras; and an image of Óscar Alberto Martínez Ramírez and his daughter, Valeria, who drowned in the Rio Grande trying to cross over to the United States (Le Duc). Before I showed the slides, I discussed with students the distressing nature of the images and the importance of acknowledging how the individual and collective trauma of these tragedies can affect us on a very personal level. I emphasized that there was nothing wrong with turning away from the slideshow, because recognizing the unbearable pain of these images helps us acknowledge the often desperate situation of refugees worldwide. I asked students to reflect on the images in relation to Hamid's narrative and gave them five minutes to jot down notes based on their reflections. Then I divided the class into groups and gave them another five to ten minutes to discuss their observations.

I then showed students images of refugees during India's traumatic Partition, pointing out the resonances in the mirroring of crowded bodies huddled together on boats, on the roofs of trains, and in tent cities. I noted that while the faces of Syrian or African refugees may differ from ours, the faces of South Asian refugees for me form a bridge to deeper empathy. The recognition of the similarities of the images of refugees from different communities in different contexts helps us extend our empathy from the communal to the global. Similarly, the "haunting" parallels between the tragic drownings of Valeria and Kurdi and the drowning of migrants attempting to cross the Rio Grande from Mexico to the United States enabled a more personal connection for students with the global refugee crisis.

In the ensuing discussion, one student mentioned that when people hear she lives in a border town, they immediately assume that her city is dangerous because of its proximity to Mexico and because of the influx of immigrants. The student pointed out that she has family in Mexico and that her perspective on why some Mexicans look to cross the border is different. As a citizen of a Hispanic-majority border town, she did not see her hometown as a dangerous place. The student also said that her grandmother, who does not speak English fluently, has to deal with racial stereotyping more than she does. This is a sentiment that students have often expressed to me, sometimes stating that they serve as interpreters for older family members who are uncomfortable speaking English. A few students have noted that because their parents were immigrants, they wanted their children to speak predominantly in English in order to avoid an accent and anglicized their children's names to help them better assimilate into

American society. Students brought these personal experiences to bear on the class discussion, adding nuances to the lives of migrants beyond Hamid's representation of the global diaspora.

Analyzing the Trope of Doors in the Novel

To better understand the trope of the doors in Hamid's novel, I designed a class activity inspired by a student interested in creative writing:

> Imagine you are one of the characters in Mohsin Hamid's *Exit West*. While we may not be in a war-torn country, we are experiencing some of the anxieties of Saeed and Nadia because of the ongoing pandemic. If you had access to one of the "doors" that take you to a different place, where would you hope to go? Whom would you take with you, and why? What would you take with you in your backpack? If you ended up in the place where you wanted to go, what would you do there? If you ended up in a place that you hadn't expected, what would your first steps be?

While students noted the lack of specificity regarding geospatial location and the complete elision of the migrant experience of the Middle Passage, the characters of Saeed and Nadia, lacking that specificity, seemed to some more relatable, particularly since students themselves, in the midst of the COVID-19 pandemic, were beginning to wish for magical doors to escape the constraints and anxieties of social distancing and stay-at-home orders. Students engaged in a spirited debate on the trope of the doors. One student pointed out that the doors, by eliminating the immigrant's journey, brought refugees closer to the citizens of the countries to which they migrated. The student clarified that because immigrants/refugees often have traumatic journeys, whether those journeys involve crossing a river from Mexico to South Texas or crossing an ocean, that trauma defines them not only in their own minds but also in the minds of the citizens of the host country. Hamid, the student felt, was attempting to bring the refugees and the citizens closer by eliminating the trauma of the Middle Passage.

There has been significant debate over the novel's central trope of "doors": some scholars have critiqued the erasure of the migrant's journey, while others have appreciated what they see as Hamid's desire to "demilitarize cross-border migration, in an attempt to normalize this 'crisis' and reintegrate displaced people into everyday life" (De Bruyn 6). Mai-Linh K. Hong, in a thought-provoking discussion of the global "refugee regime," lauds Hamid's ironic use of doors as "a clever, dramatic, and tongue-in-cheek literary device for highlighting the spurious and random-seeming nature of refugee life and refugee aid" (41). Similarly, Amanda Lagji acknowledges that the trope "collapses the friction of time and space that actual refugee movements entail" but argues that Hamid reproduces "the pain, struggles, and difficulties migrants face" in Saeed and Nadia's experience of transporting through the doors (225). Michael Perfect, however, analyzes the trope at length and notes his discomfort with a literary conceit that erases the traumatic journeys of refugees "to side-step all too conveniently the suffering of the very people at the centre of that crisis" (196). I summarized the arguments of De Bruyn, Hong, Lagji, and Perfect to show students that in their reflections, they were already in conversation with scholars in the field. For students who may have family members who have experienced border crossings, the discussion of Hamid's attempt to "normalize" the refugee experience was important.

Analyzing the Differences in Migrant Experiences Based on Location, Class, and Gender

In our discussion of the novel, the recognition of its relatability became an important point in identifying the intended readers of the novel. The class debated the suggestion that *Exit West* may speak more to metropolitan readers in "First World" nations, particularly in its attempt to change the perception of migrancy. For individuals who have recently migrated or who live in developing nations and hope to one day migrate for better opportunities, the concerns over borders as expressed in the narrative do not have the same resonance. In addition to identifying the metropolitan middle-class sensibility of the novel, students discussed the different experiences of migration based on the gender identities of Saeed and Nadia. One student argued that she would have expected the woman to be more "conservative," and this led to a discussion of how Nadia, because of her gender constraints, had a greater urge to be independent and to embrace a more cosmopolitan modern identity. As a result, she was the one to first desire escape through the "magic doors," while Saeed was more traditional, more religious, and more family-oriented in his outlook.

In this essay I have provided only a synopsis of the thought-provoking discussions by my students. What particularly stood out to me, as has been the case since I started teaching at Texas A&M University, Kingsville, was students' ability to follow my lead in recontextualizing the decontextualized global diaspora of the novel using their personal experiences and familiarity with the reality of border crossings. Such a gesture requires admirable courage and honesty from students as they sometimes voluntarily share personal details to situate abstract discussions of diaspora theory. While I look to introduce students to academic vocabulary and thoughtful considerations of literary-critical theory, I want to embrace and encourage this ability, informed by students' regional, cultural, and sociohistorical backgrounds, to personalize the political and recontextualize the global in the South Texas classroom.

Note

1. Derrida states in *Aporias*, "A plural logic of the aporia thus takes shape. It appears to be paradoxical enough so that the partitioning [*partage*] among multiple figures of aporia does not oppose figures to each other, but instead installs the haunting of the one in the other" (20).

Works Cited

Anzaldúa, Gloria. *Borderlands / La Frontera: The New Mestiza*. Aunt Lute Books, 1987.

Arbello Marrero, Floralba, and Fred Milacci. "Voices from the Academic Trenches: Academic Persistence among Nontraditional Undergraduate Hispanic Students at Hispanic Serving Institutions." *Journal of Ethnographic and Qualitative Research*, vol. 12, 2018, pp. 219–32.

Bilston, Brian. "Refugees." *National Poetry Day*, nationalpoetryday.co.uk/poem/refugees/. Accessed 12 Dec. 2020.

De Bruyn, Ben. "The Great Displacement: Reading Migration Fiction at the End of the World." *Humanities*, vol. 9, no. 1, 2020, https://doi.org/10.3390/h9010025.

"Denice Frohman - Borders." *YouTube*, uploaded by Button Poetry, 8 Apr. 2014, www.youtube.com/watch?v=CNK7Hn5_hLQ.

Derrida, Jacques. *Aporias*. Translated by Thomas Dutoit, Stanford UP, 1993.

Hamid, Mohsin. *Exit West*. Penguin Books, 2017.

———. "Mohsin Hamid Discusses 'Exit West,' His Acclaimed Novel about Migration and Refugees." Interview conducted by Kristina Dorsey. *The Day*, 23 Sept. 2018, www.theday.com/article/20180923/ENT10/180929980.

Hong, Mai-Linh K. "Navigating the Global Refugee Regime: Law, Myth, Story." *Amerasia Journal*, vol. 46, no. 1, 2020, pp. 34–48. *Taylor and Francis Online*, https://doi.org/10.1080/00447471.2020.1776571.

"Interactive Campus Data." Office of Institutional Research, Texas A&M University, Kingsville, 23 Dec. 2022, www.tamuk.edu/oira/institutional-data/Interactive-Campus-Data.html.

Kichka, Michel. "Aylan Kurdi." *Kichka*, 9 Mar. 2015, fr.kichka.com/2015/09/03/aylan-kurdi/.

Lagji, Amanda. "Waiting in Motion: Mapping Postcolonial Fiction, New Mobilities, and Migration through Mohsin Hamid's *Exit West*." *Mobilities*, vol. 14,

no. 2, 2018, pp. 218–32. *Taylor and Francis Online*, https://doi.org/10
.1080/17450101.2018.1533684.

Le Duc, Julia. "Photo of Drowned Migrants Captures Pathos of Those Who Risk
It All." *The New York Times*, 25 June 2019, www.nytimes.com/2019/06/25/
us/father-daughter-border-drowning-picture-mexico.html.

Malcom-Piqueux, Lindsey E., and John Michael Lee, Jr. *Hispanic-Serving Institutions: Contributions and Challenges*. College Board Advocacy and Policy
Center, Oct. 2011. *ERIC*, files.eric.ed.gov/fulltext/ED562686.pdf.

Perfect, Michael. "'Black Holes in the Fabric of the Nation': Refugees in
Mohsin Hamid's *Exit West*." *Journal for Cultural Research*, vol. 23, no. 2,
2019, pp. 187–201. *Taylor and Francis Online*, https://doi.org/10.1080/
14797585.2019.1665896.

Radhakrishnan, R. *Between Identity and Location: The Cultural Politics of Theory*.
Orient Longman, 1996.

Vela, Margie, and Paul Gutierrez. "The Hispanic Population and Hispanic Serving Institutions." *JEP: eJournal of Education Policy*, fall 2017. *ERIC*, files.eric
.ed.gov/fulltext/EJ1169366.pdf.

Binod Paudyal

Resisting Racialization: Mohsin Hamid's *The Reluctant Fundamentalist* in Ethnic Studies Courses

I teach Mohsin Hamid's *The Reluctant Fundamentalist* and other South Asian diasporic literary works in my Asian American studies courses, specifically to examine issues concerning the global war on terror, racialization of Muslims, and migrant and refugee crises. While I have taught *The Reluctant Fundamentalist* in different Asian American studies courses, such as Asian American Experiences and Asian American Cosmopolitanism at Northern Arizona University and Introduction to Asian American Studies and South Asian American Literature and Culture at University of Maryland, I can imagine teaching the text in a range of other ethnic studies courses focusing on issues of racialization and social justice. But for the purpose of this essay, I discuss my approach to teaching *The Reluctant Fundamentalist* in the Introduction to Asian American Studies course. I do this for two reasons. First, my approach to teaching Hamid's novel offers a theoretical and pedagogical framework for understanding the identity politics and exclusionary ideologies of the contemporary United States. Second, it helps teach students how South Asian diasporic authors like Hamid deal with issues of social justice by imaginatively subverting the epistemology of the hierarchical binary that constructs Muslims as other.

Since the Introduction to Asian American Studies course is cross-listed with American studies and fulfills the University of Maryland's general education requirement, it draws students from all disciplines with diverse interests and disciplinary trainings. I teach *The Reluctant Fundamentalist* toward the end of the semester, placing it under the topic "Asian Americans in the Post-9/11 United States." The course is structured around historical and contemporary Asian American experiences, so students have already been introduced to key issues and watershed moments in Asian American history. I spend two weeks (four seventy-five-minute class sessions) on the novel: I use the first session to discuss historical and theoretical concepts around the discourse of "us" versus "them" and the next three class sessions to analyze key issues in the novel. For the first session, I assign the introductory chapter of Edward Said's *Orientalism* (1–28) and Kent Ono's essay "Asian American Studies after 9/11." During the discussion, I ask students to reflect on any preconceived notions they may have of people of Islamic faith and ask them how they first learned about Muslims. Not surprisingly, most students shared that they had first learned about Muslims in school through discussions of the terrorist attacks of 9/11. My students' collective response reflects Amaney Jamal's finding that most Americans have come to know and learn about Islam and Arabs through the prisms of terrorism and barbarism, and a sizable percentage of Americans clearly believe that there is a fundamental clash of values between "us" and "them" (122). I remind students that following the events of 9/11 (and the more recent political shift in the United States since the 2016 US presidential election), South Asian Muslims and Sikhs (indeed, all Brown people from South Asia) have been mistakenly perceived as Arabs. They have become victims of hate crimes, racial profiling, physical assaults, and even murder because of their physical resemblance to people from the Middle East. This discussion helps students understand that post-9/11 American popular cultural production, which functions as an aspect of American Orientalism, tends to homogenize South Asian Americans—who might appear Muslim or Arab—into a single category, that of "terrorist," and treats them as what Sunaina Maira calls "the objects of intensified suspicion and surveillance" (333).

Although different Asian ethnic groups have been treated differently and have experienced different levels of prejudice in the United States as a result of the country's divergent colonial and imperial practices and foreign relations with respect to various Asian nations, framing the othering of South Asians in the post-9/11 era (and more recently, anti-Asian hate crimes and expressions of prejudice largely against East Asian Americans) within a larger historical context shows how the racist scapegoating of all Asian Americans has been an ugly part of American history. It is worth noting that anti-Asian prejudice and violence has intensified during times of crisis (including US tensions with Asian nations). For example, the treatment of South Asian Sikhs and Muslims after 9/11 and now of Chinese Americans (and East and Southeast Asians in general) conjures up memories of the internment of Japanese Americans and of the Chinese Exclusion Act. If Orientalism is an ideology that constructs the other in opposition to the "superior" West (and the American self for that matter), as Said argues (7), the history of American racist scapegoating of different Asian American ethnic groups—a systemic propensity, when confronted with a problem, to deflect the problem by blaming it on the other—itself constitutes American Orientalism.

With this contextual backdrop established, I frame Hamid's *The Reluctant Fundamentalist* as a response to the racist conflation of South Asian Americans (and Muslims in general) with terrorism and the intensified Islamophobia in the post-9/11 era. I demonstrate how the novel is a de-Orientalist text, to borrow Brett Levinson's concept (22), that critiques and dismantles Orientalist discourse about South Asian Muslims and Middle Easterners as potential terrorists, principally through what I call a "reverse-Conradian" narrative technique that speaks back to the Western power. The dramatic monologue in the novel carves out a space in which Changez, the Pakistani other, not only delivers his message to the silent American interlocutor but also illuminates American Orientalist discourse as a reflection of America's adherence to its presumed singularity, democracy, and uniqueness.

Throughout the novel, Hamid uses various globally recognized stereotypes in order to dismantle and redefine the political and cultural implications of these stereotypes. In doing so, Hamid positions his novel as a type of writing back, a form of creative resistance that disrupts the post-9/11 American discourse that tends to characterize Muslims and Arabs as inherently violent and hostile toward Americans. Such framing of the novel offers an alternative collective future by positioning the reader in a subject position. This approach helps students understand that Americans were not the only victims of the terrorist attacks of 9/11 and that this catastrophic event has had far-reaching and devastating impacts on South Asians living in both the United States and South Asia. As such, my primary goal in teaching Hamid's novel is not only to challenge the idea about racialization of Muslims, about xenophobia, but also to show how we as teachers of ethnic studies can subsequently use the classroom as a space for social transformation and imagining more just ways of life.

I direct students to the key passages in which Hamid engages with popular stereotypes of Muslims in order to help students begin to question certain misperceptions concerning South Asian Muslims and those whom xenophobes characterize as Muslims based on phenotype. For example, the novel begins in Anarkali, a formidable neighborhood of Lahore, as Changez, the narrator, offers to assist an unnamed American character who is cautiously seeking something not revealed to the reader. Changez tells him, "Do not be frightened by my beard: I am a lover of America" (Hamid 1). This strategy playfully foregrounds the suspicion, distrust, and fear of the silent American interlocutor, exhibiting Hamid's use of the stereotype of a bearded man, who is thus potentially a suspicious terrorist. What is also striking about the novel's opening is that Changez introduces himself as a "lover of America," subtly poking fun at the general misconception and fear generated by the image of a bearded man in the imagination of Americans. Although the reader does not actually hear the American speak, Changez's frequent comments about the interlocutor's reactions and gestures show that the American is very cautious and almost pathologically paranoid, anticipating danger from anyone and any direction. From the time Changez and the American listener sit in a corner of the restaurant until the end of the novel, when Changez walks with him to his hotel, the narrative makes the reader alert to the possibility of imminent danger. The reader is then momentarily relieved after seeing that every time the American becomes filled with terror, Changez reassures him that there is no danger.

Hamid's use of a de-Orientalist strategy—that is, the projection of a globally established terror threat from Muslims followed by the revelation that this threat is just an illusion—not only suggests that the American interlocutor is preoccupied with fear and terror of violence from Muslims but also illustrates that such terror is manufactured, merely the product of negative stereotypes about Muslims by American media and cultural discourse. To examine Hamid's deliberate use of globally recognized stereotypes of the violence-prone Muslim, I invite students to consider the term *fundamentalism* in relation to two separate but interrelated instances in the novel: Changez's claim that he is a "lover of America," and his pleasure upon seeing the Twin Towers collapse (Hamid 72). When students read that Changez smiles while watching the collapse of the Twin Towers on television in Manila, they instantly suspect that he is a "fundamentalist," a terrorist sympathizer and thus anti-American, and disagree with his claim that he is a "lover of America." But I remind them that Changez's pleasure upon seeing the collapse of the Twin Towers and the massacre of thousands of innocents, as he confesses to the American listener, actually comes from the surreal and surprising news that "someone had so visibly brought America to her knees" (73). I also remind students that the term *fundamentalism* not only is unique to certain terrorist groups with roots in Islam, as Hamid shows throughout the novel, but also refers to the guiding principle of many institutions and companies in the American corporate world and of the novel's fictional company Underwood Samson.

In the last session, we discuss how Hamid's novel helps us reconsider the epistemological, thematic, and geographic scope of Asian American studies by offering new ways of thinking about and understanding identities in the twenty-first century, a century marked by the global war on terror and complex global conditions, and by challenging the dominant US-based paradigms of what constitutes Asian American studies. I ask students to consider Changez as the embodiment of a new Asian American subject produced by the new sociopolitical circumstances of a post-9/11 world. The novel's engagement with and articulations of the racial logic of 9/11 reflect the category of a new Asian American by reenvisioning the primary agendas of Asian American studies. I invite students to characterize Changez as a new Asian American subject because, unlike the traditional conception of an Asian American, he is foreign-born, of Islamic faith, and has a sense of belonging to the United States but does not embrace Americanism and its so-called melting-pot ideology, rejecting his previous participation in neoliberal US capitalism, which he calls the "project of domination" (Hamid 156)—and what we might call neocolonialism—and cultivating his distinct ethnic identity as a bearded Muslim man.

While students find Changez's actions ostensibly anti-American, toward the end of the novel, they realize that Changez is not an enemy of the United States. I explain to students that the United States Changez claims he is in love with at the beginning of the novel, therefore, is not the one that excludes South Asian Muslims and looks back to its past; instead, it is the one that recognizes its origins in immigration and is responsive to the interconnected contemporary world, characterized by diversity and heterogeneity and mobility of people and their cultures and religions. To make this point evident, I ask students to consider the love triangle between Changez, Erica, and Erica's dead lover, Chris, as a political allegory.[1]

As reflected in the names of the characters, Erica represents America, Chris represents Christianity and America's past, and Changez, the non-white immigrant, represents the changing demographic landscape of the United States. Although Changez and Erica fall in love soon after the death of her first and longtime boyfriend, Chris, whom she describes as having "an Old World appeal" (Hamid 27), they are able to have sex only when Changez asks her to pretend that he is Chris.

Once we read Erica as contemporary America, Chris as old-world white America, and Changez as the changing demographic landscape of the United States, the contemporary reality, students can decipher the allegorical meaning the novel suggests—the failure of the melting-pot notion of multiculturalism, which tries to contain multiplicities only on its own terms. Erica (America) can allow Changez, a South Asian immigrant, to cross her borders only if he assimilates to old-world America (i.e., if he becomes Chris) and completely erases his ethnic identity. To further prove this point, I direct students to Erica's manuscript, which her mother gives to Changez after her disappearance. As he reads the manuscript, Changez notices that he is not a part of Erica's story; she found her past memories more valuable than Changez. Erica (and thus, allegorically, America) is unable to accept the present reality—as illustrated by her inability to make Changez a part of her story. But her attempt to escape from the present in order to live in a long-lost past results in a tragedy. Erica's suicide suggests that her longing for the white Anglo-European world is simply impossible to attain in twenty-first-century America, where diverse immigrants keep and maintain their ethnic and cultural identities. Here I tell students that perhaps acceptance of Changez could have rescued Erica from the conundrum of the past, enabling her to move forward and enjoy her new life and the changing world.

This discussion helps students understand that Hamid's novel allegorically suggests the need in the twenty-first century for the United States to move forward—instead of turning back "into myths of [its] own difference, assumptions about [its] own superiority" (Hamid 165). The novel points out these new possibilities mainly through its allusion to Joseph Conrad's Kurtz waiting for Marlow in *Heart of Darkness*. Changez tells his story to the American interlocutor for the first time. His narrative shows that he clearly knew that the American was a CIA agent on a special mission. But why, I ask students to consider, does Changez trust and tell his story to the American? Does the American interlocutor believe his story, particularly his assertion that he is a "lover of America"? Hamid does not answer these crucial questions explicitly in the novel, and students come up with different answers. But I remind them to consider the most important clue to the above questions: Changez's confession to the American interlocutor that he was "like a Kurtz waiting for his Marlow" (182). Here I briefly summarize the plot of Conrad's *Heart of Darkness*, assuming that the majority of students have not read the novella. I then discuss how considering Hamid's use of a literary allusion from *Heart of Darkness* can help us understand Changez's decision to tell his story to the American interlocutor because he already knew that he was on a list of suspects—for his "admittedly intemperate remarks," blaming America for inflicting "death so readily upon the inhabitants of other countries" and frightening "so many people so far away" (182)—and the interlocutor was a CIA agent on a mission, sent to him, as Marlow had been sent to find Kurtz. The narrative situation, however, is reversed in *The Reluctant Fundamentalist*: it is the visiting Marlow who narrates the story in *Heart of Darkness*; in Hamid's novel, it is Changez who tells his story to the American visitor.

Marlow and the American are sent to Kurtz and Changez, respectively, but the parallels do not end there. Additionally, both Kurtz and Changez are rebels who resist the expectations imposed on them: Kurtz abandons his company's orders and builds his own empire among natives of Congo, and Changez refuses to serve corporate America. The reader doubts whether the American interlocutor, who embodies Marlow, will carry Changez's story to the United States and introduce Changez not as an "enemy" but as a "lover of America" because there is a suspicion that he might assassinate Changez. Nevertheless, what is important is that, unlike Marlow, who tells the story of Kurtz and Africans from an Orientalist perspective, Changez tells his story from a non-Western perspective, thereby illuminating for students several stereotypes and misunderstandings about Pakistanis and Muslims in the American imagination. Changez particularly urges the American "not [to] imagine that we Pakistanis are all potential terrorists, just as we should not imagine that you Americans are all undercover assassins" (Hamid 183).

Teaching South Asian diasporic literary texts such as *The Reluctant Fundamentalist*, written in the wake of 9/11, offers us a new way to reconceptualize Asian American literary studies by exploring overlaps between South Asian and Asian American studies. Although Hamid's *The Reluctant Fundamentalist* narrates Changez's personal story, his personal story becomes universal in that it reflects the predicament of South Asians living in the United States and beyond in the post-9/11 era. Changez does not conform to the traditional notion of Asian American identity based on historical and cultural knowledge practices of East Asians. Instead, Changez can be understood as a new Asian American subject, a Muslim immigrant born in Pakistan, whose identity is still in the making. As Lisa Lowe compellingly argues, "Rather than considering 'Asian American identity' as a fixed, established given, perhaps we can consider instead 'Asian American cultural practices' that produce identity; the processes that produce such identity are never complete and are always constituted in relation to historical and material differences" (64). Understood in this light, Changez's identity represents an Asian American identity influenced by the shifting social and political circumstances of a post-9/11 world, circumstances that render that identity in a constant state of flux and evolution. These shifting social circumstances and relations in the post-9/11 United States, as Ono argues, are the minimum requirements needed to reconceptualize the field of Asian American studies (448). Ono reminds us that the terrorist attacks of 9/11 are an opportunity to rethink the parameters of the field and to understand the complexity of all that Asian American studies represents (448). In this context, I suggest that teaching *The Reluctant Fundamentalist* in ethnic studies courses can help us reconceptualize Asian American studies by examining the ways in which the global war on terror and Islamophobia within and beyond the United States have changed the face of Asian American studies and conceptions of Asian American identity. It can also help us renew the foundational social justice and civil rights agendas at the origins of Asian American studies in today's shifting social, racial, and political circumstances.

Note

1. A number of critics have already pointed out the allegorical meanings of the names, reading Erica as America, Chris as Christopher Columbus or Christ, Changez as representative of the demographic changes in the United States due to new non-white immigrants, and Underwood Samson as corporate America (e.g., Chakravorty; Hartnell; Morey). But I interpret these names allegorically to explore our understanding of a new Asian American identity (and the changing conceptions of American identity) in an era of transnational connections and in the context of the global war on terror.

Works Cited

Chakravorty, Mrinalini. *In Stereotype: South Asia in the Global Literary Imaginary*. Columbia UP, 2014.

Conrad, Joseph. *Heart of Darkness*. Edited by Paul B. Armstrong, W. W. Norton, 2006.

Hamid, Mohsin. *The Reluctant Fundamentalist*. Harcourt, 2007.

Hartnell, Anna. "Moving through America: Race, Place and Resistance in Mohsin Hamid's *The Reluctant Fundamentalist*." *Journal of Postcolonial Writing*, vol. 46, nos. 3–4, July-Sept. 2010, pp. 336–48.

Jamal, Amaney. "Civil Liberties and the Otherization of Arab and Muslim Americans." *Race and Arab Americans before and after 9/11: From Invisible Citizens to Visible Subjects*, edited by Jamal and Nadine Naber, Syracuse UP, 2008, pp. 114–30.

Levinson, Brett. "The Death of the Critique of Eurocentrism: Latinamericanism as a Global Praxis/Poiesis." *Orientalism and Identity in Latin America: Fashioning Self and Other from the (Post)Colonial Margin*, edited by Erik Camayd-Freixas, U of Arizona P, 2013, pp. 19–34.

Lowe, Lisa. *Immigrant Acts: On Asian American Cultural Politics*. Duke UP, 1996.

Maira, Sunaina. "Youth Culture, Citizenship, and Globalization: South Asian Muslim Youth in the United States after 9/11." *Asian American Studies Now: A Critical Reader*, edited by Jean Yu-wen Shen Wu and Thomas C. Chen, Rutgers UP, 2010, pp. 333–53.

Morey, Peter. "'The Rules of the Game Have Changed': Mohsin Hamid's *The Reluctant Fundamentalist* and Post-9/11 Fiction." *Journal of Postcolonial Writing*, vol. 47, no. 2, 2011, pp. 135–46.

Ono, Kent A. "Asian American Studies after 9/11." *Race, Identity, and Representation in Education*, edited by Cameron McCarthy et al., 2nd ed., Routledge, 2005, pp. 439–51.

Said, Edward W. *Orientalism*. 1978. 25th anniversary ed., Vintage Books, 1994.

Suhaan Kiran Mehta

Pakistani Anglophone Diasporic Literature in Writing-Intensive Seminars

I taught writing-intensive seminars for four years at Case Western Reserve University, a STEM-focused institution in Cleveland, Ohio. These classes, either led individually or taught collaboratively, fell in the ambit of the Seminar Approach to General Education and Scholarship program. In existence since 2004, the program will be replaced with new general education requirements starting in fall 2023. To fulfill the program's requirements, all incoming undergraduates were required to take a sequence of three general education, predisciplinary writing courses—a first seminar followed by a couple university seminars ("Course Sequence"). I was an independent instructor of record for first seminars on topics related to my research interests in South Asian literatures with titles such as The South Asian Immigrant Experience, Fictions of the British Empire, and Partition Fictions. Additionally, for three semesters—spring 2014, 2015, and 2016—I led a university seminar titled Literature of 9/11 that emerged from my dissertation on 9/11 fiction and film from Pakistan and the Pakistani diaspora. Using examples from my Literature of 9/11 classes in particular—by relying on course syllabi, lesson plans, assignment prompts, and my recollection of classroom activities—I discuss how my teaching in a general education program advanced its key learning outcomes. I focus, for the most part, on critical thinking and academic writing and somewhat briefly on oral communication. I then discuss how I organized virtual visits of Pakistani authors to my classes. In the final section, I explain how I plan to teach Pakistani anglophone diasporic writing in a senior literature seminar at my current institution, the University of Colorado, Colorado Springs—a public regional university in the Southwest.

Why Study Pakistani Anglophone Diasporic Literature?

One of the objectives of my university seminar on 9/11 literature was to emphasize that 9/11 was part of a complex chain of events. These include America's covert involvement in the anti-Soviet Afghan jihad in the 1980s and the global war on terrorism in Afghanistan and Iraq beginning in 2001 and 2003, respectively. Pakistani anglophone diasporic texts such as H. M. Naqvi's *Home Boy*, Kamila Shamsie's *Burnt Shadows*, Mohsin Hamid's *The Reluctant Fundamentalist*, and Nadeem Aslam's *The Wasted Vigil* offer rich representations of the many dimensions of 9/11. I assigned *The Wasted Vigil* in spring 2015 and 2016 because Aslam poignantly depicts the catastrophic effects of foreign invasions and local autocracies on quotidian Afghan lives over a period of about two decades. Given that the link between *The Wasted Vigil* and 9/11 would not be apparent to all students, I planned my course schedule to ease students into Aslam's novel.

Situating Pakistani Anglophone Diasporic Literature

At the start of the semester, I set a template of proceeding from the local to the global. On the first day of class, I played clips from Steven Rosenbaum's *Seven Days in September*, which pieces together video recordings of the immediate aftermath of the terrorist attacks on the World Trade Center. This documentary effectively captures the confusion, anger, and grief of individuals trying to process the day's tragic events. Subsequently, students watched a few short films from a collection titled *September 11*, which foregrounds international and immigrant perspectives on 9/11. Alejandro Iñárritu masterfully uses sound to convey the horror of people jumping to their deaths from the burning towers. In Ken Loach's take, an exiled Chilean author based in London writes a letter to the kin of those killed on 9/11. He reminds them of the military coup led by General Augusto Pinochet against President Salvador Allende with the tacit support of the US government on 11 September 1973.[1] Mira Nair's film is based on the true story of a Pakistani American emergency medical technician, Mohammad Salman Hamdani. Hamdani becomes a terror suspect after he goes missing on 9/11, until it eventually transpires that he rushed to ground zero to save lives. Samira Makhmalbaf's film shows how an Afghan teacher and her students, who are refugees in Iran, express solidarity with the victims of 9/11. Students had to rank the film they found most and least enjoyable and explain their choices. The ensuing class discussion anticipated some of the topics they would encounter later in the semester, such as America's militarism overseas, post-9/11 Islamophobia, and the Afghan refugee crisis. Also, the order in which I presented the material in the first week was a primer for how I organized the remainder of the course readings.

Students read Jess Walter's novel *The Zero* before reading *The Wasted Vigil*. Walter represents the traumatic effects of 9/11 on Americans through the disorienting experiences of a cop named Brian Remy. At the same time, the novel is critical of how a tragedy was exploited to normalize a culture of hypersurveillance. Having thought about 9/11 in the American context, we proceeded to Aslam's Afghanistan-based novel, *The Wasted Vigil*. Given Aslam's nuanced portrayal of typically unsympathetic characters, students encountered a potentially unfamiliar perspective on a contentious topic ("Mission"). I shall illustrate this with a specific example from my spring 2016 class. On one occasion in Aslam's novel, a character named Casa provides instructions to a young man named Bihzad—the namesake of the celebrated Persian miniaturist who lived in the fifteenth and sixteenth centuries—on carrying out a suicide mission (45–50). To facilitate discussion I asked students the following: How does Aslam represent the consequences of suicide bombing and the character of the suicide bomber? For the first part of the question, I got students to consider lines such as "the survivors [of the bombing] had in all probability needed time to comprehend fully what just had taken place. The souls will need longer still, [Marcus] knows, and they may not begin their howls for months and years" (Aslam 54). With regard to the second part of the question, I wanted students to notice how Aslam humanizes Bihzad by providing his backstory. As a case in point, the narrator says, "Bihzad and Casa . . . had then talked about their childhoods: the hunger, the refugee camps, the deaths one by one of the adults around them due to various causes, the orphanages, the beatings and worse, the earning of daily bread as beggars or labourers in the bazaars" (49). Students appreciated how Aslam depicts the suicide bomber as a three-dimensional figure without condoning his depraved actions. Students' ability to make this distinction demonstrated their ability "to think critically" and to engage in "ethical deliberation" ("Mission").

At times, students took the lead in situating a South Asian anglophone diasporic novel like *The Wasted Vigil* by presenting historical material to their peers. In spring 2016, I had each student do research on a relevant topic such as "The Afghan Mujahedeen," "The Revolutionary Association of the Women of Afghanistan," and "The Military-Industrial Complex." Toward the end of the semester, they presented their findings in a five-minute talk modeled on PechaKucha, a form of presentation comprising twenty *PowerPoint* slides, where each slide is displayed for only twenty seconds ("About"). The criteria for evaluating presentations included articulating a clear argument, spelling out key takeaways, using visuals imaginatively and resourcefully, and effectively engaging the audience. Following their presentations, students had to respond to questions by their peers and me; this assignment honed their oral communication skills ("Mission").[2] A student once remarked that the PechaKucha format helped them stay on point and deliver a concise presentation.

Writing about Pakistani Anglophone Diasporic Literature

Besides effective oral communication, another crucial learning outcome of the program is to be able to write persuasively for various audiences ("Mission").[3] I would get students to think about the element of audience by having them reflect on the "so what" question. Undergraduates at Case Western enrolled in a semester-long writing course to satisfy a general education requirement may not necessarily be attuned to the scholarly conversation on Pakistani anglophone diasporic literature. Therefore, I suggested that students could respond to the "so what" question by exploring connections between the representation of topics such as immigration, 9/11, and Islamophobia in the primary text and the representation of such topics in other types of media. This would extend the scope of their analysis beyond the course material and situate it in a larger ecosystem, one with which student writers and their readers were more likely to be familiar.

Using published scholarship as a model often enabled me to have a conversation about various elements of academic writing, including answering the "so what" question. In spring 2015 and 2016, I chose Eoin Flannery's piece "Internationalizing 9/11: Hope and Redemption in

Nadeem Aslam's *The Wasted Vigil* (2008) and Colum McCann's *Let the Great World Spin* (2009)." This article fit well with my course theme because it examined two perspectives on 9/11 by immigrant authors, including one from the Pakistani diaspora. Flannery argues that authors such as Aslam and McCann "deal with 9/11 in elliptical ways" and "provide geographically and historically displaced narrative responses to the terroristic outrages and, by implication, to the impassioned subsequent reactions and repercussions" (295). While discussing Flannery's response to the "so what" question, we talked about how he connects his analysis of *The Wasted Vigil* and *Let the Great World Spin* with reflections on the relationship between aesthetics and violence; drawing on the words of the Irish poet Seamus Heaney, Flannery contrasts the "redemptive moral value" of "art" with "the destabilizing values of murderous terrorism" (314). If I were to use this article again, I would also ask students to look at the author guidelines available on the website of the journal *English*, where Flannery's article was published. Journal contributors are informed that essays are "aimed at readers within universities and colleges and presented in a lively and engaging style" ("Instructions"). In other words, articles in *English* would be of interest to literary scholars in general and not just to specialists of Pakistani anglophone diasporic literature. This would help students better understand why Flannery responded to the "so what" question in a particular way and, more broadly, how to write for "both discipline-specific and broader audiences" ("Mission").

Connecting with Pakistani Anglophone Diasporic Authors

Though students wrote analytical papers in my courses, I also wanted them to gain insight into the process of creative writing. After our class discussions on particular novels, I arranged online video-chat sessions with authors. The Pakistani authors H. M. Naqvi and Kamila Shamsie spoke to my students about *Home Boy* and *Kartography* in my South Asian Immigrant Experience and Partition Fictions courses, respectively. The author of *The Zero,* Jess Walter, and the author of *The Corpse Washer*, Sinan Antoon, joined us in my Literature of 9/11 class. Ngũgĩ wa Thiong'o connected with my students in my Fictions of the British Empire class and engaged them in a conversation about his book *A Grain of Wheat*. With the exception of Shamsie, whom I had met when she visited the Case Western campus in April 2016, I sent cold emails to the authors. (Cold emailing has yielded mixed results. Other writers not mentioned here did not respond to my invitation for a virtual conversation with students.)

Shamsie spoke to my students on *Skype* from London in fall 2016. Students came prepared with questions for her that they submitted to me at the end of the class period. She spoke on a range of issues, including the genesis of *Kartography*, the significance of historical knowledge, and the need to reject easy explanations for complex situations. Students appreciated being able to connect with Shamsie, as evidenced in their thank-you notes to her, which I compiled and emailed to her after the session. Above all, students' comments showed how Shamsie's perspective enriched students' critical assessment of the novel. I have continued to reach out to creative writers while teaching at the University of Colorado, Colorado Springs, and in fall 2021 I used department funds to offer an honorarium to each guest. A senior colleague has encouraged me to avail of campus-wide funding resources if I continue to invite writers to speak to my students. I would like to offer a fee to writers to acknowledge the time that they are making for my students and me.

The writing program at Case Western provided me with the space to teach to my strengths while factoring in student resistance to general education courses. In my current capacity as a global anglophone specialist in the English department at the University of Colorado, Colorado Springs, my audience is made up predominantly of English majors.

Pakistani Anglophone Diasporic Literature in a Senior Literature Seminar

In the final section of this essay, I comment on how I plan to teach a course on 9/11 and Pakistani anglophone diasporic literature as a senior seminar. The course will foreground the following questions: How does Pakistani anglophone diasporic literature affect our understanding of 9/11? How do characters in these texts complicate the post-9/11 dichotomy of the "good Muslim" versus the "bad Muslim" that Mahmood Mamdani has written about?[4] How does the trajectory of some of the characters reveal a shift in the perception of South Asian Americans as model minorities, as Sunaina Maira has suggested?[5] Drawing on Judith Butler, what is the relationship between collective national grief and transnational empathy in anglophone Pakistani literature?[6] What makes tragedies in certain parts of the world more visible than those in others? How does the global orientation of Pakistani anglophone diasporic literature, including its attention to Afghanistan, interrogate our commonplace understanding of living in a post-9/11 world? To help students grapple with these questions, I will have them read four primary texts: Aslam's *The Wasted Vigil*, Kamila Shamsie's *Burnt*

Shadows, Hamid's *The Reluctant Fundamentalist*, and Naqvi's *Home Boy*. I will also include scholarly works that historicize contemporary Pakistani anglophone diasporic literature and critically evaluate its visibility in the twenty-first century global literary marketplace (Kanwal and Aslam; Cilano; Chambers; Clements; M. Shamsie). By the end of the course, students will have expanded their awareness of noncanonical literature, cultivated a deep understanding of how various forms of trauma and resilience are mediated in fiction, developed a multidimensional understanding of 9/11 and its aftermath, learned about the major debates on fields of study such as Pakistani anglophone diasporic literature and the literature of 9/11, and advanced their critical thinking, reading, and writing skills. To demonstrate how students will realize some of these outcomes, I turn to Kamila Shamsie's *Burnt Shadows*, a novel that spans several cities and decades.

Though I am sketching out a future course, my approach to *Burnt Shadows* will be consistent with how I frame conversations in my literature classes at the University of Colorado. My students or I put together discussion questions and make them available to the entire class ahead of time. If students put together the questions, they email these to me a couple days before class, and after tweaking them, I send them to everybody. Questions are always paired with relevant passages from the reading, so students know that claims have to be supported by textual evidence. For instance, there is a moment in *Burnt Shadows* when Raza is forced to travel undetected from Afghanistan to Canada, where he can reconnect with his mother, Hiroko. Raza has been working as a translator for Arkwright and Glenn, a private military contractor fighting America's global war on terrorism. After he is wrongly accused of killing another character, a former CIA agent named Harry Weiss-Burton, Raza decides to flee from Afghanistan. At one point in his journey, Raza travels with undocumented migrants under the planks of a wooden boat:

> Raza peered down. There was no space between one body and the next, the men laid out like something familiar, but what? What did they remind him of? . . . It was only when the captain slammed down the hatch, extinguishing all light, that he knew what the line of bodies made him think of—the mass grave in Kosovo. . . . Raza closed his eyes. In all the years he had sat around campfires with the TCNs [Third Country Nationals] listening to their tales of escape from one place to another, in the holds of ships, beneath the floorboards of trucks, it had never occurred to him how much wretchedness they each had known. (K. Shamsie 342–43)

Several questions emerge from this passage:

> What are some of the images or words that come to mind when you hear the word *immigration*? How does this passage reinforce or complicate your initial associations?
>
> Why does Shamsie call attention to TCNs in this passage and elsewhere in the novel?[7]
>
> Seeing migrants in the boat reminds Raza of "the mass grave in Kosovo" (342). What do you make of this comparison?[8]

Circulating questions ahead of time provides meaningful structure while giving ample opportunities to students to shape the trajectory of the conversation. At the start of class, students typically discuss questions in small groups. Then each group shares their thoughts with everyone, and I pull threads from students' responses to pose follow-up questions. The class activity centering on *Burnt Shadows* will especially further two of the five learning outcomes of the senior literature seminar I plan to teach at my current institution: understanding how trauma and resilience are represented in fiction and cultivating a complex understanding of the global war on terrorism. The discussion questions will also help students address one of the queries animating the course, namely why some tragedies have greater visibility than others. While conceptualizing this exercise, I draw on Ken Bain's discussion of how to create a "natural critical learning environment" (100) by posing thoughtful questions and guiding students to provide responses (100, 103).

At Case Western, I integrated my scholarly interests with the student learning outcomes of the general education program. At the University of Colorado, I remain committed to improving student writing through rigorous feedback and one-on-one student-teacher conferences. Because the learning outcomes in a senior seminar for English majors are different from those articulated for a general education program, my students and I can devote more time to the conceptual questions animating South Asian anglophone diasporic literature.

Notes

I thank my former colleague Dr. Erika Olbricht for her characteristically kind and thoughtful feedback on this essay.

1. The CIA was directed by President Richard Nixon in September 1970 to stop President Salvador Allende, a "socialist parliamentarian" (Kornbluh 1), from becoming Chile's president, but its covert mission failed (29–30). The US

government then recalibrated its goals and decided to carry out "a long-term expanded effort to destabilize the Chilean government" (80). This strategy "create[d] a 'coup climate' in which the overthrow of Chilean democracy could and would take place" (114). These conditions contributed to the Chilean military's success in violently overthrowing Allende's government on 11 September 1973 (113–14).

2. Students benefited immensely from my colleagues Dr. William (Bill) Doll and Dr. Sarah de Swart's informative and lively workshop on how to make effective presentations.

3. One of my co-instructors at Case Western, Professor Barbara Clemenson, would helpfully point out to her students that a paper's grader is not the same as its reader.

4. In *Good Muslim, Bad Muslim*, Mahmood Mamdani writes that President George W. Bush implied in one of his post-9/11 speeches that all American Muslims were guilty of terrorism until proven otherwise (15). He adds that the uncritical use of the categories "good Muslim" and "bad Muslim" by President Bush reveals a superficial political understanding of the contemporary world (16). In H. M. Naqvi's novel *Home Boy*, the obituary of a character named Mohammed Shah, killed during the 9/11 attacks, reveals the pervasiveness of the "good Muslim / bad Muslim" dichotomy (Morey, ch. 4). Shah's colleague Michael Leonard is quoted as saying, "Everybody thinks all Muslims are fundamentalists. . . . Mohammed wasn't like that. He was like us, like everybody. He worked hard, played hard" (Naqvi 270).

5. Maira writes that the perception of Muslim South Asians changed after 9/11 "from being 'good' minorities—although with 'foreign' cultural traditions—to potentially 'bad' or militant minorities who could be a threat to the nation" (176).

6. Butler asks whether the "situation of mourning" can "supply a perspective by which to begin to apprehend the contemporary global situation" (28) and subsequently comments that "[m]indfulness of . . . vulnerability can become the basis of claims for non-military political solutions, just as denial of this vulnerability through a fantasy of mastery . . . can fuel the instruments of war" (29).

7. To provide context about the role of TCNs in the war on terror, I will assign Sarah Stillman's "The Invisible Army."

8. Students will have read Julian Borger's short report on unearthing a mass grave in Rudnica, Serbia—yet another instance of Slobodan Milošević's war crimes against Albanians.

Works Cited

"About Us." *Pecha Kucha*, www.pechakucha.com/about. Accessed 30 Dec. 2020.

Aslam, Nadeem. *The Wasted Vigil*. Vintage Books, 2008.

Bain, Ken. *What the Best College Teachers Do*. Harvard UP, 2004.

Borger, Julian. "Kosovo Albanian Mass Grave Found under Car Park in Serbia." *The Guardian*, 10 May 2010, www.theguardian.com/world/2010/may/10/kosovo-albanian-mass-grave-serbia.

Butler, Judith. *Precarious Life: The Powers of Mourning and Violence*. Verso, 2004.

Chambers, Claire. *British Muslim Fictions: Interviews with Contemporary Writers*. Palgrave Macmillan, 2011.

Cilano, Cara. *Contemporary Pakistani Fiction in English*. Routledge, 2013.

Clements, Madeline. *Writing Islam from a South Asian Muslim Perspective*. Palgrave Macmillan, 2016.

"The Course Sequence." *SAGES*, Case Western Reserve U, 7 Feb. 2017, sages.case.edu/2014/12/05/the-course-sequence/.

Flannery, Eoin. "Internationalizing 9/11: Hope and Redemption in Nadeem Aslam's *The Wasted Vigil* (2008) and Colum McCann's *Let the Great World Spin* (2009)." *English*, vol. 62, no. 238, 2013, pp. 294–314.

Hamid, Mohsin. *The Reluctant Fundamentalist*. Harvest, 2007.

"Instructions to Authors." *Oxford Academic*, Oxford UP, 2023, academic.oup.com/english/pages/General_Instructions.

Kanwal, Aroosa, and Saiyma Aslam, editors. *The Routledge Companion to Pakistani Anglophone Writing*. Routledge, 2019.

Kornbluh, Peter. *The Pinochet File*. New Press, 2003.

Maira, Sunaina. *Missing: Youth, Citizenship, and Empire after 9/11*. Duke UP, 2009.

Mamdani, Mahmood. *Good Muslim, Bad Muslim: America, the Cold War, and the Roots of Terror*. Doubleday, 2005.

"Mission and Student Learning Outcomes." *SAGES*, Case Western Reserve U, 10 Apr. 2019, sages.case.edu/2015/01/20/learning-outcomes/.

Morey, Peter. *Islamophobia and the Novel*. E-book ed., Columbia UP, 2018.

Naqvi, H. M. *Home Boy*. Shaye Areheart, 2009.

September 11. Directed by Samira Makhmalbaf et al., Empire Pictures, 2002.

Seven Days in September. Directed by Steven Rosenbaum, Anchor Bay, 2004.

Shamsie, Kamila. *Burnt Shadows*. Picador, 2009.

Shamsic, Muneeza. *Hybrid Tapestries: The Development of Pakistani Literature in English*. Oxford UP, 2017.

Stillman, Sarah. "The Invisible Army." *The New Yorker*, 30 May 2011, www.newyorker.com/magazine/2011/06/06/the-invisible-army.

Walter, Jess. *The Zero*. Harper Perennial, 2006.

Part VII

The Forms of Diaspora:
Nonfiction, Film, Television,
Digital and Creative Writing

Subhalakshmi Gooptu

Teaching Memoirs: Nonfiction as Public Discourse in South Asian Diasporas

Introducing nonfiction writing in a literature class always has its surprises. After weeks of persuading students of the value of literary writing and fictional representation, when I transition to nonfiction, I encounter faces filled with a sense of deep confusion. Despite this, in these moments students time and again engage with the complex relationship between fiction and nonfiction to broaden and often challenge their notions of literary mediation and representation. I first began working on this essay while teaching an extract from the South Asian diasporic writer Julietta Singh's memoir, *No Archive Will Restore You*. In our discussions, I asked students to contemplate the following question: Should we read fiction and nonfiction differently? Over two years of teaching a general education literature class, in which I assign nonfiction alongside novels, poetry, and theory, has fortified my pedagogical approach to introduce multiple genres in undergraduate classrooms.

The nonfiction genre is hardly new to the South Asian canons. V. S. Naipaul, Michael Ondaatje, Salman Rushdie, Amitav Ghosh, Pico Iyer, and Arundhati Roy are widely celebrated for their contributions to public discourses through nonfiction writing. However, the teaching of South Asian nonfiction has not been widely explored. A special issue of *Safundi:*

The Journal of South African and American Studies titled *Beyond Rivalry: Literature/History, Fiction/Non-fiction* is instructive in examining the long-standing separation of nonfiction and fiction in literary canons of postcolonial nations and the complex relationship between history and the teaching of literature (Barnard). The issue is especially valuable because it embraces fiction and nonfiction as correlated mediations of South African histories. In a similar vein, I do not attempt to replace fictional texts but instead assemble syllabi that bring together fiction and nonfiction writing as literary mediations of South Asian diasporic pasts and presents.

Given the distinct but growing body of scholarship on nonfiction, especially memoirs, creative autobiographies, and graphic narratives (Kersten and Dallacqua; Pedri), along with an established corpus of teaching the craft of creative nonfiction in the United States (Young; Bloom), it is hardly surprising that scholarship on South Asian and South Asian diasporic nonfiction has grown in recent years (Mezey; Rao; Hai; Azar). Its focus on the relationship between nonfiction, the literary market, and digital media opens up yet another avenue of interrogating digital circulation and transformations of nonfiction through the burgeoning field of digital humanities (Risam; Murray). Additionally, the growing body of nonfiction in South Asian languages and their English translations, specifically a renewed interest in memoirs by Dalit writers, highlights the relationship between language, representation, and identity.

Surveying contemporary nonfiction writing corroborates the rising prominence of South Asian interlocutors on a global stage, interlocutors who distinguish themselves by traversing the binaries history/present and political/personal in their distinctive ways. The intention of this essay is twofold: to make a case for teaching nonfiction from South Asian diasporas, specifically memoirs, and to envision the future of South Asian literary studies through this pedagogical strategy. In the first part of the essay, I narrate two experiences of teaching South Asian diasporic nonfiction. In the second part, I delve into a broader discussion of what this new pedagogical framework offers to instructors of South Asian diasporic literature. In courses I taught over two years, I introduced nonfiction to students with varying degrees of familiarity with different genres of writing, the strongest familiarity being with novels, as students self-reported in their presemester surveys. While these were introductory literature classes, usually made up of freshmen and sophomores completing degree requirements, there were also some social sciences majors and English minors. The first year I taught the course, my class comprised primarily white students and a few international students (which reflected the university's demographics). The following year, when the course was cross-listed with women, gender, and sexuality studies, many more students in the class identified as Black, Latinx, and Asian as well as women and nonbinary, and there were also many more international students. In the first iteration of the course, I assigned Amitava Kumar's *Passport Photos*, and in the second year, *Good Talk*, by Mira Jacob.

In this essay I examine the specific challenges, questions, and discussions arising from classroom topics, including the relationship between fiction and nonfiction, questions of language and power, and genre-specific approaches with special focus on South Asian diasporic writing. Throughout the essay I center three broad implications:

> Compared with novels, short fiction, and poetry, how does nonfiction writing unfold the relationship between genre and cultural theory?
>
> How can we examine conceptions of circulation and circularity through the genre of nonfiction writing?
>
> In what ways can reading nonfiction in a literature classroom enable students to reflect on their own digital and cultural literacy?

Languages of Nonfiction

Kumar's *Passport Photos* is an encyclopedic, experimental reflection on living and being in the diaspora. Assembling photographs, poetry, and analytical reflections, Kumar organizes the book as a passport with chapters titled "Name" (58–81), "Place of Birth" (82–99), "Nationality" (148–71), "Identifying Marks" (196–215), and so on. The first chapter, however, is titled "Language" (16–35). After introducing how this "forged passport" (ix) works like a book, the first chapter highlights an element that is missing in passports: "My passport provides no information about my language" (17). By posing the question of why a person's language is not included in their passport, I ask my class to reflect on what it means to begin a memoir with something that is ostensibly missing. Some students recognize techniques of defamiliarization, but for the most part they are drawn to the photograph that follows this section—a sign from a grocery store that reads as follows: "WE SALE ALL CAN BEER IN HEER" (18). Kumar's reflection on the importance of *broken* language leads to a broader, class-wide discussion about how language and power are inextricably linked in the diaspora. Picking up on the humor of the misspellings, students consider how this photograph demonstrates that English is spoken as a global language. This tension between language and diasporic privilege is most visible when Kumar navigates works by Rushdie, Naipaul, and Ghosh to argue that the passport—much like fiction—transports the reader. Students are usually quick to point out the issues in this equivalence by bringing to our attention the differences in power and agency that are involved in international travel due to visas and their restrictions. Following this section, Kumar deftly shifts from a pointed dialogue about language and place as experienced by immigrants from the film *Falling Down* to the tragic story of Vincent Chin's murder in 1982, and his critical insight is not lost on students: language has the power to destroy and cause harm. As we explore the history of the murder of Chin—a Chinese American man who was misrecognized as Japanese—an important discussion on racial and ethnic difference develops. Kumar's crucial encapsulation holds these different threads together: "If, on one hand, the meanings of words like *passport* and *visa* are tied to dreams and fantasies, they are also, on the other, inextricably woven into the fabric of power and social prejudice" (21). I urge students to notice how Kumar assembles a familiar photograph, a popular movie, and a news excerpt to overlay his commentary on language and race. We then close-read Kumar's excerpt from Krisantha Sri Bhaggiyadatta's poem "Aay Wha' Kinda Indian Arr U?." This satirical epic poem lists the multitudinous identities that are collapsed under the umbrella of "Indian" identity: "the Indian wearing a salwar or a sari, a turban or a pottu," "the sponsored Indian whose husband owns her," "the Indian hiding in a women's shelter," and so on (qtd. in Kumar 22–23). Alternating verses with conversations from a visa interview, Kumar curates a multigenre reflection on difference in identities through language. Eventually, students reach a collaborative moment of recognition that despite the absence of "language" on a passport, it is impossible to overlook its shadow in Kumar's anecdotes.

The format of the hybrid narrative—which incorporates photographs, news clips, performance pieces, and analytical reflections—is effective in alerting students to the intentional assemblage. Kumar's own biographical details create space for a deeper historical consideration as well. For instance, photographs of Kumar's place of birth in Bihar launch an intertextual conversation about language learning in educational spaces around the world. Navigating Rushdie's "Good Advice Is Rarer than Rubies" along with a discussion of Michelle Cliff's *Abeng*, Kumar reflects on the potential and politics of creative appropriation of language that results from the legacy of colonial education. The chapter closes with a familiar photograph from the United States–Mexico border that students find enticing: a sign that reads "Caution" in English and "Prohibido" in Spanish (Kumar 30). Citing the poet and activist Guillermo Gómez-Peña's "Border Brujo"—"I speak in English therefore you listen / I speak in English therefore I hate you" (qtd. in Kumar 34)—Kumar addresses the role of language in the exclusionary politics of the United States. Ultimately, Kumar uses these critical anecdotes to point toward the relationship between language and power and toward the transformative potential of language when forged into a "weapon of protest" (25).

Leveraging Kumar's hybrid technique shapes students' discussions in unique ways. For instance, reading across the different genres contained in the memoir invigorates reflections about nation, language, diaspora, and race without falling back on plot progression or character analysis. This alerts students to intertextual references, temporal expansiveness, and emphasis on linguistic differences in Kumar's oeuvre. Perhaps most importantly, students are able to translate for themselves how language and power shape and taint their lived experiences. Finally, concluding with a discussion of the circulation of memories in the nonfiction genre motivates students to reflect more intentionally on circulation of written text (literary or otherwise) both geographically and digitally.

Diasporic Circulations

Jacob's *Good Talk* typifies the overlapping, recursive, and circulatory nature of diasporic writing. The graphic memoir traverses the author's childhood in New Mexico, her time as a writer in New York City, and her strained marriage amid increasing political polarization. Its most engaging parts are conversations with her biracial son, Z, whose curiosity drives the memoir. The palimpsestic overlaying of stock images, the author's personal photographs, illustrated strips, and colloquial dialogue forces students to contend with the juxtaposition of what they see and what they read. The seeming lack of emotionality of the words and the characters is repeatedly disrupted by striking backgrounds. I have found it useful to begin teaching *Good Talk* with an overview of the histories and traditions of graphic narratives and by asking students to reflect on their prior experience with reading graphic narratives. Some formal aspects of a graphic narrative are familiar to students, thus the relationship between form and the nonlinear narrative structure lend themselves to vibrant discussions about Jacob's work.

When teaching living writers of any genre, I encourage students to trace the ways the words of those writers circulate outside assigned texts. In this case, I ask students to create a biographical note for Jacob—textual or visual—that could accompany *Good Talk*. These biographical notes range from traditional notes to *Instagram* posts that incorporate the author's social media presence. This becomes an opportunity to facilitate small-group discussions about how images layered under words can reveal broader themes. For instance, in chapter 2, "Indians in America" (Jacob 21–31), photographs of Jacob's parents in their homes in India, Rome, and Albuquerque and of Jacob's childhood mingle with images of American landscapes and flight maps. These images are disrupted most notably by a *New York Times* headline on the assassination of Martin Luther King, Jr. (28)—an ominous portent amid images of adventure and exploration. I have found that students can more effectively contextualize the histories of South Asian migration through this section than through historical notes that center legal histories without critiquing model minority myths. Much like Kumar's work, *Good Talk* focuses on discussions of race, but such discussions are rooted in complex frameworks of the post-9/11 era in New York.

Chapter 10, titled "Winter 2015" (Jacob 80–86), sheds light on the limitations of binary racialization that lead non-Black people of color to ignore their own role in perpetuating anti-Blackness. Focusing on a conversation between the narrator and her son, students debate the roles of individuals and institutions in upholding racist systems. During these conversations, I find it useful to pause and spotlight reflections by students of color who wish to consider their racialized positionalities within these complex discussions. The chapter is framed by a backdrop of evolving images of New York's Chinatown as the narrator explains to her son how systemic power shapes racism in the United States. In response to her son's question, "Are we racist?" (80), the narrator replies, "Racism is about using power to keep other people down" (82). This dialogue leads to the narrator asserting, "I wouldn't call it racist because of the whole system thing. . . . We're in the middle place where sometimes we get treated badly and sometimes we do it to other people" (84–85). Ultimately, Z, the narrator's son, insists through childlike catechism that measuring racial superiority on the basis of financial success is racist. I find it useful here to ask the class to delineate who they see as encompassing the pronouns *we, us,* and *they* in the chapter. This close reading becomes an opportune moment to decode the complexities of South Asian (diasporic) Brownness in the post-9/11 era without eliding the inextricable global anti-Blackness that haunts this interaction in Jacob's memoir. We also focus on how the images of Chinatown in the background of this conversation alert readers to the multiple diasporas that are interlocked within racial formations in the United States. Students learn to see how this graphic memoir enables a meditation on the refracted racialization of South Asians in the United States against the conditions of global anti-Blackness (Tuszynska; Thomas). Building on this, students notice how the narrator of the memoir does not address her own participation in anti-Black microaggressions, which complicates her responses to her own son. In further critiquing the memoir, the class notices that Jacob's writing does not engage with post-9/11 war-on-terror codifications that make the narrator and her son vulnerable to state prejudice, hate crimes, and connected violences. These limitations in *Good Talk* can be addressed in conversation with valuable scholarship on terror and representation (Puar; Deb). The memoir ends with an emotional monologue by the narrator, who, as a South Asian American, is acutely aware of the ways the state incriminates, weaponizes, or rewards middle-class immigrants. Together, these moments offer instances of reflection on the circulation of racist language in quotidian exchanges. More crucially, using digital humanities pedagogy such as n-grams and digital mapping tools, students reflect on how racialization and racialized terms are coded in digital formats. These reflections include references to the ways that digital blackface is deployed in memes, videos, and GIFs for humoristic effects in digital spaces and social media that depict transnational South Asian diasporic experiences. I have found that layering conversations about language, race, and digitality enable students to consider how literary and, more broadly, textual circulation behaves. Additionally, considering the various representations of queerness, embodiment, and sexuality in the memoir boosts discussions about diasporic circulation, enabling students to see how these categories transform over time and space. When we finally return to the biographical notes that were developed in small groups, we consider the circulatory nature of the nonfiction genre—defined by its digital and technological crossings. Not only do these diasporic writers of nonfiction move imaginatively and spatially between contexts in the Global North and Global South, their writing also enables students to discern the circulatory nature of South Asian diasporas.

Holding Space for Nonfiction

Given the heterogenous contours of diasporic histories and identities and the potential for nuanced interrogations of textuality and circulation, holding space for nonfiction in a South Asian diasporic literary corpus becomes essential. Some examples of works that offer dynamic approaches to teaching this growing corpus include Sujatha Gidla's *Ants among Elephants* and Rajiv Mohabir's *Antiman*, which center caste, queerness, and amorphous transformations in the diaspora. Through environmental narratives, Sonali Deraniyagala's *Wave* tackles human loss in the face of the 2004 tsunami in Sri Lanka, while Aimee Nezhukumatathil's highly acclaimed *World of Wonders* transforms the tradition of nature writing to interrogate belonging in the diaspora. Memoirs about sexuality, embodiment, and queer identity form a notable portion of the corpus: for instance, Fariha Róisín's illustrated journal *Being in Your Body* and Abeer Y. Hoque's *Olive Witch* navigate Bangladeshi diasporic identities, whereas Samra Habib's *We Have Always Been Here* is a coming-of-age memoir about being queer in Pakistan and Canada. These join a growing body of queer and trans memoir writing that includes Siddharth Dube's *An Indefinite Sentence* and Aparajeeta Duttchoudhury and Rukie Hartman's collection *Moving Truth(s)*. Finally, memoirs by the activists Deepa Iyer (*We Too Sing America*) and Anjali Enjeti (*Southbound*) and by the more seasoned authors Nikesh Shukla (*Brown Baby*) and Asma Gull Hassan (*Red, White, and Muslim*) contemplate the legacies of a post-9/11 era in North America and echo the writings of Meena Alexander (*Fault Lines*).

As with South Asian literary fiction, and global anglophone writing more broadly, the teaching of diasporic nonfiction involves a recognition of otherness, differences, and opacities (Cooppan) as well as a commitment to rigorous historical, geographic, and political contextualization (Srikanth). Moreover, memoirs reveal a negotiation of memories, affects, histories, and literary mediation (Avieson et al.; Dillon; McNeill and Douglas). Thus, teaching nonfiction has several advantages: first, it exposes undergraduates in introductory courses to different genres and styles; second, it helps demystify the relationship between fiction and historical context; and third, it reveals literature as an economy, both in its circulation and syntactic content (Brouillette). Creative nonfiction has found a place in intellectual spaces in the United States, whether it be in creative writing classes, common core readings at the secondary education level, or first-year orientations at universities. For instance, memoirs like Alison Bechdel's *Fun Home* and canonical creative nonfiction like Jamaica

Kincaid's *A Small Place* empower hesitant readers as they enter higher education institutions and are guided by instructors with critical expertise to recognize the role of the writer in contemporary society (Gardiner). For instructors, the personal and political nature of nonfiction writing also presents opportunities to contemplate the "bodied effects" (Chatterjee 81) of teaching identity and positionality. As a South Asian woman of Indian origin, I am consistently alerted to the ways in which my gendered and raced identities (Bannerji; Dasgupta) form an integral part of my pedagogical rationale, which is invested in anti-imperial and anti-racist thinking and praxis. In teaching Kumar's and Jacob's nonfiction, I dismantle the scripts of colonial, global, and neoliberal histories that bind my identities through collaborative considerations of the ethical imperatives of reading and writing. Therefore, whether it be in courses on South Asian literature or global nonfiction writing, the inclusion of South Asian diasporic nonfiction allows undergraduates to reflect on their own positionalities and identities in relation to the writer and instructor and prepares them to engage in discussions of power and representation in classrooms beyond ours.

Works Cited

Alexander, Meena. *Fault Lines: A Memoir*. Feminist Press, 2003.

Avieson, Bunty, et al., editors. *Mediating Memory: Tracing the Limits of Memoir*. Routledge, 2017.

Azar, Tawnya. "Inside and Outside the Literary Marketplace: The Digital Products of Amitav Ghosh, Arundhati Roy and Salman Rushdie." *South Asian Review*, vol. 40. no. 3, 2019, pp. 190–205.

Bannerji, Himani. *Thinking Through: Essays on Feminism, Marxism, and Anti-Racism*. Women's Press, 1995.

Barnard, Rita, editor. *Beyond Rivalry: Literature/History, Fiction/Non-fiction*. Special issue of *Safundi: The Journal of South African and American Studies*. Vol. 13, nos. 1–2, 2012.

Bloom, Lynn Z. "Coming to Life: Teaching Undergraduates to Write Autobiography." *A/B: Auto/Biography Studies*, vol. 32, no. 1, 2017, pp. 75–86.

Brouillette, Sarah. *Literature and the Creative Economy*. Stanford UP, 2014.

Chatterjee, Piya. "Encountering 'Third World Women': Rac(e)ing the Global in a U.S. Classroom." *Pedagogy*, vol. 2, no. 1, 2002, pp. 79–108.

Cooppan, Vilashini. "The Ethics of World Literature: Reading Others, Reading Otherwise." *Teaching World Literature*, edited by David Damrosch, Modern Language Association of America, 2009, pp. 34–43.

DasGupta, Kasturi. "Negotiating the 'In Between' Space: Third World Women in American Higher Education." *Transformations*, vol. 10, no. 2, 1999, pp. 24–29.

Deb, Basuli. *Transnational Feminist Perspectives on Terror in Literature and Culture*. Routledge, 2015.

Deraniyagala, Sonali. *Wave: Life and Memories after the Tsunami*. Alfred A. Knopf, 2013.

Dillon, Brian. *Essayism: On Form, Feeling, and Nonfiction*. New York Review Books, 2018.

Dube, Siddharth. *An Indefinite Sentence: A Personal History of Outlawed Love and Sex*. Atria Books, 2019.

Duttchoudhury, Aparajeeta, and Rukie Hartman. *Moving Truth(s): Queer and Transgender Desi Writings on Family*. Flying Chickadee, 2015.

Enjeti, Anjali. *Southbound: Essays on Identity, Inheritance, and Social Change*. U of Georgia P, 2021.

Gardiner, Judith Kegan, editor. *Approaches to Teaching Bechdel's* Fun Home. Modern Language Association of America, 2018.

Gidla, Sujatha. *Ants among Elephants: An Untouchable Family and the Making of Modern India*. Farrar, Straus and Giroux, 2017.

Habib, Samra. *We Have Always Been Here: A Queer Muslim Memoir*. Viking, 2019.

Hai, Ambreen. "(Re)Reading Fawzia Afzal-Khan's *Lahore with Love*: Class and the Ethics of Memoir." *Pakistaniaat: A Journal of Pakistan Studies*, vol. 3, no. 2, 2011, pp. 29–51.

Hassan, Asma Gull. *Red, White, and Muslim: My Story of Belief*. HarperOne, 2009.

Hoque, Abeer Y. *Olive Witch: A Memoir*. HarperCollins India, 2016.

Iyer, Deepa. *We Too Sing America: South Asian, Arab, Muslim and Sikh Immigrants Shape Our Multiracial Future*. New Press, 2017.

Jacob, Mira. *Good Talk: A Memoir in Conversations*. Random House, 2018.

Kersten, Sara, and Ashley Dallacqua. "Of Studious Babies, Talking Rabbits, and Watercolor Activism: Using the Comics Form to Consider Nonfiction." *Journal of Children's Literature*, vol. 43, no. 1, 2017, pp. 17–26.

Kumar, Amitava. *Passport Photos*. U of California P, 2000.

McNeill, Laurie, and Kate Douglas, editors. *Teaching Lives: Contemporary Pedagogies of Life Narratives*. Special issue of *A/B: Auto/Biography Studies*, vol. 32, no. 1, 2017.

Mezey, Jason. "Franchises and Fetishes: Critiquing State Power in Arundhati Roy's Nonfiction." *South Asian Review*, vol. 29, no. 2, 2008, pp. 56–82.

Mohabir, Rajiv. *Antiman: A Hybrid Memoir*. Restless Books, 2021.

Murray, Simone. "Charting the Digital Literary Sphere." *Contemporary Literature*, vol. 56, no. 2, 2015, pp. 311–39.

Nezhukumatathil, Aimee. *World of Wonders: In Praise of Fireflies, Whale Sharks, and Other Astonishments*. Milkweed Editions, 2020.

Pedri, Nancy. "What's the Matter of Seeing in Graphic Memoir?" *South Central Review*, vol. 32, no. 3, 2015, pp. 8–29.

Puar, Jasbir. *Terrorist Assemblages: Homonationalism in Queer Times*. Duke UP, 2007.

Rao, Nagesh. "The Politics of Genre and the Rhetoric of Radical Cosmopolitanism; or, Who's Afraid of Arundhati Roy?" *Prose Studies*, vol. 30, no. 2, 2008, pp. 159–76.

Risam, Roopika. "Torrents of Tweets: Teaching the Ibis with Digital Humanities." *Approaches to Teaching the Works of Amitav Ghosh*, edited by Gaurav Desai and John Hawley, Modern Language Association of America, 2019, pp. 186–96.

Róisín, Fariha. *Being in Your Body*. Abrams Noterie, 2019.

Shukla, Nikesh. *Brown Baby: A Memoir of Race, Family and Home*. Bluebird, 2021.

Singh, Julietta. *No Archive Will Restore You*. Punctum Books, 2018.

Srikanth, Rajni. "Overwhelmed by the World: Teaching Literature and the Difference of Nations." *Pedagogy*, vol. 7, no. 2, 2007, pp. 192–206.

Thomas, Ebony E. "'We Always Talk about Race': Navigating Race Talk Dilemmas in the Teaching of Literature." *Research in the Teaching of English*, vol. 50, no. 2, 2015, pp. 154–75.

Tuszynska, Agnieszka. "Who Needs Race Talk, Anyway? Teaching African American Literature to Students of Color in Anxious Times." *MELUS*, vol. 42, no. 4, 2017, pp. 164–91.

Young, Jennie. "Creative Nonfiction in the First-Year Writing Classroom: To Colonize or Theorize?" *Writing on the Edge*, vol. 29, no. 1, 2018, pp. 59–70.

Matthew Spencer

Amitav Ghosh's *The Great Derangement*, Close Reading, and Moments of Recognition

Close reading is a basic inquiry skill deployed at every level of English education, but it holds a special place in higher education, where it is encouraged in students as the primary mode of engaging with a text. More importantly for this essay, close reading is a gateway to recognition. I refer to "recognition" in the sense in which it is evoked by Amitav Ghosh in *The Great Derangement: Climate Change and the Unthinkable*, as "a passage from ignorance to knowledge" (4). However, recognition is not the discovery of something new; "it arises rather from a renewed reckoning with a potentiality that lies within oneself" (5). The conception of these moments, which harkens to a psychoanalytic understanding of perception, forms the backbone of how, in Ghosh's formulation, people may come to realize their place within the overlapping systems that make up the greater structure of global climate change. Key within this structure is the flow of migrant bodies and the reaction to this movement in the wealthy nations of Europe and North America. While much of Ghosh's oeuvre deals with diaspora and diasporic consciousness, what makes Ghosh unique among contemporary South Asian writers is his engagement with a climate diasporic consciousness emergent in this era of the Anthropocene. Migrants continue to travel across borders for the

258

same reasons as they always have—safety, opportunity, and so forth—but now that movement is increasingly colored by the effects of global climate change. Furthermore, Ghosh emphasizes the role desire plays in motivating migrants to risk the journey to a new life. Using Ghosh's concept of moments of recognition as a guiding principle in course design and instruction, specifically in courses dealing with global climate change, allows students to tie close reading to their own experiences living in the Anthropocene and to build a deeper understanding of their entanglement with others. However, this practice is far from the surface-level discussion resembling a recreational book club into which some literature classes devolve. Instead, students come to realize their own place within the phenomenon of climate change and the extent to which climate change is affecting and will affect the global movement of people across national borders, a realization that hopefully leads to an interrogation of what it means and would look like to create greater equity on a worldwide scale.

While *The Great Derangement* is a unique text that borders on the scholarly, it maintains the distinctive, adept blend of fiction and nonfiction that Ghosh cultivates in earlier works such as *In an Antique Land.* It condenses much of his thinking on global climate change that formed through the Ibis trilogy and *The Hungry Tide* and is best encapsulated in his novel *Gun Island.* While his views on climate change can be found in his earlier works, *The Great Derangement* has the greatest pedagogical potential when paired with works within or adjacent to the realm of climate fiction. Such a pairing allows students to not only identify concepts such as the climate uncanny as narrative tools in novels but also use their understanding of moments of recognition to build a stronger understanding of how climate fiction works to expound the stark urgency of global climate change. A major tool used to illustrate this urgency in works of climate fiction is the movement of peoples and the creation of climate diasporic consciousness. I derive this concept from the work of Vijay Mishra, who uses the term "diasporic imaginary" to refer to "any ethnic enclave in a nation-state that defines itself, consciously or through self-evident or implied political coercion, as a group that lives in displacement" (14). He elaborates on this concept and the role diasporic communities play in construction of place: "Nations are not fixed entities, national cultures are not absolute cultures, they are not governed, like religion, by perennial, universal values. Nations and cultures are products of their multifaceted histories, and they grow and change with the times. Diasporas tell us much about the evolution of cultures" (20). In this way, diasporic communities, such as the Bengali community living in Venice in *Gun Island*, play a vital role in writing the present and future of a place, redefining what it means to be a part of that place. Additionally, this framing helps students when they, along with Deen, the protagonist of the novel, encounter the Bengalis in Venice. They share Deen's surprise but then come to their own moment of recognition as to why the Bengalis are there, what they are doing, and why it matters.

What makes *The Great Derangement* especially useful in a variety of undergraduate teaching scenarios, then, is the way in which it distills a range of discourses—environmental, postcolonial, spiritual, economic, historical—into a coherent work with a clear viewpoint that illustrates to students the ways in which we are all products of a global diaspora not only of people and cultures but also of ideas, beliefs, and lived relationships to the environment. This proliferation of genres is also clear in Ghosh's fiction writing: he has described the novel as "a meta-form that transcends the boundaries that circumscribe other kinds of writing, rendering meaningless the usual workaday distinctions between historian, journalist, anthropologist, etc." ("Amitav Ghosh: *The Glass Palace*"). Incorporating this varied approach into instruction and learning using moments of recognition as a pedagogical tool grants written inquiry renewed, existential importance within the academy.

I have invoked moments of recognition in two very different courses: a dual enrollment class on climate fiction in a dual credit high school setting and a writing and research first-year composition course in a university setting. In both cases, this framework served the invaluable purpose of allowing students to come to their own personal reckoning with the reality of climate change without having it forced upon them. This educational Trojan horse functioned through mindful implementation of close reading and reader response in our group discussions. In this way, Ghosh's book serves as a threshold text for understanding how difficult, nebulous concepts can be approached through an eclectic form of writing that combines research and academic discourse with personal narrative and deeper rumination on unseen forces. Once students were able to grasp Ghosh's ideas and understand the clever way in which they are presented, they felt freed to expand their own authorial voice, whether they were writing about literary texts or their own interests.

To understand how Ghosh's ideas can be used in the classroom, it is vital to first outline them. Ghosh refers to recognition as "a passage from ignorance to knowledge," and so, "[t]o recognize, then, is not the same as an initial introduction. Nor does recognition require an exchange of words: more often than not we recognize mutely. And to recognize is by no means to understand that which meets the eyes; comprehension need play no part in a moment of recognition" (*Great Derangement* 4–5). This kind of abstract inspiration leads one to begin to view the world through a new lens that does not immediately reveal meaning and, so, is not the flashing-light-bulb eureka moment often associated with a sudden influx of knowledge. Andreas Malm offers a parallel concept:

> We are only in the very early stages, but already our daily life, our psychic experience, our cultural responses, even our politics show signs of being sucked back by planetary forces into the hole of time, the present dissolving into past and future alike. Postmodernity seems to be visited by its antithesis: a condition of time and nature conquering ever more space. Call it the warming condition. (11)

Both Ghosh and Malm offer a way to conceptualize a shifting perception of the world, its multiple, overlaid systems, and the ways in which we are entangled with them. This is an alteration in orientation that leads one to develop new forms of knowledge in a new paradigm that one did not previously recognize. This potentiality is akin to a prior awareness that is the lost other of the flash of noticing that occurs at the moment of recognition.

As previously mentioned, these moments can spark understanding of one's place in the greater structure of global climate change. According to Ghosh, in these moments, "it dawns on us that the energy that surrounds us, flowing under our feet and through wires in our walls, animating our vehicles and illuminating our rooms, is an all-encompassing presence that may have its own purposes about which we know nothing" (*Great Derangement* 5). Such moments are often observable in writings that directly address climate change, such as Elizabeth Kolbert's *Field Notes from a Catastrophe*. In the opening chapter of the book, Kolbert travels to Alaska, where she encounters sinkholes created by thawing permafrost that sometimes swallow houses (15–16). This chapter of the book is the first text students encountered after reading selections from *The Great Derangement*, and we had discussed the environmental uncanny as a uniting concept for the semester. We discussed the uncanniness not only of the images but also of knowing that such processes as the thawing of permafrost are taking place. One student found themselves struggling to explain how it made them feel but then arrived at an apt observation: "It sounds like the end of the world." What that student was experiencing was a spark of recognition in which previous notions of what the end of the world would look like combined with the new knowledge from Kolbert's essay to shift the way in which they experienced the world around them. Kolbert's retelling of her moment of recognition and my student's moment of recognition both illustrate how lived experience and literature can combine to increase not just knowledge of climate change—after all, I found surprisingly little resistance of denialism among students—but also awareness of one's place within it that not only implicates or condemns but also leads to more productive questions: for instance, "What do we do now?"

Key to the impact of these events is the way in which they reveal the hitherto unknown agency of the nonhuman and those systems that lie outside our control. In Kolbert, the human impact is emphasized, and the effect of that impact is damage to the landscape. However, the reality lurking behind the recognition of this impact is that its effects ultimately turn back on humanity. For instance, consider an example Kolbert gleans from a talk with a climate scientist: if you rock a rowboat, it will eventually settle back to equilibrium (34). If you rock it too hard, it may flip, but being upside down is just another form of equilibrium. Whether or not you stay in the boat or drown is of no consequence to the boat. This metaphor is the best I have encountered for pithily explaining the progress of climate change and its threat to humanity. Proceeding into Ghosh's fiction from this point has proven productive, and students are better prepared to engage with his unique style of storytelling and his sly rhetoric.

Ghosh's first novel following the publication of *The Great Derangement, Gun Island,* is a distillation of his thinking on global climate change into novel form, a culmination of his scholarly and authorial thinking—especially since the publication of *Sea of Poppies,* the first volume of the Ibis trilogy. One way in which *Gun Island* serves this function is by challenging reality and the limits of human understanding of the natural world. A major way in which the novel challenges representation is through the improbable and the uncanny, through events that seem unbelievable, even when they occur in fiction. The events are so far outside the realm of our normal experience that they challenge our ability to suspend disbelief. Ghosh posits that the improbable has been barred from the realm of serious fiction since the emergence of the novel as a genre. He cites this exclusion as a major factor in why the serious novel is unequipped to deal with the reality of climate change. Instead, the novel must avoid the outlandish to maintain verisimilitude and not alienate its audience or, worse, drag them into the muck of genre fiction. In doing so, the "serious novel" bars from its pages just the sort of unlikely events that occur in the real world every day. As an example, Ghosh refers to the experience of a tornado in Delhi that occurred in his youth, the first of its kind on record. The event is so improbable that Ghosh wagers that if he included it in a piece of fiction it would be too unbelievable. This encapsulates what he refers to as the irony of the "realist" novel: "the very gestures with which it conjures up reality are actually a concealment of the real" (*Great Derangement* 22). I have students read this section of *The Great Derangement* as a primer for later texts because of its depiction of an unprecedented yet viscerally real event related to climate change. This builds a foundational understanding that helps students identify similar moments in texts such as the Kolbert essay or Jesmyn Ward's novel *Salvage the Bones*, in which Hurricane Katrina is a looming presence.

The concealment of the climate uncanny is exactly what Ghosh works against in *Gun Island*. As Ghosh posits in *The Great Derangement*, to include uncanny climate events in fiction is to flirt with expulsion from "the mansion in which serious fiction has long been in residence" and be banished to the "humbler dwellings that surround the manor house—those generic outhouses that were once known by names such as 'the Gothic,' 'the romance,' or 'the melodrama,' and have now come to be called 'fantasy,' 'horror,' and 'science fiction'" (24). Many works within the burgeoning genre of climate fiction suffer this fate and are kept at the margins because, as Ghosh suggests, the improbable is not the realm of "serious fiction." *Gun Island* eschews this trend in part by portraying a story that is deeply enmeshed in the now: the effects of climate change are just beginning to be observed on a mass scale, first in vulnerable areas such as the Sundarbans; smartphones and social media connect everyone from banking sharks on Wall Street to fishermen in the Sundarbans and are a major part of networks that allow for the migration of people around the globe; the refugee influx into Europe—long faded from the news and, subsequently, the minds of many people—continues, causing social upheaval on the continent. As the protagonist, Deen, experiences multiple events that cannot be explained by modern science, students share his confusion, but as the novel builds toward its climax, they begin to find the uncanny in the mundane and, furthermore, begin to see the uncanny *as* mundane. This is a crucial shift in outlook that is needed in an era of man-made climate change and one that is easier to develop by reading fiction than by reading the latest climate report. While it is certainly reasonable and sometimes necessary to use climate reports or similar documents to contextualize this moment in history, students enjoy engaging with fiction far more, and the mundane strangeness of a work like *Gun Island* encourages deep engagement with the text. When they read the novel, they are wrapped up in the mystery and strange happenings along with Deen, and they seek resolution to the multiple mysteries. In investigating them, they experience moments of recognition. For instance, when Deen's airplane is flying over the Venetian Lagoon, leading Deen to compare it to the Sundarbans, the vulnerability of the ancient city is made evident; something so seemingly eternal is revealed to be marked for destruction. Ghosh takes the effects of climate change from the realm of local tragedy to global existential threat, emphasizing the urgency of the situation for students. In these moments, it becomes apparent that not all future climate migrants will be from the impoverished, formerly colonized areas of the world, and climate diasporic consciousness will develop in a far more diverse portion of humanity that could come to include students themselves as well as people they know.

A similarly important aspect of the novel is its interrogation of human migration and the forms that migration takes. In particular, the story of Tipu and Rafi and of the blue boat of refugees heading for Italy serve as vital teaching moments concerning how world governments could or should deal with mass migrations caused by climate change. Furthermore, Ghosh does not shy away from including the lure of wealth and comfort in his analysis. Global culture has been homogenized by the hyperconnectivity of the Internet and proliferation of smartphones, and, as Ghosh has noted, "Culture generates desires—for vehicles and appliances, for certain kinds of gardens and dwellings—that are among the principal drivers of the carbon economy" ("Amitav Ghosh: Where"). This sentiment is similar to Mishra's explanation of how in a globalized world "the act of displacement makes diasporic subjects travelers on the move, their homeland contained in the simulacral world of visual media" (3–4), and, as such, "[w]e need to look at people's corporeal or even 'libidinal' investments in nations (as denizens or as outsiders)" (21). Ghosh's conception of diaspora, then, consists of a tripartite understanding of motivations that often overlap. The first motivation involves the legally sanctioned, documented movement of those who travel about the globe for work, education, or other state-recognized pursuits. The second involves the unsanctioned movement across borders by war and climate refugees seeking safety. The third involves the similarly unsanctioned movement driven by desire. This desire that drives migrants to embark on dangerous journeys is, then, not merely one of survival, although that is surely the primary concern, but also one of want. Ubiquitous visions of the ostentatious wealth in some metropole of Europe or North America, such as those seen by Tipu in *Gun Island*, continuously stream to the smartphones of individuals around the globe. Unpacking this desire is key to students' understanding of the novel and leads to useful discussion questions: How can we expect people not to want that kind of existence, and who are we to deny them the opportunity of obtaining it? Of course, the role of mass consumption in the perpetuation and worsening of global climate change complicates the conversation, so what, then, might a more equitable approach not just to migration but also to consumption look like? The second question recalls one a good friend asked me in a discussion about scientism that I often think about and ask my students in turn: "What is there in science that tells us why climate change is bad?" After all, the earth is not going anywhere; we are. But while we are here, writers like Ghosh seem to be urging us toward a new paradigm for understanding how we connect to one another and to our planet. These are new realities born of a brave new time, so what could be a better jumping-off point for a class full of the same young people who will continue to struggle with extreme weather and severe biosphere disruption, and whose children, if they have them, may be the first generation born into a brave new world? We, as educators, did not ask for this role but find ourselves increasingly saddled with it, and the work of writers like Ghosh can help us see the broader picture while also giving us the tools to transfer that mode of thinking to our students.

To close, I wish to briefly return to the concept of the improbable versus the believable. In interviews following the release of *The Great Derangement*, Ghosh revealed that the scene in Venice in which the protagonist is almost struck by a falling masonry stone but is warned by a construction worker in Bangla is drawn from experience ("In Venice" 6:20). Unlike the Delhi tornado, which he wrote was too unbelievable to occur in fiction, he decided to include this experience in the novel. This suggests the same confluence of what is traditionally thought of as "the weird" with the "the realist," and this combination is present throughout the novel. As the writer Roy Scranton has noted, echoing Ghosh's thinking in *The Great Derangement*, "[I]n order for us to adapt to the strange new world, we're going to need more than scientific reports and military policy. We're going to need new ideas. We're going to need new myths and new stories" (19). By taking the unlikely seriously, Ghosh suggests that the truth is, in fact, stranger than fiction, and the onus is now on fiction to conjure new stories that help us live in the new world on the horizon. Then the responsibility will fall on educators to relate those stories to students in effective ways in order to arm them against the darker impulses of a changing planet such as xenophobia, ecofascism, and base human selfishness. By making space for the uncanny within the mundane, we open our minds to a world reenchanted by anthropocentric action. In doing so, we make it clear that the spectacular events of climate fiction will find their way into our lives, and when they do, we will be better prepared to face them and forge viable futures in the face of destruction.

Works Cited

Ghosh, Amitav. "Amitav Ghosh: *The Glass Palace*." Interview conducted by Michelle Caswell. *Asia Society*, 2023, asiasociety.org/amitav-ghosh-glass-palace.

———. "Amitav Ghosh: Where Is the Fiction about Climate Change?" *The Guardian*, 28 Oct. 2016, www.theguardian.com/books/2016/oct/28/amitav-ghosh-where-is-the-fiction-about-climate-change-.

———. *The Great Derangement: Climate Change and the Unthinkable*. U of Chicago P, 2016.

———. *Gun Island*. Farrar, Straus and Giroux, 2019.

"In Venice, I Heard Bangla Everywhere: Amitav Ghosh on 'Gun Island.'" *YouTube*, uploaded by The Wire, 19 June 2019, www.youtube.com/watch?v=r5RbdChKMv4&t=382s&ab_channel=TheWire.

Kolbert, Elizabeth. *Field Notes from a Catastrophe: Man, Nature, and Climate Change*. Bloomsbury, 2006.

Malm, Andreas. *The Progress of This Storm: Nature and Society in a Warming World*. Verso, 2018.

Mishra, Vijay. *The Literature of the Indian Diaspora: Theorizing the Diasporic Imaginary*. Routledge, 2007.

Scranton, Roy. *Learning to Die in the Anthropocene: Reflections on the End of a Civilization*. City Lights Publishers, 2015.

Madhurima Chakraborty

Joke's on Us:
Indian Americans, Comedy,
and Writing America

There are few South Asian American or international South Asian students at Columbia College Chicago, the arts and media school where I teach: in ten years, six students who identified as being of South Asian descent have taken my class. Additionally, when I taught Indians Writing America as a section of Topics in the Novel in fall 2017, we did not as yet have an English major, which meant that the reading-intensive novels course was considered a heavy lift. I was excited to teach the course, which I saw as a chance to introduce immigrant writers' invention and examination of the concept of "America" to students. At the same time, I was also concerned about being able to convince students that Indian American literature was relevant to their major areas of study. In the end, I chose to include stand-up comedy by Indian Americans in hopes that the addition of this format, likely to be more familiar to students at my college, would provide a respite from the reading schedule while exemplifying immigrant narratives in another form.

In the end, however, stand-up comedy was more than merely another example; in fact, it was a key discursive tool in our discussions about the relationship between ideas and aesthetics. The use of Indian American stand-up comedy helped buttress questions about immigration,

267

belonging, authenticity, and representation that we saw emerge in novels such as Bharati Mukherjee's *Jasmine*, Chitra Banerjee Divakaruni's *Mistress of Spices*, Jhumpa Lahiri's *The Namesake*, and Sohrab Homi Fracis's *Go Home*. Because arts and media students at Columbia College Chicago are generally savvy and practiced critical consumers of popular culture, they were attentive to the quick messages that filtered through in both the content and form of stand-up comedy and were able to trace the resonance of ideas across the genres. In particular, because I had titled the course Indians Writing America, we were able to organize our discussions if not around craft per se, then at least around the work of story building; the clear performative aspect of stand-up also clarified, in turn, the process and narrativization of the predominantly realist fiction. Looking back at the end of the semester, it was also clear to me that this focus on storytelling, which helped us see the concept of "America" itself as a narrative, also helped destabilize the idea that ethnic literature and ethnic comedy participate in a direct or unmediated relationship with immigrant lives. Still, as a set of cultural texts that is often interpreted as sociological statements, comedy continues to pose the same kinds of exegetical challenges for students as fiction does.

The title of this essay points to the visual proximity of *US* and *us*, which is ironic given the vast separation between dominant and immigrant communities, a recurring topic for the Indian American writing and comedy that my fall 2017 class examined. In effect, through close investigation of texts in that class, students thought about whether it was possible to truly transform the narrative that cast immigrants and their unfamiliar ways as the necessary object of suspicion and ridicule, even in jokes that immigrants themselves tell, into a critique of the majoritarian fundamentals of American nationalism. In subsequent courses such as Comedy and Justice and Asian Comedy and Immigration, I have been able to reframe the questions we asked in the fall 2017 class about the possibilities that inhere in comedy, stand-up in particular, for uncovering and refracting philosophical concerns of other cultural forms. In Asian Comedy and Immigration, I once again paired comedy (predominantly stand-up) with more traditional literary forms such as fiction and poetry. Though this essay focuses on that first course, Indians Writing America, my experience in subsequent courses has confirmed that comedy can be a powerful theoretical interlocutor when teaching South Asian anglophone diasporic writing, especially in institutional contexts where there isn't a well-established cohort of traditional literature students interested in South Asian literature.

Representation and Double Consciousness:
Russell Peters and Bharati Mukherjee

I have always found it challenging to teach Mukherjee's *Jasmine* because it is a book so easily and unhesitatingly consumed by students. Unless I point it out, my overwhelmingly non–South Asian and non–South Asian American students miss that the titular protagonist is Punjabi, whereas the author herself is Bengali. Beyond signaling an easy criticism of identity politics, this distinction is significant because it troubles a documentary assessment of the novel. Yet, even when I call attention to this difference between the author's and protagonist's ethnic identity, it seems to some students that I am splitting hairs, since what separates two ethnicities in India seems to be irrelevant or at least insignificant given the larger opposition between India and America as framed in *Jasmine*. The idea of an inherent divide between the two countries is an indefatigable theme of Mukherjee's novel, which has been commonly understood in terms of its easy binarism. Even in an essay such as Vanita Reddy's, which seeks to recover a nuanced feminism in the novel where others have seen Orientalist tropes, the novel is ultimately beholden to readings that understand it as a national allegory.

In our class discussions, as in the writing assignment for the novel, I encouraged students to think about the constructedness of binarism as a literary tool that is contextualized not only through the author's national identity but also through her positionality as one of the first prominent South Asian American writers. In Indians Writing America, I introduced Gayatri Chakravorty Spivak's analysis of representation as a way to emphasize Mukherjee's craft. In "Can the Subaltern Speak?," Spivak points out the double meaning of *representation*—though these meanings are demarcated in German by separate words, they are collected in one word in English, allowing for a slippage between *representation* as literary symbol and *representation* as political proxy (275–79). As students become increasingly comfortable with the idea that representation matters, Spivak's delineation is an important reminder that there are different kinds of representation and that, in fact, literatures of certain communities, such as South Asian diasporic ones, carry a particular kind of representative burden that is simultaneously symbolic and standing in for entire communities.

The question of representation was brought into sharp relief with the pairing of Mukherjee's novel with the comedy of Russell Peters. Peters's jokes are dependent on his situating himself as a representative of the

Indian community writ large (with little to no distinctions drawn between Indians in different geographic areas or of different ethnicities), even as he inhabits a mainstream, hyperreal white audience's perspective of all ethnicities as other. Interestingly, both Mukherjee and Peters came to be residents of the United States via Canada; in this, their relationship to the United States is thus mediated another degree, though their experiences as being twice in diaspora as it were—once as Indian Canadians and again as Indian (US) Americans—is not readily apparent to some readers and viewers.

Peters is known for his brash, ethnic humor; the subjects (or, more accurately, objects) of his comedy are cast in the broadest vaudevillian terms. Lawrence Mintz traces different elements of ethnic humor in vaudeville, foregrounding the idea that these elements—such as familiar behavioral stereotypes regarding immigrants, humor based on their misunderstanding of language, and so on—both predate vaudeville and cast a long shadow on twentieth-century American comedy; he also notes that this is not restricted to American humor (19). Still, Mintz's outlining of the typically American vaudeville has interesting ramifications for how we may draw Peters into a lineage of comedy in which white, almost deracinated perspectives are normalized and all people of color, immigrants or not, are cast as essentially different and abnormal. Peters has said that he doesn't have a polished set, and his performances seem to support that assertion, since his routines habitually include significant crowd work (Peters). However, he also turns to the most obvious punch lines in this riffing with a consistency that suggests practice and uniformity if nothing else. Even as students were able to see the stage presence and charisma Peters brought to his routine, they were largely put off by the way he mocked the voices and behavior of people from other communities; his caricatures registered as simple bigotry milked for laughs.

What students found more complex was how and why Peters represented his own community—as a singular, monolithic group of Indians. First, though students believed that the other communities Peters joked about were deployed as exaggerated stereotypes, it was less clear to them if Peters was caricaturing his own community to the same extent. After watching his routine "Accents," for instance, students seemed to trust that Peters's depiction of his own community was more authentic; in fact, even if they were uncomfortable with his mocking, students did not question his right to speak of and for other Indians. Additionally, in routines such as "Somebody Gonna Get Hurt Real Bad," Peters used his father as a proxy for this generic Indianness, and it was clear to students that there was an affection there, an appreciation for his father's (heavily accented) wit, an appreciation that was absent in Peters's description of other immigrant communities ("Russell Peters"). In a different course, a student also pointed out that by first making fun of immigrants and especially their accents in "Accents," Peters earned the right to then make fun of his white Canadian audience. That is, white accents as well as white Canadian behavior qua whiteness were more easily available to him as a punch line because he had just directed the exact kind of generalizing critique at immigrant communities and at himself. Contradicting the more commonly held opinion in the class that Peters was laughing at himself and his own people with statements like "we know what [the Indian accent] sounds like" ("Accents" 0:32), a student pointed out that Peters may in fact not be laughing at himself at all. Clearly, Peters's accent was very different from what he was reporting his father's to be and from the accent he used to characterize romantically unsuccessful Indian men. Therefore, the class concluded, even though he uses the pronoun "we," the audience understands that Peters is not like his father, is not like these other men, and in that way is above the joke he's leveling at them.

Considered separately, *Jasmine* and Peters's comedy routines functioned in our class in much the same way one assumes they would in other circumstances, as texts that speak to completely different audiences and that can be analyzed for the truth of immigrant lives they discuss. However, when we considered Peters's comedy in conjunction with Mukherjee's novel, the common concern of representation became clear—that it was our reading protocol that transformed the authors' literary representations, their choices to create fictional figures and characters, into a form of representation as political proxy. In thinking of both texts together, as thematic interlocutors, I argued to students that the easy binaries found in each text are also a function of how each of these authors, not really having any predecessors who could find footholds for them, were operating in an atmosphere similar, though not analogous, to what W. E. B. Du Bois has described as the "double consciousness" of Black Americans, who are affected by "this sense of always looking at one's self through the eyes of others, of measuring one's soul by the tape of a world that looks on in amused contempt and pity" (194). Emphasizing for students the very different contexts of our class's topics versus the early decades of post-manumission in which Du Bois was writing, I nonetheless encouraged students to find guidance in Du Bois's explanation of the double consciousness for how we may interpret the work of artists such as Mukherjee and Peters. Du Bois's description of this simultaneous self-awareness and awareness of contexts, I argued, gives us valuable insight, albeit a century later and in a drastically different politico-cultural context, into these artists, who have had to not only consider their own creative inclinations but also negotiate these inclinations with an understanding of how they would be received and of the exegetical contexts in which their work would be framed.

Students watched Peters's comedy weeks after we discussed *Jasmine*; yet, despite the belated introduction, they were able to reflect on the novel to think about the content—about, say, how each author may have characterized the clash of cultures. More importantly, by tracing how these narratives were shaped by form, by intended audience, and by the contexts of production and circulation, students were also able to theorize how form and genre refracted these messages through prisms of authenticity—which is to say, we deliberated on how authenticity could not be assumed and how a tacit or articulated claim to authenticity is one of the many frameworks that could adjust our interpretation of the texts.

Second Generations and "Thirdspaces": Jhumpa Lahiri's *The Namesake*, Hasan Minhaj, and Hari Kondabolu

If *Jasmine* is easy for students because of its familiar theme of immigrant lives as embodying the clash of national identities, then Lahiri's novel *The Namesake* inspires equally enthusiastic responses since students find the quandaries of the protagonist, Gogol Ganguli, relatable. The novel inevitably invites some simplistic class discussions about Manichaean notions of tradition versus modernity and what it means to belong to India versus the United States; however, it also offers up more complex readings of cultural interactions in clear ways. In fact, positioning the novel alongside the comedy of more nuanced Indian American comedians such as Kondabolu and Minhaj allowed us to consider why we are attracted to binary analytical frameworks in the first place.

I have argued elsewhere that despite conventional analyses of *The Namesake*, the novel presents the space for second-generation immigrants neither as an always incomplete mimesis of a distant home nor as a yearning to be in identity with the hostland. Instead, Lahiri articulates through Gogol Ganguli that his place, instead of being at the interstice between India and America, is actually a third space altogether; the space may be imbued with the heritage of different cultural practices, but it is nonetheless a discrete entity (Chakraborty). In introducing students to the possibility of thinking beyond binary interactions, I was able to draw on Edward Soja's idea of "thirdspace," an idea that itself pulls from various postcolonial and philosophical theories, including its homonym, "third space," a concept developed by Homi K. Bhabha, to suggest that this spatial concept may help us, as a metaphor, think of consequences of transculturation in more plural, multidirectional terms.

In Indians Writing America, we spent a fair amount of class discussion interrogating the extent to which terms most relevant to the course—*India* and *America*—were *the* determining frameworks of the novel or whether they were in fact too baggy as concepts to speak to the cultural particularities we saw emerge in the novel. Certainly, a close examination of the novel encouraged students to conclude that India and America writ large are not the sources of Gogol's conflicting allegiances. For instance, we traced the examples of Indianness, only to conclude that it is really a more specific ethnic Bengali identity—in fact, the immigrant practices of being Bengali on the East Coast of the United States—that Lahiri describes. Further, Lahiri does not characterize these practices as traditional or repressive in any clearly discernable way. A student pointed out in our class discussion that Gogol's parents let him change his name whenever he decides he wants to and that they respect this decision by using his name in public. The student suggested, moreover, that it is largely Gogol's own anxiety that propels the tension in the novel.

We also discussed how it is not a real, complex United States that appeals to Gogol. In thinking about Gogol's attraction not just to Maxine but also to her parents and their lifestyle, my predominantly American students talked about how they did not really see their own lives reflected in Maxine's. The elite lifestyle described in the novel—with Manhattan brownstones and elegant dinner parties with European food and select guests—gave us an opportunity to think about the function of this hyperreal America in the novel. We discussed the ease with which students allowed that lives wholly unfamiliar to them, or to people they knew, could be proxies for their nation; in turn, this conversation gave us the opportunity to revise initial assessments that the novel was underpinned by themes of homeland versus hostland or the clash of essential cultures. Addressing the inadequacies of such binarism head-on, we were subsequently able to move to a discussion that helped us see shifts and nuances in cultural practices as South Asian diasporic subjects build on the narratives that have come before them.

Minhaj's Netflix comedy special *Homecoming King* and Kondabolu's comedy album *Mainstream American Comic* address some of the same themes of second-generation Indian Americans inhabiting and developing cultural spaces for themselves that are fundamentally syncretic. Students pointed out that these comedians work through rather than against or around cultural heritages, consequently making the argument that they are inevitably entangled in multiple lineages. Though their perceived national origins are hypervisible to their audiences, and for this reason, among others, are inescapable in their comedy, both Minhaj and Kondabolu draw on a variety of popular cultural influences, political concerns, and family dynamics, demonstrating that their ethnic identities encompass all these variances. For instance, Minhaj presents his subjectivities in multiple ways in his process of identifying with the demographically heterogeneous audience: he is Brown, Indian, a person of color, an immigrant kid, Muslim, and South Asian. Further, through his constant references to popular culture—not only to Drake, BMX bikes, and X-Men but also to Trayvon Martin and Laquan McDonald—Minhaj claims all cultural, social, and historical specificities as part of his lineage. Through quick jokes and rapid-fire allusions, Minhaj helped students retrospectively identify a sense of heterogeneous cultural traditions in *The Namesake*.

Students were inclined to attribute this complexity to Kondabolu's and Minhaj's status as second-generation immigrants; like Lahiri, the comedians speak of the waxing and waning of community affiliations in their homelands rather than the clear separation of former and current home that we see in *Jasmine*. At one point, I reminded students that Peters, who we had thematically connected to Mukherjee, was also a second-generation Indian Canadian. Did his comedy complicate our diagnosis of second-generation immigrant comedy necessarily being more complex? The discussion that followed allowed students to examine, once again, our affection for generalizing the stories of immigrants. I also argued that one of the many lineages that Minhaj and Kondabolu are part of (and building) is that of Indian American stand-up comedy.

Part of how these comedians construct the narrative is through a meta-awareness of their roles as comedians, which students noticed was expressed in their routines. There is a moment in Kondabolu's album *Mainstream American Comic* when, as an explanation for why he doesn't use accents when he's talking about his parents, he says, "I think about what my mom's been through in this country, right. People saying things like 'take that dot off your head,' or 'why are you wearing bedsheets out of the house,' or 'why don't you shut up and make me food,' and this is just stuff me and my brother said to her growing up. Can you imagine what she dealt with out of the house?" ("My Mom" 1:55–2:10). This self-directed joke recognizes the role that second-generation immigrants play as they align themselves with dominant cultures; in this way, Kondabolu's comedy, which often includes fleeting references to how jokes function in general, is also an allusion to a particular past of Indian diasporic comedy. In Indians Writing America, I shared a chapter on Kondabolu by Rebecca Krefting (*All Joking Aside* 196–230), which notes that Kondabolu employed the broad humor of accents and stereotypes in his early years as a comedian. Consequently, students understood that the joke cited above was an allusion both to the community-mocking history of South Asian diasporic comedy writ large—Peters's comedy being particularly paradigmatic—and to Kondabolu's specific history of participation in that comedic mockery.

Ruining the Joke: Challenges, in Conclusion

In the early weeks of the literature courses in which I use comedy, I am always excited by stand-up's potential as a theoretical interlocutor with which we can unlock some of the complexities of novels. And, as I argued above, the generic and formal contrasts between the two forms clarify, through juxtaposition, the familiar and conventional reading protocols that readers bring with them, especially students who analyze novels by BIPOC writers through simplistic lenses. However, one of the challenges that I continue to face in pairing Indian American stand-up with literature is that, like any other genre, the nuanced and complex authors are far fewer than the facile ones. Further, in some ways the truncated format of stand-up comedy also distills our defensiveness, so the challenge that inheres, for instance, in critiquing a novel for its troubling politics, becomes that much more pronounced in the case of quick texts whose point is to make us laugh, especially since nothing ruins a joke quicker than an explanation.

As I continue to teach courses that look at comedy and fiction in conjunction, I have to note the persistence of the neatly packaged tale delivered by the stand-up comedian, structured into setup and punch line. In the case of Indian American comedians, it is worth remembering that it is Peters and not Kondabolu—and not even the more popular Minhaj—who has repeatedly sold out shows in Las Vegas; the currency of vaudevillian humor remains strong.

Works Cited

"Accents by Russell Peters." *YouTube*, uploaded by Russell Peters, 1 Nov. 2016, youtu.be/z4KhEj0ai5E.

Bhabha, Homi K. *The Location of Culture*. Routledge, 1994.

Chakraborty, Madhurima. "Adaptation and the Shifting Allegiances of the Indian Diaspora: Jhumpa Lahiri's and Mira Nair's *The Namesake*(s)." *Literature/Film Quarterly*, vol. 42, no. 4, 2014, pp. 609–21.

Divakaruni, Chitra Banerjee. *The Mistress of Spices*. Anchor Books, 1998.

Du Bois, W. E. B. "Strivings of the Negro People." *The Atlantic*, Aug. 1897, pp. 194–98.

Fracis, Sohrab Homi. *Go Home*. Knut House Press, 2016.

Kondabolu, Hari. *Mainstream American Comic*. Kill Rock Stars, 22 July 2016.

Krefting, Rebecca. *All Joking Aside: American Humor and Its Discontents*. Johns Hopkins UP, 2014.

Lahiri, Jhumpa. *The Namesake*. Houghton Mifflin, 2003.

Minhaj, Hasan. *Homecoming King*. Directed by Christopher Storer, Netflix, 2017, www.netflix.com/title/80134781.

Mintz, Lawrence E. "Humor and Ethnic Stereotypes in Vaudeville and Burlesque." *Ethnic Humor*, special issue of *MELUS*, edited by John Lowe, vol. 21, no. 4, winter 1996, pp. 19–28.

Mukherjee, Bharati. *Jasmine*. Grove Press, 1989.

"My Mom (Accent Not Included) by Hari Kondabolu." *YouTube*, uploaded by Kill Rock Stars, 9 July 2016, youtu.be/MIBYXkqz1I0.

Peters, Russell. "Interview: Russell Peters on His No-Holds-Barred Comedy and How He Turns Stereotypes into Humour." Conducted by Soumya Rao. *Scroll.in*, 31 May 2019, scroll.in/magazine/925157/interview-russell-peters -on-his-no-holds-barred-comedy-and-how-he-turns-stereotypes-into-humour.

Reddy, Vanita. "Beauty and the Limits of National Belonging in Bharati Mukherjee's *Jasmine*." *Contemporary Literature*, vol. 54, no. 2, 2013, pp. 337–68.

"Russell Peters - Somebody Gonna Get Hurt Real Bad." *YouTube*, uploaded by Just For Laughs, 18 Mar. 2016, youtu.be/Adz4l5qEpD4.

Soja, Edward. *Thirdspace: Journeys to Los Angeles and Other Real-and-Imagined Places*. Blackwell Publishing, 1996.

Spivak, Gayatri Chakravorty. "Can the Subaltern Speak?" *Marxism and the Interpretation of Culture*, edited by Cary Nelson and Lawrence Grossberg, U of Illinois P, 1988, pp. 271–313.

Robyn Carruthers and Asha Varadharajan

Extimate Pedagogies, Intimate Texts: Teaching Digital South Asian Diasporas

While teaching South Asian diasporic literatures, we have observed that our students often seize on diasporic texts as a form of confession, keen to translate narrative into experience and locate that experience within an identity-based (trans)national politics.[1] The digital contexts in which South Asian diasporic formations are increasingly emerging, however, manifestly disrupt the assumptions on which such an approach rests. As Roland Barthes argues, the writerly text resists interpretation as simple transmission of the interior to the exterior, being both indeterminate and infinite, a "galaxy of signifiers" rather than "a structure of signifieds" (5). Although the production and circulation of diasporic literature always implies a network that exceeds the (trans)nation, pulling a range of diasporic subjects, translators, publishers, gatekeepers, cultures, and readers into relation, new digital contexts for the production and circulation of texts offer unique opportunities to interpret and mobilize South Asian diasporic literature as a "galaxy of signifiers" that resists being consumed as raw or even mediated experience. Online platforms showcase distinctive combinations of revealingly intimate and explicitly social registers that invite seemingly immediate as well as tightly orchestrated interaction from necessarily highly connected and dispersed participants. For these reasons, digital contexts shift who might be considered a participant, and how they might participate, in diasporic formations through writerly texts in ways that complicate the confessional impulse behind facile pedagogical approaches to diasporic literature.

Acknowledging this disruption to conventional approaches to diaspora, this essay intervenes in South Asian diasporic studies by theorizing what we term an "extimate pedagogy." Our use of this term is indebted to Jacques-Alain Miller's articulation of "extimité" ("extimacy") as the presence of the exterior in the interior, the opaque at the heart of the intimate. We put into conversation two contemporary South Asian diasporic writers whose work can be defined by extimacy's paradox—the famed (or notorious) Instapoet Rupi Kaur (*Milk and Honey*, *The Sun and Her Flowers*, *Home Body*) and her equally controversial literary counterpoint Meena Kandasamy (*Touch*, *Ms Militancy*, *The Gypsy Goddess*, *When I Hit You*, *Exquisite Cadavers*). Our purpose is to consider the pedagogical implications of the extimate aesthetics these two women writers explore and embody, with attention to the digital platforms through which their works circulate. This pedagogical consideration, therefore, does not derive from a set of techniques previously adopted in the classroom but instead evolves from an analysis of the different connotations *extimacy* assumes in Kaur's and Kandasamy's performance of (digital) diaspora and from a consideration of how these writers reciprocally shape extimacy as a pedagogical frame. In this way, we introduce extimacy as a diasporic aesthetic with the most pedagogical potential for illuminating new digital diasporic formations and imagining a place in them.

Extimacy and Pedagogy

In the preface to *Exquisite Cadavers*, Kandasamy expresses her frustration that *When I Hit You* was described "offhandedly and repeatedly as a memoir," thus "side-stepping the entire artistic edifice on which the work stood" (1) and defining her "solely" (1) by her experience as "raped Indian woman, beaten-up wife" (2). She thus asserts her rejection of the approach to understanding her diasporic text as simply a confession—a neat transmission from interiority to exteriority that equates the writerly text with a record of (victimized) diasporic experience. To evolve a pedagogical strategy that would instead give Kandasamy the "autonomy of deciding the genre to which the book . . . belonged" (2), we recall Miller's description of Jacques Lacan's work on extimacy as a "teaching" (75) rather than

a dogma and Miller's insistence on extimacy's "contradictions, its antino-
mies, its deadlocks, its difficulties" rather than its coherence (75). Miller
suggests that "a teaching implies a back-and-forth motion between work
and experience" (75). Conceiving of extimacy in the context of *When I
Hit You* as this movement "between work and experience," autofiction
and memoir, art and life, our pedagogy emulates this seesaw motion in order to communicate how diasporic literature not only transmits diasporic
experience but also performs the work that allows writers (and those with
whom they are brought into relation through the writerly text) to inhabit,
interrogate, and transcend the diasporic condition.

Kandasamy should be placed in a back-and-forth conversation with
Kaur, whose poetry moves in the opposite direction, from opacity to (orchestrated) transparency. Kaur's manipulation of social media transforms
the register of intimacy into that which "grounds what is common, what
conforms" (Miller 79) rather than that which registers alterity. Kaur's and
Kandasamy's experimental genres and modes mimic diasporic states that
are fluid and transitional, states of becoming rather than being, states that
are reflective of potentiality rather than perceived and fixed identities. Our
pedagogy thus begins by asking, and requiring that students ask, how
Kandasamy and Kaur renovate the possibilities for diasporic narratology
and poetics through their articulation of extimacy in the canny metafic-
tions they produce.

The dialectic between intimacy and extimacy we have begun to explore acquires different connotations in the context of diaspora studies,
which students must consider as part of our proposed extimate pedagogy.
Robin Cohen and Carolin Fischer explain the relation between diaspora as
a "category of self-identification" and diaspora as a "category of external
classification" as the "tension between the emic (the perspective of the
subject) and the etic (the perspective of the observer" (2). This tension
is of course powerfully displayed in the title of Kandasamy's *When I Hit
You*, which is expressed in the voice and words of the abusive husband
in the autofiction and from the perspective of the observer rather than
the observed. The subtitle switches that perspective while retaining the
tension between exteriority and interiority—the "young wife" emerges in
the third rather than first person, as portrait rather than proxy, and still as
young wife rather than adult woman, her personhood deferred and uncertain. But the "writer as a young wife" implies an alternative temporality,
one in which the portrait is finally hers to sketch rather than for others to
paint. This alternative temporality is already manifest in Kandasamy's earlier

publication *Ms Militancy*, but the shifts traced by the titles of the author's autofictions intimate her awareness that the emic is always hard-won and never stable. The tension between the emic and the etic becomes fascinating and pedagogically valuable in Kaur's writings because Kaur solicits rather than defies the gaze, and as her notoriety gains momentum, her diasporic identity becomes in turn authored by her fans and critics alike.

But how can students inhabiting different subject positions within multiple diasporic formations navigate this relationship between the emic and the etic? How can they articulate the relations between identity and affiliation in the (trans)nation to which they may or may not belong, or belong differently than the authors of the texts they are studying? How can they understand and perform the politics of location and dislocation implied by these questions? We suggest that they consider how the erroneous conflation of territory, identity, and belonging to which Cohen and Fischer allude has significant consequences for Kaur's and Kandasamy's status as diasporic authors. Kaur immigrated to Canada at the age of four; she is a Sikh migrant and settler whose relation to the politics of Khalistan and the Indian nation-state remains a fraught one. Kaur's tactical focus on the gendered Sikh body, her honoring of past generations, and her careful crafting of ethnic loyalties become crucial components of a persona that might otherwise seem merely singular, displaced, feminist, and cosmopolitan. Kandasamy adds a further twist to the tension between dispersal and belonging. She might be described as a recent entry in the annals of South Asian diasporic literature because she still divides her time between London and Chennai and was already an established figure before she made her reputation in London. Kandasamy's life as an activist, her advocacy of Dalit causes, and her branding as Maoist rebel place her in an adversarial relation to the Indian nation-state that she fearlessly indicts. Her frank explorations of desire and sexuality and excoriating accounts of marital rape and domestic violence also challenge the patriarchal status quo that masquerades as tradition. As her deployment of epigraphs from well-known international women writers indicates, Kandasamy imagines her writing as an inventory of affiliations across borders; the tissue of quotations that bind her work together serves as a homage to any woman anywhere who is "sitting down to write her story" (*When* 245). Students should approach both Kaur's and Kandasamy's writings for how they might be perceived as symptomatic of the depth and complexity that *diaspora* signifies. Our extimate pedagogy asks students to utilize external typologies to comprehend internal complexities.

Extimacy and the Digital Diaspora

We contend that students should navigate this extimate politics of location and dislocation, should perform this back-and-forth between emic and etic aspects of Kaur's and Kandasamy's diasporic works and experiences, in and through the digital contexts in which these diasporic writers and their writerly texts circulate. Our pedagogical practice aligns, therefore, with the new context of popular online platforms—*Instagram*, *Twitter*, *Facebook*, blogs, *YouTube*, and *Reddit*—in which digital diasporas take shape. Because digital diasporic networks can be formed around a homeland not as a place of origin but rather as a point of reference (Ponzanesi 985), they incorporate actors that do not necessarily belong, in the traditional sense, to an ethnically or culturally defined (trans)nation. Belonging within this digital diasporic space, therefore, hinges not only on identity and geography but also on participation. Participants in—rather than members of—the digital diasporic network can orient themselves to the (trans)nation in a wide variety of ways but always as a "connected user" (Ponzanesi 978) and not merely a dislocated subject.

Miller's attention to extimacy as a teaching, a back-and-forth motion between work and experience, informs how the idea of diaspora can be approached pedagogically given this participatory and performative context of (digital) belonging: it invites an exploration of the kind of work entailed by these digital networks along with the kinds of experience they reflect, circulate, and produce. Rather than approach these diasporic networks as constellated around a (trans)national homeland, we think it would be far more productive to orient a pedagogy to the ways participants evolve or challenge the distinction between exteriority and interiority, self and world, surface and depth, feeling and action, as part of extimacy's back-and-forth motion. We must ask students, in their role as participants, to reflect on how they manifest and shape the work and experience of virtual and embodied diasporic performance on and through these digital platforms.

Before speaking to specific examples of how students can be asked these questions, it is worth positioning Kaur and Kandasamy as diasporic performers in order to introduce some considerations our pedagogy must address in this regard. Both writers act as virtual and embodied performers and invite participation in diasporic networks, but they do this in different ways. Kaur's emergence as an Instapoet whose style is explicitly shaped by social media—most significantly *Instagram*—makes her the more obviously and intrinsically *digital* diasporic figure. Pedagogical practice should therefore attend to the way Kaur's "digital style" (Alinejad 189) intersects with her diasporic style. Digital styles perform extimacy's back-and-forth movement between work and experience; they digitally expand the writerly texts that produce diasporic subjects. Our pedagogy, therefore, attends carefully to case studies of Kaur's digital diasporic style both on- and offline as well as to the ways this style has been emulated and parodied as part of extimacy's back-and-forth motion.

Kandasamy's form and style of writing have no comparable integration with a digital platform as Kaur's do with *Instagram*. The conversations on her social media feeds are far more political than literary in tone, and her writing emerges and circulates principally offline—in traditional print formats. Nevertheless, Kandasamy serves as a literary and stylistic foil to Kaur in the way she registers intimacy as extimacy. Where Kaur leverages the back-and-forth motion of extimacy to ostensibly expand the scope and degree of intimacy registered as increasingly shared experience, Kandasamy does so to challenge that directionality. Our pedagogical strategy therefore solicits the articulation of these differences as part of a broader exploration of diasporic subjectivity, the evolution and disruption of identity and community, and the possibility of interpretation as affiliation rather than identification that our understanding of digital diaspora entails.

Concretely, this means asking students to participate in real-life digital conversations and to be attentive to the questions that our analysis of Kaur's and Kandasamy's intimate texts have raised. For example, both Kaur and Kandasamy use their digital networks to advance their activism: they fashion their selves as specifically female activists, linking their intimately registered writings with social change and asking a digitally connected public to participate in this process. Notably, both Kaur and Kandasamy performed this work of digital extimacy in the case of the Indian farmers' protests of 2020–21. Kaur used her digital platforms to circulate a wide variety of commentary on the issue, positioning herself as a warrior in the poem "a little louder." Students could be asked to participate in the related digital conversations taking place on these platforms as part of an engagement with Kaur's broader use of the warrior trope to fashion herself as committed to a form of female solidarity that is diasporic as well as universal. Kaur not only adopts the persona of a warrior to characterize the strength found in her intimate depths, writing that her experiences "pulled a warrior out of me" (*Home Body* 43), but also mobilizes that warrior persona in her public activism as part of extimacy's back-and-forth motion between (private) experience and (public) work. Students could then compare and contrast Kaur's approach with that of Kandasamy, whose "militancy" offers an alternative construction of female power and resistance.

By participating in this real-life case, students must also participate in a back-and-forth motion, reflecting on the relationship between their own experientially linked but diverse positionalities and the work they produce in participating in this diasporically inflected and forming conversation. Through their back-and-forth approach, they will ultimately be able to add their analysis of these diasporic authors' work to the online conversations, specifically as it pertains to the way they perform extimacy, and thus participate in the digital diasporic formation itself. They will come to understand diaspora as a condition of dwelling in the world that demands participatory conversation with all the potential challenges and conflicts that entails: there is no easy transmission of interior to exterior. They will recognize the consequence that our theorization of the digital diaspora reveals: they are all connected users in a digital sphere who need to learn to navigate their positionality and perspectives in relation to this diaspora, as its preferred interlocutors.

We should emphasize that students must engage across virtual and embodied contexts as part of this extimate pedagogical approach and should reflexively attend to the relationships between these contexts. Kaur's poems, for example, operate differently, though still in relation to one another, in their various forms: in Kaur's poetry collections, they are read as part of a self-help-style narrative arc from wounded to healed; on *Instagram*, they appear not only more piecemeal but also more shareable and available for immediate social interaction; printed on merchandise, they invite audiences to literally style themselves in Kaur's words. While Kandasamy's writing appears in more traditional printed form, her persona on *Twitter* allows her to offer both politically engaged commentary and snarky comebacks to her detractors as part of her digital diasporic performance. When students participate not only in the scholarly conversations that extend from considering these writers primarily in their print forms but also in the broader conversations that these writers invite on digital platforms, they are forced to perform work that is both critical and creative. They may emulate the intimacy Kaur solicits or reject it through the use of irony, mockery, or travesty. (Kaur's recognizable style has been the subject of parodic memes.) They may join both Kaur and Kandasamy in political dissent in relation to events such as the Indian farmers' protests.

This kind of participation allows students to perform the work and gain the experience that defines extimacy in a digital diasporic world.

Our pedagogical approach does not deny the value of traditional writing assignments for such a course. Topics for such assignments, however, evolve out of this broader approach to the South Asian (digital) diaspora and reflect our engagement with extimacy. Both authors dismantle the borders between art and life; that is, self is as much a matter of style as it is of living and being. An extimate pedagogy foregrounds this dialectic between work and experience in order to challenge the presumed transparency of showing and telling. The writing assignments for this course thus focus on the question of genre and mode: autofiction versus autobiography versus Instapoetry and Instafiction, the function of epigraphs in Kandasamy, ostensible ethnic or local color in both Kaur and Kandasamy, and interiority and exteriority or opacity and transparency and their relation to sympathy, empathy, and critical understanding or knowledge.

We decided to collaborate on this essay because, while we both identify as women and as Canadian, we occupy different subject positions: professor (Asha) and graduate student and instructor (Robyn); reluctant native informant (Asha) and intellectually and culturally curious white postcolonial scholar invested in doing the cultural homework necessary to negotiate otherness (Robyn); middle-aged (Asha) and not yet middle-aged (Robyn); middle-class (both); a proponent of print culture and live rather than virtual dialogic classrooms (Asha) and digitally savvy and open to digital networks and assemblages (Robyn); drawing from exclusively academic professional experience (Asha) and incorporating previous work experience in civil government and corporate cultures and domains (Robyn). We embody the traffic between selves and worlds that Kaur and Kandasamy exemplify and that we hope to model in our pedagogy.

We designed this pedagogical approach to appeal to undergraduates in Canadian institutions and are aware of how intersectionality varies across student demographics. Kaur's and Kandasamy's straddling of words and worlds, their forays into translation and transculturation, are likely to resonate with students who belong, more or less, to their generation, who themselves inherit forms of displacement and dispossession, and who contend with woke and cancel cultures from positions of privilege and marginality. Since the diasporic imaginary has long since been defined as "unhappy" (Mishra 1), we focus on authors whose works, while hardly innocent of yearning, melancholia, and trauma, are equally fierce and poised. These latter qualities will make them inviting rather than intimidating to their potential audience.

Ultimately, this pedagogical strategy is about understanding what it means to be a migrant and settler subject and understanding the complex overdeterminations that constitute our place in a multicultural and global world. Our extimate pedagogy asks students to recognize that they live in a diasporic reality, with all the plurality, bones of contention, and possibilities for connection that implies, and they can and must interpret and participate in it. Because extimacy requires that one take difficulties seriously, as conditions of possibility for engagement rather than as impasses that preclude it, our proposed pedagogy is designed to foster an "arduous conversation" (Kureishi) rather than a tame dwelling in difference.

Because both Kaur and Kandasamy stand in an ambivalent relation to the nation-states they inhabit, Indigenous students may take inspiration from the authors' methods: these students may use the authors' critical distance from migrant and settler positions to articulate their own positions while nuancing Kaur's and Kandasamy's take on racialization, dispossession, gender politics, and cultural mythologies to reflect Indigenous concerns. Finally, our deployment of extimacy is a response to the growing emphasis on lived experience as a means of counteracting dominant narratives. We chose these authors precisely to ask what "lived experience" means as a weapon and as a way to reshape both the vocabulary and the genre of anglophone diasporic literary expression.

Note

1. We use parentheses in *(trans)nation* and *(trans)national* throughout this essay not simply to indicate that such an identity-based politics can be both, or either, transnational or national but also to recognize that these terms are so mutually constituting and implicating in our contemporary diasporic reality as to be conceptually inseparable, even reciprocal. The nation and the transnation are not alternative political orientations, but interdependent ones.

Works Cited

Alinejad, Donya. *The Internet and Formations of Iranian American-ness.* Springer International Publishing, 2017.

Barthes, Roland. *S/Z.* Translated by Richard Miller, Noonday Press, 1974.

Cohen, Robin, and Carolin Fischer. "Diaspora Studies: An Introduction." *Routledge Handbook of Diaspora Studies,* edited by Cohen and Fischer, Routledge, 2020, pp. 1–10.

Kandasamy, Meena. *Exquisite Cadavers*. Atlantic Books, 2019.

———. *Ms Militancy*. Navayana, 2010.

———. *When I Hit You; or, A Portrait of the Writer as a Young Wife*. Atlantic Books, 2017.

Kaur, Rupi. "a little louder for the people in the back." *Twitter*, 29 Nov. 2020, twitter.com/rupikaur_/status/1333134812287168514/photo/2.

———. *Home Body*. Andrews McMeel Publishing, 2020.

Kureishi, Hanif. "The Arduous Conversation Will Continue." *The Guardian*, 19 July 2005, www.theguardian.com/world/2005/jul/19/religion.iraq.

Miller, Jacques-Alain. "Extimité." *Lacanian Theory of Discourse: Subject, Structure, and Society*, edited by Mark Bracher et al., New York UP, 1994, pp. 74–87.

Mishra, Vijay. *The Literature of the Indian Diaspora: Theorizing the Diasporic Imaginary*. Routledge, 2007.

Ponzanesi, Sandra. "Digital Diasporas: Postcoloniality, Media and Affect." *Interventions*, vol. 22, no. 8, 2020, pp. 977–93, https://doi.org/10.1080/1369801X.2020.1718537.

Amina Gautier

"A Temporary Matter":
Jhumpa Lahiri and
Creative Writing Pedagogy

Creative writing instructors who teach fiction often assign the published works of authors to reveal the individual craft components of a short story and to model how various craft elements function both separately and together. We lead discussions of published works where we ask students to analyze how, in terms of structure, craft, and execution, a text achieves its purpose, and we encourage students to envision and articulate possible alternative modes of execution. This prepares students to ask similar questions of their peers' story submissions, informs their own processes of revision, and importantly conveys the significance of authorial selection. As R. V. Cassill suggests in *Writing Fiction*, "A writer reading must be forever aware that the story exists as it does because the author chose his form from among other possibilities" (7). Therefore, facilitating discussions and exercises in which students engage in envisioning other possibilities reinforces the value of authorial selection and the knowledge that "no choice of character, action, language, names, or anything else is an isolated one" (8). Such an awareness is crucial for students to understand the ways and means by which short stories are shaped. Originally published in 1998 in *The New Yorker* and later included in her debut collection, *Interpreter of Maladies* (1999), Jhumpa Lahiri's short story "A Temporary Matter" is an exemplary text for teaching the intricacies of point of view and for imparting the significance of authorial selection to creative writing minors, majors, and MFA students in undergraduate and graduate fiction workshops.[1]

"A Temporary Matter" depicts the relationship stalemate between Shoba and Shukumar, an Indian American couple residing in Cambridge, Massachusetts, who are notified that "for five days their electricity would be cut off for one hour, beginning at 8 PM" for localized municipal repairs (Lahiri 1). A pregnancy loss six months earlier has destabilized their marriage, and their inability to process their grief manifests in their avoidance of each other. Shoba detaches herself from their home, working later hours and treating their house "like a hotel" (6), while Shukumar sets up his office in the nursery and works from home, reclusively spending entire days inside and "not even leaving to go get the mail, or to buy fruit or wine at the stores by the trolley stop" (2). The planned outages temporarily force the couple, who are "experts at avoiding each other in their three-bedroom house" (4), into each other's company: "Tonight, with no lights, they would have to eat together" (8). Told from Shukumar's point of view, Lahiri's story explores the aftermath of the couple's pregnancy loss and encourages readers to expect a reconciliation that never comes. The story's unexpected ending prompts in-depth class discussions on point of view. Lahiri's pairing of a chronologically linear narrative structure with Shukumar's limited third-person point of view manipulates reader expectations, thus demonstrating the importance of authorial selection to the development of a short story.

In *Imaginative Writing: The Elements of Craft*, Janet Burroway dubs point of view "a slippery concept" (55) yet one of the two most important skills for a writer to master. Lahiri's masterful and strategic execution of point of view and use of "indirect description," or the method of having one character describe another (Cassill 23), eludes most students, and most readers, who, as a result, misidentify the story's viewpoint character. The major challenge of helping students unpack the story's ending is that they do not perceive that "A Temporary Matter" is told from Shukumar's perspective, that his perspective is the only one presented, and that his perspective is unreliable. Because the story opens as Shoba reads aloud the repair notice, students misidentify her as the viewpoint character and do not notice that she is indirectly described by Shukumar. As she reads the notice, Shukumar sees that her lipstick has worn off and that her eyeliner has smudged and "left charcoal patches beneath her lower lashes"

(Lahiri 1), observations Shoba would not be able to make about herself without the aid of a mirror. Nevertheless, readers miss that Shoba is filtered through her husband's eyes, both in the story's present action and its flashbacks, for several likely reasons, which include the story's focus, the distraction of Shoba's ubiquitous presence, and the persuasiveness of Shukumar's intimate knowledge. First, readers who may not expect to read a story about pregnancy loss solely from the father's viewpoint may simply assume Shoba's viewpoint has also been included. Second, even in scenes where Shoba is not physically present, Shukumar's thoughts are about her; his preoccupation renders Shoba ever present, which makes it easier to overlook the lack of access to her inner thoughts and motivations. Third, Shukumar's wealth of minute and concrete details about Shoba's intimate habits, such as the fact that "she curled her fingers tightly when she slept, that her body twitched during bad dreams. He knew it was honeydew she favored over cantaloupe" (16), proves both distracting and convincing. Because students learn so much about Shoba, they believe they learn about it from her perspective.

To better understand Lahiri's nuanced maneuvers, it is important to have students review what they have already been taught about point of view, whether that means revisiting John Gardner's definition of "psychic distance" in *The Art of Fiction: Notes on Craft for Young Writers* (111) or the five principal narrative points of view listed in Ursula LeGuin's *Steering the Craft* (84–90) or using some other instructional handout. This review should be followed by an exercise that encourages students to replicate and distinguish among various forms of point of view (first-, second-, and third-person objective; limited omniscient; omniscient; peripheral; etc.) and their accompanying levels of psychic distance. An exercise in which students explore alternative viewpoints by reimagining and rewriting brief expository sections of "A Temporary Matter" will help them properly identify the viewpoint character by means of practical application. For example, we may take Shukumar's remarks on Shoba's nightly visit to the nursery-cum-study—"He knew it was something she forced herself to do" (Lahiri 8)—as our selection. Asked to rewrite this sentence from Shoba's first-person point of view, students might produce something akin to "I forced myself to visit my husband in the nursery," whereas having them rewrite it in her limited third-person point of view might yield "She forced herself to visit him here." Continuing to reimagine and rewrite the same sentence from Shoba and Shukumar's alternating limited third-person points of view (à la Katherine Anne Porter's "Rope") or from an omniscient point of view would further demonstrate to students the absence of Shoba's perspective and help them conclude by a process of elimination that Shukumar is in fact the story's viewpoint character.

Lahiri's structuring of the story encourages readers to expect that the utility repairs will play a role in ending the couple's stalemate and moving them toward resolution, but her privileging of Shukumar's point of view prompts readers to equate resolution with reconciliation. By beginning with the repair notice, Lahiri deliberately structures the story's conflict around the five nights of repairs and encourages readers to draw parallels between the downed power line and the couple's stalled relationship, suggesting that both will be simultaneously set to rights. To readers, the outage-induced contact seems cathartic, pushing the couple's grief to the surface and their avoidance to a head as they share previously undisclosed secrets over dinner. The first night appears to effect a change in Shoba, who "came home earlier than usual" (Lahiri 14), and in Shukumar, who foregoes his reclusiveness to go out for groceries. Toward the fifth day of repairs, Shoba and Shukumar's relationship appears to improve: "Something happened when the house was dark. They were able to talk to each other again" (19). Their tenuous rapport moves them from awkwardness on the first night to kissing on the third and making love on the fourth, a progression that is halted when the repairs are completed ahead of schedule. Shukumar's perspective invites readers to share his hope that his and Shoba's problems "would pass, that he and Shoba would get through it all somehow" (5), and since he believes these nights are moving them toward reconciliation, readers follow suit. Structurally, because Lahiri's story promises five days of repairs, the premature completion preempts and disrupts the couple's last night of confessions, leaving Shukumar and readers "disappointed" (20). Following on the heels of the couple's night of sexual intimacy, Shoba's announcement of her plans to move out disorients students and other readers who expected the couple to reconcile. Like Shukumar, students are surprised when they discover that the nights of confessions were Shoba's way of preparing to announce her departure:

> All this time she'd been looking for an apartment, testing the water pressure, asking a Realtor if heat and hot water were included in the rent. It sickened Shukumar, knowing that she had spent these past evenings preparing for a life without him. He was relieved and yet he was sickened. This was what she'd been trying to tell him for the past four evenings. This was the point of her game. (21)

Whether or not students feel "sickened," like Shukumar, they are brought up short by Shoba's revelation, feeling betrayed and confused by what they initially regard as a plot twist or trick ending.

Therefore, to appreciate the narrative tension that exists between the story as Shukumar understands it, where he and Shoba are heading toward reconciliation, and the reality that he and Shoba are headed for a separation, if not a full-scale divorce, we must explore the function of Shukumar's subjective viewpoint. What exactly does telling the story from his viewpoint achieve that another viewpoint could not? In an offshoot of the previous exercise, students can be tasked with simply locating, rather than rewriting, textual examples of Shoba's and Shukumar's points of view. Whether working singly or in groups, students come up empty-handed when they seek narrative evidence of Shoba's thoughts, yet they find a plethora of examples of Shukumar's thoughts, among which are the following: "She used to look this way sometimes, *Shukumar thought*, on mornings after a party" (Lahiri 1–2; italics mine); "Each time *he thought* of that moment, the last moment he saw Shoba pregnant, it was the cab *he remembered* most" (3; italics mine); "*He thought* of how long it had been since she looked into his eyes and smiled" (5; italics mine); "In the dimness, *he knew* how she sat, a bit forward in her chair" (11; italics mine); and "The birthday candles had burned out, but *he pictured* her face closely in the dark, the wide tilting eyes" (14; italics mine).

Compiling such a list concretely demonstrates that readers are firmly housed in Shukumar's inner thoughts, and the last two examples reveal the highly subjective nature of his observations. As the couple eats dinner together in a room whose darkness is relieved by only a handful of birthday candles, the absence of light prevents Shukumar from seeing Shoba. Thus, Shukumar does not actually "know" how she sat; he is merely guessing from previous observations. Similarly, since darkness obscures Shoba's face, Shukumar must instead "picture" it. In both examples he relies on memory and projects past actions and observations onto the present scene, never questioning the accuracy of his description as he replaces his wife's current presence with past observations of her. His practice of viewing Shoba through a lens of the past and basing his present interactions with her on her habits and routines before the pregnancy loss enables him to read reconciliation into their shared confessions. Completing this exercise prepares students to recognize Shukumar's projections as well as their complicit acceptance of his conclusions.

Shukumar's limited third-person point of view allows Lahiri to make use of indirect description, to introduce bias, and to mask events that occur in plain sight. Therefore, the exercises, coupled with the understanding that the effects of indirect description mean that "the good reader will expect the indirect to be less reliable, more *biased* than the direct" (Cassill 23), prompt students to question Shukumar's narrative reliability and interrogate their own presumption of his objectivity. Equipped with this new awareness, students revisit formerly overlooked details and in them find new meaning. Shukumar's "facility for absorbing details without curiosity" (Lahiri 4) now seems especially damning. Shukumar's ability to absorb details has been falsely read as introspection, and his lack of curiosity, which initially quelled readers' own curiosity and kept readers from questioning his interpretation of events or considering alternative outcomes, now appears as willful blindness on his part. Students' reexaminations uncover a body of examples that retroactively explain how Shoba pulled off her meticulous planning without detection, and they read new motivation into her habits. Shoba's "capacity to think ahead" and her innocuous tendency to save her bonuses in a separate bank account and to "prepare for surprises, good and bad" (6) now seem portent. Students who recall that Shoba previously lied about her whereabouts to go to a bar with a girlfriend and escape Shukumar's visiting mother now surmise that Shoba was apartment-hunting when Shukumar assumed she was working late or at the gym. Because Lahiri privileges Shukumar's point of view and because Shukumar lacks curiosity, the truth about Shoba's actions, motivations, and whereabouts are discreetly concealed from the reader until Shoba reveals them herself through dialogue. However, students now see that the signs of her unhappiness and withdrawal were depicted plainly but were ignored or misinterpreted by Shukumar. Shukumar misreads Shoba's domestic disinterest, evinced by her failure to finish sewing lace into curtains (6), as proof of her lingering depression, when her detachment is actually an indicator of her impending departure. Why bother to decorate or sew lace curtains for a home one intends to vacate? Shukumar also misreads their sexual intimacy on the fourth night as a sign of rekindled romance rather than the farewell it is. Although their night of lovemaking fills Shukumar with anticipation for the next day's confessions, students who revisit this scene in which Shoba and Shukumar make love "with a desperation they had forgotten" and in which Shoba "wept without sound" (19) see that their encounter is far more mournful than romantic.

Lastly, students' reappraisal of the story's ending must address their unquestioning conflation of resolution and reconciliation. Although the story's structure implies that both the electricity and the couple's relation-ship will be set right within the same span of time, repairing a relationship is not synonymous with reconciling one. Shoba's announcement of her departure shows the ways in which Shukumar's perspective masked an equally viable alternative and challenges students to reevaluate their ex-pectations and redefine their understanding of resolution. For Shukumar, repairing the relationship means getting past the grief and reuniting, but for Shoba, a proofreader trained to spot and correct mistakes, repairing the relationship means ending it. Despite Shukumar's surprise at Shoba's revelation, students come to see how Shoba prepares her departure before our very eyes and that Lahiri's ending is not actually achieved through a trick or plot twist at all but through a sophisticated and nuanced execution of point of view that challenges readers every step of the way.

Note

1. Because Lahiri's story makes subtle and sophisticated moves in its execution of point of view, "A Temporary Matter" is most successfully taught in the second half of the semester, after students have read other stories with more clear-cut and straightforward points of view and after they have read and discussed other pub-lished short stories by writers of the South Asian diaspora, such as Akhil Sharma's "If You Sing Like That for Me" and Chitra Banerjee Divakaruni's "Mrs. Dutta Writes a Letter." Because Sharma's story is set entirely in Delhi and Divakaruni's is set in San Francisco and includes nostalgic flashbacks to Calcutta, interspersing these stories among stories of writers from other backgrounds curtails potentially reductive readings such as viewing Lahiri's story as representative of the South Asian diasporic experience.

Works Cited

Burroway, Janet. *Imaginative Writing: The Elements of Craft.* 3rd ed., Pearson Longman, 2007.
Cassill, R. V. *Writing Fiction.* 2nd ed., Simon and Schuster, 1975.
Divakaruni, Chitra Banerjee. "Mrs. Dutta Writes a Letter." *The Best American Short Stories 1999,* edited by Amy Tan, Houghton Mifflin Harcourt, 1999, pp. 29–47.
Gardner, John. *The Art of Fiction: Notes on Craft for Young Writers.* Vintage Books, 1991.
Lahiri, Jhumpa. "A Temporary Matter." *Interpreter of Maladies,* by Lahiri, Houghton Mifflin Harcourt, 1999, pp. 1–22.
LeGuin, Ursula K. *Steering the Craft: Exercises and Discussions on Story Writing for the Lone Navigator or the Mutinous Crew.* Eighth Mountain Press, 1998.
Sharma, Akhil. "If You Sing Like That for Me." *The Best American Short Stories 1996,* edited by John Edgar Wideman, Houghton Mifflin Harcourt, 1996, pp. 282–306.

Nidhi Shrivastava

Recovering the Gendered Violence
and Trauma of Partition in the Me Too Era

The 1947 Partition of India, one of the bloodiest migrations in the history of the Indian subcontinent, resulted in one of the largest migrant crises in history. Caught in the midst of genocidal violence, arson, massacres, forced conversion, riots, abductions, and sexual violence, the refugees often never made it to their destination. It is estimated that between 200,000 and two million people perished during the Partition, and about 75,000 women are thought to have been forcibly raped and abducted (Butalia 3). Yet, Partition is seldom taught at the high school level or in undergraduate courses in North American universities, and undergraduate students typically have no prior awareness of the cataclysmic event.

In this essay I address this gap through my pedagogical philosophy and expound a postcolonial feminist pedagogical approach to teaching the Pakistani American author Bapsi Sidhwa's semi-autobiographical novel *Cracking India* and its film adaptation, *Earth*, directed by the Indo-Canadian filmmaker Deepa Mehta. Speaking to a transnational audience, both the novel and the film allow for collective and individual engagement with memories of a traumatic past through the older Lenny's recollection of the Partition. They also allow students to engage with the concept of "postmemory" (Hirsh), a concept that is essential in helping students understand and explore current debates in Partition studies. Although Sidhwa and Mehta have been the subjects of criticism (Desai 78–79; Neutill 76–77; Sidhwa, "Making Up"), their works appeal to students who are unfamiliar with the Partition, and they generate meaningful and dynamic classroom discussions on the themes of South Asian diasporic experiences; child narratives; representation of genocidal violence, trauma, and sexual violence; adaptation theory; the voice and agency of Ayah in Sidhwa's *Cracking India*; complicated masculinities and nationhood; and the realistic depiction of unspeakable violence in film.

My pedagogical goal is twofold. First, I aim to create awareness among undergraduate students of global events, especially of the 1947 Partition, which is not widely known in the New England region, where I teach. Unlike in Canada and other parts of the United States, where the Partition and other historical events such as the 1914 incident involving the *Komagata Maru* steamship and the tragic crash of Air India Flight 182 are memorialized in literature and outside of it, the myriad experiences of raped and abducted women are met with silence in this region because the conversations surrounding them tend to bring feelings of discomfort and shame. For the most part, students and even faculty members in my university, to an extent, are unaware of the Partition's relevance in global history. Second, I aim to make visible the many forms of gendered and sexual violence that women experienced during the Partition. In the Me Too era, there have been efforts to venerate victims of sexual violence in the diaspora of other genocides but not of the Partition (Saidel and Brutin 11). By teaching about the genocidal violence that occurred during the Partition, students gain awareness and share this knowledge with their peers and communities.

To establish a postcolonial theoretical framework, I refer to the scholarship of Urvashi Butalia and of Ritu Menon and Kamla Bhasin. The work of these scholars focuses on the reconstruction of the silent voices that are often elided or reduced to statistics in official and historical accounts of the Partition. Informed by witness accounts, oral narratives, and government documents, their scholarship serves as a lens into the lives of women who were part of or witnessed the atrocities that occurred during and after the Partition. I situate the Partition within the broader context of global genocides to underscore the value and significance of this cataclysmic event. This has been an effective pedagogical strategy because it not only recognizes the Partition at a global level but also helps students contextualize the

Partition as a historical event that took place within years of the Holocaust. I introduce Sidhwa's novel and Mehta's film after we read narrative texts about the Holocaust, such as Olga Lengyel's *Five Chimneys: A Woman Survivor's True Story of Auschwitz*. This pedagogical strategy helps students see a clear link between the genocidal violence that took place during the Partition and the violence that took place during other genocides.

For instructors teaching in the Me Too era, at the pinnacle of digital and hashtag activism, it has become crucial to reclaim marginalized, silenced voices, especially the voices of victim-survivors who were affected by significant political events such as genocides and war. Their experiences are often silenced in the broader conversation of the Me Too movement and thus require our attention in the classroom. As was the case with the Holocaust and the Rwandan genocide, there was a period of silence in the aftermath of the Partition.

The gendered violence that occurred during the Partition emerges repeatedly in South Asian diasporic writing and culture as part of the history that the South Asian community continues to grapple with. The Indo-Canadian authors Shauna Singh Baldwin and Anita Rau Badami explore the psychological, social, and somatic experiences of the Partition in their novels. More recently, the Indo-Canadian author Sohan S. Koonar published *Paper Lions*, an epic multigenerational novel about a family deeply affected by the Partition. Koonar's novel focuses on the Sikh experience of the Partition, but there is no mention of women's experiences.

As the above examples demonstrate, the authors who conjure the specter of Partition are primarily based in Canada. In the United States, the 1947 Partition Archive was established in 2010 (www.1947partitionarchive .org). The archive's goal is to document, preserve, and share eyewitness accounts and oral testimonies from all ethnic and religious communities. When teaching *Cracking India* and its film adaptation in the future, I will require students to explore this digital archive in order to learn more about the collection and preservation of testimonies and about the stories that are and are not being shared on public platforms. As a complement to this activity, students will read a chapter in Anjali Gera Roy's *Memories and Postmemories of the Partition of India* titled "They Stuttered: Non-narratives of the Unsayable" (84–105), which discusses how language operates in popular culture, literature, and testimonies. As Roy notes, "While narrating their stories, survivors' memory works by eliding traumatic experiences or transforming them into acts of agency but is betrayed by language that screams, stammers, stutters, or comes to a halt" (85–86). Since the goal is to uncover the silenced voices of women who have been raped and abducted, the exploration of digital archives will call further attention to the gap that exists in the Partition archives. Whereas the USC Shoah Foundation has encouraged scholars such as Lauren Cantillon to pursue research focused specifically on women's narratives of sexualized violence during the Holocaust (Pitic), similar research projects have not yet been conducted in the 1947 Partition Archive. While the archives have thus far collected more than 10,600 oral interviews in various vernacular languages, we still do not have access to them (Svensson 221). Therefore, we cannot explore and study the raw testimonies of those who may have witnessed instances of gendered violence or experienced it themselves. In the Indian context, Ted Svensson notes that the "heritage landscape relating to Partition has . . . been marked by a dearth of more formalised and official remembrance efforts" (217). Svensson argues that "[c]ontemporary efforts to memorialise the Partition" in India are examples of "dissonant heritage" (219). The term "dissonant" implies that the event is memorialized differently by various groups. Indeed, while there is an effort to remember Partition in the South Asian diaspora, this effort is scattered and selective. The South Asian diaspora continues to struggle to find the language to speak about the gendered violence that occurred during the Partition. Here, Parvinder Mehta's argument is critical because it suggests that to examine the key ethical and moral arguments raised by Partition writers, we have to acknowledge "the representations of history and social sufferings, coded within the rubric of shame, dishonor, trauma and acceptance" (39). By examining Sidhwa's text and Deepa Mehta's film with the ultimate goal of making visible the many forms of trauma that women experienced, we are recognizing the narratives that have been ignored or silenced because of shame and dishonor.

Set in Lahore in the years leading up to the Partition, *Cracking India* recounts the coming-of-age experience of Lenny, an eight-year-old polio-stricken Parsi girl, during the 1947 Partition. She witnesses the formation of distrust between the ethnic communities as the tense sociopolitical conditions indicate the imminent reality of Partition. Sidhwa's novel and Mehta's film also focus on the love triangle that involves two Muslim men, Dil Nawaz (also known as the Ice Candy Man) and Hassan, who are both in love with the Hindu Ayah, also called Shanta.

Sidhwa's and Mehta's positionality, as a South Asian diasporic author and a South Asian diasporic filmmaker, respectively, allows them to explore and engage in topics that would be considered sensitive or taboo in the communities in their home countries and in the South Asian diasporic community. Both Sidhwa and Mehta are often questioned because they are seen as outsiders in their home countries and, simultaneously, bear the responsibility of being cultural informants in their host countries. For example, Sidhwa faced anger in response to her novel because of her choice to shed light on the narratives of women who have been raped or abducted, which she discusses in an interview with Isabella Bruschi, noting that this topic "is something nobody talks about, nobody: it is such a dishonour to admit that a woman in one's family was raped" ("Making Up" 144). Because this subject has been silenced both in India and in the diaspora, Sidhwa leverages her position not only to recognize and write about the gendered violence that occurred on women's bodies during the Partition but also to preserve memories of her experience growing up next to a recovered women's camp. Sidhwa admits that the topic is "so hush-hush . . . no one wanted to mention or admit to" it (144). Mehta's diasporic status has also left her open to criticism from scholars, audiences, and film critics alike. Jigna Desai, for example, writes that "Mehta is caught in the neither/nor of diasporic (displacement). . . . Mehta's status as a Canadian is questioned. Similarly, Mehta as a diasporic intellectual playing native informant is interrogated by South Asians . . . in regard to her alienation from, and lack of intimacy with, the homeland" (78). I encourage students to frame the discussion of Sidhwa's and Mehta's subjectivities in the context of literary trauma theory. A central claim of trauma theory is that "trauma creates a speechless fright that divides or destroys identity," but a novel (or film) about trauma calls attention to the fact that the "geographic place of traumatic experience and remembrance situate the individual in relation to a larger cultural context that contains social values that influence the recollection of the event and the reconfiguration of the self" (Balaev 149). In other words, trauma theory helps students understand how Sidhwa and Mehta use the medium of literature and film to make sense of the collective trauma of the Partition. Ultimately, both the novel and the film address the cultural silence surrounding the trauma and raise difficult questions about the lives of women who were raped or abducted.

Although some of the criticism that Sidhwa and Mehta have faced is justified, both works create an opportunity for students to learn about sexual and gendered violence during the Partition. In the novel and film, Lenny is coping with multiple traumas, including her struggle to come to terms with polio, that color her perception of her surroundings and the people she interacts with. Lenny's experiences and her own limitations also help us explore trauma associated with disability and self-perception. Because of her perspective as a Parsi, Lenny shows that people from all communities were equally responsible for the violence that took place at the time of the Partition. Students are drawn into both the novel and the film because they are able to relate to Lenny's indirect experience of genocidal violence, especially when they see evidence of the psychological impact of such violence—for instance, after witnessing the dismemberment of a Hindu man during the Lahore riots, she later tears apart one of her dolls in a similar manner.

The focus then shifts to Dil Nawaz, who undergoes a transformation when he loses his relatives during their journey to Gurdaspur. The class pays specific attention to the fact that the film focuses on his sisters, who are brutally mutilated after being murdered, before turning to his trauma. We then discuss the moment when he proposes to Shanta in *Earth* (Ayah in the novel), stating that he will become an animal if she refuses his marriage proposal (1:01:44–1:03:44). This leads to an interesting discussion about the factors and conditions that lead people to become perpetrators of genocide. It is not until the end of the film, when students observe Ayah's untimely abduction and disappearance into the abyss, that students realize that, ultimately, the character who has been made unreal *is* Ayah in the film adaptation. In other words, after Ayah's abrupt abduction, the film ends with the older Lenny recounting her kidnapping and not knowing about Ayah's fate (whether she marries Dil Nawaz or is left in a brothel). The audience is left without closure regarding her character.

As part of our discussion of the film's ending, I assign feminist scholarship by Menon and Bhasin to help students consider the role of the Indian state in the recovery operations of the abducted women. Reading Menon and Bhasin's article with the film's ending effectively demonstrates the complex and nuanced lives of the women who were raped and abducted and helps students see Ayah in a new light. Although I agree that the film's ambiguous ending is sensationalized to entice viewers, students can engage deeply with the subjects of rape and abduction because both texts provoke curiosity to learn about the lived realities of gendered violence during the 1947 Partition.

We then turn our attention to Sidhwa's novel. Many students reflect that Ayah is assertive and is able to speak to Lenny's godmother (a character, as we discuss, who appears only in the novel) when she meets with Lenny and his godmother at Ice Candy Man's brothel. Ayah exclaims, "I cannot forget what happened" (Sidhwa, *Cracking India* 273), recalling her violent abduction, and declares, "I am past that, *I am not alive*" (274; emphasis added). In the end, she returns safely to Amritsar with the help of Lenny's family. Kavita Daiya has suggested that Mehta's film marks Ayah's "death as a social subject, a citizen, and an agent" (62). Ambreen Hai is critical of Ayah's lack of agency in the novel. She contends that in Ayah's narrative, her "fate after rape is to be found or to be packed off by other women, not to be acted upon. There can be no 'life after rape' or accession to subjecthood for Ayah in Sidhwa's text" (Hai 405). I draw students' attention to the following quotation from Hai's article. Drawing on the work of Rajeswari Sunder Rajan, Hai states that narratives that focus on survival and continued existence redefine the subjecthood of victims of rape: "To center the narrative elsewhere is to disallow rape from being the single shaping force of the subject and of the narrative itself" (403). Our class discussion turns to what "life after rape" really means and whether Rajan's criticism is indeed true. Students and I generally agree that Ayah has more agency and voice in Sidhwa's novel than she does in the film adaptation. I then show students scenes from *Pinjar* and *Tamas*, which helps them see the multitude of realities that women encountered during the Partition. They see that abducted women were often rejected by their families and that many of them were willing to participate in mass suicide. Students are reminded of how the filmmaker's editorial choices can affect how we perceive characters, and they consider the film's message as it relates to Ayah's sudden abduction, which reduces Ayah to a statistic among numerous women whose identities were permanently erased from national memory, leaving many students without a sense of closure.

Sidhwa's novel and Mehta's film are fundamental in the South Asian diaspora because they make the Partition accessible to those who may be unaware of the cataclysmic event. Both *Cracking India* and *Earth* provide an in-between space as cross-cultural texts whose language, nuances, and specifically, characterization of Lenny as an older woman recalling the harrowing events of the Partition—rendering her similar to Holocaust survivors giving testimonies—make their narratives relatable. I have had perhaps only two students of Indian descent in my classes over the years. One of them, in her weekly journal entry, shared with me that before she read *Cracking India*, she had been unaware of the history of Partition, since it had not been discussed in her family. This is further evidence that conversations on gendered violence are silenced in the diaspora. We must turn to works such as Sidhwa's and Mehta's to begin conversations on the lives of women who were raped and abducted in order to confront our history so that we can begin to heal.

Works Cited

Balaev, Michelle. "Trends in Literary Trauma Theory." *Mosaic*, vol. 41, no. 2, 2008, pp. 149–66.

Butalia, Urvashi. *The Other Side of Silence: Voices from the Partition of India.* Duke UP, 2000.

Daiya, Kavita. *Violent Belongings: Partition, Gender, and National Culture in Postcolonial India.* Temple UP, 2008.

Desai, Jigna. "Homo on the Range: Mobile and Global Sexualities." *Social Text*, vol. 20, no. 4, 2002, pp. 65–89, https://doi.org/10.1215/01642472 -20-4_73-65.

Earth. Directed by Deepa Mehta, Hamilton Mehta Productions, 1999.

Hai, Ambreen. "Border Work, Border Trouble: Postcolonial Feminism and the Ayah in Bapsi Sidhwa's *Cracking India*." *Modern Fiction Studies*, vol. 46, no. 2, 2000, pp. 379–426, https://doi.org/10.1353/mfs.2000.0028.

Hirsh, Marianne. *The Generation of Postmemory: Writing and Visual Culture after the Holocaust.* Columbia UP, 2012.

Koonar, Sohan S. *Paper Lions.* U of Toronto P, 2019.

Lengyel, Olga. *Five Chimneys: A Woman Survivor's True Story of Auschwitz.* 2nd ed., Academy Chicago Publishers, 1995.

Mehta, Parvinder. "A Will to Say or Unsay: Female Silences and Discursive Interventions in Partition Narratives." *Revisiting India's Partition: New Essays on Memory, Culture, and Politics*, edited by Nalini Iyer et al., Lexington Books, 2016, pp. 35–53.

Menon, Ritu, and Kamla Bhasin. "Recovery, Rupture, Resistance: Indian State and Abduction of Women during Partition." *Economic and Political Weekly*, vol. 28, no. 17, 1993, pp. WS2–WS11.

Neutill, Rani. "Bending Bodies, Borders and Desires in Bapsi Sidhwa's *Cracking India* and Deepa Mehta's *Earth*." *South Asian Popular Culture*, vol. 8, no. 1, 2010, pp. 73–87.

Pinjar. Directed by Chandra Prakash Dwivedi, Lucky Star Entertainment, 2003.

Pitic, Badema. "Lauren Cantillon Lectures on Women's Narratives of Sexual(ized) Violence during the Holocaust." *USC Shoah Foundation*, 9 Apr. 2021, sfi.usc.edu/news/2021/04/30871-lauren-cantillon-lectures-womens -narratives-sexualized-violence-during-holocaust.

Roy, Anjali Gera. *Memories and Postmemories of the Partition of India.* Routledge, 2020. Routledge Studies in South Asian History.

Saidel, Rochelle G., and Batya Brutin. *Violated! Women in Holocaust and Genocide.* Remember the Women Institute, 2018.

Sidhwa, Bapsi. *Cracking India*. Milkweed Editions, 1991.

———. "Making Up with Painful History: The Partition of India in Bapsi Sidhwa's Work: Bapsi Sidhwa Interviewed by Isabella Bruschi." *Journal of Commonwealth Literature*, vol. 43, no. 3, 2008, pp. 141–49.

Svensson, Ted. "Curating the Partition: Dissonant Heritage and Indian Nation Building." *International Journal of Heritage Studies*, vol. 27, no. 2, 2021, pp. 216–32, https://doi.org/10.1080/13527258.2020.1781679.

Tamas. Directed by Govind Nihalani, Blaze Entertainment, 1988.

Notes on Contributors

Umme Al-wazedi is professor of postcolonial literature in the Department of English at Augustana College. Her research and teaching interests encompass postcolonial literature, British literature, (Muslim) women writers of South Asia and the South Asian diaspora, Muslim feminism, and postcolonial disability studies. She has published in *South Asian Review*, *South Asian History and Culture*, and *Women's Studies: An Interdisciplinary Journal*. She is also the author of several book chapters. Her coedited book *Postcolonial Urban Outcasts: City Margins in South Asian Literature* was published in 2016.

Anita Baksh is professor of English and former director of the Women, Gender, and Sexuality Studies program at LaGuardia Community College, City University of New York. Her teaching and research interests include Caribbean literature, gender, feminism, postcolonial theory, and composition. Her publications have appeared in *The Journal of West Indian Literature*, *WSQ*, *Caribbean Quarterly*, and in such collections as *Indo-Caribbean Feminist Thought: Genealogies, Theories, Enactments* (2016).

C. S. Bhagya is lecturer (education) in English at Brunel University London and a tutor at the University of Oxford. Her academic work has been published or is forthcoming in the *Journal of Postcolonial Writing*, *Wasafiri*, *Oxford Research in English*, *Postcolonial Text*, *Contemporary Literature*, and *The Oxford Handbook of Modern Indian Literatures*. Her pedagogy-focused writing can be found in the *English Review* magazine and the open educational resource hub *Writers Make Worlds*. She is currently working on a monograph based on her doctoral work, tentatively titled "Tropes of Exception: Representations of the Emergency (1975–77) in Indian Literature."

Dharitri Bhattacharjee teaches South Asian and Indian Ocean history at Western Washington University. She has published in *South Asian History and Culture* and *History Compass* and, for a broader audience, in *The Wire* (India) and *Caravan Magazine*. She created a digital archive of South Asian voices, *Stories to Tell*, which is hosted by Western Libraries and *South Asian American Digital Archive*. She produces and hosts a podcast called *Grit and Grub* on local business history and is working on her first documentary, *The Limits of History*.

Mushtaq Bilal is a postdoctoral researcher at the University of Southern Denmark's Hans Christian Andersen Center. He is the author of *Writing Pakistan: Conversations on Identity, Nationhood and Fiction*. His work has appeared in academic journals such as the *Journal of World Literature*, *Comparative*

Literature Studies, and *Angles: New Perspectives on the Anglophone World* and in newspapers such as *The Washington Post*, the *Los Angeles Times*, and *Dawn* (Pakistan). He has taught Pakistani literature to undergraduates, general members of the community, and officers of the American foreign services.

Robyn Carruthers is a doctoral candidate in English at Queen's University in Canada. Her dissertation project, *Foreign Relations: Contemporary Travel Writing and the Poetics of Foreign Space*, reimagines how travel writers and their works interpret who, where, and what is foreign. Her further research and pedagogy focus on new directions for postcolonial studies in a global and planetary context, life writing at the intersection of the real and the fictional, the digital humanities and bookish Internet culture, and debates surrounding the postcritical turn in scholarship.

Chandrima Chakraborty is professor in the Department of English and Cultural Studies and director of the Centre for Peace Studies and the Global Peace and Social Justice Program at McMaster University. Her research is on public memory, nationalist history, masculinity, and religion, with a focus on the literatures and cultures of South Asia and the South Asian diaspora. She held the honorary title of University Scholar at McMaster University (2017–21) and was elected to the Royal Society of Canada's College of New Scholars, Artists and Scientists in 2019. Her publications include *Masculinity, Asceticism, Hinduism: Past and Present Imaginings of India* (2011), *Mapping South Asian Masculinities: Men and Political Crises* (2015), and *Remembering Air India: The Art of Public Mourning* (coedited 2017).

Madhurima Chakraborty is associate professor in the English and creative writing department at Columbia College Chicago. She is the editor of *Global South Asia: South Asian Literatures and the World* and a special issue of *South Asian Literature* titled *South Asian Literatures in the World*. She is coeditor of *Postcolonial Urban Outcasts: City Margins in South Asian Literature* and a special issue of *South Asian Review* titled *Nation and Its Discontents*. Her scholarly work has been published in *Journal of Postcolonial Writing*, *Literature/Film Quarterly*, *South Asian Review*, and *Journal of Contemporary Literature*.

Esther Daimari is assistant professor in the Department of English at Tezpur University. Her research interests include landscape and literature, contemporary South Asian fiction in English, Partition literature, and English literature from Northeast India. She has published articles in *South Asian Review*, *Southeast Asian Review of English*, *Journal of the School of Language, Literature and Cultural Studies*, *Dibrugarh University Journal of English Studies*, and *Muse India*.

Mayuri Deka is associate professor and chair of English studies at the University of the Bahamas. She has published and presented numerous papers in the area of American literature, with a focus on multiethnic identities, postcolonial literatures, popular culture, and pedagogy. She is in the process of writing a book on prosocial pedagogy and social justice. She has taught a wide range of American and world literature, including multimodal texts from popular media.

R. Benedito Ferrão is assistant professor of English and Asian and Pacific Islander American studies at William & Mary. His edited volume *Goa/Portugal/Mozambique: The Many Lives of Vamona Navelcar* (2017) accompanied a retrospective show he curated of the artist's work in Goa in 2017–18.

Robin E. Field is professor of English at King's College in Wilkes-Barre, Pennsylvania. She is the author of *Writing the Survivor: The Rape Novel in Late Twentieth-Century American Fiction* (2020) and coeditor of *Transforming Diaspora: Communities beyond National Boundaries* (2011, with Parmita Kapadia), *Critical Perspectives on Chitra Banerjee Divakaruni: Feminism and Diaspora* (2022, with Amritjit Singh and Samina Najmi), and *#MeToo and Modernism* (2023, with Jerrica Jordan). She is managing editor of the journal *South Asian Review*.

Amina Gautier is professor of English at the University of Miami. She specializes in nineteenth-century American literature and African American literature. Gautier is the author of three short story collections, *At-Risk, Now We Will Be Happy*, and *The Loss of All Lost Things*, and a recipient of the Pen/Malamud Award for Excellence in the Short Story. Her critical essays and reviews have appeared in *African American Review, The Cambridge Companion to the American Short Story, Critical Insights: Frederick Douglass, Daedalus, Journal of American History, Libraries and Culture, Nineteenth-Century Contexts*, and *Whitman Noir: Essays on Black America and the Good Grey Poet*.

Subhalakshmi Gooptu is assistant professor of world literature at the Fashion Institute of Technology, State University of New York, where she teaches courses on global anglophone and postcolonial writing, transnational and migration literatures, and labor studies. In her courses, she centers insights that arise from looking across and between different genres, forms, and media. She is currently working on her first book project, "Stories Women Carry: Labor and Reproductive Imaginaries of South Asia and the Caribbean," drawing from her dissertation.

Nalini Iyer is professor of English at Seattle University. She teaches courses in postcolonial South Asian and African writing, diaspora studies, and transnational feminisms. Her books include *Other Tongues: Rethinking the Language Debates in India* (2009), *Roots and Reflections: South Asians in the Pacific Northwest* (2013), and *Revisiting India's Partition: New Essays in*

Memory, Culture, and Politics (2016). She has also published articles in *ARIEL*, *South Asian Review*, and *Tulsa Studies in Women's Literature*. She is the chief editor of *South Asian Review*.

Maryse Jayasuriya is professor of English at the University of Texas, El Paso. She is the author of *Terror and Reconciliation: Sri Lankan Anglophone Literature, 1983–2009* (2012) and the editor of *The Immigrant Experience: Critical Insights* (2018). She also guest-edited a special issue of *South Asian Review* on Sri Lankan anglophone literature (2012).

Feroza Jussawalla is professor emerita at the University of New Mexico, Albuquerque. In her forty years of teaching in the United States, she also taught at the University of Utah and at the University of Texas, El Paso. She is the author of *Family Quarrels: Towards a Criticism of Indian Writing in English* (1984). She is the editor of *Conversations with V. S. Naipaul* (1999) and coeditor of *Interviews with Writers of the Postcolonial World* (1997), *Emerging South Asian Women's Writing* (2017), *Memory, Voice, and Identity: Muslim Women's Writing from across the Middle East* (2021), and *Muslim Women's Writing from across South and Southeast Asia* (2023). She has numerous published articles and poems, and her collection of poems, *Chiffon Saris*, was published in 2002.

Dinidu Karunanayake is assistant professor of English at Elon University, where he researches and teaches global anglophone postcolonial literature, Asian American literature, human rights, genocide, memory, and diaspora. His work has appeared in *South Asian Review*, *ICES Research Papers*, *The Subjects of Human Rights: Critical Asian and Asian American Studies*, and *The Oxford Encyclopedia of Asian American Literature and Culture*.

Rajender Kaur is professor of English at William Paterson University. Her research and teaching interests are interdisciplinary and focus on early American studies, postcolonial theory, and gender, class, and social justice issues in South Asian and South Asian American literatures and culture. Her articles and book reviews have appeared in a host of scholarly journals, and she is coeditor most recently of *India in the American Imaginary, 1780s–1880s* (2017).

Suhaan Kiran Mehta is assistant professor in the English department at the University of Colorado, Colorado Springs. He has published scholarly articles on Indian and Pakistani anglophone print and visual texts. He has taught previously at Case Western Reserve University, Ohio State University, and St. Xavier's College, Mumbai.

Aniruddha Mukhopadhyay is associate professor of English and graduate coordinator at Texas A&M University, Kingsville. His work focuses on representations of marginalized identities in Dalit and South Asian diasporic literatures. He has published an article on animal representations in Dalit autobiographies in *South Asia: Journal of South Asian Studies*, several book reviews in the *South Asian Review*, and creative fiction in the *Langdon Review of the Arts in Texas*. He serves as web manager for the South Asian Literary Association and is the president-elect of the Conference of College Teachers of English.

Binod Paudyal is a senior lecturer in the Asian American Studies Program at the University of Maryland, College Park. His research and teaching interests include Asian American studies, comparative race and ethnic studies, Asian American literature and film, and global diaspora and postcolonial studies. His current research projects focus on identity politics, invisibility, and undesirability in the twenty-first century, which is marked by the global war on terror, migrant and refugee crises, and complex global conditions.

Pallavi Rastogi is professor of English at Louisiana State University. Her first book, *Afrindian Fictions: Diaspora, Race, and National Desire in South Africa*, was published in 2008. Her second book, *Postcolonial Disaster: Narrating Catastrophe in the Twenty-First Century*, was published in 2020. She has coedited a collection of essays, *Before Windrush: Recovering an Asian and Black Heritage within Britain* (2008), and two special issues of the journal *South Asian Review* titled *Precarities, Resistance, and Care Communities in South Asia* (2018) and *Writing South Asia in Disastrous Time* (2023). She has published articles in various scholarly journals and anthologies.

Manav Ratti is professor of English at Salisbury University. He is the author of *The Postsecular Imagination: Postcolonialism, Religion, and Literature* (2013). His other publications include "A Postsecular Poetics of Dislocation: Secularism and Religion in the Indian-American Poetry of Meena Alexander" (2021) and "The Intersections of Postcolonialism, Postsecularism, and Literary Studies: Potentials, Limitations, Bibliographies" (2022).

Asma Sayed is Canada Research Chair in South Asian Literary and Cultural Studies in the Department of English at Kwantlen Polytechnic University. Her interdisciplinary research focuses on postcolonial and diaspora studies, the South Asian diaspora in Canada, Indian Ocean studies, critical race studies, and Indian cinema. Her publications include five edited or coedited books and numerous articles in a range of periodicals, anthologies, and academic journals.

Alpana Sharma is professor of English and chair of the School of Humanities and Cultural Studies in the College of Liberal Arts at Wright State University. She publishes and teaches in the areas of anglophone postcolonial literature and theory, South Asian women's writing, South Asian diasporic literature, and Indian cinema. She has also published her poetry in the journals *Postcolonial Text* and *Journal of Postcolonial Writing*. Her essay "Intimations of Modernity: The Legacy of Toru Dutt" appeared in the Modern Language

Association's Options for Teaching volume *Teaching Anglophone South Asian Women Writers* (2021).

Nidhi Shrivastava is a lecturer of English in the Department of Languages and Literature at Sacred Heart University. Her research focuses on the Me Too movement, Hindi cinema, censorship, the figure of the abducted and raped woman, Indian rape culture, and the 1947 Partition of India. She coedited the volume *Bridging the Gaps between Celebrity and Media* with Jackie Raphael and Basuli Deb, and her academic research has also been published in *South Asian Review*. She contributed a chapter in *#MeToo and Literary Studies: Reading, Writing, and Teaching about Sexual Violence and Rape Culture* and has several forthcoming publications, including contributions to a collaborative volume titled *Gender Violence, the State, and Society: Perspectives from India, Japan, and South Africa*.

Matthew Spencer is a lecturer in English at Auburn University. His research deals primarily with ecocriticism, depictions of global climate change, and environmental activism in American and anglophone literatures. His current work seeks to trace a genealogy of environmental radicalism in the American literary tradition from transcendentalism to contemporary mass movements advocating action to mitigate the effects of climate change.

Asha Varadharajan is associate professor of English at Queen's University in Canada. Her current research focuses on forced migration and involuntary displacement. Her work has appeared in the *Dictionary of Literary Biography*, and her most recent publications comment on the crisis of the humanities, the subaltern in the present era, sexual violence and human rights, decolonizing pedagogies, and the legacy of the Frankfurt school. In 2021 she received the Queen's University Principal's Promoting Student Inquiry Teaching Award.